To

Granny,

love from Em, I do hope you like this – sorry it was the best I could get. x x x

16.11.73.

Taylor - Jones,
Chennell Park.

ONLY THE WIND WILL LISTEN

Reith of the BBC

Also by Andrew Boyle

NO PASSING GLORY (Cheshire, V.C.)
TRENCHARD, MAN OF VISION
MONTAGU NORMAN

ANDREW BOYLE

ONLY THE WIND WILL LISTEN

Reith of the BBC

HUTCHINSON OF LONDON

HUTCHINSON & CO (*Publishers*) LTD
3 Fitzroy Square, London W1

London Melbourne Sydney Auckland
Wellington Johannesburg Cape Town
and agencies throughout the world

First published 1972

This book has been set in Bell type, printed in Great Britain on antique wove paper by Ebenezer Baylis and Son Limited, The Trinity Press, Worcester, and London, and bound by Wm. Brendon, of Tiptree, Essex

ISBN 0 09 113820 5

To all who helped or hindered
John Reith in his predestined courses
this book is admiringly dedicated
as a small tribute to the BBC
on its fiftieth birthday

'. . . And God said
Prophesy to the wind, to the wind only, for
Only the wind will listen . . .'

Ash Wednesday—T. S. Eliot

Contents

	Preface	11
	Prologue	15
1	The Boy	29
2	The Misfit	39
3	The Warrior	55
4	The Seeker	85
5	The Opportunist	103
6	The Visionary	138
7	The Hostage	179
8	The Autocrat	215
9	The Paternalist	247
10	The Outsider	296
	Epilogue	329
	References	353
	Index	359

Preface

I FIRST MET John Reith at the suggestion of Lord Trenchard, the controversial 'Father of the RAF', on whose life-story I had begun work in the late summer of 1955. 'I once had a fine quarrel with Reith', boomed Trenchard. 'You should see him.' I did; and I was amazed by Reith's extraordinary capacity for remembering the obscurer details of the row. It had arisen over the BBC's plans for erecting a new transmitter which, so Trenchard contended, was too high for the safety of his pilots and aircraft. Reith at first refused to comply with the demand that the mast be lowered. In the end the two men reached a compromise which enabled the BBC to have its transmitter and its founder to earn the enduring respect of Trenchard.

It was an episode of marginal interest only, but I had to marvel at the almost caressing fashion in which Reith lingered over it. The memory seemed to spark off many others, and I was detained for so long that, finally, I had to make my excuses for breaking off that original interview. It led to the growth of a relationship between John Reith and myself which lasted until his death, for I responded to his pressing invitation that I should 'call again whenever you feel like it'. John Reith lived almost wholly in the past during these declining years. I enjoyed the gloomy yet often sharp exhilaration of his company. He read the typescript of my Trenchard biography with a sternly approving eye, already well aware of my interest in the contradictions of his own outsize personality. He was so obviously at odds with the world and himself that nothing then or later could shake my resolve to discover why. What puzzled me most was Reith's conviction that his public, and to some extent his private, life had been a ghastly failure. I knew from his somewhat disappointing memoirs, *Into the Wind* and *Wearing Spurs*, that he possessed a high talent for self-justification; my conversations with him revealed also a profound taste for self-condemnation. Those conversations enabled me at last to find the key to his character, without which no complete or coherent biography would have been possible.

My personal knowledge of the man has been sharpened by many unpublished letters which have recently come to light in collections of private papers. For access to these important new sources I am indebted to Mr. A. J. P. Taylor and his assistants in the Beaverbrook Foundation Library, who let me use the fascinating Beaverbrook correspondence with Reith; to the librarian of Nuffield College, and to Dr. Cameron Hazlehurst of the Queen's College, Oxford, who guided me to the half-sorted papers of Lord Gainford and to those of Lord Aberdeen; and to Mr. Charles Curran, the BBC's Director-General, as well as the archivists at Caversham Park, for freedom to consult the corporation's voluminous record at the normal, outside researchers' fee; to Professor Asa Briggs for reading my draft manuscript with scholarly care, and to Mr. Donald Stephenson for performing the same task with admirable detachment on behalf of my employers at Broadcasting House.

The numerous men and women whose paths crossed Reith's crowd the pages of this biography. I am grateful to them all, but have space to register my thanks to only a few. The late Sir P. J. Grigg, Sir Desmond Morton, Sir Kingsley Martin, Lord Trenchard, Lord Chandos and Mr. Ronald Norman, indirectly helped, while they were alive, to refine my understanding of Reith's relationship with the political worlds of Baldwin, Ramsay MacDonald, Neville Chamberlain, and Sir Winston Churchill. So, in their respective ways, did Sir George Bull, Mr. Malcolm MacDonald, and Mr. A. J. P. Taylor. I owe much also to the relatives, the friends, the critics and the disciples of my subject, whose recollections of Reith at various stages of his career proved invaluable. The names of Lords Boothby, Shinwell, Mancroft, Runciman, Moran and Longford; of Lady Davidson, and Lady Elliot; of Janet and Mary Adam-Smith; of Mr. Harold Macmillan, Mr. Harold Wilson, Mr. Selwyn Lloyd, Mr. Malcolm Muggeridge, Mr. Oliver Whitley, Mr. Harmann Grisewood, Mr. Val Gielgud, Sir John Lawrence, Sir William Haley, Sir Adrian Boult, Sir Gerald Beadle, Sir Lindsay Wellington, Sir Harold Hartley, and Sir John Masterman, must do duty for the multitude of other witnesses who inspired me with evidence of substance.

I must also express thanks to the authors and/or publishers for permission to quote from the following works: *English History, 1940–1945*, by A. J. P. Taylor (Oxford University Press); *The History of*

Broadcasting in the United Kingdom, by Asa Briggs (Oxford University Press); *Into the Wind* by J. C. W. Reith (Hodder and Stoughton); *Wearing Spurs* by J. C. W. Reith (Hutchinson); *On England* by Stanley Baldwin (Allan); *Geoffrey Dawson and Our Times* by Evelyn Wrench (Hutchinson); *The Decline and Fall of Lloyd George* by Lord Beaverbrook (Collins); *Beatrice Webb's Diaries 1924–1932* (Longman); *King George V* by Harold Nicolson (Constable); *The Life of Neville Chamberlain* by Keith Feiling (Macmillan); *Lloyd George: a Diary* by Frances Stevenson (Hutchinson); *One Thing at a Time* by Harman Grisewood (Hutchinson); *Diaries and Letters* by Harold Nicolson (Collins); *Years in a Mirror* by Val Gielgud (Bodley Head); *Prospero and Ariel* by D. G. Bridson (Gollancz); *Churchill: The Struggle for Survival, 1940–1965* by Lord Moran (Constable); *The Brabazon Story* by Lord Brabazon (Heinemann); and *Memoirs* by Lord Chandos (Bodley Head).

I add my concluding words of thanks to Sir Robert Lusty and Harold Harris of Hutchinson, to my literary agent Mr. Graham Watson of Curtis Brown, to my long-suffering colleagues on *The World at One*, and to Christina, who, as usual, was always at hand to see the whole thing through.

Putney—Hurstwood Farm (*Sussex*)

Prologue

1

ON THE way to the brilliantly lit Bute Hall elderly members of Glasgow University's academic court gathered their robes about them and lowered their heads against the stiff, cold wind. Only one man in the straggling procession seemed impervious to the darkening day and the first leaden touch of winter. Head slightly tilted, chin upthrust, as if to display like some old campaign ribbon the deep scar tissues that had disfigured his left cheek for half a century, John Reith strode forward with the rigid bearing of an antiquated guardsman. The bleak conditions suited him well, so that the swirl of dead leaves rustling and crackling underfoot, the plaintive cries of gulls wheeling towards the eternal throbbing sounds from the distant river, even the casual stares of the few bystanders, might have been theatrical props laid on for his special benefit. It was the afternoon of the last Friday in October 1966, and Reith's genuine sense of homecoming complemented a natural sense of satisfaction. The honour of being installed at last as Lord Rector of this ancient university was all the more keenly felt because as a youth he had been denied the opportunity of studying at any higher seat of learning. Besides, he had come armed with something positive to say.

The incidental point that, in keeping with their rowdy tradition, most undergraduates probably regarded the ceremony as a ludicrous charade, and therefore as a fitting occasion for mischief, did not seriously occur to him. Nor did the unspoken apprehension of several members of the governing body, that Reith's indifference might in itself provoke a shambles, begin to touch the new Lord Rector-elect.

His self-confidence was, as usual, supreme. Why should he bother to ponder the fate, ten years before, of Richard Austen Butler, then Britain's Lord Privy Seal, whose face and gown had been liberally spattered with flour during his installation speech? Reith at least had no political axe to grind. Even if he had, he could claim without immodesty that he would certainly not have been humiliated like Butler. Any politician unwise enough to have come moralising at the height of the Suez Crisis had got less than his desserts in emerging with a whole skin. It had served 'Rab' right, in his view, for being so naïve.

During the formal somewhat stilted introductions Reith sat hunched on the platform, his eyes screwed up in discomfort against the strong glare of the lights rather than in distaste at the empty oratorical banalities. He had always believed in plain speaking, and he was in the mood now to select from a lifetime of experience some home-truths for the minds and hearts of these undergraduates. After all, they had paid handsomely in advance by inviting him to become their spokesman and official representative. How could the most intuitive member of the university court be expected to appreciate his extravagant sense of occasion, in which elation, astuteness, nostalgia, the irrepressible zest of the actor, and the sad wisdom of an ageing seer jostled for pride of place? Reith had travelled far, done much, and endured innumerable frustrations in his seventy-six years. As he rose now and towered above the lectern, waiting like a good conductor for the expectant buzz to die away, he had no doubt whatever that the audience was already his for the taking.

He began playfully enough:

'Well', he exclaimed, staring around with mock ferocity, 'am I not far too old to be Lord Rector of this university?'

The end of the phrase was drowned in a responding wave of sound.

'Yes, yes, far too old', they shouted; but the involuntary gestures and nervous signals of professors, senior officials and lesser fry beside him on the platform Reith either did not notice or chose to ignore. Waving his arms like windmill sails in an appeal for silence, he regained control of the student body at once. Then his voice rose to a dramatic pitch of earnestness:

'For God's sake, don't misunderstand me. And don't think I'm talking down to you, because I'm talking up. Life is before you, whereas I am now near the end of it; and you want the life that is really worth living—of happiness because you love and are loved, because with all your success and achievement you have been of great service to others and to the country.'

The rolling cadences and the tone of his voice were reminiscent of a Presbyterian preacher warming to his theme, yet Reith also brought an eerie prophetic quality to his plea that the young men and women listening to him should strive 'to find some inspiring, guiding determining ethic, some rules for life, which will enable you to rise to the awful but lovely challenge of today'. Somehow, beneath the air of pleading certainty, there lurked a hint of elaborate humility and remorse. Why else should he ask himself aloud whether his words could carry across the 'long, wild stretch of years' behind him to convey anything that made sense?

Like the students below, he belonged to this city, had been suckled and bred in it. Though he had left long ago to live and find fame far away, he was conscious now of being back home. Not many yards from this place he had picked buttercups and daisies as a child in the grass of the West End Park. When he was older, walking home at night along the High Drive towards his father's manse, he had often strained his ears hopefully just in case 'the wind had a message for me from the everlasting hills'. Alas, life had since taught him that direct communications from the Almighty could not be relied upon because the human spirit was a fickle receiver. Even so-called success in life often turned out to be a snare and a delusion:

'As to the success in life of any individual, only herself or himself can judge: their judgment is absolute. The judgment of others is relative and quite likely of no value whatsoever. He and she whom public opinion regards as successful may know themselves to have failed, or at any rate to have fallen far short of what they might have been or done. Perhaps what they most desired in life they failed to secure'—and as if to demonstrate that these truisms were the stuff of his own existence, Reith added with an austere shrug: *'C'est moi qui parle.'*

The belief in his own failure as a public figure was as strong in him as the haunting feeling of frustration which had dogged him intermittently down the years, even before his withdrawal from the BBC. Yet as the founder and first Director-General of that unique and still vastly influential institution, John Reith had set the unmistakable stamp of his own flawed personality on the Britain of his day. Was it a bad conscience or just a Calvinistic acceptance of doom which made him sound at certain moments rather sorry for himself? And could it be the defiant hope of a man trying to redeem the squandered years in the little time still left to him which induced him to say:

'Many of us were under earnest Christian instruction when we were young, with varying effects in after years. But we haven't begun —nor have the churches in my view—to take Christ seriously, his

2

person and his message. In particular we haven't begun to comprehend the mystery and the magic of the indwelling Christ—therein *via*, the way, therefrom *veritas*, the truth. I know this to be true and I long for you to discover for yourselves what I have come to realise so late.'

Some definite and compelling form of religious faith, Christian or otherwise, was a key factor in any real success or service or happiness. The danger of mankind becoming absorbed with things rather than with conviction was all too apparent. It could lead to the damnation of an individual or of a whole society as surely as it had led to the downfall of Imperial Rome.

'The burden, I suppose, of what I am trying to say to you young men and women is—for God's sake prevent it. . . . I warn you that you are going to find yourselves up against almost incredible inefficiency, incapacity, stupidity, unreliability and indifference.' Reith was suddenly rounding on his so-called betters, the politicians and faceless advisers behind them who had punitively taxed his patience in the past. He had come to realise the hopelessness of confrontations with men who were the embodiment of such vices, but he recommended the young not to despair. Democracy was busy confounding itself by pretending that all men had equal gifts and qualities. Let them take it from him, John Reith, that the young especially had a duty to be best and to excel all others:

'Is that undemocratic or in any way repugnant?' he asked. 'The mini-men won't like it and, of course, they've all got votes. . .'"

He ended his address as suddenly and artlessly as he had started, leaving any mischief-makers in the stunned crowd of students no time for a last-ditch demonstration. Instead, applause broke out. It thundered on, startling the gulls and pigeons outside as the academic procession left the Bute Hall and straggled into the gloom again. It had been a weirdly uneventful but moving ceremony, particularly in view of the new Lord Rector's statement of his own hypnotic but highly unfashionable convictions.

2

Reith's instinct, on first receiving the invitation to stand, had been to turn it down flat. The Lord Rectorship was traditionally, he knew, an ornamental position without powers; and while he delighted in the business of dressing up, and had a connoisseur's taste for all branches of ritual, he realised clearly what complete fools most previous Lord Rectors had usually managed to make of themselves. Whatever happened, his unerring dignity would forbid him to play for cheap laughs and sink to such a level of pathos. His misgivings were genuine, but still he was sorely tempted to apply, and in the end he succumbed. He had stood as an independent candidate, yet several public men of note had refused to subscribe to the campaign fund of those Scottish Nationalists among the student body who sponsored him. Once or twice he had trembled on the brink of withdrawal, notably when Lord Caradon and Mr. Iain Macleod entered the lists against him. The possible intervention of Spike Milligan had worried him less:

'As to Lord Caradon', he wrote, 'I certainly said that I thought he might be reluctant to stand against me; I would say so still; but I suppose he knows that I am a candidate and, therefore, I am wrong. I am surprised, though—knowing him—*not* surprised . . . Macleod I have never met. I have always disliked him by sight and repute . . . I never heard of Spike Milligan but my secretary has just told me he is a comedian-actor, whatever that might be. This may surprise you, but I can be almost incredibly ignorant, particularly about people in whose activities I am not interested.'

Yet his interest, when stirred, could carry him to a point that astounded and captivated his youthful promoters in Glasgow. The seemingly endless stream of telegrams and letters from Reith in London, his readiness to present all references (down to a copy of his birth certificate), his almost embarrassing candour about his own self-doubting, sometimes caused them short and wakeful nights. A few of the 'campaign testimonials' that floated in from the famous resembled the gushing unselfconscious praises of teenage bobbysoxers in honour of their favourite pop stars:

'If I had a vote, I would give it to Reith', ran a typical paean from a distinguished Scottish academic. 'Because? I know him and I like him. I admire the cut of his jib. He is a big man. He looks and talks as if he had authority. He is a great Scot, a man of wide and varied experience. Moreover and forbye, he is, for me, a non-party politician. (As a citizen I am interested in politics: but I regard party politics as a game like tiddledywinks or snakes-and-ladders—useful when the rain prevents one from doing anything else.) Yes, it would be Reith for me. . . .' When his name eventually came out at the top of the ballot he had felt more alarmed than flattered until he hit on a characteristically complex way both of justifying himself and of retrieving the situation by that extraordinary inauguration speech.

All his life John Reith had been a dreamer. Unlike the common run of men, however, *his* dreams were spurs to action. Not even in moments of aberration did he treat them as escape hatches from reality or as mere opiates to soothe anxiety. The source of his dreams he accepted quite simply as providential; and, until middle age, at any rate, his faith in them had grown through practice into certainty. The habit of communing, as he supposed, with the infinite was a habit he had acquired in boyhood during long, solitary holiday walks among the foothills of the Cairngorms. There, in the clear mountain air, the wind had sometimes seemed to speak, and he had learnt to interpret the language of destiny. Above the world of men he had caught inspiration meant for himself alone.

He would have been shocked by suggestions that such wishful communings amounted to sheer self-indulgence, since he had long believed implicitly that the dreams of John Reith were short-cuts to lofty ends. He was glad now, an old man who dreamed mostly of the past, that Glasgow University students had chosen him. He would have refused any nomination from Edinburgh, and quite reasonably. For the capital city of Scotland saw enough of him already. As a long-standing Member of the Queen's bodyguard, and latterly as Her Majesty's Lord High Commissioner, he held sinecures enough there for his palate. The dark, magnificent rooms in Holyrood were at his command; he had colourful uniforms to wear with his decorations on state occasions, persons of distinction to entertain in the season, and sufficient pomp to dignify all ceremonial functions. Being head-over-heels in love with symbolism, he drew deep enjoyment from official visits to Edinburgh—much more than he could hope to find in the plebeian atmosphere and surroundings of the common rooms at Glasgow University.

Still, the attractions of the Lord Rectorship had beckoned him like a beacon. For emotional reasons Glasgow was the centre where the Reith family had flourished for long generations before his birth. In the Victorian heyday of commercial expansion his grandfather had raised a large family and put the city of his adoption in his lasting debt by turning the Clyde into a great artery for sea-borne traffic. That huge, bearded patriarchal figure, whose gentle severity John Reith could still discern whenever his memory peered through a selected loophole in the oblivion of childhood, had worked as an engineer on the river. He had shown vision during his quarter of a century as general manager of the Clyde Navigation Trust, but Glasgow had forgotten that he ever existed. Its ingratitude was as base as the insensitivity of those pious gentry who had similarly ignored what the Presbyterian Church still owed to the Reverend Dr. George Reith, grandfather's noblest son. How like the churchgoers, he thought, to leave nothing but a cemetery headstone as a memorial to his revered father. Only in the last four years of a selfless life dedicated to the spreading of Christ's kingdom had this Presbyterian minister begun to understand the yearnings and powerful impulses that animated his own youngest son; but John Reith still felt at times the grip of his father's benign influence on him. The passage of the years had weakened it, of course, but as a younger man it had guided him from beyond the grave through many a crisis.

In returning as Lord Rector, Reith felt that he was paying respect to these two forbears whose greatness lay in their goodness and integrity of purpose. The knowledge gave him occasional twinges of guilt. His own demonic will had impelled him to seek wordly fame. It had not brought him happiness. The fact that he was now trying to make vicarious amends by reviving the name of Reith in this city would probably have struck both his father and his grandfather as an empty gesture of filial piety, but John Reith could not be absolutely sure. His father had been fond of saying that there were many routes to the Kingdom of God. Could it not be argued that coming home like this to put a little hard-won wisdom at the disposal of Glasgow's undergraduates was a move which his father would have blessed in an age of unprecedented permissiveness?

So Reith's dialogue with himself went on, an uneven compound of pride, self-abasement, perception and guilt. The dream he had constructed from these contradictory elements, being as fragile as a bubble, slowly disintegrated within weeks of his installation. He noticed, for instance, that the majority of students treated him with the indifference of total strangers. As they continued to steer clear of him, his hopes of reaching them, of befriending the receptive, of stirring them to start thinking of the true meaning and purpose of existence, gradually began to fade. Only then did it cross his mind that his vague plan of firing a mob of undergraduates with enthusiasm for outdated values might be a ludicrous piece of self-deception. Short of emulating John Wesley and converting the Bute Hall lectern into a permanent pulpit, he could not have succeeded in winning over a single young man or woman; and as Reith had no aspirations as a preacher, he decided to discard the dream.

His disappointment did not endure. He had no quarrel with any of the students, even those rowdier ones who eyed him ostentatiously from a safe distance and made half-audible, impertinent remarks about the mistaken policy of importing fossils and ancient monuments as Lord Rectors. John Reith did not appear to notice or to care, though naturally he did—and deeply. For he was suddenly made aware of playing the principal part in a farce which he had devised and wished upon himself. He was even more stricken by failing his father and grandfather in a specific task of retribution. The sour taste of failure was too familiar for him to delude himself further, so instead of yielding to tantrums, Reith resigned himself to another bizarre situation. He took whatever compensations he could from concentrating his attentions on a few girl students who were quick to discover an unexpected chink in the apparently impregnable armour of this outwardly grave and dignified old man. Was it feminine intuition or just the mischievous cruelty of the adolescent mind which induced them to fawn on him and hold up to ridicule his weakness for a pretty face or a good figure?

Perhaps Reith had aged more than he knew. For here again he either did not seem to mind the absurd figure he would sometimes cut, when seen chucking one particularly pert young lady under the chin or listing like a wounded giant as he tried to walk with a playful arm thrown over another's shoulder. He was reconciled to the hollow nature of his official position when Malcolm Muggeridge, elected the following spring to the vacant rectorial chair of Edinburgh, paid him several neighbourly calls. Being meticulous in the discharge of even the slightest duties, he had much advice to offer Muggeridge, who was taken aback by the tedious irrelevance of most of it. The fires of Reith, the earnest zealot, had been mysteriously damped down. The last echoes of an inaugural speech, which the new Lord Rector of Edinburgh, for one, had praised for its weird frankness, had died away so that it was possible to believe that the spirit of the speaker himself had been overtaken by some fell affliction. The truth, of course, was more prosaic. John Reith had merely perceived that he could do nothing but go through the motions as though his office meant something to him, while all the time his spirit was a prey to the black sense of hopelessness which had afflicted him for as long as he could remember.

3

It rarely happens that the popular conception of an eminent public figure matches the inner reality. Reith, notably at the height of his controversial BBC career, had often been caricatured as a relatively uncomplicated creature. Nobody appeared capable of seeing beyond the man's undoubted strength of will, uncompromising manner, and utter solemnity of outlook. In fact, Reith was altogether more complex and less inhuman than the mass of his critics, admirers, enemies and disciples could ever have conceived. His inscrutability, of course, was carefully contrived to hold the inquisitive at bay; and it effectively masked the vulnerable, uneasy, tangled core of the man within. By keeping his public and private lives in rigidly separated compartments, he was able to seal himself off from unsought attention, so that none but a handful of relatives and close friends had any notion of his basic weaknesses. These alone could think of him at intervals as a person of exceptional gifts who was apparently also something of a God-fearing hypocrite.

Reith's vain attempt at Glasgow to placate fate and his ancestors, and especially to prove himself a credit to his father's memory, was bound up with feelings of profound remorse. His conscience was only part of the trouble: any sorrow he might conjure up at the recollection of past faults, notably his puzzling association with younger women in his latter years, could not allay the underlying despair which seemed increasingly to exclude all light from his soul. The same John Reith who dreamed hopefully and on the whole positively, secure in the knowledge that the hand of providence was shaping the dream, was equally a prey to a darker fatalism. He feared that he was foredoomed to damnation, and that no good works would avert that calamity. Whether he had Knox and Calvin to thank for the resulting desolation of spirit, or whether he could have blamed some defect of heredity, Reith did not pause to enquire. It would have made no difference anyway.

A leading neurologist who administered electric shock treatment to him in his eighty-first year was amazed by Reith's willingness to discuss the immediate if superficial cause of a recent but sustained bout of depression: the patient confessed that he was anxious about an unmarried woman for whom he felt particular affection. His regard for his wife, whose saint-like patience he had so frequently overstrained, flowed on a different level. Her understanding and devotion did not make him feel any better, however. His acrobatic falls from grace tended to affect him most deeply in old age when there was too much time for considering the hurt they brought to others; but then he would be struck by another reflection. What possible difference would it have made if he had lapsed a million times, since his fate in the next world was already fixed?

'Keep close to your Saviour, dear boy', his father had advised him in one of the last letters he wrote to him. 'Nothing else is worth while, as the years will tell. We are not here to get great things for ourselves but to make the world a better place for others. Keep hold of the hand of Jesus: no other hand will help you.'

His father would have been appalled by the terrible finality of John Reith's twisted view of God's plans for him, but then the minister had been an erudite theologian with a mind of his own. His son could still recall that a Roman Catholic thinker of sensitivity and depth like John Henry Cardinal Newman had meant more to his father than a host of orthodox Presbyterian sages. But neither Newman nor his father could teach him how to shrug off the demon of self-doubt which, unknown to anyone but himself, had begun to torment him as a boy at home. Because he worshipped both his parents from afar, being too shy and tongue-tied to mention the terror that accompanied his childish superstitions, he got no reassurances from the two people above all others most fitted to exorcise the demon. He had learnt too early how to fend for himself. Self-willed even then, he had shut himself off from the warmth and light and trust which might easily have transformed him into a balanced human being.

Yet the question must be asked: what would have happened if Reith's father had succeeded in penetrating the boy's reserve and solving the worst of his problems? It is probable that John Reith's vast contribution to the educational and cultural life of Britain would, in that case, have been neligible. If in his adolescent days he had conquered the driving impulse to trust nobody but himself, there might have been no BBC as we know it. Could anyone else except the untamed John Reith, whose contemporaries could respect the magnitude of his achievement as the creator of British broadcasting while disliking his style and omniscient manner, have surmounted so many obstacles? What other rival could have summoned up such unique organising ability? Where else could any Government have turned for the sure touch of a visionary who upheld the intrinsic importance of Christian values in any system of public service broadcasting—no matter what his own private relationship might be with God? Certainly nobody but Reith could have inspired such loyalty or set such impeccably lofty standards, rejecting from natural disdain all things that were vulgar, unseemly and pretentious.

Despite a hypersensitive nature, Reith showed toughness and resilience in his dealings with politicians and bureaucrats, and his monumental gift for riding out storms and surviving setbacks was at least partly explained by the secret canker which gnawed at his vitals. For if he could stand that, he could stand anything. He admitted some years before leaving the BBC that he was a victim of accidie, that morbid affliction of the spirit which the medieval monks were so fond of describing; but by then he had more leisure for brooding. Long before he had schooled himself to live with an ailment for which no doctor or priest could prescribe. Sometimes it had struck at him without warning like summer lightning, even when he was preoccupied with constructive work, and its effect had been to turn the whole world sour. Yet nobody fully realised what he suffered, and he would not have thanked anyone who did know for commiserating with him.

As it was, the link between Reith's accidie and his doomed sense of foreboding was never established by his contemporaries. Well-meaning friends would often complain that he was altogether too addicted to the habit of magnifying his failures and writing off his triumphs; but they had no glimmering of the tormented being whose triumphs tasted like ashes in the mouth. There was no petulance in the way he kept repeating himself on the subject, and those who criticised him for seeking to win sympathy did him a mild injustice. John Reith had outgrown flattery and was beyond false humility: he simply knew that his successes were as pointless as his failures.

What betrayed him as a profoundly unhappy man was his inability to laugh or raise the tiniest smile at the inconsistencies and ludicrous cavortings of 'the mini-men' who had somehow come to dominate public life since he left it behind. This became an obsession with him in his final years and was all the more surprising since he so clearly regarded himself now as the most obnoxious mini-man of all. Yet his jaundiced opinions of people and events and trends were usually outrageous enough to amuse the studious listener. Only when I stumbled on the tragic root of the matter, and came to comprehend at last the true reasons for his melancholy, did I find it impossible not to pity him. How could any man in his condition find anything amusing? In his rambling, sharp and often elliptical way, Reith could be a fascinating conversationalist. He could switch on the charm and be both wise and witty in certain moods. Lacking any authentic sense of humour, however, he was usually destructive in his railings against life. There were too many fools about, and he had never been able to suffer fools gladly.

In warning the Glasgow undergraduates that 'he or she whom public opinion regards as successful may know themselves to have failed', John Reith was already doodling with his own epitaph. And the ringing French phrase, '*C'est moi qui parle*', so reminiscent in tone of that other giant from Colombey-les-Deux-Eglises who had wrestled better with a wider destiny, was Reith's nearest approach to acknowledging openly that he had rejected himself. Whatever might be pleaded in mitigation, he had placed the black cap on his head and passed final sentence with the pitiless candour of the self-condemned. Judgment Day had long passed. Death would merely bring confirmation of the sentence.

The careers of nearly all great men of action are shot through with an element of the theatrical. Not infrequently it goes far towards explaining what they achieved in terms of what they were as individuals. The most intriguing fact about John Reith's career is that his highly developed feeling for the theatrical predominated to a degree probably unmatched by any other public figure in the Britain of his day. Not even Churchill managed in peacetime to build his own theatre at public expense, dream up his own modern morality play, cast himself in the role of actor-manager, and seriously contrive to reach audiences of millions whose tastes, attitudes and values were affected as never before by the rigid standards laid down by this one man. Yet Reith knew that all the time he was presenting a play within a play, and that however successful his appearances might be on the narrower, worldly stage, no amount of applause would save him from his predestined fate when the final curtain came down. In the absolute sense Reith was his own Hamlet.

There are no clear clues to this sombre state of mind in his two autobiographical volumes, *Into the Wind* and *Wearing Spurs*; nor would we expect to discover any references to it in the detailed and solidly factual volumes of broadcasting history on which Professor Asa Briggs is still working. It might have been assumed as a matter of course that much insight into the intricate movements of Reith's mind could be obtained in the incredibly lengthy diary which he started to keep before the First World War. This must have run to more than five million words by the time of his death, yet the entries shed little conclusive light on the diarist's fundamental beliefs, hopes, fears, fixations, as he set down the doings of each day rather like a careful accountant determined to balance the books to the last halfpenny. These massive tomes, when suitably edited, will undoubtedly demonstrate Reith's proficiency both in getting things done and in faithfully recounting every minute particular of the process. Yet most of the relevant extracts have already appeared in the books mentioned above. The private record he kept studiously left out all but a few passing references to the dark and prolonged night of his soul.

The purpose of the present study of John Reith is to complete the fragmentary likeness which emerges from the autobiographical material by unravelling the hidden knots and strands of his unusual personality. Whether he would have been pleased with the result must remain a matter for conjecture, in spite of his avowed liking for the unvarnished truth. Once, in conversation with him, I ventured to remark that there were too many bad self-portraits by public men and that the majority of them ought to have been forcibly restrained from putting pen to paper.

'Does that apply to me?' he asked sharply.

'I'm afraid in some ways it does', I admitted.

'Why?' he persisted.

'Because you always managed to dodge the really important issues. I mean—when you were apparently just on the point of revealing something very personal and revealing about yourself, you suddenly dried up or went off at a tangent.'

'Yes', he cried triumphantly, 'but that was the whole idea!'

He was not unaware that I had a vested interest in him both as an experienced biographer, who liked delving deep, and as a comparatively young friend who accepted at face value his repeated protestations that he had 'never been fully stretched', but who persisted in wanting to discover why. This book provides the answer to this and other crucial questions by trying to separate the man from the myth. The qualities in his make-up were many and conflicting: with the inexhaustible vigour went a native shrewdness, with the towering arrogance a touching humility; and if his courage sometimes bordered on recklessness, his ambition for worldly fame was offset by the deadweight of a progressive and almost pathological despair.

The evaluation of these factors will enable others to understand John Reith for what he was, and to assess his achievements with a kindlier and more objective eye than could this eccentric genius who had earned his own footnote in history at least a quarter of a century before he died.

1
The Boy

1

John Reith came into the world prematurely and with a struggle late one summer's night. After the slow agony of delivery came the first feeble cries of the new baby, echoing in his mother's ears like an uncertain hymn of praise. Mary Reith's confinement had not been easy, but now the pain and discomfort receded in the warm afterglow of relief and happiness. A neat, strongly practical woman, whose striking good looks were beginning to fade, she had held in careful check during her ordeal the anxieties natural to an expectant mother in her forty-second year. An unsentimental piety had been her mainstay throughout; for her habitual trust in God was as total as her unqualified acceptance of this latest and joyous manifestation of His will. So on the night of July 20, 1889, had she not the right to relax for a while and marvel in speechless gratitude at the gift of another son?

Her husband leaned over her. He could permit himself again the luxury of a smile which illumined and softened the ascetic lines of his face. The Reverend Dr. George Reith was six years older than Mary. Tall, clean-shaven, and severely handsome, he moved with the dignity and grave assurance of a judge. He loved his wife and family dearly but without possessiveness; and the happiness he shared with his wife at the arrival of their seventh child, a sublime feeling which shone in his slow, rare smile of benediction, was George Reith's immediate way of thanking the Giver of all good things, life included, for a further mark of Divine favour.

To the minds of this gentle but austere and unworldly couple the suggestion of an unwanted pregnancy would have been not merely blasphemous but quite unthinkable. They had grown close together during their twenty-five years of marriage, and the spiritual outlook they shared was uncommonly pure. The big grey manse where they lived in the West End of Glasgow stood next door to the College Church, one of most fashionable and well-to-do Presbyterian parishes in the city. George Reith had been appointed to this desirable incumbency not long after being ordained—an indication, perhaps, of the high hopes then placed in him by his superiors. He had since earned local renown as a preacher, a liberal theologian, an organiser, and an untiring promoter of good causes. There was little of the ambitious, self-seeking cleric in his make-up. Indeed his tolerance for the foibles and the errors of unenlightened souls of other persuasions may have precluded him from moving further up the Presbyterian ladder in an age notorious for the divisions still existing between the Christian churches. It was also an age which set great store by outward appearances.

Many people went to church because it was the done thing; but this did not commit anyone to the pretence that Christian precept could be translated into daily practice at every turn. The ideals which men and women solemnly mouthed together on the Sabbath seldom had much bearing on their actions as individuals during the rest of the week, a fact which saddened the heart of George Reith and gradually drove him to redouble his own efforts as one who taught by example as well as word. His form of Christian teaching was not of the exclusive kind, despite a life-long attachment to the articles of the Presbyterian establishment. Rigid and dour as he invariably was in his personal interpretation of the moral law, yet for the apathy and backsliding of weaker brethren he could always find forgiveness since his God was merciful as well as just. Whether John Knox would have endorsed such breadth of mind in a late-nineteenth-century Scottish disciple must be a moot point; but how far the subtle tolerance of George Reith ever succeeded in shaking the traditional belief of his own people in their predestined status as the Lord's elect remains equally a matter for conjecture.

Because he saw no distinction between a person's public and private life, and took such pains to discourage it as a minister, George Reith's code of conduct was imposed on his children as soon as they learned to talk and think for themselves. Family life, as a result, had always tended to become a rigid and sometimes unnatural extension of the way of life laid down by their father from the pulpit next door. The atmosphere was cheerless. Adherence to an inflexible timetable, with meals and prayers, recreation and religious instruction at set hours, produced in the older children a spirit of superficial compliance. The goodness of a father and mother so selflessly dedicated to the service of outsiders did not automatically evoke a comparable goodness in their offspring. Too often left alone to look after younger members of the family while their parents were otherwise engaged, too overburdened with cheerless observances from which there was no escape, the older sons and daughters of the Reiths outwardly conformed because they had to. But like prisoners biding their time they longed for freedom and meanwhile sought distraction from the unbending regime of home life wherever they could find it.

The birth of a baby brother so much younger than themselves provided a pleasant enough distraction in 1889. The event broke the domestic routine in their holiday house at Stonehaven. Their mother spent more time with her children. And when the family returned to Glasgow, the novelty of helping to dance attendance on her, first in the nursery before John was weaned, then later while he was learning to crawl and toddle and walk, provided an interlude of happiness. For Mary Reith's next youngest child was already ten years old. In the process, of course, the new baby became the focal point of interest and attention. It was surprising that such strict parents as the Reiths should not have foreseen that, by allowing this process to continue, they ensured that the infant soon became thoroughly spoilt.

2

Out of the dusk of infancy John Reith retained in after-life only two significant flashes of memory. As his father was fairly comfortably off, he could afford domestic help. There were daily servants for the upkeep of the manse and a nurse who lived in and helped Mary Reith until John was old enough to go to preparatory school. On one occasion he went out for a walk with his nurse to the neighbouring park where the wild eyes of buttercups and daisies sparkled in the grass. He was three years old, and wanted a bunch to carry home to his mother.

The nurse at first insisted, quite wisely, that he should pick the things for himself, but he pulled a face, flatly refused, then explained why she must do it: 'John's too fat', he lisped. The nurse yielded to his natural quickness of wits and John returned home in triumph. He scored a similar victory over the evangelist preacher, Gypsy Smith, who came to visit the boy's father one day and was persuaded to take John on his morning constitutional. The boy led him across the park to the streets and a convenient baker's shop, bought himself a large, sticky cake, thanked the assistant behind the counter and turned to leave without paying. 'Where's your money?' demanded Gypsy Smith. 'In your pocket, Gypsy,' John Reith replied.[1]

What his parents made of these impulses of childish self-indulgence is unrecorded, but John was certainly not punished. In any other household, at any other period, it might have seemed a harsh and heartless business to have been even reprimanded; but his brothers and sisters would never have expected the slightest concession to bad behaviour when they were his age. So if John could indulge himself in small ways and get away with it, it must have been because the chasm of a whole decade between the baby and his sister, Beth, induced everyone, including his parents, to treat him with special favour.

The first five years of his existence, despite John Reith's assertions to the contrary when he was much older, proved to be years of unclouded happiness. He did his parents, and especially his mother, an unintended injustice in depicting the entire period of childhood as one of misery, since he grew very close to her when he was small and somewhat pampered. A sturdy, talkative boy with a developing will of his own, he was far too absorbed in the black and white realities of the narrow yet fascinating universe he inhabited to notice how much his elders were enslaved by the clock and the church-bell. The demands on them of regular worship and a stifling religious upbringing meant nothing as yet to a child whose natural worship was confined to his mother who taught him his prayers, tucked him up each night, and comforted him when the bogey man behind the nursery curtains troubled his dreams.

The break in this carefree routine came with an abruptness that puzzled and distressed the boy about the time his father decided that John was old enough to start his schooling. For the first time, at the still tender age of five, he was caught up in the grinding round of life as the other children knew it. No longer could he expect to find consolation at his mother's side: his father, still a distant figure of vague power and authority, suddenly emerged as the real ruler of the manse. The word of the Reverend Dr. George Reith was law, and though he seldom appeared except at meals and prayers his unseen presence weighed heavily on John, who strove unwillingly to emulate his brothers and sisters in obedience to the regulations and an inflexible time-table.

John Reith realised that his childhood had ended when he discovered with a shock that his brothers and sisters were no longer in any mood to humour his whims. Having helped to spoil him, they now turned on him as if on the latest recruit to a regiment which prided itself on excessive discipline. If it was unfeeling of them thus to take advantage of the youngest member of the family, George and Mary Reith deserved the lion's share of the blame for failing to anticipate the inevitable. As parents, they lacked both the leisure and the resilience to understand that John's petulance and sullen behaviour were partly their fault—and partly the fault of their older children, who, having been sternly repressed at that age themselves, could see no reason why John should not suffer likewise in turn. And since these insensitive brothers and sisters had experience enough to know most of the tricks of trouble-making, and were not above sneaking on him at times, the unfortunate boy suffered doubly. For when he did break the rules there was nobody in the manse, nobody in the whole wide world, to whom he could now turn for comfort. Even his mother, the one person he continued to adore with lonely, fanatical ardour, appeared to lose all sympathy for him whenever he did wrong.

3

By his own reckoning, it must have been between his sixth birthday, while he was learning the three R's at Park Preparatory School, near his home, and his tenth, when the silk-hatted masters of Glasgow Academy were beginning to treat him as a difficult pupil, that John Reith became an avid and accomplished dreamer. At first the practice proved a necessary escape mechanism: surrounded by so much restriction and opposition at home and at school, the boy naturally turned in on himself and allowed free play to the fires of an extremely active imagination. As he grew older, however, everything served as fuel for the furnace; and by some enchanted process of alchemy, everything touched by his vivid fantasy could be turned to fairy gold. Time had no meaning or terrors for him in this private universe where the people and the realities of everyday existence were not excluded but simply transmuted and made more tolerable. As architect and supreme controller of the dream domain the young John Reith could enter or leave it at will. It was a haven of refuge in moments of stress, discouragement or discontent. It was also a place, or more precisely a state of mind, to which he could transport himself instantly under favourable conditions. The solemn thundering of organ music, the harmony of voices singing a favourite psalm in church, even a colourful phrase spoken by his father from the pulpit during a sermon, somehow seemed to inflate his spirit like a balloon and lift him to that other world.

His power of imagination grew by what it fed on; and if there was a certain plainness and lack of variety about the diet at the College

Church manse, this did not diminish his appetite. The house was full of books, not just the leather-bound tomes of theology and other esoteric subjects which lined his father's study, or the dull volumes prescribed by teachers at school, but a small treasure trove of novels and adventure stories approved by his parents. The heroes and villains of Sir Walter Scott became early if distant acquaintances; but the two characters whom he idolised on first meeting, and rapidly identified himself with in his own romantic wanderings through the region of make-believe, were Tom Sawyer and Huckleberry Finn. He often longed for the day when he, like them, would strike out on his own and demonstrate to the rough, hostile world beyond the manse and school his capacity to endure and overcome adversity. It was no accident that John Reith's affection and regard for these sharp-witted, lively creatures of an American author's fertile invention lasted for the rest of his life, so that in his eighty-first year Reith admitted to me that he could still discover fresh things to marvel at in the 'homely, common-sense philosophy of Mark Twain',[2] particularly as expressed through the children of his genius.

Perhaps because of the intense atmosphere of religion in the home, the boy drew little direct consolation from prayer or spiritual exercises, despite the vigilance of both parents. He was not especially pious by nature, the one stimulus to concentration of thought and emotion being his superstitious dread of an avenging God which had been acquired at a remarkably early age. The notion that divine justice might be tempered with mercy was a frail but tempting straw he could not bring himself to clutch at; for John Reith knew that the all-seeing eye of the Almighty could never be taken in by human presumptuousness or pretence, and this tendency to exaggerate the heinousness of his own undoubted failings was precociously strong in him. What was the use of telling God you were sorry for your faults when you knew quite well that the very next moment you would probably fall again? And where lay the sense in staking everything on the outside hope of a death-bed reprieve almost by the toss of a coin, since God's foreknowledge enabled him to say in advance: 'Heads I win, tails you lose.'

So, much too early in life for comfort, this unusual boy got caught in the cruel trap of an ancient theological dilemma about the extent of man's free will. If the circumstances of his upbringing did nothing to relieve its emotional grip on him, it should be stated, too, that this was because the dark and simple superstitions of Calvinism had been bred in his bones like a hereditary disease, just as his romantic imagination was partly an endowment from the Stuart grandmother on his father's side of the family.

The Reiths came of stern, unyielding Presbyterian stock; and John was naturally proud of his ancestors. His grandfather, the first general manager of the Clyde Navigation Trust, had died when John was only four months old; but the old man's doings and sayings were so often mentioned at home that he seemed to live on like a familiar, guiding spirit. The family photographs amplified the frequent word-of-mouth descriptions of him, so that fifty years later his grandson admitted to having 'heard and read so much about him as almost to have known him. Courageous, masterful, inflexible, shrewd, he ruled the river.' A will of steel coupled to a daring, original outlook had enabled this rugged elder to prevail over men 'of lesser prescience and of other ideals'.

Grandfather George Reith, like his clergyman son, was 'very tall, of commanding dignity and presence, of frightening austerity of countenance. He was of the Covenanter breed, intensely—but in child-like simplicity—religious. There was an absolute rigour of obedience to what he held to be his Master's will. In his public life he never forgot that he was a citizen of the Kingdom of God. Beneath the forbidding exterior there was a kindly, tender heart which children—and mendicants—soon uncovered. There is no memorial to him in the city of Glasgow, despite what he did for it. He was among the very last of his caste; the same was later said of my father. They both had a potent influence on me; an *ex pietate* compulsion. While it held, I was secure'.[1]

4

At the time he wrote those words, in 1948, Reith was secure only in his established renown as the BBC's founding father and as an ex-Minister of the Crown somewhat less than normally effective. Like many a modern autobiographer, he allowed little of his true self to slip through between the lines; yet the implication that his father and grandfather exerted a benign if waning influence on him for many years requires some qualification. The standards of simple goodness and excessive piety they set him in his lonely and bewildered boyhood were already far beyond his reach. A sullen youngster, constantly on the defensive, he gave the impression of someone prepared to be disbelieved because even among his brothers and sisters he was like an unarmed scout cut off in hostile territory. Neither school nor church offered any relief or comfort to him: in the classroom his masters regarded him as an inattentive boy lacking in application and taste for hard work; in the family pew his feverish sense of awe made him only too well aware of the Lord God's omnipotence and his own helplessness. There were crumbs of consolation to be picked up from his bright daydreams, of course; and in the religious instruction given on the afternoon of every Sabbath by his mother he learnt impotently to admire the sweet wholesomeness of her faith. How much his frustrated emotional attachment to her entered into the boy's religious confusion can only be conjectured. What cannot be doubted is that some of the rich, spiritual optimism of this remarkable woman rubbed off on her youngest son:

'To the alien, manifold and exacting duties of the lady of a Scottish manse', he wrote, 'she brought a spirit of resolute and rare devotion. . . . She too was shy; she too had sorrows enough. But she was gallant and of buoyant faith. All, she was convinced, would come right in the end. . . . Sunday afternoons with my mother are among the precious memories of home.'[1]

His father and mother were seldom at home during the long weekday evenings after school. John Reith followed the set pattern and whiled away the time in his bedroom, reading or trying to catch up with his studies. The habitual sense of isolation served only to heighten misunderstanding and so embitter relations with his brothers and sisters; and increasingly John Reith found himself hankering to escape from the unhealthy atmosphere of home:

'My mother was a saint and my father, well, he was saint-like. They were so preoccupied with good works and the care of others outside the manse that they were more often out than in. The servants could not keep the peace so they kept out of the way as well. I did not get on with my brothers and sisters, and two or three of them I deeply disliked.'[2]

The anti-social instincts of the young John Reith became more pronounced in adolescence. There came a moment of crisis when the masters at Glasgow Academy were obliged to tell his father that they had done all they could for him. Scholastically he was no dunce, but in eight years of intermittent striving he had displayed little aptitude or stomach for learning. 'Undistinguished and unsatisfactory' were his own honest epithets for performance, 'impatient, independent, intolerant' for general conduct. On the rugby field his tall, lean, tense figure, the classic figure of a teenager who had outgrown his strength but held his own by cunning and sheer doggedness, could on occasion strike terror in opponents older than himself. He loved the game; but a wayward streak of vindictiveness in his nature made him a dubious sportsman. Nobody at this period of formation could ever have said of John Reith, by way of premature epitaph, 'he always played the game—and he always lost it'. His loss was graver than that.

He was still only fifteen when two boys about his own age went absent from school for several days on end. Subsequent enquiries showed that their truancy was the direct result of Reith's bullying of both; and, on being confronted with the accusation, he neither denied it nor manifested any contrition. His father, greatly disturbed by this culminating proof of the boy's undesirable characteristics, responded to advice and withdrew him from Glasgow Academy. The hard-and-fast decision was taken to send him to an English public school. The problem boy accepted the blow to his pride in the fatalistic mood of a prisoner condemned to transportation for a petty misdemeanour.[3]

'Something of the sort had been threatened for some time', he recalled. 'There were several suggestions as to what should be done with me; one brother had even suggested a training ship for the mercantile marine. . . .'

This drastic remedy was averted by the persuasions of John's eldest brother, now vicar of a Norfolk country parish, who claimed to know the very place where the tantrums, the temper and the studied rebelliousness of the young could be curbed without forfeiting the advantages of a formal education. Gresham's School was close enough to his living for him to keep a weather eye on the boy's progress, but he had little doubt that the headmaster and staff, of whom he spoke highly, would manage well enough to handle the Reith family's misfit. So all the arrangements were made, and in the late summer of 1904 John became a reluctant public schoolboy in a land he balefully regarded from the outset as foreign.

'I was', he observed, 'entirely moral but otherwise vexatious and difficult. . . . The ordered procedure of the place was subjected to some strain.' Once again the long reach of retrospect, however carefully adjusted, fails to do more than scratch the surface: for John Reith underwent so much misunderstanding and stern discipline before settling down at Gresham's that any fifteen-year-old of simpler moral fibre might well have cut short the ordeal by running away. The headmaster, whom he learnt slowly to respect and admire, conceived an immediate dislike for an outspoken boy whose contempt for traditions and rules was spiked with thinly disguised defiance. There were several painful interviews with Mr. G. W. S. Howson, who, in the outraged judgment of John Reith at the time, proved himself to be not 'one of the great headmasters of the country' but a bigoted and despicable tyrant.

'The mere fact that I was Presbyterian and a Scot seemed to offend him; and I had the unprecedented effrontery to question and resist some of his principles of management. I reciprocated his dislike with great cordiality.'[2] Until the Christmas term of his second year at Gresham's the boy kept up his front of resistance to authority, enduring the rebuffs and punishments handed out to him as part of the tribute that individualistic virtue must always pay to high-minded, eccentric viciousness. Then, perhaps despairing of changing him, Mr. Howson began to treat him with more leniency; and the months before John's seventeenth birthday passed in a haze of relative contentment. The ordeal, though it solved nothing fundamental, had taught John Reith to depend utterly on himself and to offer a grudging trust only on the most beneficial terms obtainable.

As a prefect during his final year he brought a measure of whimsy to his interpretation of discipline; but it was his keenness and efficiency in the cadet corps which earned him promotion and much praise, possibly convincing the school staff that John Reith's refusal to become a conformist concealed a contrary sense of responsibility. If he did not shine at lessons, his taste for history and English set him apart. When he said his last goodbyes in July 1906, nobody would have quarrelled with his retrospective verdict that he was going out into the world 'still immature and unformed', leaving parents, teachers, brothers and sisters very doubtful indeed about his future.

2

The Misfit

1

THAT SUMMER of 1906 was the darkest and most confusing period yet for the returning public schoolboy. Well before the end of his last term at Gresham's, John Reith was prepared to acknowledge that his parents had chosen wisely in sending him there, despite the knocks and occasional ridicule he had to take for wilfully parading his alien status as a Presbyterian and a proud Scot. In a calculating yet masterful fashion he had easily acquired the prefect's knack of supervising the lives, and correcting the wayward tendencies, of boys who were mostly younger, smaller and more timid than himself, gaining the grudging approval of the headmaster for his efforts. Without question he had most enjoyed the activities of the officers' training corps, in which he reached the rank of sergeant.[1] The rough training had shown the need for discipline, rousing his patriotic ardour and firing his love of drilled precision. It gave him an almost sensual thrill to hold a target steadily in his sights and to score a bull's-eye with a firm and final squeeze of the trigger; the ecstasy, though momentary, surpassed the demanding pleasures of demonstrating his physical strength and irrepressible urge to win untidier and less convicing victories on the rugby field.

Even in the classrooms at Holt there had been marked improvement of a kind. History and the classics became his favourite subjects, and though he could have wished at times that Euclid had been smothered at birth, John Reith had a quick head for figures. The thirst for knowledge had wakened late in him; but it went deep and was tinctured with an anxious, hopeful longing. Would his father respect his wishes?

Would the evidence of his belated application at Gresham's be conclusive enough? He desperately wanted to continue his studies. Yet, characteristically, he would not demean himself by unbaring the hopes and fears that alternatively beset him to anyone in authority at Holt. That would have smacked of weakness or of seeking an uncovenanted favour; his stiff pride forbade it. So he had said his goodbyes, stifling a secretive and genuine regret at leaving a place which had taught him self-respect, and returned to Glasgow with uneasiness pricking his mind behind the impenetrable mask of cheerfulness he wore as he faced his family again.

Within a few days of unpacking his trunk John Reith's inner world suddenly came tumbling down about his ears. He had never felt happy in the past when his father summoned him into the manse library 'for a talk'. It was not that he detested having to hear the one-sided litany of reproaches for faults, heinous and small; he seldom could deny them anyway. But in the presence of this self-assured, noble and seemingly omniscient man, whose severity was as gentle as his patience, John Reith invariably grew tongue-tied. He was prepared this time for something more constructive than the familiar dressing down. He therefore waited with less than his usual apprehension for his father to speak. Looking older and more severe than the boy could remember the Reverend Dr. George Reith handed him a single sheet of paper ruled out in the printed, oblong spaces of a school report, and invited him to read it. Mr. Howson's assessment of John Reith's qualities and academic attainments in his final year at Gresham's struck the subject as fairly unflattering, but it certainly called for less drama and controlled indignation than followed the son's swift, unsurprised scanning of its main critical points. His father took the report back and announced his verdict.

'You will not be continuing your studies', he said with slow emphasis. 'That's perfectly clear.'

It was as if he had hurled a thunderbolt, bringing down the ceiling and the contents of his bookshelves on the unsuspecting head of his son. John Reith was too stunned to reply. Everything he had done at Holt during the previous year had been directed to the one aim of proving himself worthy to complete his education at a university. Now he realised with a sense of bitterness that he might as well have idled away every moment. Was it conceivable that his father did not understand or care? Did it matter now in any event? Long practice enabled him to hide his anguish behind a stony face and downcast eyes. He refused to show by word or gesture what he thought about this cruel decision. He let that eloquent tongue drone on, half listening to the explanations and recriminations of a person who sounded like any other unfeeling stranger. The money spent on sending John Reith to a university would be money wasted, said the voice. Where lay the sense in seeking to reason or argue with someone so revered, whose mind on a matter of such tremendous importance was already made up? That would have served as little purpose as throwing himself on the floor, kicking and screaming, until his elder brothers were summoned to carry him struggling to his room.

'We shall have to think and pray hard about your future', his father concluded. 'Whatever is best for you will be arranged. But remember, my boy, you will never be or do anything useful in this world until you start thinking how you can serve others and learning to work with a will.'[2]

Even in his seventeenth year, though he experienced much trouble in curbing his temper, John Reith saw that there were moments when it was convenient to avoid pressing home the truth. Here, in loathsome and unacceptable form, was one such occasion for reserve. He had stood in superstitious awe of both parents, and especially his father, for as long as he could remember. The Reverend Dr. George Reith, so godly and selfless in thought and deed, had represented far more than any mere servant of the Almighty: in the constricting atmosphere of the manse he was God's deputy, and the mind of this late-developer invested him with quasi-divine majesty and power. Every scolding and punishment the boy had ever received from him was not only deserved but providentially designed for his own good. Now in a terrible flash of recognition John Reith saw through the haze of superstitious awe. If he appeared as contrite and submissive now as in any previous crisis, an element of realism stiffened his attitude. How, he wondered, could God permit such mistakes to happen? He knew beyond doubt that his father was wrong, and the insidious knowledge led him to question and gradually to reject the sweet childish assumption that this pillar of saint-like wisdom could read his heart more easily than a well-thumbed book from the library. So at one shattering blow the boy was both reduced to the edge of despair and infused with a strange, new conviction that his father was just another fallible mortal. John Reith was growing up, both because of, and in spite of, his surroundings.

'It was decided that I should become a mechanical engineer', he recalled a lifetime later. 'I knew it was wrong. I was not at all mechanically-minded. Abhorrent the idea was. I wanted to go to a university—classics, philosophy, physics, literature, history—almost anything that was an intellectual rather than a manual pursuit. My desire was entirely vague; and, as was pointed out, there had been no special signs of scholarship.'

Too striken with frustration to speak out on his own behalf, he had too little of the natural rebel in him to run away. Had the idea occurred to him, he would have spurned it like any evil temptation because he still felt himself to be a prisoner of circumstances beyond his personal control. His mother, serene and thoughtful, had ceased to act as his confidante. She complied with her husband's high-handed treatment of the boy, choosing to temper it in her own discreetly refined way by steering the conversation to neutral topics at meals and trying hard to draw her youngest son out of his shell. In neither course was she successful. The rest of the family were united in their tactless determination to reconcile John to his grey future as an apprentice in the big locomotive works at Hydepark on the dingy eastern approaches to the city.

'My father said he believed in every man learning a trade', John Reith wrote. 'One brother said it would take the nonsense out of me, another that steam was the basis of all power. The family doctor intervened. It must have been my mother's doing. I was too young and too tall to go straight into the works; it would overtax my strength, he said—and I let him say it.'

He resented the cruelty of his brothers and sisters who seemed to gloat over him in his misery. The spoiled brat of the family was at last getting his just desserts. He hated them for their sanctimonious spleen, longing for the day when he could turn his back on them for ever. His only safe defence meanwhile was silence: at least in the bosom of this odd family he kept his own counsel and trusted nobody but himself. Let them all say, if they wished, that he was the misfit; the problem child who refused to be his age; the big, hulking baby who was 'all set for failure or at best mediocrity'. His father unwisely took the view, and the others dutifully followed his lead as if God had spoken.

If only by some miraculous gift of insight the mistrustful old man could have pierced the blank wall of indifference with which the boy confronted everyone, his rigid opinion might have softened a little. How could any minister and natural father, imbued with such firm faith in the mysterious workings of Providence, have failed to respond with compassion to the revelation that his youngest son's spiritual life was in a hopeless muddle? It may well be that children today still grow up into sceptics because religion has been stuffed down their throats at too tender an age. John Reith certainly belonged to a generation which suffered much from the practice, yet his circumstances made the process of erosion one which was at once more agonising and more bewildering. Having been brought up so close to the Throne of Grace, his spirit now tended to recoil from sacred things like a queasy stomach overburdened with rich food. Instead of yielding, however, he was impelled by a lively and over-scrupulous conscience to resist a temptation which could have come only from the devil. His predicament was scarcely improved by the doubts he also began to feel about his father's sympathetic awareness of the problem; this godly person, whom the boy had once invested with the gift of an unerring omniscience, seemed totally insensitive to the unwitting suffering he caused his son.

In a household so strictly regimented and enmeshed in unending religious routine, any boy of spirit would have been bound to react sooner or later. The tragedy in John Reith's case was that the reaction should have caught him bending, since at this awkward stage in his development the onset of doubt served to intensify his feelings of guilt. He had difficulty enough trying to control an explosive temper without having to put up with bullying and teasing; but he found it impossible to describe the dull aching sensation of being caught in a deeper trap not of his own making. Endowed with the physical strength of a man, his emotions were still as immature as a child's and the lip-service he paid to religious observances produced no consolation. As imperceptibly as air expelled from the lungs, the joyless deity of the manse was receding from John Reith as Someone who cared as little about the pain He inflicted as did his own father. Was a God like this entirely credible, no matter what revenge He might eventually return to take?

Edmund Gosse was writing in that very year of his own equally ungrateful upbringing in the care of a father whose piety proved much narrower than the Very Reverend George Reith's:

'Through thick and thin I clung to a hard nut of individuality, deep down in my childish nature', said Gosse in *Father and Son*. 'To the pressure from without I resigned everything else, my thoughts, my words, my anticipations, my assurances, but there was something I never resigned—my innate and persistent self. Meek as I seemed and gently responsive, I was always conscious of that innermost quality . . . that existence of two in the depths who could speak to one another in inviolable secrecy.'[3]

So John Reith learnt the wisdom of confiding in himself alone, without shedding the remorse he had increasingly felt since attaining the use of reason.

2

The Reiths as a family had their traditional way of spending the summer holidays. Instead of going to the seaside, or to some foreign spa which would have been too expensive and ostentatious for a minister of the Kirk, the Reverend Dr. George Reith invariably took his wife and children to the same small place in the highlands north of the River Dee but not many miles from his own Kincardineshire birthplace. Aviemore has since changed almost out of recognition: then there were no ski-slopes, no modernistic hotels for cosmopolitan visitors with a liking for winter sports, no good road-links or fast rail services. It was the sleepy, ageless character of this delightfully remote village, with its one spartan hotel in a single street of granite cottages, which drew back the Reiths every year as though to their roots. For two whole months they would while away the long days in the mountain air; and when John accompanied his parents to Aviemore at the end of July 1906 he was as relieved as they must have been at the prospect of a break from the wearying deadlock of minds and hearts at home.

His happiest memories were of warm sunlight filtering through the firs on the slopes beyond the village, of staring at his distorted reflection in trout-streams as he lay spreadeagled on the bank with his nose just clear of the fast, clear water, of dreaming away the hours in books of adventure stories when the rain came down and threatened to wash Aviemore away. Now he had returned to seek respite from the latest miseries in store for him: at least for this interlude there need be no bickering with sisters and brothers, no stern admonitions from his father; in his own company he might find solace from the glum forebodings which seemed to crowd his brain like vultures. He *knew* that his father had committed a blunder in choosing a career for which he, the youngest and most vulnerable son, had neither the aptitude nor the taste; and the blunder had greatly diminished his father's authority and prestige in his eyes. Yet John Reith was prepared to submit and obey him from a kind of reflex habit of devotion. He resolved not to ruin this break for his parents or himself by raising the subject or by appearing sulky and disgruntled. If they would leave him to his own solitary devices, he would repay the compliment.

So he took to the winding paths through the trees to the bare flanks of the Grampian foothills on long, wearying walks which sometimes lasted most of the day, remembering how his father had led him first to the crest of Cairngorm at the age of seven. And as if by way of recompensing him for the private bargain he had made, the sheer exertion of climbing seemed progressively to clear his mind of its settled melancholy. He could picture himself in the guise of one or other of the romantic heroes in the books he always turned to like drugs: Rob Roy or David Balfour, hardened by troubles greater than he had to face, might have crossed this beautiful empty wilderness intent only on accomplishing their perilous missions through thick and thin. At Gresham's he had more recently dipped into the poetry of Wordsworth. Its appeal was immediate and compelling. Snatches of verse echoed in his mind as his eyes took in the glories of nature around him, his ears the loveliness of birdsong. A sense of peace would momentarily descend. The world of home and church, with its deadening routine of superficial piety and hidden discontents, looked smaller and slightly less hopeless when set in this sublime perspective. John Reith suddenly detected in the atmosphere the heady scent of hope. Why should he remain so downcast by his father's mistaken judgment? He could emulate his own private, fictional heroes in their strength of purpose and endurance. He might even win through in the end.

The God who ruled the manse and his parents' every conscious move had become a more shadowy and less credible figure of late. When John Reith strode through the Rothiemurchus forests, the God Who reigned there seemed at once a kindlier and more reasonable Being perhaps because he was almost palpably in touch with His creation. Certainly the signs of majesty and power needed no pointing with rubrics and organ music and sermonising. They filled the senses and the spirit without cloying, and while the spell remained John Reith could shake off the doom-laden fear which penetrated his immature religious belief like the prongs of a devil's pitchfork. The feeling of uplift came most clearly when the background noises of nature were drowned by the whistling of the wind in the trees. If proof were required that inside this young man was a suppressed mystic struggling to get out, it can be found in John Reith's frank admission that he stopped in his tracks and frequently strained his ears 'just in case the wind had a message for me from the far hills'. There was no blasphemy in the inspired thought that the kindlier God he had encountered on the heights might wish to speak: and whether His word reached the supplicant or not, the young man was already defiantly convinced that his destiny lay in his own hands. The wind, the trees, the sky, the primeval rocks and every living thing in that unspoilt landscape seemed to tell him: 'Trust yourself and all will be well'.

The people in the village could not be counted friends, though he exchanged the ordinary courtesies with them. He wanted and sought no companions among youths of his own age; he was too self-conscious about the rift with his father, and in any case he enjoyed loneliness as much as others enjoyed gregariousness. It was the same in Glasgow, after that wondrous escape from everyday reality, once he started attending classes at the technical college. His fellow-students were socially rather mixed, not a few of them lacking the manners he had firmly instilled into younger and forgetful boys at Gresham's. John Reith had no wish to befriend anyone in an institution he already detested, nor did the place particularly tempt him to make unnecessary enemies. But he did hit back with venom when one coarse-mouthed student provoked him by jeering at 'the wee boy from the kirk'. The joke was never repeated. John Reith retaliated at once, grabbing the young man by the collar and shaking him like a rag doll and threatening to beat the living daylights out of him on the spot. The rest of his classmates acted prudently after that, leaving the excessively tall, gaunt and rather angular son of the manse to go his own lonely way. His one outlet for pent-up energies was on the college rugby field. There this morose young man demonstrated how uninhibited, co-operative and even generous he could be when his mind was wholly concentrated on striving to win a match, no matter how loaded the odds might be against him. In class his teachers were even less successful than his parents in piercing the mask of indifference he habitually wore. He did not slack or malinger, but his work lacked enthusiasm and precision. Without any facility for drawing, he did not disguise his distaste for having to illustrate complicated engineering mysteries he did not understand. As an innate aptitude for higher mathematics was also required, Reith felt quite lost. The effort seemed far beyond his powers of comprehension; yet he settled down with determination to employ an exceptionally retentive memory in the mechanical task of learning a multitude of necessary formulas by heart.

Broader subjects like natural philosophy attracted him because they had more relevance to life and the unfolding of its manifold meanings. His brain assimilated knowledge of the kind with an appetite of true appreciation. By contrast he was increasingly incensed by the pointlessness of 'purely technical' problems. Of what earthly use were these to any human being with a serious interest in life? He wondered at times whether mechanical engineers as a breed could be as deadly dull as their specialised branch of learning suggested, and with the speculation there would rise like heartburn a sense of grievance against his teachers. For the first time John Reith revolted against them and the rubbish they purported to teach. They in turn resented his arrogance—and freely exposed his ignorance. The reports which reached the Reverend Dr. George Reith indicated that the boy, far from making progress, was rapidly earning the reputation of a dunce and a nuisance. All his reproofs, however, seemed to leave his son unmoved; and he was sometimes left questioning what he had done to deserve such hard ingratitude from someone he loved.

It was a protracted period of great unhappiness for father and son, the rift between them widening until it seemed that nothing could ever bridge it again. Yet the points at issue were trifling in themselves and merely symbolic of a deeper divide. Of what importance were a master's criticisms of this young man's apathetic performances in class beside the damning self-criticism John Reith could have offered his father had they been on open terms with each other? Candour was out of the question, however, for someone forced by the unreal conditions of his existence to lead a double life. Outwardly conforming at home to the monotonous rhythm of meals, religious services and study, the youngest son of the manse followed his own wayward impulses whenever the front door closed behind him and he walked off by himself. His behaviour, on the whole, was innocent enough; but what motivated it as a rule was a powerful sense of defiance. He knew that his father misunderstood him, as well as what was vital for his development as a person; he accepted the absurd future that had been chosen for him, but his resentment ran deep. All he could hope for from the experience was to learn how to endure and persevere without complaining. So, like a stranger in the bosom of his own family, John Reith retreated more and more into the disordered world of his own dreams and superstitious nightmares. In seeking freedom and a limited privacy, he was conscious at the same time of turning his back on the precepts he had been taught to accept since childhood. His conscience, as a result, did not cease to torment him.

Emerson once wrote of a witty medical friend who asserted that the Creed of an over-zealous Christian was most probably located in the duct of the bile. The physician deduced that if the patient's liver were diseased, then the latter must be a Calvinist. The conceit may be scandalously far-fetched, yet the unrelieved religious gloom shared by many extremist disciples of both Calvin and Knox down the centuries does suggest a canker of the spirit which appeared to affect the human liver also. John Reith, however, had enjoyed robust health from infancy. Apart from a bout of whooping cough, he was immune to the colds and sniffles and common ailments of adolescence, possibly as a consequence of his spartan upbringing. On the other hand, and almost certainly as a result of a bad conscience, he had cultivated by his eighteenth year an outlook on life of almost morbid cantankerousness. He still took care to preserve appearances. Because his father was a prominent figure in the public life of Glasgow, John Reith himself had become, in a sense, an object of mild interest to the numerous friends and well-wishers of the Reverend Dr. George Reith. This reinforced the young man's resolve to play two or more roles like an indifferent actor, posing with a difficult smile for the passing edification of a kindly visitor or passer-by from his parents' wide social circle, baring his teeth in flashes of contemptuous anger at the unappreciative staff of the technical college, and wearing a martyr's halo at home in the unfriendly company of his own sisters and brothers. He was truly himself in the solitude of his room; but when he gazed at his reflection in the distorting mirror of conscience, John Reith invariably loathed what he saw. At such timeless points in his unhappy youth he feared for his immortal soul, as if the gloomy superstitions of his Covenanting forefathers had been bred in the bone—and the Christian teaching and example of his godly parents no longer counted for anything.

3

One familiar effect on the mind of prison conditions is to telescope the passage of time. A spiritual jail may be worse in that respect, for life can glide across the surface of the measured hours with apparent smoothness and yet fail to touch the prisoner. The eight years spent by John Reith between the technical college and the Hydepark engineering works were equivalent to eight years spent in a kind of self-imposed solitary confinement. The sequence of events became blurred; the highlights of relief and hope were so few that their exact dating hardly matters. Yet these years proved to be crucial in the making of a man with whose character and public reputation the world rightly conjures today. Nor is it necessarily by accident or oversight that Reith himself skated lightly over the period in his memoirs. It was not a question of his selectively wiping out by a trick of will what he wanted to forget: it was more a matter of his being unable to recall from that dark limbo much beyond the desolation of spirit which sheer determination taught him to live with.

The studies originally intended as a prelude to the engineering apprenticeship were unsuccessful. He did his best, but at his own pace and in his own unattractively rebellious fashion. So, by the late summer of 1909, when he set off from the manse just before five o'clock one morning to meet his new employers and fellow-apprentices, John Reith was as unsure of his future as ever. In a fit of desperation he had recently broken his silence and habitual self-reliance to plead with his father for the chance to do something else:

'I'd like to join a railway. I'm sure the management side would interest me.'

He had seen an advertisement in a newspaper, inviting applications for jobs on the Caledonian line. He had gone to much trouble over the letter; and his momentary jubilation was great when he received a favourable reply. They were looking for youths with ambition; vacancies existed, though the initial pay would be low and the precise duties somewhat vague. As his single ambition then was to escape from the deadening routine laid down for him, he struck out for a change in his own defence. But his father's judgment was crushing and final:

'So you'd like to join the Caledonian railway? Yes, and be a railway clerk for the rest of your life.'

No counter-argument was possible. It was quite true that John Reith's paternal grandfather had worked his way to the top on the railways. His whole career, however, had been one of single-minded resolve to succeed. He had first acquired the skills of a wheelwright in his native village, then the qualifications of a lawyer; and his experience led in the end to his becoming general manager. The minister of the College manse did not have to hammer the moral home. He had tried in vain a hundred times to warn John of the folly of calculated idleness. He simply dismissed his son and his hair-brained scheme without further ado.

'It was', Reith concluded many years later, 'presumably an indication of his estimate of my capacity.'

There could be no escape. As he still gave no evidence of possessing or wishing to acquire the qualities deemed necessary for rising high, John Reith was offered no alternative but to learn a trade—the hard way. In that household the word of his father was law; and with outward submissiveness he accepted it, for all the bitter inward sense of being misused.

A 'gentleman apprentice', forsooth! He would not be left in peace by the tough, coarse-mouthed youths who signed on with him, of that he was assured by the elder brother who never let pass the slightest opportunity of teasing him. At last he would meet his match, and serve him right. It was high time somebody handy with his fists took him to one side and taught him a good lesson.

'He expatiated, seemed to gloat, on what they would do. I was frightened, so frightened that defensive measures were adopted in advance.'

Out of his slender pocket money, John Reith bought himself a muffler and a workman's skip-cap. Discarding collar and tie on his first day at the plant, he signed on wearing the cap 'at an aggressive angle', the face framed between the peak and the rough folds of the muffler was twisted into a scowl of fixed ferocity. It was, once again, the unnatural actor's way of disguising what he truly felt. To quote his own words, it was 'colossal bluff—but it worked'. On one

4

occasion only, and this occurred well into the long, five-year sentence of unrewarding labour in the locomotive shops, did John Reith completely lose control of his temper and raise his hand menacingly to a young man who had tried his patience too far.

By and large, his relationships with others at the works were correct rather than cordial. The first two months, during which the actor's muffler and skip-cap were replaced in favour of more conventional articles of attire, inevitably proved to be the most taxing. Some brains have a natural affinity with the ingenious processes of building, stripping, maintaining and repairing engines, so that the underlying principles come easily and their strict application to some minute, intestinal part in a corner of the grimy shop can be as thrilling and satisfying as a laboratory experiment to the born scientist or a successful minor operation to the diagnostic skill of a good doctor. Since John Reith's mind simply seized up when he handled bits and pieces of machinery and passed them on to a trained fitter or foreman, he felt as out of place as a foreign stowaway trapped in a ship's engine-room. The 'acute crisis' he went through at first was merely a repetition of that dreaded sense of being displaced and misunderstood which had haunted him intermittently since the inglorious end of his schooldays. Rising before five o'clock each morning, walking to the tram-stop, brooding on his fate as the jolting, noisy vehicle crowded with listless early-shift men in overalls rumbled into the still city, the young man knew that by a savage twist of irony 'an awful mistake' was being compounded for his imaginary good.

He emerged slowly from the initial bludgeoning of mind and senses with noise, the sickening smell of oil, the incomprehensible engineering jargon, and the passive performance of subordinate, menial tasks with a small, unambitious resolve. At least he would still not run away like a coward. Apart from anything else, there was nowhere else to go. If he stuck it out, endured the long hours and the din, continued to slog away at the neglected theoretical side in evening classes before dropping exhausted into bed after eleven each night, even a brain so allergic to the marvels of mechanical things would surely soak in a little useful knowledge. That minute, hard grain of determination was enough; and it grew by what it fed on: the rough companionship of foremen and fellow-apprentices on the job and at meal-breaks taught him gradually how to fend for himself, without (except in the solitary instance already mentioned) any loss of self-respect or self-control. A man less blinkered by prejudice and more proof against self-pity would no doubt have acquired greater tolerance and understanding of others than John Reith's temperament and background allowed. At any rate he gradually overcame the innate suspicion with which he had always been accustomed to treat fellow-human beings of his own age; and as he relaxed, so a measure of confidence in himself as well as pride even in distasteful work started to develop.

The winters, of course, were the worst times. He did not mind getting up in the darkness and virtually living all day, too, under artificial light. Nor did his tough, lean body shrink from the icy blasts. He could boast, without undue exaggeration, that he hardly noticed the cold either. In fact, some masochistic streak in his make-up enabled him to find exhilaration in the harsh touch of the year's cruellest season. The harder the frost, the more he enjoyed it. If he was expected to endure as the price of initiation to the business of earning his keep, he would endure with a defiant cheerfulness which was no longer entirely hollow. John Reith realised this with a rare flash of thankfulness when walking along the high drive towards his father's house. The biting wind from the north was always worth listening to carefully, in case it carried a whispered message for him from the God of the Eternal Hills. By a quirk of temperament, he could extract from the effort one more gleam of hope for the future.

The other lasting compensation was his one evening a week talking, thinking and schooling himself in military lore as a keen member of what was to become the Glasgow University Officers' Training Corps. When he joined the contingent in 1906, almost at the same time as he entered the technical college but with vividly contrasting enthusiasm, it was then part of the First Lanarkshire Rifle Volunteers. Characteristically, he would remember the summers of his drably protracted youth for the few days spent under canvas, carrying out training exercises as the sergeant in command of a section. He was justifiably proud to be 'one of the first three' considered suitable for the rank, worked with a will to pass the necessary tests which secured him certificates of efficiency, and generally took the arts and disciplines of a profession he had not hitherto thought of entering with a solemnity which his men found trying, and others of equal or higher rank in the University Company largely comical. Walter Elliot, for a while an exact contemporary of his at Glasgow Academy, was invariably pleasant and complimentary, but conceded to his intimates that John Reith somehow had the fatal combination of attributes which turned him into 'a crashing bore'. The two young men were sufficiently dissimilar in outlook and disposition to remain only casual acquaintances. Elliot's easy and sophisticated manner attracted Reith as little as Reith's laconic and usually depressing opinions attracted Elliot.

'I doubt whether his father's manse entirely explained the phenomenon of John Reith', this flippant comrade-in-arms was fond of saying to his friends. 'When he told me that before going to the academy he'd been sent to Park Preparatory School, a select institution for small girls, I felt I understood him better. The experience has surely marked him for life.'[4]

Yet at the end of the summer training camp in 1910 the lugubrious Reith thought he could afford to smile for a change with unfeigned happiness. Three members of the cadet company, including Walter Elliot and the future playwright, James Bridie, pressed upon him what he described as 'an unsolicited testimonial', praising him for devotion to duty and for less probable qualities. So prized a possession shone like a diamond among the untidy dross of these years: Reith treasured it as such, reproducing it word for word in his memoirs:

'This is to certify', it ran, 'that we, the undersigned, after full and careful consideration and many opportunities of observation, have come to the conclusion that Sergeant John Charles Walsham Reith, a Section Commander of Section Four, A Company, Glasgow University Contingent, Officers' Training Corps, is not only the most efficient Sergeant in the aforesaid Corps, but also the only Sergeant in the Corps with the smallest right to pretensions of honour, manliness or good-fellowship. We furthermore decided to give to him this testimonial of our unqualified respect and esteem. We should go further but our pen is done.' The signatures of O. H. Mavor, Walter E. Elliot, and R. R. Archibald certainly followed; but the exuberance of Elliot, a practised hand, may be detected in the clear-cut style of the writing. Some who knew Elliot well, and who knew also of his ambiguous regard for Reith, believed that he wrote the reference with his tongue in his cheek. If so, the recipient did not suspect anything worse than flattery. The very idea that he might have been the victim of an elaborate jest in dubious taste mercifully never even entered his head.

'In my OTC section was a medical student, two or three years younger than I', wrote Reith. 'With him the military life was the grand passion. Often on Saturday evenings we walked far into the then pleasant country to the north-west of Glasgow, returning along the deserted Great Western Road long after midnight. The talk was invariably and exclusively of army affairs and war; we had little else in common. . . . The war on which we had so often speculated by the Kilpatrick Hills or the Campsie Fells was a liver issue than we knew. One of us was killed and the other nearly so within a mile and within a week of each other.'

Any young man who left home for work at 4.45 each morning and seldom returned from evening classes before 11.30 at night could be excused for not being as politically well informed as companions who enjoyed a less restricted life than he did. Too turned in on his own troubles for the luxury of surveying the wider world, John Reith relied for his slender grasp of politics and international affairs on hearsay supplemented by what he cared to extract from the staid journals taken at the manse. His father had the good churchman's judicial pessimism about politics and politicians; but since his word no longer had the force of divine law to a disenchanted youngest son, the Reverend Dr. George Reith's observations on the perils of peace cut little ice with him. Besides, they seldom met now, except on the Sabbath. But the prospect of war, especially one in which Britain would have to fight against a major European power, seemed absurdly remote as the expansive Edwardian period ended. Despite Germany's manifest ambition to challenge Britain's traditional sea power, the enormous wealth and strength of the nation in the full flush of her imperial destiny seemed to rule out the serious possibility of hostilities. So even if his father, an instinctive patriot like Reith himself, had approved of soldiering as a career, he would have firmly disapproved of any premature entry into a profession which then appeared to offer no outlets whatever for martial ardour. The fact that his son chose to spend a few hours of his little spare time each week drilling with the OTC contradicted nothing: far better that than dissipating his energies on pleasure-seeking.

After receiving the King's commission in the 5th Scottish Rifles in February 1911, however, the young man became slightly disillusioned with his brother officers in this recently renamed Territorial unit. They were mostly men of comparative leisure, whereas he was not. They took for granted too many things which he could and would not assume or allow so lightly. John Reith, groping his way out of the darkness still encircling him in the dungeon of an excessively prolonged youth, was too easily embarrassed and affronted by other men's conventional values. His consuming prejudices were impassioned enough to make a bonfire of conventions, for the self-pity and frustration of the deprived smouldered on beneath the various masks he now wore like faces for all seasons.

He believed against reason that some high destiny still awaited him. And the more resolutely he endured the pricks and stings of life, the readier he would be to answer the eventual call to greatness. The contrary drives of starved affection and fierce aversion, between which he was still caught like a victim on the rack of conscience, did not blur this vision. The longing to prove that he, too, would dominate and lead men, not as his father did but in his own fashion, increased during the last two or three years of his apprenticeship. He kept a careful note of his small triumphs. Nor did he disdain boasting at home about them. It must have meant a great deal to this spiritually lopsided man of twenty-five when he was able to record in the summer of 1914 that his time had come:

'There I was—like a ship engined, manned, equipped (more or less so) ready to sail—without sailing orders or course. Pathetic, tragic, desperate it was. Not just physical self-confidence. Every sort. I was now sure I could do things. Almost anything.'[1]

His major achievement, he knew, had been to complete the marathon training scheme. Quite apart from earning him his qualifications as a tradesman fitter, it had redoubled his mystical belief in himself and his future:

'They said I was one of the best apprentices they had ever had. I had worked in almost every department. I had taken pride in my work. . . .'

His militia certificates of proficiency, one of which had entitled him to sew a gold star over his sergeant's stripes, were equally the symbols of a limited success that had been slow in coming; just as the King's commission set the seal on his ability and right to command men in battle. To the Walter Elliots of this world, John Reith might be a tedious fellow, to be taken only in small, discriminating doses. To himself, especially on the eve of war, he was already reaching for the stars. The incidental fact that his mind had long been a battlefield remained a terrible secret between him and his Maker.

3

The Warrior

1

IT WAS towards the end of July 1914 that John Reith heard for the first time since boyhood the whispered call to greatness. For the best part of six months he had been earning a modest living in London as a junior member of Pearson's, the engineering contractors. The job was hard, fairly exacting, but not uninteresting: amidst mounds of rubble and the gigantic disarray of heaped raw materials he had been helping to direct the labours of a small army of skilled men who were working against the clock to finish the new southern extension of the Albert Dock on the Thames at North Woolwich. His father, of course, remained irreconcilably opposed to the whole preposterous idea. The Reverend Dr. George Reith still feared the worst for his youngest son, unable to believe that John could fend for himself like the more adaptable inhabitants of a remote and alien city. When the young man had suddenly announced the previous January that he intended to look for suitable employment in England, after his hopes of finding anything locally had been rebuffed, his father said scornfully:

'You'll come back—with your tail between your legs.'[1]

John Reith departed, vindicating in his own simple but resolute fashion the gibe of Dr. Johnson that the finest prospect before a Scotsman is the highroad to England. Nor did he return even to witness the installation of his father late that spring as Moderator of the General Assembly of the United Free Church of Scotland, for the executive head of Pearson's had just rewarded Reith's keenness by increasing his pay from thirty to forty shillings a week: and, as the young man put it himself, 'I was too conscientious to ask for leave.'

Conscientious he might have been, restlessly ambitious he unquestionably was. The pinpricks of his father's implacable anxiety on his behalf were easily shrugged off at this distance, and he tried to reassure both parents that all was, and would be, well in his regular letters home. One day, however, in casual conversation with Pearson's subagent on the Albert Dock site, Reith discovered with a start of indignation that the wretched man was earning only five pounds a week after fifteen years' service with the company. He decided there and then to ask for an afternoon off. Pearson's, he swore to himself, could stew in their own juice from now on. Meticulous to a fault, Reith wrote for an appointment with the rival engineering concern of Nobel's. He saw their managing director one afternoon before the end of June and agreed to join them as soon as possible, after promises of advancement somewhat more in keeping with his own high if still unearned expectations. Meanwhile, he carried on thanklessly at North Woolwich, counting the days until he could decently turn his back for ever on the ungrateful firm of Pearson's. Then, suddenly, John Reith's delicately attuned ear picked up the thrilling sound of distant thunder. It was warm that July, but no freak summer storm could have provided effects so gloriously spectacular as those foreseen by Reith in the imminent approach of Armageddon.

On July 29th, 1914, a single word in the diary he had begun to keep with fidelity some time after his twenty-first birthday vividly illumined the romantic escapist's sensation of tingling hope. That word was 'WAR'; and because its staccato brevity seemed wholly inadequate to convey all it meant to him, Reith dignified the word like a proud child by conferring on it the mortuary honour of large capital letters. He was not an avid reader of newspapers, but his nimble mind fastened quickly on essentials; and through the confusing haze of diplomatic moves and counter-moves, of warnings and counter-warnings, and finally of mobilisation orders to the armed forces of the contending European powers, there shone for Reith like a shaft of sunlight the sudden prospect of a new, exciting career as a warrior. While Lord Grey, Britain's Foreign Secretary, struggled for nearly a week longer to stave off the inevitable conflict, the immature young man eagerly anticipated the only conceivable outcome. For Reith had ears only for the language of destiny. His mind feasted on the prizes and perils of a battlefield outside the mind. It called to him like innocence.

'Here was something tremendously exciting', he explained without guile years after the event. 'In a sense I had been looking forward to war—and for years. Now it was coming. It was an entirely personal affair—no thought of what it might mean to home, or country or civilisation. I was a week over twenty-five, and in a thoroughly unsettled state anyhow'.[2]

From his nursery days onwards John Reith had loved things military. Perhaps this was wholly natural for a boy of Covenanter stock, reared on the Bible with its frequent evocations of the God of Battles. He had played with lead soldiers as a child, in common with thousands of other children, though the pleasure he drew from lining them up and ordering them into decisive conflicts was probably less common. When he was eight an elder brother, who roused his envy and admiration by appearing once a week on drill nights in the kilted uniform of a Lanarkshire volunteer, had gratified a deep desire by teaching him how to hold, load, and fire an air-gun. The lesson was not forgotten. It had come in useful later in the cadet corps at school and in the territorial unit where he was distinguished as much for his stiff ardour on the parade ground as for his lack of small talk and social graces off it. In fact the officers' mess held no attractions for this suspicious son of the manse, who took little trouble to hide his disapproval of gossip or risque jokes from colleagues unhampered by his awkward burdens of uncertainty and guilt. To Reith, as to the young David or the young Cromwell, military training was too serious a matter to be mixed with the inane distractions of the world. His aloof, somewhat disdainful manner hardly made him popular; and Walter Elliot, one of the few contemporaries to penetrate the mask of Reith's shyness, had felt bound to dismiss him merely as a tedious fellow with a one-track mind. Nevertheless, events at last appeared to vindicate the young man's sure intimation of a call to arms for which he had so long prepared himself.

The diary entries failed to dwell, as might have been expected, on Reith's conviction that war would be for him a time of great fulfilment. This may appear surprising in a person whose ability to spell out the signs of his private language of destiny was by now so marked. His diary, however, seldom lived up to expectations because it differed in substance and intention from the kind of record which someone of Reith's introspective nature might have been tempted to keep. Some diarists are virtually compelled by nature to write down their secret thoughts, regardless of the prying eyes of posterity, since the very act of committing them to paper releases pent-up emotions. Very seldom in the voluminous bulk of John Reith's diary, and not once during these early years of trial, does he rinse out his conscience or parade his inner feelings. The reason for that, in the judgment of this writer, lies in the exceptionally odd combination of motives and circumstances which prompted him to open this personal journal.

A sadly demoralised young man, spiritually at odds with himself and the world about him, grimly resolved not to yield, John Reith started to recount his happenings in the mood of someone searching for his own identity. If therefore he was for ever seeking to justify his actions, it was in no petulant or egocentric spirit. His primary aim was far simpler: by registering every event that had hindered or helped him during the day just ending, he strove to learn not only what manner of person he was, but how he might profit tomorrow by these minor triumphs and setbacks. To put them down on paper was to relive them—and in reliving them he gained that incidental margin of comfort which diarists often seek for its own sake. This process of total recall accounts for the enormously detailed style of Reith's narrative. Perspective is missing, even where events of real importance overtake him; and perspicacious readers even of the abridged edition of his experiences as a soldier, published only five years before his death, may have wondered why so much needless space was devoted to scrupulously circumstantial descriptions of people, places and incidents which seemed to lead nowhere at all.

I was asked by Reith to read the manuscript many months before he decided to approach a publisher. He received in due course an injudiciously frank critique, stressing that there were more currants than pudding in the concoction as it stood: with some ruthless editing, some good rewriting, and some clarification of cloudy but intriguing reflections, he would produce an unrecognisably better book. Reith did not take too kindly to the final point:

'What precisely do you mean?' he asked.

'In several key sections the best parts are the blanks. You seem to be just on the edge of unfolding something most revealing, then you dry up.'

He smiled a little austerely. 'That is very observant of you', he said, 'but I shall leave it.'[1]

Absorbed every night in his recording angel's task of noting every twist and turn of the day, Reith had discovered a painless means of applying balm to an uneasy spirit. Yet this was no exercise in moral stock-taking. The diarist's concern was less with conscience, a force he chose to grapple with in decent privacy, than with self-justification at the superficial mundane level. He was patiently building a living theatre to re-enact the tedium of real life; and if much of that tedium seeped into the diary, spoiling what little drama there was, this did not matter in the slightest to John Reith. He had hit on a necessary device for warding off the demon of self-doubt; if nobody believed in him, he could still learn how to believe in himself. Every date, name, person, place and incident in Reith's journal helped to fortify the make-believe structure of his faith.

One of Reith's first acts on settling in London had been to write a letter to his Glasgow territorial unit, resigning his commission. He received no reply and assumed that there had been an oversight. Now, on the eve of hostilities, he wondered if he would be crossing to France with the 5th Scottish Rifles. Contrarily, he hoped to defer his call-up. For, as he remarked: 'It was at that particular time inconvenient for me to go to war. I was about to depart on holiday with a friend.' So Reith wrote off again to his territorial adjutant in Glasgow, 'telling him that, though I had resigned, I was all for war and for going with the 5th, but, if mobilisation were only a sort of precaution, I did not want to miss this holiday. . . . I thought I was being very good and patriotic and that they actually had no claim on me at all.'[2]

The telegram which came back in response to his quaintly naive message cut Reith to the quick. It curtly ordered him to report for duty at once, otherwise dire consequences would follow. Puzzled and indignant, he took the overnight express to Glasgow, collected his uniform and equipment from home, was greeted coldly by the adjutant, who then left him cooling his heels for twenty-four hours. Then he appeared before the commanding officer and all his brother officers to explain his dilatory behaviour. Two telegrams had been despatched to him. He had ignored the first completely and replied only to the second. Why? Accusing eyes were upon him, but Reith's bafflement was genuine. He surmised that the original message must have gone to the wrong address. Might it not be a good idea if someone produced the counterpart? This was done, the commanding officer scrutinised it with care, and admitted that the wire had been misdirected. Nobody commiserated with Reith for missing his holiday. Instead the commanding officer, no doubt referring to Reith's unsociable behaviour in the past, issued a dismissive word of advice:

'Now you're here, Mr. Reith, you will, I trust, do your best to help the regiment.'

On August 29th, the first wartime Sunday, the entire battalion, led by its band, marched down Glasgow's Great Western Road to church. On many a Friday night during his years as an apprentice Reith had swung along this route, head erect, at the side of his company commander. He had never enjoyed it because of the caustic remarks from passing strangers. The company commander, as it happened, was so small that his cap hardly reached Reith's elbow, and the spectacle had invariably evoked the ribald if rather obvious wit of local ruffians to whom apparently nothing was sacred. Reith noted earnestly in his diary:

'We had been playing at soldiers before. Now we were soldiers, status and potentialities recognised.'[2]

He was being slightly premature. Though orders arrived which plainly stated that the battalion would shortly 'proceed to war station', the move was long in coming. Such was John Reith's mood of sustained euphoria, however, that his diary treated every step and stop on the circuitous route to Flanders as a realistic prelude to the great adventure. After all, his was a territorial unit mobilised for war. To a man, the entire unit reacted as though already 'on active service', which meant on paper that severe penalties, even the death sentence, awaited delinquents who defied authority or shirked their bounden duty. Reith did not neglect to tell his men 'the awful import of the term "on active service" '. It was eerie and disturbing to be handed an identity disc stamped with his name, initials, rank, religion and unit, a graven token of his new condition as an equal candidate for death or glory. Then, at a stroke, the 'crass stupidity' of authority threatened to disband the 5th Scottish Rifles and ensure that the cherished identity disc would have to be handed back.

The commanding officer announced that a special battalion was to be formed at once for combat service overseas. Rather sheepishly he recommended his officers to join it. Reith refused, in common with most of his colleagues, defiantly electing instead to volunteer for foreign service with his own unit. Nearly six uncertain weeks passed, weeks spent in an otherwise enjoyable holiday-like atmosphere, guarding a viaduct and an aqueduct at Larbert on the main railway line from Perth to Glasgow. Being in charge of a detachment nearly sixty strong, Reith ruled it in his own style, dispensing praise, blame, exhortations and rough justice to the assembled soldiers each Sunday morning after early church parade. Once he had the temerity to reduce a lance-corporal to the ranks, regardless of the fact that he had no right to do so, yet no superior questioned this high-handed decision.

'I do not know', he admitted, 'what powers I was supposed to possess in the matter of punishment or privilege. I certainly exceeded in both.'[1]

Whatever else happened, he was single-minded in his resolve to make it *his* war. The bad auguries he had feared at the beginning, because of his delay in responding to the mobilisation call, were fast receding. Then two wholly unforeseen happenings confirmed his faith in the utter fitness of things as they were. The first, in the form of a revised order from General Headquarters, announced towards the end of September that the 5th Scottish Rifles would not be disbanded after all: those muddled men with red tabs had evidently had second thoughts. As if this relief were not enough, a second spin of the wheel of destiny the very next day made Reith the proudest man in the battalion. An orderly approached him, saluted, and handed him an envelope. He opened it and found written instructions authorising him to take over and reorganise the battalion's transport section. His amazement momentarily offset his joy. Why John Reith rather than anyone else? Could it be that his superiors recognised his powers of leadership which, like his superb self-confidence, he had never doubted himself? He did not pause to enquire. Now, at long last, a dream which had recurred since childhood, when his war-games with lead soldiers on the nursery floor were invariably resolved in gorgeous chaos by charging cavalry, had come true as well. From now on, like Prince Rupert, he would be entitled to the honour of wearing spurs.

On a lower level of perception, Reith suspected that the honour had come his way through a fortuitous misunderstanding. Because he longed to ride, several of his brother-officers had, in the past, heard this normally uncommunicative man wax almost lyrical on the subject of horsemanship. Naturally, they assumed that he was a capable horseman already. Once, indeed, during the training manœuvres of 1912, when he had also watched with mild incredulity his first military aircraft, piloted by Charles Longcroft and navigated by Hugh Trenchard, circling low overhead to spy out the land, he had actually been 'volunteered' into mounting a horse. A brigade major had appeared leading the field commander's mare by the bridle and asking whether any officer present could ride.

'Yes, sir. Reith can ride', someone had answered.

'Splendid', said the brigade major.

There had been nothing for it but to approach the 'large and forbidding' animal, get on her back with every appearance of being in control, and move off gingerly in the direction favoured by the mare. As this coincided exactly with the instructions of the brigade major everything went well until Reith rounded a convenient bend in the road. His troubles started at the first crossroad where, according to the brigade major, he had to turn right for the appointed rendezvous with the field commander. The mare had other ideas. She moved straight ahead at her own easy pace, the helpless Reith having no alternative but to obey or risk being thrown. He stayed mounted until the mare reached the camp. The brigadier fortunately did not miss his horse so nobody called the unskilled rider to account; yet from that day onwards the imagined horsemanship of John Reith became enshrined as fact among the officers of the battalion.

If the dignity of wearing spurs was hardly something he had earned, he did not now question the wisdom of the commanding officer who may also have remembered the tall, intense young man in shirt-sleeves, supervising the horse-drawn transport as the battalion entrained at Glasgow for its annual camp during the last two summers of peace. Perhaps that had helped to clinch it, for it must also have dawned on his superiors that Reith was at his best when left to his own initiative. On this last score the new transport officer had no doubts at all. To quote his own boastful words:

'I would have accepted the command of the battalion or brigade or division without the least hesitation—and would probably have done very well at it.'[1]

The overweening conceit of a shy, basically immature but ruthlessly self-confident man rings out in that admission; but unlike many of his contemporaries Reith was also imbued with the vision, the panache and the eye for essentials which tore obstacles aside like cobwebs. This was his 'first real job'. He tackled it with an enthusiasm tempered by guile. The fierce drive of ambition which had been bottled up during the long years of waiting for the call to arms was released at last. It either amused or infuriated those fellow-officers who still tended to regard him as a tiresome crackpot with no manners. Yet Reith could say without dissembling nearly fifty years after the event that no other post he ever held in his career was so utterly satisfying as the post of battalion transport officer. It offered him a taste of power, and he used it.

The weeks of preparation for the final move to France were agreeably busy. He flung himself recklessly into the business of making his mark. The initial problem, that of justifying the appointment itself by learning to ride a horse, was solved in becoming secrecy with the connivance of a friendly transport officer from an adjoining unit. How often we shall find, as Reith's life unfolds, that at important turning points it is the stranger who proves a sounder ally than the familiar! A quiet field just outside Larbert, a reasonably docile mount, a drill manual and a patient instructor enabled him in the space of a few days to parade on horseback for a long route march with the entire brigade. His composure was good. Only his unusual height in the saddle set him apart from the rest, yet inwardly he quaked with anxiety for fear of being pitched off. His luck held. It was assisted by his judicious refusal, criticised by the more casual as carrying zeal beyond the norm, to dismount for any reason at any stage. Why run the risk of getting off when he would certainly fail to get on again with all the ignominy of having to accept a helping hand?

Reith's next step, a harder one, was to shake up the transport section. In his judgment it needed a thorough overhaul. The methods he adopted created an outcry; yet that risk he gladly ran. He was convinced of it when he held his first parade. One look at the sergeant and other NCOs told him the worst. There was nothing for it but to 'lose' them for a start. So, without consulting anyone in authority, Reith set about appropriating volunteers. He did not mind greatly whether his chosen replacements knew anything about horses. Working from the principle that what *he* had learnt inside a week others could acquire more gradually, he simply went about earmarking men who were smarter, keener and more spirited than the unenthusiastic, dishevelled rabble he had inherited.

Some of the best, naturally enough, were recruited from the ranks of the detachment which had been lately guarding the Larbert railway viaduct under his orders. A corporal previously attached to him promptly responded to Reith's solicitations. This man, in turn, signed on an ex-shipping clerk and an ex-stockbroker, each of whom happened to have the desirable qualification of understanding horses. The procedure was unorthodox but effective; and there were indignant protests from Reith's late company commander. The official complaint castigated Reith's high-handed tactics. It was pitched in strong terms. For if poaching were not enough, the new transport officer also contrived to dump what he described as 'misfits' on other unsuspecting companies with no desire or house-room for displaced persons.

Fortunately for Reith, the battalion adjutant, who normally went by the book but had become uneasy about the decrepit state of his transport, defended these moves, even advising him where he might hand-pick further recruits. There was further bad feeling as a result; and the chorus of criticism reached a crescendo when a corporal piratically recruited was promoted overnight to transport sergeant at Reith's behest. Others received unexpected stripes in due course. Reith was content. This reliable nucleus was precisely what he needed to rebuild a unit that would work his way. He did not care about the resentment of people who put such store on appearances. He ignored their snubs and relished his unpopularity as an unrepentant nonconformist. Rightly or wrongly, Reith consoled himself that this was preferable to being treated in the mess as a soft, complacent nobody. He had a brusque retort and a sardonic twinkle in his eye for those officers, mainly superiors, who took him aside in vain attempts to warn him off. Armies were not, and could not, be run on these lines, he was told. Yes, he would reply, but if there were rules governing such matters, surely the battalion adjutant should know that rules were invented for fools to keep and wise men to break.

The simple expedient of annexation, costly as it proved in terms of personal esteem, transformed the transport section. The adjutant himself grew a little uneasy at the single-mindedness of Reith who had the leaven at last, in his own biblical phrase, for 'an undisciplined lump' of nearly fifty soldiers. By precept and example, he ensured that the leaven raised the morale and standards of the unit. In times of peace, no territorial battalion like the 5th Scottish Rifles was entitled to its own transport, so that the job had to be improvised and mastered from scratch. This in itself enabled John Reith to justify free poaching on other men's preserves, since only the battalion would benefit when it eventually reached the frontline. The last and finest of his recruits was an older man called Robert Wallace, already a lance-corporal with a high reputation as a competitive marksman, who claimed to know a good deal about handling horses from his rural upbringing yet to whom at first sight Reith took an unaccountable dislike. Soon the battalion transport officer realised how badly he had erred. For Wallace became the most dependable of all his NCOs and, because of Reith's almost atavistic aversion to convention, Wallace also gradually became the nearest thing to a friend this friendless being had discovered in all his twenty-five years.

2

'It is rather a shock to your mother and me to find that you are off to the Front', wrote the Reverend Dr. George Reith, 'and we can only pray God to be with you every moment. . . . You are doing a great work in defending your country—one of the greatest honours that can come to men in this world. Our country's glory and good name are committed to your care for a time; the mere thought of that should inspire you with high resolve to do all you can. God is on our side as we contend for honour and faithfulness among nations; and we shall be on His side if in our own hearts we repent of our national sins and seek that this terrible business be overruled for our spiritual welfare as a people. Keep close to Christ, dear boy. No ill can befall you then.'[3]

This first letter from home reached Reith in Armentières half-way through November 1914. He had been in France for about a fortnight, and the early strangeness was wearing off. The tingling excitement and sense of anticipation remained. Every contrivance he had employed to revitalise his 'private army' had been thoroughly vindicated by the smoothness of subsequent events. Larbert now seemed a long way off. They had left for Broughty Ferry on the River Tay at short notice only three weeks earlier. Every item of equipment had been accounted for, neatly stowed aboard the long train to Dundee, unloaded, and just as efficiently reloaded when the battalion received the order: 'Proceed overseas at once'. Once again, he had experienced a nagging grievance that the War Office planners paid too little respect to the convenience of John Reith. For on the first Sunday of November 1914, comfortably billeted in the West Manse at Broughty Ferry with the local minister and his wife, he had been looking forward to a little holiday among friends.

He had knelt next to the minister's pretty daughter, Kitty, in the family pew during divine worship, hoping that closer acquaintance might rapidly overcome the awkward, almost uncontrollable shyness he felt in the company of young women. It was not to be; the evening meal had been dramatically interrupted by the movement order; and he had broken the news to his father on the telephone at midnight, mentally prepared again to spend the small hours on horseback, supervising the reloading of the battalion's goods and chattels.

The estrangement between father and son had evaporated with the coming of war like mist in the morning sun. Now that John Reith had found not only a role but an unmistakable sense of fulfilment, the old causes of friction on either side no longer counted. The contrast in their respective attitudes to the purpose and meaning of armed conflict did not affect the heightened regard each felt for the other. To Dr. Reith this was a holy war, a veritable crusade; to his son it was a magical challenge, no less solemn or inspiring for being a private affair of the heart. Nor was it hard for him to go along with the religious convention that the Lord favoured the cause of righteousness and would smite the hosts of the Philistines. The thought that Christians on the enemy side probably believed just as fervently that the same puzzled overworked diety would bless their arms with ultimate victory was too subtle to have occurred to Reith in his exalted frame of mind. His God, in any case, was given to communicating through the sign language of destiny; and Reith's destiny, he was sure, lay here in France.

He had not seen a dead man yet, only a dead horse which had succumbed on the train travelling south to the port of embarkation. A startled and protesting group of porters had gathered as Reith and his men dragged the carcase out of the horse-box and left it sprawling untidily across the platform at Newcastle Central. One uniformed official said in some agitation that the express from London was due in at any moment, adding gratuitously that the station-master simply 'would not have it'. Reith did not argue. He just stared back, as if to imply that if the station-master did not want horseflesh the porters were all at liberty to share it among themselves. Two other vignettes which stayed sharply etched in his memory were the noisy and perilous crossing of London in the swaying driver's seat of a two-horse dray, and the magnificent sunrise that had greeted his tired eyes two days later as he caught his first glimpse of the French coast from the deck of a troopship standing off Le Havre. The wind was fresh but it bore no message, not even the faint grumble of gunfire. Somewhere away to the east lay the real battlefield. Momentarily he wondered when his battalion would reach it, and what fate held for him then.

Had Reith but known it, the war on a front stretching from the English Channel virtually to the Alps was entering a long, hard winter of stalemate. While he had been absorbing the elements of his job in Scotland, the larger moves and counter-moves of the opposing armies had passed him by. Yet he needed no maps or communiqués to describe the nature of the fighting when, towards the end of the battalion's slow and tortuous progress to Armentières, Reith noticed a thin, bedraggled line of infantry returning from the trenches —'the remnants of the London Scottish'. The unit had only just emerged from Messines, and the ordeal showed in the faces of the survivors:

'Stupidly we were not halted but some of them walked beside us and gave us bits of their story. We were tolerably smart; they were unshaven, weirdly clad and caked in mud. They had already made their name glorious. What would we do?'[2]

There was awe in this chance encounter near the town of Bailleul, and next day a similar thrill of nervous hope pulsed through him as another battered party matched past, this time the Scots Greys. Barbed wire, the machine gun, shrapnel from the concentrations of heavy guns which each side seemed increasingly to rely on for deafening preludes to limited and bloody advances by vulnerable hordes of men with bayonets, these were the grisly factors which contributed to an endless campaign of attrition. Reith found it all puzzling, as the first snow began to fall. The transport section settled into its temporary billet, a lunatic asylum on the edge of the deserted town of Armentières. Less than two miles from the German trenches, Reith was waited on at meals by two serving maids in a big, empty mansion whose owners had evidently taken refuge somewhere safer. This, he reflected, was an unreal, almost illusory war, 'funny but not unpleasant'. The contrasts astounded him at reflective moments. His battalion joined 19th Brigade to man part of a sector near Houplines on November 20th, and the unnatural quiet that had descended on this small area of trenches struck him as ominous. Quite typically, Reith prided himself on being 'the first territorial from Scotland' to visit the front line proper. The quartermaster of the Cameronians led the way forward at dusk, his visitor seated beside him on one of two wagons loaded with rations, equipment and mail. These were unloaded at a ration dump. Then a corporal accompanied Reith down the road towards a necklace of tiny lights strung across the flat, darkening landscape. At a barbed wire barricade he was met by the adjutant and second in command of the Cameronians. A burning haystack made him feel suddenly expendable and exposed as he moved to the right across a field of turnips, ready to fall flat, as these veterans instructed him, 'if firing starts or a star shell goes up'. In the small headquarters, half hut and half dugout, he spent the best part of an hour listening to the experiences of the colonel and other officers, grateful for that privilege as much as for the chocolate they showered upon him before he left. Pleased with himself at 'feeling no fright when crossing the exposed ground' on his way back, he realised that it was 'no question of being brave' but 'a matter of nerves or temperament or both'. Yet it was equally interesting to 'walk across a turnip field knowing that at any moment one will stop walking for the most conclusive of reasons'.[2]

Reith never hesitated to obey his impulses and go out of the way to meet friendly strangers beyond the circle of overfamiliar faces in the battalion mess. The mannerisms of his brother officers so grated on his nerves at times that he normally preferred, and sought the company of his NCOs. From neighbouring senior officers of the Service Corps he received much sound advice, from the brigade's veterinary officer many useful, practical hints—as well as a bay mare for his private use. Touched by their willingness to help, Reith 'got quite a kick' out of consorting casually with professionals who knew their business. For the present, he was unconcerned at the carping of colleagues in the battalion at his frequent absences. How were they to know that he had already set his ambitious heart on securing the vacant post of transport officer to the 19th Brigade, and that his perfectionist ardour was directed solely towards that unlikely end?

'Most thrilling to hear the shells whistling through the air and to wonder where they're going to land', he wrote to his parents before that particular kind of thrill began to wear thin.[3] Reith was happier now about the vital role of transport in conditions of static winter warfare. The dangers, especially in the early evening when the wagons rumbled down roads within bullet-range of the enemy, seemed to be as real as in the trenches, though Reith had a secret aversion to the idea of being impaled on a German bayonet. For that reason alone he thanked his stars at having been spared the ordeal of going over the top after standing to for hours, ankle or knee deep in thick Flanders mud. On the last night of November, at his own private request, he clambered cautiously forward with an officer of the Argylls into the desolation of No Man's Land and watched a rather blasé sapper party blow up a ruined cottage often frequented by enemy snipers. Reith was both elated and impressed, particularly by the coolness of the burberry clad officer who sauntered back after the explosion to inspect the demolition:

'I remembered that I was an engineer. I wished I could be a sapper, especially if Bob Wallace and the others could have come with me.'

There was in Reith's make-up a rich vein of the frustrated actor. No element of the morbid lurked beneath his craving for peril, however, only a childlike longing to be tested under fire and not found wanting in courage or proficiency. The restlessness to win the approval of true professionals ran like quicksilver through him, prompting him no longer merely to wish but to scheme for some dramatic part of greater importance. That was one side of his nature, by now the most dominant and consistent side. Yet there was another less obvious side which hinted at chains still capable of holding him captive in some dark cellar of his psyche. The taciturn giant who cut a slightly eccentric figure in jodhpurs and spurred gumboots, striding through the muddy streets of the empty town on wet days, a huge umbrella borne aloft like a standard to protect his glengarry from the rain, could also behave like a bashful schoolboy when the incongruous or the unexpected happened.

One morning he opened a parcel from the family of a former school friend at whose home in Kent he had stayed briefly during two summer breaks from his engineering apprenticeship. His friend's sister, a gay, attractive girl, had caught his eye only. He talked to her, went walking with her, occasionally quoted poetry to her, but 'had never even kissed her on the cheek'. Yet here now, among the gloves, chocolates and other gifts, was a startlingly good and evocative photograph of the creature. Reith's reactions were undoubtedly confused. The more he gazed at her image, the more he liked it—'and the less I liked the situation'. Clearly he could not keep it. What if a stray bullet killed him and the picture came to light among his possessions? What would his parents say? Perhaps the best course would be to burn it, yet that too would be misinterpreted if he survived and ever had to own up to the deed. Reith was still studying the photograph in perplexity when Whitelaw, the ex-shipping clerk whom he had rescued from the ranks and now prized as an excellent NCO, entered the room. Reith showed him the girl's likeness and explained his romantic dilemma.

'I'd be happy to have that on me', said Whitelaw, 'dead or alive.'

Somehow the words clinched the problem immediately. Reith let Whitelaw go—then 'in solemn and almost sacramental style' he placed the picture on the fire and watched it slowly burn to ashes.[1,2] The ritualistic phrase used by Reith pinpoints both the style and the complex mentality of a man for whom half-measures were seldom good enough. Admittedly, Reith possessed an exceptionally tidy mind. Like the housekeeper in one of Georges Bernanos novels, he regarded dust and debris of every sort as something to be annihilated rather than kept under control.

The habit of periodically clearing out his room at home and discarding all litter and useless papers was the shorthand expression of this fiercely uncompromising attitude to the flotsam and jetsam of life. Only his inordinately detailed war diary was safe from the flames. So little did it disclose of his tortured inner self that Reith sent regular batches of entries back to Glasgow in the care of an army chaplain for his parents to browse through at will. He believed in travelling light. Why should he encumber himself now with evidence from the past which could be misconstrued, however innocent it was in fact? Above all, Reith believed in travelling after his own star with a craggy indifference to the feelings or the separate fate of non-travellers. For on his predestined journey through the fire he had to go alone.

Rumours of advances, of enemy withdrawals, of imminent unit movements to suit, were a constant source of debate and speculation at the front. How the rumours arose it was impossible to say, but invariably they spread like wildfire. Reith grew accustomed to discounting them on principle, until the December morning when one of the least plausible rumours of all confounded his scepticism. King George V had arrived in Flanders, according to the whisper, and would be inspecting the battalion despite the fact that half of it was then on duty in the trenches. Nevertheless, the remainder of the unit received orders to smarten themselves up for a special parade. Reith persisted in suspending belief as he stood at ease in front of the transport section, half expecting the almost inevitable apparition of another interfering brasshat with time on his hands. When two closed cars approached, and the door of the leading car was held open, his eyes widened in astonishment as the small, neat, bearded figure of the King stepped out, followed by the Prince of Wales. It was a unique, unforgettable moment to watch the Monarch move along the line of officers, saying not a word but shaking hands with each of them in turn. One of the unspoken embarrassments from which Reith had suffered since youth was that his superiors, whether parents, teachers, foremen or prospective employers, had always had to look up at him because of his giraffe-like stance. Suddenly he felt no embarrassment as the steady eyes of George V turned upwards into his own. Again no word passed the royal lips, but the look seemed to speak volumes: 'I can't find words to say what I feel', was what that regal look conveyed to Reith. 'You may be killed—considering the length I've got to look up to you, you'll probably catch it on the head. I represent what you're fighting for. Good luck and a safe return home.'[2]

Armentières was subjected to an intensive bombardment later that same week. More than a thousand shells rained on the town from nightfall to the following morning. From his billet Reith drove a cart containing his kit through the full fury of it, reflecting that the missiles 'seemed to pursue us as if some malign power, thunderbolts in hand, hovered overhead, watching our puny progress'. The lunatic asylum where the horses were stabled had not been hit, so he despatched a cyclist to headquarters at Houplines for instructions to move off out of the target area. The message from the adjutant urged Reith, in effect, to do as he thought best. With shells exploding close by all the way, he led his section into the open country-side until the onslaught of the artillery died just before dawn. Reith's billet came through intact, and there on Christmas Day he ignored army regulations and gave a special dinner party to his NCOs and the transport men on duty. A strict teetotaller himself, as he remained for several years, Reith did not stint the champagne for the others. On the last day of 1914 the battalion having been pulled back out of the line for a spell, Reith had a rare bout of despondency. The old black devil of melancholy possessed him, and he was in no mood for the nostalgic revelries of Hogmanay. Yet he would not have exchanged his job or his status for everything because, in his heart, Reith knew that on balance he had never been so content in his life.

What he seemed constitutionally incapable of recognising was that he had been spoiled by his own luck during the first five months of war. As a specialist officer, he was excused parades. He was spared the rigours and the perils of the trenches. He was largely his own master. So far this had enabled him not only to choose his own acquaintances but to avoid the attentions of his nominal superiors. The battalion adjutant, for instance, who had lately been taking more notice of his activities, did not seem to care greatly for the aloof and independent posture of the transport officer. Suspecting as much, Reith gave an even wider berth to the 'nasty little man' in the imaginary interests of harmony.

His grievances against the adjutant amounted to the merest pin-pricks, yet these were sufficient to make Reith see red. There was the small matter, for instance, of the Rifle Brigade, newly-arrived in the sector and on the look-out for good stables. Their transport officer had persuaded the amenable colonel of Reith's battalion to order his transport section out of some excellent quarters they had just acquired. Suspecting a bluff, Reith went straight to his colonel, the adjutant happily being absent, and got permission to stand his ground until the would-be squatters produced a signed requisition from higher authority. The Rifle Brigade's representative had quite a shock when Reith said firmly: 'No chit, no stables,' and refused to budge. He sat on his horse barring the way, unmoved by threats of being hauled up before 'the general'. He was still sitting when the rifle brigade's unit commander gave up and led his men away. Later the adjutant expressed distaste for the needless friction Reith had caused by these undiplomatic and irregular methods.

'Reith's job is to obey orders', was his tart comment. On another occasion Reith was wallowing in a hot bath when the adjutant sent an urgent note asking him to explain why two of the section's horses were not properly groomed. Fuming with indignation, he poured more hot water into his tub and worked off his wrath by singing at the top of his loud and none-too-musical voice selected verses from some of the more bloodthirsty Psalms:

O Lord my God in thee do I
My confidence repose:
Save and deliver me from all
my persecuting foes;
He made a pit, and digged it deep,
Another there to take;
But he is fall'n into the ditch
which he himself did make.
Upon his own head his mischief
Shall be returned home;
His violent dealing also down
On his own pate shall come.[2]

Possibly there was a hint of envy in the attitude of the adjutant, for Reith's efficiency earned him for a short spell the honour of acting as transport officer for the whole brigade. This duty proved doubly onerous as he went down with dysentery through drinking polluted water, yet insisted on staying off the sick list in case he missed anything. Shortly after returning to the battalion, early in February, Reith received a stern reprimand from the adjutant for abusing the proper channels of communication in addressing a petty complaint *direct* and in somewhat offensive terms to a senior officer. Clearly the antagonism between the two was coming to the boil; and during a local attack some nights later they had a public disagreement. To an earth-shaking cacophony of fierce shelling and persistent small-arms fire, Reith sat patiently at the head of his column, waiting for two companies of the battalion to parade. As the soldiers fell in behind their officers, there was a lull in the bombardment. Reith moved forward slowly, only to be stopped in his tracks by the voice of the adjutant:

'Where the devil have you been, Reith, and why isn't transport out?'

The man was evidently beside himself with indignation, and his unusually hectoring tone momentarily struck Reith dumb. Then, recovering himself, he reminded the adjutant that transport had been patiently standing by for the best part of ten minutes. This evoked no response of any sort, and in a flash Reith's quick temper exploded:

'You've no right to talk to me like that and accuse me in the middle of a battle of not being on the job,' he shouted. Then savagely spurring his mare and turning her head, he galloped away in a shower of sparks. Within an hour, the order to stand down came through, followed almost at once by the adjutant in person. Somewhat crestfallen, he said to Reith:

'I've come to apologise to you. I was in the wrong tonight.'

The unexpected admission threw Reith into instant confusion. He was so embarrassed that, according to his own account, 'I lost control of the situation. . . . Then he gave me a jaw about my temper; said I went hunting around for trouble, putting people's backs up and jumping down their throats. . . . I certainly gave him credit for coming but felt he spoilt it completely by the line he took.'[1,2]

Not for the first or last time, Reith found himself at a disadvantage when suddenly confronted by an unsympathetic individual in whose image he invariably enjoyed sticking outsize pins. The encounter left him feeling cheated and a little foolish. Only too vividly aware that his own self-conscious clumsiness had played into the other's hands, he wondered to what extent the long memory of the adjutant would hold the incident against him; and he had very good reason to do so. For the long-suffering adjutant, without saying it in so many words, was offering the overbearing young officer a final chance to knuckle down and conform.

Weeks went by without further trouble between the pair. Each seemed content, for the present, to keep well out of the other's way; and a prolonged lull along the front also helped to preserve a semblance of tranquillity behind it. When the chance of short leave was offered, Reith jumped at it, the six days he spent at home passing all too rapidly in a rosy haze of happiness. Time and distance had miraculously healed the rift with his father: now that his youngest son had shed the awkwardness and the tiresome petulance of a child who refused to grow up, the Reverend Dr. George Reith enveloped him in his affectionate attention. The difficult past was forgotten, and the joy of reunion with both parents remained a fragrant memory to John Reith for many months to come.

How thrilling it had been on his first Sunday to stride down the aisle of the College Church, head erect and spurs ringing out, with every eye in the congregation on him as he advanced on the family pew. The fulfilment of a vivid childhood dream had been well worth waiting for. It was rewarding in a less self-indulgent way to call on the relatives and friends of his men, often in the company of his father and mother, and to realise what consolation his small gestures of friendship brought to all of them. During that week of unconfined bliss, he knew that the lost years were rolled away as if nothing had ever come between his parents and himself. They were growing old; but age had not changed them; and more than ever he envied them their serene confidence in the mysterious ways of Providence. The pattern of his own religious outlook was much less conventional and simple than theirs: he cultivated a possessive faith in himself; it rested on the intuitive certainty that he was predestined by a God whom in other respects he feared to carry out some important task in life.

It was not in Reith's nature to wonder whether he might not be guilty of sheer presumption, or at any rate of self deception. His genius lay in identifying his own strong impulses with the otherwise inscrutable promptings of Providence. He could more easily have flown like an angel than have sat passively waiting with prayerful patience for things to happen. A young man with his true ear for the music of personal destiny had no doubts about the way ahead: his business was to *make* things happen and to keep the gnawing worm of remorse at bay. Yet he still clung to the practice of praying on his knees before going to bed at night. Even if God had already earmarked him for damnation, he could still seek inspiration for the mission required of him on earth. To this private religious feeling was added an undiminished attraction for formal ritual which led him on occasion to arrange Communion services for his men in the most improbable surroundings behind the front.

Soon after his return from leave, Reith acquired a particularly fine thoroughbred bay mare from the divisional veterinary officer. One of his NCOs declared that the animal was the living double of a champion called Sailaway which had won the Ayr Gold Cup the year before, so Sailaway Reith's new mount was named. He quickly mastered her. He also noticed that the hated adjutant whose horse was lame cast covetous eyes on her, but persisted in riding everywhere on her broad back. His flexible code of behaviour condoned the scrounging of extra mounts and surplus feed for them, but it forbade the telling of lies. His men were instructed never to deny the truth about ill-gotten gains if asked point-blank by the authorities.

On Easter Sunday evening Reith took the fateful step of drafting and sending off to the relevant senior officer of the divisional train a request for the removal of an incompetent farrier sergeant. He did not begin to question his right to act without consulting the ever watchful adjutant, because the man he wanted to fire belonged to the Army Service Corps, not to the battalion as such. Reith had several times rebuked this individual for slackness and lack of leadership. Like a bad apple in a barrel, the apathy of the sergeant had corrupted others, including a particularly notorious offender whom Reith found one morning standing 'roped to the wagon wheel of cart', in expiation of his (and the still more guilty sergeant's) military misdemeanors. The case for getting rid of a consistently poor NCO was reasonably strong, and Reith's request for his dismissal went through at once. Then, without warning, the adjutant struck back with a vengeance.

First, he demanded a written explanation of Reith's conduct. This left him dissatisfied. He had no wish to be reminded that transport officers always dealt direct with the Service Corps at divisional level about matters of common concern. The adjutant therefore sent for him. It was a stormy interview. The almost pathological dislike Reith felt for this 'nasty little man' now made it impossible for him to keep a civil tongue in his head. When the adjutant urged him once more to explain why he had behaved so improperly, Reith sat down heavily and stared at him in astonishment. The adjutant promptly shouted: 'Stand up.' Reith obliged him, and from his full height glared down at his persecutor.

'I won't give you any further explanation', he said. 'I'll give it to the commanding officer if required.'

'You can certainly see him if you wish', said the adjutant. Reith realised that this time he had gone too far, but he resented the warning that he might now expect to be removed from transport and packed off to the trenches as an exemplary punishment.

Within an hour Reith went to see his commanding officer, fearing the worst because he knew the man was no better than putty in the adjutant's hands. He could scarcely admit to being surprised at the bland verdict:

'You are returned for duty forthwith.'

'In that case, sir', said the impenitent Reith, 'I wish to see the brigadier.'

The brigadier sent for him a few days later, the last round of the farce being played out in the presence of Reith's silent accusers, the soft, compliant commanding officer and the hard, overtaxed adjutant. The brigadier complimented him on his efficient handling of transport which, he said, was not in dispute. However, since the battalion commander had decided that Reith must resume ordinary duties, there was nothing which he, the brigadier, could or would do about it.

Reith saluted, then followed his persecutors out of the room, blasting their souls to hell and back in his heart as he walked three paces behind them all the way to headquarters.

'I did not then reproach myself for my inexplicable failure before the general', he wrote of this setback. 'I was still too bewildered and utterly disconsolate.'[2]

That night, on the hard floor of his new billet John Reith slept badly. The small room above a busy *estaminet* in the centre of Armentières was shared with five others. When at last he dozed off, he dreamed of Sailaway, the bay mare in a thousand. The chances of riding her would be few from now on, but Sailaway was safe at any rate from the adjutant's clutches. A well-disposed veterinary officer had promised to look after her for him; as far as the battalion was officially concerned, Sailaway could no longer be accounted for. She had simply vanished into thin air.

The company officers went out of their way to be kind and helpful, but suddenly the fun had gone out of Reith's private war. No man six feet six inches tall could feel exactly safe or comfortable standing or crouching in a trench with his boots covered in thick, sticky mud:

'A platoon, forsooth', he had written in an access of disgust at his demotion. 'No horses. Nothing of any interest. It was a loathsome war now.'

Yet he did not linger in the trough of despondency. The scene had shifted, but nobody could deny him a new part in the drama. Even if the trench parapets were inconveniently low, he had no qualms. The duties were straightforward and monotonous: two hours on watch, then dawn stand-to when all officers turned out. After the stand-down a bald report had to be written on 'the tactical situation'. During his first few days and nights on watch Reith was criticised by his company commander for unnecessarily exposing himself to enemy fire:

'Are you wanting to get killed just to spite the adjutant?' he asked shrewdly.

'Oh no', Reith replied. 'I'm not in the least wanting to get killed. I don't much mind if I do, but I think I would like to kill him first. Am I likely to get the chance?'

The company commander gave him an odd look:

'I wouldn't put it past you,' he said.

Reith's parents had been kept fully informed of his troubles with the adjutant. One day he was sent for by the battalion commander.

'I have had a letter from Dr. Reith', he said, 'about the circumstances of your leaving transport. You may tell your father that I have received it but that I cannot answer it.'

Reith replied without a second thought: 'My father is not accustomed to having messages of that sort, sir. I shall not give it.'[2]

There was no response from the battalion commander, so Reith saluted and left him to his thoughts. He was making the best of the anticlimax. The respect of his men he gained at once by keeping a close eye on their welfare and placing them on their honour to write letters which needed no censorship from him. But, with his own welfare in mind, he next sought out the nearest headquarters of the Royal Engineers. There he told his story and outlined his qualifications to the commanding officer who promised to put in a favourable word for him at brigade. Reith then formally applied for a transfer to his own commanding officer. It was during a bout of influenza early in May that Reith received on his sick-bed an official message which gave him more pleasure than any he could recall since the instruction to take over the battalion transport eight months before. The engineers had not overlooked him; their local chief wanted to see him personally next day. Weak from lack of food, Reith was driven to the sappers' headquarters and told that his application had been 'strongly recommended' by the brigadier; as far as they were concerned, he could join the Royal Engineers in the field once all the paper formalities had been completed. These appeared to be endless. Nearly a month passed. Then a note arrived from the War Office. Was the recipient willing to become a member of the Royal Engineers? If so, would he kindly sign in the place indicated. Meanwhile, the tedium and the intermittent risks continued to corrode his spirits, though he recovered quickly in his billet when the company pulled back for periodic rests. On a June Sunday afternoon, seated in a corner of a field, he found himself pondering yet again over his obsessive dislike of his two wretched superiors.

'If I could convince myself that the Christian and strongest course would be to forgive the blasted CO and adjutant, or anyhow not to cherish feelings of such animosity, I might perhaps bring myself to do it. But I could not so convince myself, possibly did not want to. Life was dull now, and a vendetta of this sort brightened things up a little. . . .'[2] Without a target as tempting as the adjutant, Reith would have been quite lost. The black hound of depression might well have seized him by the throat, squeezing out of him that new zest for life with which the war and its theatrical part in the attainment of his destiny had filled him. Yet it is equally certain that a man of Reith's appetite for self-righteous display would have found another victim just as easily. Fools were born every minute; the need to invent what already existed in profusion on the battlefield therefore did not arise. His mind was swift and merciless in leaping to conclusions which, in broad terms, would be justified both by events and by history. As has already been noted, a minute sector of the huge, immobilised western front was scarcely the best vantage point for any detached assessment of Allied strategy or tactics. Yet here Reith's nimble leaps from the particular to the general, however much one may suspect him of strengthening the core of his argument with a generous dash of hindsight, were unconventional and wholly in character. The extravagant conceit of an unknown young Scottish territorial lieutenant, who accepted it as a matter of course that he could have run a division as well as any general, deserves to be weighed in the scales against the unflattering verdict of posterity on most of the military leaders in the First World War:

'Like marionettes we were', he wrote in a mellower mood many years afterwards. 'Fortunately we saw only what happened on our own tiny stage—though things often happened there which were not conducive to confidence and peace of mind. What of that war is remembered now? Tragedy of death and wounds and incapacity, of inconsolable bereavements. Its utter fatuity. The train of complications, economic, social and political. And its inefficiency. Inefficiency in result is recognised. Less has been said about inefficiency in management. . . . Efforts and costs of all kinds in the 1914 war were utterly disproportionate to results. . . . One wonders how many of those who are commemorated on the memorials which star the land have simply paid the price of inefficiency.'[4]

His mood in 1915, as spring ripened into summer, and with still no confirmation of his transfer to the Royal Engineers, lacked all charm. He became a sharp thorn in the flesh of the middle-aged and somewhat cautious company commander, whom he additionally distrusted as a friend of his elder brothers. This officer rebuked him repeatedly for taking short-cuts that exposed himself and others less flamboyant to the fire of enemy snipers. Indeed the quiet-spoken major's sympathy for the adjutant and the battalion commander steadily grew as he vainly tried to discourage the restless spirit of a man who did not seem to know how to live and let live, and who always questioned the methods laid down by authority. The frustrations of Reith therefore grew also. Yet soldiers in the front line appeared to admire him for his independence of mind as much as for his concern with their morale. He had marvelled one night to discover two sentries sound asleep at their post. Instead of reporting them he let them sleep on and stayed beside them until they stirred. The shame and contrition on their faces in the moment of awakening was, he felt, condign punishment enough. So long as he dictated and applied the rules, Reith could show more mercy than justice. A conformist at heart, despite his disconcerting attempts to play the natural rebel against constituted authority, what he had most liked in the case of the sleeping sentries was making exceptions to strict disciplinary regulations which he would never have dreamed of violating himself.

Of course, he persistently offended against the proprieties which ordinary people held sacred. Some of his brother officers considered that Reith lacked good taste as well as manners, for he enjoyed worrying aloud over difficulties like a greedy mastiff gnawing at a bone. He also took delight in cutting a dash and trying to appear different and out of the common run. The yellow shirts he wore off duty were as striking as they were well cut. In the trenches he sported a dark blue rugby shirt, on the breast pocket of which was emblazoned the red lion rampant of Scotland. What critics failed to grasp was the importance of symbolism in the pattern of his thinking and acting. The shirt was a proud relic of his brief membership of the London Scottish Rugby Club which he had joined early in 1914. But for the war, he convinced himself, he would have played full-back for them, and perhaps even for his country.

'I thought', he wrote with imagined modesty, 'that the way was clear to the fulfilling of a great ambition.'[2]

Conspicuous he might be, perhaps slightly vulgar too, in his love of self-dramatisation; but, apart from a weakness for exposing his ungainly form in the trenches, and a childish longing to lead a daring raid which would demonstrate his martial valour, Reith proved a conscientious and competent infantry officer. Few of those who knew him best would have been prepared to wager on his survival. For John Reith had an unerring instinct for drawing the line between reality and melodrama in the wrong place; and to this extent he proved more of a liability than an asset to an infantry unit in the front line. Despite his lengthy fulminations to the contrary, the practical judgment of Reith the warrior lacked consistency. For the competing urges of Reith the romantic were too strong at times to be adequately resisted.

3

He suffered several near-misses that summer during routine spells of trench duty. The sector remained comparatively quiet on the whole, and casualties in the battalion were remarkably low. He was 'badly sniped at' one night while crawling out to a forward listening post, but had to acknowledge that 'one never really knew how close the bullets came'. By now he was reconciled to wearing his identity disc, carefully smothering the string in mercury ointment each morning as a deterrent against lice. With his fetish for detail, Reith had no time for idling during the long night vigils. He delighted in moving from point to point at speed in the small perimeter which it was his responsibility to protect. There was wire to be inspected and reinforced, firestep sentries to be visited, No Man's Land to be patrolled. The dogged endurance of the men struck him as no less remarkable than their crude unpretentiousness. He often stopped for a whispered conversation with them until a starshell went up, in a trice bathing the whole front in its weird, unnatural light. Then the sharp silhouettes of wire, of trench lines, even of the shadowy shapes of men caught unawares and frozen to the spot, would appear in focus. Sometimes the whizzing bullets would follow.

When dawn began to finger the eastern sky, and the familiar scene of siege warfare slowly assembled itself before his weary eyes, Reith often felt stirring within himself a poignancy that was almost sensual:

'One felt close to ultimate realities, buoyed up by a profound and unassailable conviction that all would be well, come what might', he wrote on one occasion, trying to recapture the feeling in words. 'I felt there were special transport facilities from the racked battlefield on which we stood to the green pastures and still waters beyond . . .'.[2]

He was still a man of wildly fluctuating moods. For the same John Reith could yield just as easily to impish whims that verged on the totally irresponsible. And when the chance finally came of scoring like an overgrown schoolboy off his adjutant, he gladly took it. The latter paid a rare visit one evening to the headquarters dugout. The burden of the adjutant's message to the commanding officer and others was the superfluous one that all wire aprons and advanced posts should be regularly and thoroughly checked. Reith sat listening with a scowl. When the visitor finished his lecture, Reith had a sudden brainwave.

'Wouldn't you like to go out in front yourself, sir?' He asked in an offhand manner which nevertheless conveyed some of the vicious scorn he felt.

'I should love to', said the adjutant somewhat unexpectedly. So Reith offered to lead the way. His mood now was one of absurd exultation. He did not mind dying himself, provided this pompous imbecile met his just end as well:

'What a dramatic end to a feud,' he reflected—and later used that revealing phrase in his diary note on a disastrous and somewhat shameful episode.[2]

Together the two men approached the first of the shallow sap-trenches. These stretched forward beyond the wire, in the direction of the German positions. There were two ways forward from the front line. The proper route lay through a hole in the parapet, which was screened off by a movable thicket of barbed wire. Reith pointed this out to the adjutant. The more normal way, he added, was over the top of the parapet, and, jumping up, he stood nonchalantly staring down at his superior in full view of the enemy. With the answer that he preferred to use 'the proper' route the adjutant went down on hands and knees, emerged from the tunnel and proceeded, still crawling, down the sap-trench. Reith now leaped up again and walked defiantly above the adjutant on the open, muddy ground. After a cursory look round they returned, each by the route of his choice. Not a single shot had been fired throughout. Reith admitted that he had 'never taken quite such a risk before'. For his part the adjutant dismissed the incident as the crowning example of this eccentric young man's 'over-weening sense of his own importance'. And who can say that this was a mistaken or unfair judgment?

4

The release of John Reith from the flat, scarred landscape of Flanders in which he had created such a chequered local reputation came not by bullet or by special messenger but by water-bottle. This happened towards the end of July 1915. His twenty-sixth birthday was spent in bed after he again contracted violent dysentery. They moved him first to a field ambulance, next to a casualty clearing station, finally to the base hospital not far from the Channel coast. The senior medical officer recommended, to his great astonishment, a period of recuperation at home when he was well and on his feet again.

Calling at the War Office in London the day after his unexpected return to England, Reith was told that his application for transfer to the Royal Engineers had been unaccountably mislaid; but before the end of his sick leave, most of which passed peacefully with his parents in a highland farmhouse, the faithful Whitelaw wrote to tell him that the transfer was through at last. It had been officially posted in battalion orders, which meant that now he had two identities. In France he had become a sapper, yet in Britain, where such things were normally arranged, he was still an infantry officer. The muddle disturbed him. It made him all the more anxious to hurry back to the front before the War Office forced him to give up the smart RE uniform for which he had been measured and fitted in Glasgow.

He had another reason for haste. At the territorial base in Rouen on September 22nd he heard rumours that 'something big was about to happen'. That day he received the formal notification which repaid the letters he had impatiently dashed off to the Adjutant General's department, to the Commander, Royal Engineers, and to the kindly veterinary officer who had been looking after Sailaway, his bay mare, for nearly six months. With it came the order: 'Proceed at once to the front'. Alighting from the train at Béthune, Reith hired a horse-drawn cab and ordered the reluctant driver to take him to the village of Noyelles. There he was informed he might find the Seventh Divisional Field Company he was looking for.

They were not expecting him, of course. Communications did not run to such luxuries as that. The field company major said that he had heard of Reith's impending arrival the night before at headquarters, but still could not understand why he had come. A subaltern from Aberdeen had already been posted to his unit and was presumably on the way, that was all. A lieutenant was apparently the last thing he wanted, as his perfunctory welcome made clear. How long, he enquired, had Reith held the rank? What, since August 1914? That was rather unfair on the other officers, since it upset the balance of seniority in the company.

'You won't like conditions out here,' the major remarked unhelpfully.

'I don't really mind the conditions', replied Reith. 'I'm fairly used to them. If you must know, I've been in France for nine months already.'[1,2]

The major was obviously staggered by this piece of information. He had no room for an extra lieutenant, particularly one brimming with self-confidence—and evidently determined to stay. Every time he wanted to speak to this very tall, spare stranger, he had to crane his neck upwards in an embarrassing fashion, so he decided for the present to say nothing more. After all, the man's papers were in order. This was the unit he had been instructed to join by the muddlers at GHQ. If Reith's cross-country journey to Noyelles had been wasted, there would be time enough to tell him so some other day. Meanwhile, the major proposed with some reluctance to use him as best he could until the subaltern from Aberdeen arrived to bring the unit to its full and proper strength.

The dugout, Reith noticed, was twelve feet under the surrounding mud. It gave him a mild sensation of claustrophobia. When he said he would like to go up and have a look round, the major commented:

'Please yourself, but you'll find it safer down here.'

From the top of parapet in the blustering wind, Reith peered around him through his binoculars. This little corner of the Loos salient, where Haig's costly attempt to penetrate the German front was still in progress, was a picture of carnage. Shells shrieked overhead, in both directions; there were corpses strewn about in untidy profusion; and half a mile away to the left he saw a Scottish unit charging across open country in their kilts towards a group of shattered houses. Many of them were mown down. It was hard to discover the lie of the Allied trenches, still harder when he went below to persuade his new commander to disclose what precisely the job of the unit might be in that inferno.

Reith's initial task was to mark out and supervise the digging of support trenches some yards behind the front line. A German counter-attack seemed to be in the offing; and as he waited in the newly-completed trenches, with bullets flying above and the stench of rotting flesh assailing his nostrils, he wondered when some real sapper work would be his. Nobody knew what was happening. Certainly the dazed and ragged remnants of British regiments withdrawing to the rear had no ideas on the subject, while the major preferred to keep his own counsel and discourage conversation. One fact Reith did hit upon by chance was that his former battalion had taken up position in the line not far away; so during a lull he visited the 5th Scottish Rifles, 'taking care that I was observed by the commanding officer and adjutant but of course without speaking to them'.

There proved to be only too much work for him to do, all of it skilled and highly dangerous work carried out under cover of darkness. By the brickstacks in a village called Cuinchy he went at the head of a sapper section to put up wire entanglements in front of the Wiltshire Regiment, while snipers tried to pick off his engineers and their infantry escort one by one. Reith realised before the task was finished that he wanted to excrete. It was not fear but forgetfulness which brought him to this predicament. Ever since his recovery from dysentery, he had been taking daily doses of chlorodine, but that particular morning he was in such a rush that he had failed to do so. However, it was neither bravado nor false modesty which induced him to step further out into No Man's Land to relieve himself. His need simply would not wait; and if any German saw him squatting, compassion may have prevented the enemy marksman from firing on a British officer caught short in front of him. During the next week Reith was machine-gunned, mortared, and shelled while strengthening the wire between the two front lines and repairing a damaged bridge across the La Bassée canal. He was once more beginning to enjoy life and its hazards. Only on October 6th did he learn officially that GHQ, in their wisdom, had posted him to the wrong unit. But he no longer cared about the thoughtless slip of somebody's pen. Even the major was becoming used to his idiosyncrasies and his wild enthusiasms.

In what turned out to be the last letter he wrote from France to his father, Reith pronounced himself in excellent health and spirits. As far as he was concerned, the war had again begun to justify itself to the romantic warrior. The business of being a sapper might be perilous and exacting but it suited him splendidly. 'I shall finish it in the morning', he promised Dr. Reith. The letter remained uncompleted. For next morning Reith took a chance too many and thus provided an alert sniper in the Cuinchy backyard with a remarkably easy target.

He had risen for a late breakfast on October 7th after a long, hard night under fire. The major told him he was going out to inspect some redoubts. Reith offered to accompany him, although he had already put on riding breeches, his best tunic and one of his yellow shirts because he was off duty that day. As they entered the trenches together, Reith knew that he ought to have changed into something less conspicuous and more suitable for the filthy conditions. Whatever happened, he was resolved to keep the mud off his clothes. The communication trench was crowded with men coming and going, so Reith climbed out and walked over the ground parallel with it, urging the major to hurry up and follow. The major prudently stayed where he was. His interest in the redoubts had dwindled. For Reith, who had jumped down to join him in the trench again, mentioned that a mine blew up in the night close to the line, probably causing havoc to the earthworks. Presently they were approaching the devastated scene. One glance showed them both the wide extent of the damage: clearly the sappers were going to have another busy night, since the parapet of the trench had entirely vanished at several points.

By now Reith's head and shoulders must have been plainly visible to any watchful enemy marksman. He continued walking just ahead of the sapper major when out of the blue a bullet hit him. Reith stumbled but did not fall. Nor did he at once lose consciousness. He was suddenly aware of a loud singing noise in his ears and of a dreadful jarring pain that enveloped his head. Then he saw the blood pouring down on to his nice, new tunic and silently cursed his luck. It took him only a second more to realise that he was still standing for the marksman to take aim again and finish him off. So now he lay down in the broken trench. A sergeant of the Wiltshires found him, and, tearing off his field dressing because Reith was not carrying one, the man tried to staunch the gaping wound on the left side of Reith's head and face.

How badly injured he was Reith could only guess as the searing pain increased. He still had the presence of mind to ask for a piece of paper and wrote on it the name and address of his mother in a trembling hand. The major knelt in the muddy trench beside him as Reith fumbled with the pencil and spelt out the three additional words: 'I'm all right.' He could not see what he had written because of the pain and the dripping blood. He was also feeling very tired, for his eyes were turned straight up into the unclouded blue sky. From a long way off he heard someone remark that he had another wound in the shoulder, and then Reith knew that he was not going to die. As he wrote of his feelings afterwards:

'I felt rather foolish. And then very angry. I was so happy, I had only had three weeks of the RE after all the fuss to get there. But in after years I have often wished that I could contemplate the blue of eternity with such equanimity as then.'[1,2]

4

The Seeker

1

FATE HAD slammed the door with brutal violence in John Reith's face; but once he knew that he was not going to die, the conviction slowly possessed him like a comforting revelation that presently another door to self-fulfilment would automatically open. The doctors who attended him left him in no doubt that his days as a warrior were over: from the first casualty clearing centre, not far behind the broken trench where he had been struck down, to the long, crowded wards of the Millbank Hospital in the heart of London where he ended his slow and confusing journey from the front, every specialist was specific on that single point. Reith refused to believe them at the start. Yet even while trying to argue helplessly against their unanimous verdict, even while fuming inwardly at the absurdity and inevitability of the blow to his secret hope, he already accepted the probability that the experts were right. Destiny had led him providentially down a humiliating, frightening blind alley only to save him from himself for some other higher task still to be discovered.

What tilted the balance of certainty in favour of hope was a significant event which happened on the second night after his inglorious and abrupt departure from the fighting zone. Reith, normally a sound sleeper, was troubled by a particularly vivid nightmare. Weakened at length by pain, loss of blood and the intense anger he felt at his own folly, he fell into a drugged doze—and suddenly found himself trapped in the full glare of an enemy searchlight. As in most grisly fantasy states of the kind, he could not move though impelled to do so both by the ordinary instinct of self-preservation and by a compulsion to accomplish the task allotted to him. German guns had smashed the forward wire entanglements. Under cover of darkness he had crept out alone to repair the damage. His arms were outstretched, his hands as busy as his fevered brain on a seemingly hopeless venture, when the beam picked him out and momentarily blinded him.

It seemed to transfix him like the thrust of a bayonet. A fly caught in a web he had spun for himself, Reith waited for the inevitable machine guns to put him out of his misery. And in that timeless moment of horrified expectancy he awoke in a lather of cold sweat, with his heart pounding madly.[1]

The nightmare had a profound impression on him because, from the dawning of his conscious life, Reith had been spared the experience of bad dreams. This relief may appear somewhat unusual in someone who had endured so much unhappiness during his childhood and prolonged adolescence, especially perhaps in the closing years of his apprenticeship when he had become a spiritual prisoner confined to his father's manse. Yet no two brains function in precisely the same way. The unconscious half of John Reith's mind, indeed, seemed to belie the agonising pressures he suffered constantly while awake. Perhaps sheer fatigue after eighteen hours' hard, grudging labour was a better preventive than he would ever admit, but habitual weariness alone could hardly have explained the freedom from disquiet in sleep. It was the exercise of naked will-power, more than robust health or the narrow play given to an otherwise powerful imagination, which enabled him to reject anxiety, much as a slot-machine rejects spurious coins, whenever his head touched the pillow. By the middle of 1914, the walls of his prison came tumbling to the ground with the trumpet-call to arms. John Reith the warrior strode out of the rubble, intent on the fulfilment of a daydream long ago shaped by destiny.

It demanded a vast outpouring of energy and thought, often on petty details; the cause was worth the effort, however, and it suffused the dark horizon of his mind with the promise of sunlit glory until the nightmare shattered his crust of composure. He could no longer repress or extinguish the sharp and bitter lesson to be drawn from this dramatic re-enactment of an accident he had brought upon himself. The awful suspense of hovering between life and death, realising that he did not deserve to escape, forced him against his will to welcome the medical verdict. Survival was preferable to extinction; the ignominy of failure was in itself a kind of dying.

The messages and brief communications that reached his distraught parents after he was wounded laid emphasis on the fury that seized him at 'ruining his best tunic', and on his frustration at being carried off the field just when he was beginning to feel thoroughly useful and happy at last. He did not unbare to them the true depths of his distress, then or later. Their view in any case was as simple and prosaic in its own way as that of the doctors: John, their youngest son, had already done more than his fair share of active service. When he did reach home about a month afterwards, his face was disfigured and still raw down its furrowed left cheek from the recently removed stitches, but he could only marvel with them, and for totally unsentimental reasons, at having got off so lightly. The bullet might just as easily have blinded or paralysed him, or even left him a mental cripple for the rest of his life.

During the earlier period of being lugged about like a sack from one gentle pair of doctor's hands to the next, Reith had gradually discovered the extent of his injury. They had seemed worried at first about his sight, but he stilled their fears as well as his own by demonstrating that he could see quite well out of both eyes. His mouth and all his teeth, too, were surprisingly intact; but he experienced much difficulty in moving his jaws to talk or eat. The nurses fed him through tubes and begged him to stop mouthing questions at them. They ordered him to keep quiet and give his wound a chance of healing. He did not see fit even to mumble at them when they rebuked him for struggling along to the toilet without assistance, but the doctors usually tried to humour the incessant inquisitiveness of the patient.

'Will I have a mark on my face?' one of them understood him to enquire after much expressive gesticulating:

'A mark on your face,' echoed the doctor in mild incredulity, and with endearing tact he indicated the extent of the injury and the number of stitches required to hold the cheek in place after the removal of bone-splinters.[1,2] He was too relieved to be alive. Had he moved his head by the merest fraction, or had the sniper's trigger-finger trembled, Reith would already have passed beyond all possibility of reflection or of self-reproach, in the manner of ten thousand others already picked off in their prime. He could envy these a little: they were at peace, all ambition and passion spent. He had to carry on, with a ravaged face. The thought kept recurring: 'How odd it will be, getting used to looking different!'[1] His parents, his brother-officers, everyone he had known and learnt to like or dislike, would recognise him in future by something other than his grotesque height—a feature which he found as embarrassing and distressing at times as he would the stunted form of a dwarf. Yet a war wound, he knew, might suit a survivor so sensitive about appearances. However it had been gained, the wearer could contrive at least to carry it with some semblance of pride, like a badge of courage. The scar might prove to be his best campaign medal of all.

It was at Millbank Hospital that Reith resigned himself to a fresh search, no matter how long it took him, for the predestined path to greatness. In spite of this, he was forced by pride to maintain a show of interest in the art of active crusading:

'I very much wanted to go back to the front and as quickly as possible', his father was informed. 'A good staff job *might* keep me at home if sufficiently busy and with real responsibility. But I'm not at all sure. I really want to go back to France again.'

Dr. Reith, as eager as his wife to drop everything and visit their son, was dissuaded by him from doing so. John Reith needed time to think out the immediate future without parental guidance, time for the raw flesh to become whole again, time above all for his angry uncertainty to abate. His parents appreciated why he was uneasy and restless. Anger, usually bottled up inside him, had always been one of his favourite counsellors, though Dr. Reith must have wondered a little at its fierce persistence even in the face of death:

'Of course it was a narrow shave', his son had acknowledged in his first, laboriously scribbled letter from bed, 'and they tell me I am very lucky. I'm very hungry as I can't open my mouth to eat anything and I've spoiled my best uniform.'[3]

Neither Dr. Reith nor his wife expected John, so fixed now in his outlook, to accept the world and his God-given place in it as they did. He lacked the serene trust which they so abundantly possessed, but the young man's strangely elaborate belief in himself could hardly fail to touch them. How they wished that he had not opposed their travelling down to meet him off the hospital train: he had implored them to stay at home, and with much reluctance they had yielded.

The two months' treatment confidently predicted by an eminent doctor soon after Reith arrived at Millbank Hospital finally dwindled down to three weeks. Skin-grafting and cosmetic surgery were undiscovered refinements then, and with so many more serious cases on their hands the medical consultants abandoned their original idea of inserting a silver plate in the side of his face. John Reith was not displeased. He disliked the passive routine and the long, empty days. He filled the hours as best he could by reading, thinking and writing short, laconic letters to a few of the people who would no doubt be glad to hear from him. One of those letters, meticulously cast like bread upon the waters, brought him an unexpected but not unwelcome visitor within a week.

The wards at Millbank were lengthy and high. There was a mild stir at the far end one morning when a smartly dressed lady, burdened with a huge bunch of roses, swept past the nurses, brushed aside their deferential reminders of the official visiting times, then asked for

John Reith by name. He had met Mrs. E. W. Moir, the wife of his former employer at Pearson's, only once before. He did not immediately recognise her, but pretended to, and presently his prehensile hopes went soaring upwards on a star which he knew was in the ascendant again. Against the odds, apparently, a boss who had once paid him so badly that Reith would certainly have left the firm but for the outbreak of war, now seemed concerned about his well-being, so concerned in fact that he had despatched this formidable but gracious envoy on an errand of mercy.

Yet, in marvelling at his good luck, Reith was partly deceiving himself. Chance did not enter the matter. Here, as in the engineering of his military preferments, there had been a customary measure of calculation. Spinning the threads of useful relationships was not a task for entrusting to coincidence. In Reith's book, human 'contacts' existed to be cultivated with industrious discretion, and Moir was only the latest example. While Reith was warming to his work with the sappers near Noyelles, his small success in repairing a damaged bridge over the canal at La Bassée had inspired him to write a descriptive note to Moir. Owing to circumstances beyond the control of either men, Moir's friendly reply to that note had only just reached Reith by circuitous routes at Millbank Hospital; and the latter's rejoinder had caused Mrs. Moir to call on him.

The well-dressed vision of beauty at the foot of his bed was not so much a promised sign conjured up by destiny as the very human response to a letter containing bad news. Moir, hard taskmaster though he might have been, obviously saw more in Reith than Reith himself could begin to allow. Yet the timing of Mrs. Moir's visit could not have been finer if Reith had personally arranged it; and in the role of the wounded hero he went for drives with the lady, visited her home, and talked a good deal about his disappointments and yearnings before his final discharge from Millbank. Both she and her husband were anxious to help him. The prospect of finding a suitable war job through the good offices of Moir, his original boss, did not strike him as far-fetched or ironic.

There were by now surprisingly few qualified engineers left in civilian life for the very many vacancies available. Volunteers for military service had depopulated the industry. The firm of Pearson, Reith discovered, was erecting a huge, new munitions factory at Gretna. The contract stipulated that it should be completed in eight months when some fifteen thousand workers would move in. The prospect of working at Gretna did not attract Reith nearly so much as the wilder idea, picked up in casual conversation with Moir, of possibly crossing the Atlantic to help the British war effort as an engineer in the United States. He was delighted to find that Moir was more than willing to back the scheme. Meanwhile, however, having been given indefinite leave from active service, Reith called at Gretna on his way home to Glasgow, accepted a temporary post without bothering to wait for War Office approval and started to earn his keep again early in December 1915.

2

A month later Moir sent a cable from New York, urging Pearson's to let Reith come and join him there at once. The firm refused. They found him too useful to release from Gretna. Then they relented, but crossed wires controlled by procrastinators at the two interested government departments in London promptly threatened to ruin everything. So, taking the problem into his own hands, Reith travelled down to Whitehall only to learn without undue astonishment that the Ministry of Munitions had been seeking him high and low for the past few weeks. Officials ushered him from one controller to another until he reached the room of George Booth, the City expert appointed by Lloyd George to galvanise and co-ordinate the efforts of a new and expanding department. Booth, like many other men of his enterprising breed and business background, preferred to trust his own judgment rather than get lost in the labyrinthine procedures of the civil service. He took an instant liking to Reith's bluntness.[4] The appointment in America was confirmed, the salary agreed, and Reith's irregular situation in the eyes of the military satisfactorily settled in a single day of breathless hustle. 'You will sail to America in a week', George Booth told him. 'Your job will be to inspect the supplies of small-arms that are being produced over there under contract. We'll pay you £500 per annum plus an allowance of £750 for living expenses.'

This was wealth beyond the rosiest dreams of John Reith. It would enable him at last to contribute handsomely to the support of his ageing parents, and yet to live himself in reasonable style. Three of his elder brothers happened to be at home, and like an actor he chose his moment to announce nonchalantly, 'I'm off to America next week', so as to create the maximum effect of consternation. He had never cared too much for any of them. One of his farewell gestures, recorded somewhat complacently in his diary, was ordering the delivery to the College Manse of several 'heavy fur coats with astrakan collars'. Then he invited his astonished father to pick the one he liked best. The son had not forgotten how, in the last year of his apprenticeship, he had been walking with his father down a Glasgow street when they met a rich acquaintance well padded against the wintry blast by such a coat: 'Would you like one of those?' he had asked. 'Not if the money came as his does', his father had enigmatically replied.[2]

Good public money paid to an ex-officer bound for a distant but promising assignment seemed to give Dr. Reith no room for scruples. His pleasure in the gift was infectious. He would no doubt have been less pleased had two small but equally significant incidents come to his attention: the first, when his youngest son ignored the friendly greeting of his former battalion commander one day in the street and cut him dead; the second, when the headstrong John Reith spent the best part of twenty-four hours attempting to track down a reckless van-driver who had knocked his father down, even approaching the police for the man's address and visiting his lodgings armed with a large, lethal wrench. Fortunately for everyone concerned, the miscreant was not there.

'If I'd laid hands on him', Reith admitted many years later, his anger rekindling at the recollection, 'I'm sure I would have murdered him'.[1]

His one slight worry on the eve of departure concerned the job awaiting him beyond the Atlantic. Honest enough to admit that he was quite ignorant about the manufacture of small-arms, he did not mind who knew that this 'bothered me not at all. There would be an expert staff. . . . It would be largely commonsense and self-confidence and there was an ample supply of the latter anyway. . . .'

On the long, slow, ice-bound voyage to New York at the end of January 1916 Reith kept warm in his berth, spending many hours more than his nightly ration in deep, dreamless slumber. Moir was at the dockside to meet him, and together they discussed at great length the broad arrangements for speeding the flow of small-arms to Britain. Surprisingly, neither of them at any point raised the important question of the existing hierarchical ladder and of their respective places on its rungs. Reith quite naturally assumed that there was nobody above Moir, who talked spaciously and with an authority that befitted the top person in any organisation; and since Moir did not even hint at any difficulties in his relationship with the British Army's local inspectors, Reith was totally unprepared for the hostile reception awaiting him in New Haven, Connecticut, where he kept his next appointment. The very name of Moir, it seemed, was anathema to Major Smyth-Piggott, the officer to whom he reported early in February. This middle-aged and mildly eccentric deputy chief inspector greeted Reith with something less than enthusiasm. Any friend and protégé of Moir's, he bluntly explained, could expect no help from him. What precisely did Captain Reith hope to do in the United States? Serve as a member of the military inspectorate of small-arms at the Remington Delaware plant outside Philadephia? Surely Captain Reith was not being serious?

'I have no intention of taking you on my staff', he said.

Reith was nonplussed. Inwardly he fumed at Moir for neglecting to mention the conflicts and underlying jealousies that had obviously arisen between himself and the uniformed inspectorate department. These, no doubt, were an extension of sharper rivalries which had meanwhile developed three thousand miles away between the War Office and that exuberant upstart, the Ministry of Munitions. Apparently, anyone from 'the Pearson racket', whether in or out of uniform, was bound to be regarded as an object of deep suspicion. Reith, who had to spend almost two months as the reluctant victim of these misunderstandings, relieved his immediate feelings by blurting out some uncomplimentary remarks about Moir, somewhat to Smyth-Piggott's astonishment. The newcomer was questioned closely about his engineering experience and his front line service, then quite suddenly the hostile attitude of the major changed.

'You're not quite what I was expecting,' he admitted. 'Trained engineers are rare birds over here and I like your style. So will the chief inspector when he gets my recommendation.'

'The chief inspector?' echoed Reith. It was the first time he had heard of him; it seemed that this mysterious colonel in New York devoted much of his time and energy to undermining the alleged empire-building activities of Moir. What weird methods these distant satraps of officialdom adopted, Reith reflected, in support of the army in the field. Major Smyth-Piggott, however, had by now shed all his enmity. He insisted on going with Reith to Philadelphia, installing him in a grander hotel than the one originally booked for the unknown and unseen protégé of Moir's, then accompanying him to the huge Remington factory some ten miles outside the city. The American managers showed them round the lathes and the long production lines, describing the bold yet intricate processes which would enable them within a few months to turn out six thousand rifles for Britain every day. Reith was as deeply impressed by their simple pride in the mammoth size of the task they had assumed as by their belief, which he shared, in the necessity for combining the best speed with the utmost efficiency. Much, of course, would depend on the British inspectors. A number of specialists from Enfield, England, had already begun to supervise output, but gradually these would train Americans recruited locally until the inspectorate reached full strength.

As the officer about to take charge of this expanding section, Reith was treated 'with great courtesy and deference'. The American managers led him to a suite of rooms. 'Your offices', they explained. 'Just let's know how you'd like them fitted out.'

They hoped to see him start shortly, just as soon as Major Smyth-Piggott gave the word that all formalities had been completed. There was the rub. The mysterious colonel, whose decision Reith had naturally assumed would be favourable, would still not relent: 'Not having this impostor at any price', he declared categorically in a message from New York.

Reith's immediate temptation was to call on this stupidly implacable colonel, tell him exactly what he thought of him, pack his belongings, and catch the earliest possible ship to England. Smyth-Piggott managed to calm him down.

'Leave the chief inspector to me', he said. 'I'll convince him if it's the last thing I do.'

It was in fact, almost the last thing he did. For, despite the careful letter which Reith helped his ally to concoct, denouncing Moir in passing for the 'false position' in which he had placed an innocent stranger, the remote colonel proved as obdurate in the end as Reith himself could be. So confident, nevertheless, was Smyth-Piggott that his appeal would do the trick that he authorised Reith to return to Philadelphia before the colonel's reply came.

'You can get yourself acclimatised', he said cheerfully. 'If it were left to me you could start work at once, but I haven't the authority to approve it.'

Reith had already decided to claim that authority as his own, so that his disgust knew no bounds when a copy of the colonel's final judgment reached him after his first few days in charge of the inspection department at the Remington factory.

'See no reason to modify decision about Reith,' it read.

There was no other honourable course now but to leave. Reith informed the puzzled American managers of his doubtful status and took several compensatory days off. Another wasted week passed, then a happy Smyth-Piggott called up Reith with the unexpected news that a major-general, newly arrived from London to unscramble the confusion caused by the rivalry between Moir and the local War Office representatives, had overruled the colonel.

'The general asks me to say that you must stay,' he added.

Reith was rather short with Smyth-Piggott, and later wished that he had sounded a little less churlish. For the very next day this unfortunate middle-man, who envied Reith his war service and never ceased to press him for details of his experiences in the field, suffered a sudden stroke and died. He had failed to win over the mysterious colonel, but Reith had to acknowledge that the failure was certainly not due to ill-will or idleness. He had meanwhile been bereft of an ally who might have become a friend.[1,5]

3

Nearly two months of uncertainty about his official standing might easily have soured Reith's personal relationships with the Americans at the factory as well as in the Philadelphia suburb of Swarthmore where he had already rented a small house. As an officer who had fought against the Germans, and who could not in any case disguise the ugly facial scar gained in his overzealous campaigning, Reith cut an unusual figure commanding instant respect. Philadelphia had been visited in the past by British civilians, Moir included; and the new factory at Eddystone, outside the city proper, had played host to several army officers senior in rank to Reith but lacking both his experience in battle and his appalling candour. He was so unlike the traditional stereotype of a Briton in the King's uniform that his hosts took Reith to their hearts virtually as one of themselves.

On his first Sunday in Swarthmore, then a fashionable but by no means wealthy district, he knew that he had found a home-from-home. There was a Friends' Meeting House as well as a Presbyterian church for the spiritual needs of a population largely of English and Scottish origin, and the minister of the kirk went out of his way to make him welcome. Many other eyes must have been fastened on him during the service; for immediately afterwards, in their friendly and direct fashion, at least half a dozen parishioners introduced themselves, satisfied their curiosity about this stranger in their midst, and invited him to visit them. It was the start of a life-long attachment to America and American ways which, but for changing circumstances, John Reith would almost certainly have pursued to the point of embracing United States citizenship.

The minister, 'a thoroughly bellicose old gentleman' in the view of his watchful visitor who had understood that the United States was still a neutral power, appeared to be the natural pivot of the community. The services he held, like the sermons he preached, were down-to-earth and very much to Reith's taste. The air of Swarthmore seemed to exude a utopian warmth and friendliness; and the beauty of that first American spring was intoxicating. The delicate greenery of the trees, the trim, unfenced lawns in front of the houses, the rising sap of a new hopefulness within himself warded off his natural tendency to depression and self-pity as the memory of his latest discomfiture began to fade. The war itself seemed very far away at times, though at others he caught himself longing for the risks and the exhilaration, even the squalor and the frequent monotony of active service. Once he had found his bearings, this American interlude, which was to last for eighteen virtually carefree months, taught him lessons of lasting value which he never forgot. He appreciated that among these civilised, amiable but vigorous people he occupied a place apart 'as a curio': no other survivor from France had so far drifted their way. And because young and old tended to lionise him, Reith responded with the verve of the born romantic, doubly pleased with the part a kindlier destiny had chosen for him.

The sensation of 'being wanted', of 'fitting in easily', enabled him equally to surmount the recurring teething troubles at the factory on the other side of the city where he worked hard all the week. Remington Arms of Delaware, the parent company, had built its plant at Eddystone to meet a British Government contract for the manufacture and delivery of two million rifles by mass-production methods. The Enfield specialists, under Reith's general supervision, were already on the spot to ensure that quality kept pace with quantity; and the standards they imposed were the strict, inflexible standards applied in Britain during pre-war days when skilled craftsmen managed to turn out in a year fewer rifles than Eddystone planned to turn out in a month. The precision required of the thirteen thousand workers was daunting. As Reith clearly saw the problem: 'The management were there to secure mass-production, but the mass-production to which they were accustomed was of the sort where .01 of an inch did not greatly matter, as in locomotives; in rifle work .0001 of an inch might matter a great deal'.[1]

Reith undertook to give fair notice to the American managers of any modifications in manufacturing techniques which might reduce or eliminate faults. The commitment demanded courage as well as firmness and diplomacy. For he was trapped between the handful of English experts, who insisted through thick and thin on perfection, and the American managers who were aggravated by any delays or setbacks in the maintenance of output.

'In May (1916) about 75 per cent of what came in to the British inspectors had to be rejected', according to Reith. 'Though the Eddystone management thought we might have been still more tolerant, the pundits at home were shocked by what was passed'.

His sympathies were with the Americans more than with the fussy recipients at home who needed the arms but would not accept anything less than 100 per cent flawlessness. He was quite satisfied, by constant trial and error on the firing range, that the American-made weapons were accurate, and felt inclined to inform London as he ruefully informed the managers and his Enfield experts:

'The damn things work, don't they? Don't you *want* to kill Germans?'[1]

Perhaps his most invidious task as an intermediary was to tell the firm at the end of May 1916, only six weeks after settling in his office at the Eddystone factory, that London wanted them to introduce a number of major changes in design which involved altering the jig-tools and machines. He broke the bad news to the managing director and his staff without beating about the bush, giving his own firm opinion that it would be wiser and probably cheaper in the long run not to get involved in fractious arguments with the Ministry of Munitions.

Half-expecting an unpleasant confrontation, Reith was amazed by the businesslike coolness with which the American directors accepted the inevitable. They promised to look into the problem immediately, all work on the assembly lines stopped, and the next day he received a formal letter stating that the alterations would be put in hand 'at once, and with no extra charge'. He admired the sound, hard-headed way in which these people knew how to cut their losses and start again, with the blessing of their financial backers. How many British firms, he wondered, would have had the guts and the belief in their own investment to react so swiftly and positively? When the President of the big arms concern of Baldwin's, Sam Vauclain, visited the plant during the mechanical alterations, this cheerful tycoon filled Reith with proud confusion by saying that the firm had decided 'to make no charge against the British Government' as 'a tribute' to the tall, plain-speaking Scot who had won the assured respect of everyone who met him.

Slowly but steadily, output started to rise that summer. Between June and August 1916 rifles rolled off the production belts at a rate that pleased even the bureaucrats in the far off Ministry of Munitions. Reith felt that he was justifying himself when the figures multiplied in those three months from five hundred to two thousand every day, proof indeed that American techniques and business methods were as good as promised. His respect grew apace for the detailed thoroughness of the planning, for the speed of its execution, and for the eagerness of everyone from senior executives to workers at the lathes to improve today on yesterday's shipments. If this was the native spirit of America, then John Reith did not mind confessing that he had fallen in love with it. He had been invited to 'feel free' and move about the factory talking to anyone he pleased, foremen or chargehands as well as directors. This he did; and in the process he learnt a good deal about the urges and aspirations of ordinary Americans. What all of them shared was a robust determination to better themselves by hard work. Their attitude broadly squared with his own.

He had a slight edge on them, of course, because destiny continued secretly to sharpen his longing for success in everything he turned his hand to; and as time passed he thought that the United States seemed an ideal country in which to seek the recognition which had so far eluded him. If New York was not America, the same could be said of Philadelphia. Yet the atmosphere of this old city, where the founding fathers of the new American republic had declared their defiance of British tyranny and triumphed against heavy odds in their battle for independence, was always intoxicating. Swarthmore, the 'Christian suburb' with its Presbyterian and Quaker descendants of the early settlers, was infinitely more romantic in its bustling reality than any of the Mark Twain stories which John Reith had read as a boy. Then he had hungered for adventure. He had envied Tom Sawyer and Huckleberry Finn their liberty to lead gay rough-and-tumble lives. If Philadelphia was not America, yet Reith's affection for its civic pride, its friendliness and its adventurous spirit helped him to understand the make-up of most Americans. He would have liked to put down permanent roots there. Repeatedly in old age he would regret having missed his chance to seek worldly fame in terms of his private American dream. So much in tune was Reith with the simple, straightforward ways of his adopted people that he never doubted his own ability to create something at least as enduring as the BBC, though probably in a different sphere, on the far side of the Atlantic.

In his catalogue of such things, Reith put efficiency and ambition high among the practical virtues which would help anyone to reach for the stars without stumbling. He marvelled at the fact that so many Americans appeared to agree with him, and that men could stand tall in that country because they accepted the challenge as part of their birthright. He liked the look and the feel of a society of free and equal citizens whose only aristocracy was one open to talents. There was enough of the romantic in his soul to see the advantages it held over countries like his own where the snobbery of caste and privilege were far too deeply rooted still. If there was a touch of the naive in his belief, it can be put down to his unworldly sentimentality. There was something of the chameleon in his character, too; and because he happened to be more of a natural conformist than a rebel, despite a powerful streak of stubbornness, Reith would in all probability have out-barnumed Barnum if he had settled in the United States. The

White House would not have been beyond his hopes had he gone into politics. The presidency of any of a dozen of the biggest industrial enterprises might easily have come within his grasp had he chosen a business career instead. The second best would never have suited this seeker of utopian riches that lay never far below the soil of God's own country.

4

What finally dissolved the bubble and brought Reith back to earth was, of course, the declaration of war on Germany by the United States in April 1917, when projects like the Eddystone factory were commandeered to enable an unprepared nation to furnish itself with arms. Right up to that point in the idyllic American interlude Reith experienced a contentment without previous parallel in a life which had so far been robbed of any joyful sense of purpose. In his own phrase, he felt himself to be 'a curio', set down in an historic city of the new world with a self-imposed task. Helping to multiply the flow of small-arms to the British forces, still locked in indecisive combat with the enemy from the Channel coast to the lines of the Somme and the Aisne, represented only the official half of his business; the whole of his leisure time, which he gave gladly, was occupied in propagating the nuances of a great civilising cause symbolised, as he knew, by his own gaunt, scarred countenance. Because fate and Whitehall had wished the rôle upon him, John Reith carried it out until the curtain fell.

The discovery in himself of a simple talent for 'playing to the gallery', and extracting every particle of drama from occasions when he was invited to speak in public, proved disconcerting and even frightening at first. The boy, the apprentice, the somewhat truculent junior officer, who had learnt unwillingly the virtue of speaking only when spoken to, learned to use the opportunities which came at every turn of saying what he badly wanted to say with the ease of a leading churchman or a visiting statesman. It had all started casually enough with an invitation from an American business acquaintance to attend a banquet given by the St. Andrew's Society of Philadelphia. He found, on arrival, 'a semi-circle of prosperous looking, white-waistcoated gentlemen, obviously waiting to welcome the guest of the evening'. To his consternation, this guest turned out to be himself. They were all expecting Captain Reith, and after the toasts two pipers led him out at the head of the company into an adjoining hall where a large audience was already seated.

'I had never attended a party on this scale, never spoken in public, was wholly unprepared. I was horrified, felt positively fraudulent. Then I realised that here was a crisis in life. . . . I must not let them down, must carry it off as if it were natural to me.'

He had held his listeners captive. The *acteur manqué* in him had sprung to his rescue, disclosing an unsuspected source of responsiveness to the mood of his audience. The temptation was strong to go on improving a talent which, in his unique situation as 'a curio' from the old country at war, could well have been exploited for the best of reasons; but he shrank from it like a timid girl from an importunate suitor.

'It was thoroughly unsettling and upsetting', he noted. 'I had better address no more gatherings, or anyhow very few.'

His father, a preacher of eloquence and nobility, had indirectly passed on to John Reith the rueful lesson that words alone seldom moved the hearts of men in any permanent or decisive fashion. Every Sunday for nearly twenty years he had sat in the family pew listening to sermons which, particularly towards the end of his schooldays when he had become a prey to superstition, helped to turn the screws tighter in the rack of his conscience. But as fear and remorse had still to be lived with, weekdays endured and normal work done, his father's words gradually lost their original impact on him. He had often heard Dr. George Reith discuss with his family or with friends the failure of the politicians to cut any ice with a public which had a sound instinct for distinguishing truth from propaganda. Now that John Reith had stumbled on his own untrained gift, he wisely refused to believe that he had no right to bury it in silence.

'I only spoke about ten times in the eighteen months. Of course I had the advantage of what was, to such audiences, the lurid and compelling background of war. Many of those to whom I spoke heard from me what their own consciences had been saying for long enough.'[1]

When it was a question of drawing on his own experiences, of relating those to the sufferings and grief of whole nations, and of trying to describe how the Allied struggle was that of civilisation against barbarism, Reith could be persuaded to speak with a fervour that came naturally. He was careful about the choice of audience and the place, being quite willing, for example, to address officer cadets at Princeton or the Pennsylvania National Guard, but refusing to address students or women. There was nothing arbitrary in his attitude. He preferred to converse with young people in person; as for the company of women, this he could tolerate when their menfolk were present, not otherwise. The prospect of having to win over several hundred American ladies crowded together was too daunting for him even to consider.

Politicians he tried to avoid as sedulously as women, but once towards the end of his time in the United States the audience at a degree-conferring ceremony enjoyed an off-the-cuff, impassioned speech from Reith that put a local congressman in his place. The United States had recently entered the war, and with provocative tactlessness the politician launched forth into a colourful account of how the Americans were about to save the world. He was certain that their intervention would tip the balance against the Germans, and that when the war ended the United States would emerge from it as the greatest power on earth. This was too much for Reith. He reminded the congressman that others had been in the field, fighting the world's and America's battles, for three years. He did not care to hear an American politician demeaning his own country by stating confidently that the United States would soon be the leader of nations. Such language was 'worthy of the Kaiser himself'. An English official present said to Reith later that he wished the floor had opened and swallowed him up. For the congressman sat, stunned and hurt, while the audience stood and cheered, and Reith resumed his seat slightly amazed at himself.

Perhaps the unblocking of his own inhibitions to declaim the moral values in which he believed was the most significant part of this happy period among people whom he liked and respected. After April 1917 Reith realised that his days on American soil were now numbered, that his dream of settling down permanently had been shattered by events. Increasingly he began to feel superfluous. The moment of proud climax had come and gone on the day the United States decided to fight. On the church lawn at Swarthmore, 'Captain Reith of His Majesty's Royal Engineers' had raised and broken the Stars and Stripes on a towering flagpole, a gesture which the watching thousands had applauded, and a fitting conclusion to the efforts of this military castaway in their midst to prepare them mentally for their decisive part in the war. Had he not acted as the unofficial instructor of a new company of the National Guard, providing them with rejected arms and ammunition 'borrowed' from the place where he worked as an inspector? His presence and very appearance had at times seemed a sort of walking reproach to local able-bodied young men, most of whom regarded war as an unthinkable calamity until it happened.

For nearly four months more Reith hung on awaiting the marching orders from London. He was relieved with one half of his being at the enforced delay in his departure from the 'paradise on earth' which Swarthmore had become in his unworldly scheme of things. Yet the stern realist in him chafed a little until American army ordnance men arrived at the end of August and took over the factory. Characteristically, Reith stole off at short notice. He gave his parents no warning of his return, walking into the College Manse one evening to find them at supper. What would replace the broken remnants of his insubstantial American dream in a Britain torn by dissent between partisans of the generals and the politicians over the conduct of the war? There was not much that he could seriously hope for now in the way of a responsible staff appointment; and despite the horrifying British casualties, the prospects of a posting to France were slight. By 'crashing in' on yet another major-general at the War Office, Reith mistakenly supposed that his persuasive tongue would secure a transfer to the Railway Operating division of the Royal Engineers, preferably on the western front; and though the transfer went through, so did an exasperating order that no more captains were required with railway engineering units overseas.

As fast as Reith moved towards a suitable opening, fate seemed to move just that shade faster and callously trip him up. Gloom and frustration descended on him, clouding his outlook and drawing out all those unbearable traits of conceit and intolerance that made life virtually impossible for others. The months he spent that long winter with an inactive unit of Royal Engineers, attached to an infantry brigade in the Norwich district were dreary and empty of incident; and even after Reith arranged a further transfer in May 1918, to the engineering department of the Admiralty, which was planning to lay a huge hydro-electro barrage from the Sussex coast at Southwick across the bed of the English Channel to the French coast, he got a chilly reception at first from the Royal Marine colonel in charge of the project. His refusal to be rebuffed by anyone, one of the facets of Reith's touchy pride, won him a favourable hearing in the end. He never believed in holding back a grievance if he could find a sympathetic listener, and his tale of woe so impressed one of the senior officers at Southwick that the colonel reluctantly took him on.

At first the work was not very complex or exacting. Speed and thoroughness of supervision were the main requirements for laying level foundations on which would rise eight enormous towers to carry the underwater cable. But Reith extended his area of interest. He enjoyed controlling and co-ordinating the work of large teams. Authority sat lightly on him when there was a clear job to be done, yet his feeling for power mattered far less to him than the almost physical satisfaction of watching a plan take shape exactly as he had envisaged that it should. The colonel next put him in charge of constructing the towers themselves. He boasted of having two thousand men and some thirty officers under his direct command, including two of his prewar superiors from Pearson's.

'I hung on till April 1919', he recorded, 'because it had been decided to complete the first two towers, and I had neither sense nor opportunity to go elsewhere. The end of the war had brought no elation. I was at least happily and busily engaged. . . .'

The mysterious towers were, as far as can be discovered, never put to any practical use. Yet the building of them called for more finesse and detailed planning ability than Reith would admit to possessing himself. What enthralled him was the interdependence of the workforce and the engineering experts: his own task was to harness all their efforts, take the necessary decisions, and stick to a schedule carefully laid down so that public money should not be idly squandered. Each tower, when complete, had to float like a ship, four decks rearing up in concrete to a height of eighty-two feet with a further eight decks of steel climbing another ninety-two feet beyond. The colossal base of this white elephant was 193 feet long and 162 feet wide. And having finished his monstrous handiwork, Reith moved on to Salisbury Plain where, it was said, a military housing scheme demanded the services of a sound engineer. Since the War Office would not countenance the elevation of a territorial captain to the vacancy of second-in-command, he decided once and for all to cut his losses and go back into civilian life. Why should he waste any more thought and nervous energy on a service which contained too many idle people chasing too few jobs?

Meticulous as always in his calculations, Reith cast his mind back and felt a surge of righteous indignation when he reflected that 'between September 1917 and August 1919—twenty-three months—I had done about six months' useful work'.[1,5] It really was high time he got out of uniform, and he did so without regret. The seeker had still to find the outlet promised by destiny.

5

The Opportunist

1

To be out of work in the late spring of 1919 was the lot of many a British ex-officer. Though the finest flower of a nation's manhood had been mown down on the battlefields, relatively few of the survivors seemed to find the transition to civilian life easy or quick. After the wild euphoria that followed the armistice, a mood of anti-climax seemed to have settled on the country. It affected the returning servicemen most of all, not because any but the simplest had fallen for the glib political catch-phrase that they were returning to 'a land fit for heroes to live in' but because the business of readjustment to the perils of peace took time. Britain's economy was still not in gear, and the Government of the day had too much else on its hands to be bothered about the widespread feeling of disenchantment. There were reparations to be extorted from the vanquished, and the map of the world had to be redrawn so that never again would the world become unsafe for democracy. Meanwhile, men like John Reith had to find jobs in a labour market that was still badly out of joint.

Two mildly conflicting reasons impelled him to go job-hunting with less than the discrimination one might have expected of a man who had benefited greatly from his experiences in the United States. The first and most pressing was the obligation he felt towards his parents, now old and in declining health, and this induced him to look for openings in Glasgow. When the post of housing director to the corporation fell vacant, Reith armed himself with excellent references and applied. He felt deeply mortified at being passed over in favour of a local sanitary inspector. There was a further rebuff to his pride after the chairman of the Gas Light and Coke Company, to whom he had been personally introduced, dashed his hopes of becoming assistant to the chief engineer in that concern by failing to consult the chief engineer himself: an oversight which naturally roused the latter's antagonism and so put Reith out of the running. He could not help recalling with a touch of anguish that this was not the first time in his thirty years that a well-disposed prospective employer had let him down by failing to observe orderly procedures, thus giving rise to unnecessary jealousies. It was a lesson in correct manners which Reith was unlikely to forget.

Torn now between impatience with being idle and concern for his parents, Reith left for London to seek something temporary, and until March 1920 was employed by the Ministry of Munitions in charge of winding up all existing contracts for rifles, machine guns, shells, bombs, fuses and grenades. The war machine was still producing the unneeded merchandise of death at a profligate pace. It could be slowed down and stopped only by patiently and skilfully renegotiating sensible terms with the armament makers. This, on a far larger scale, was almost the exact reverse of what Reith had been so happy doing in Philadelphia nearly three years before, and the irony of it did not escape him. Nevertheless, by driving good bargains and applying common sense as well as experience, he managed to save money and salvage valuable equipment that could be used again for constructive purposes. It was not the great task in life which, despite all the unfavourable omens, Reith believed would eventually come his way; but he enjoyed dealing directly with generals and senior officials and persuading them to reach firm decisions. It tickled his vanity to be listened to with care and as an equal. His salary of fifteen pounds a week was quite high by the standards of the period, but he comforted himself with the knowledge that every penny of it was well earned.

There was a second reason for Reith's anxiety to snatch at the kind of job which would not pin him down too far from home. For he had meanwhile fallen in love. He had allowed that to happen after some heart-searching, not suddenly and capriciously but with a cautious willingness to be proved wrong, which at times seriously taxed the patience of Muriel Odhams. They had originally met in Southwick at the marine engineering depot. Muriel was in the Women's Legion. He had often seen her behind the wheel of the colonel's staff car which she drove with smooth dexterity round the vast perimeter of the camp. When his parents spent their summer holiday at Southwick in 1918, instead of paying their usual visit to the highlands, Reith was introduced to her through them. He liked her calm, gentle ways.

The fact that she took at once to his father and mother, and they to her, increased the distant admiration he felt for this young woman who appeared quite capable of holding her own in a conversation without losing one jot of her shy charm. Reith might well have left Southwick months earlier than he did if Muriel had not been living there with her parents in their lovely, old home. The young couple became acquainted and met at intervals but a mutual diffidence prohibited either of them from imposing any emotional demands on the other. In John Reith's case, a pronounced timidity in the presence of women accentuated the habitual inhibitions of his stern religious upbringing; in Muriel's case, a natural delicacy was reinforced by genuine bewilderment as to the direction and strength of this unusual young man's true feelings. She grew increasingly attracted to him, but feared to tell him so. They kept one another at arm's length, and only after Reith's departure from Southwick did they begin to open their hearts to one another in occasional exchanges of letters.

The prospect of getting married had not, up to this point, stood high on the list of his priorities. Anyone so sensitively attuned to the mysterious call of destiny could scarcely have allowed himself the luxury of so major a distraction. What slowly helped to reconcile Reith to the idea was the unreserved approval of his parents who knew and liked the girl. If it had not been for the happy coincidence of their encounter with her in 1918, Reith's matrimonial plans would probably have been long deferred. Now, however, a sense of urgency lent impatient wings to his search for the type of work which would not only offer security but also release in him the single-minded will to succeed.

One of Reith's consistent traits, even when engaged on tasks which could be described in his book as being of minor significance, was an inability to tear himself away from immediate duties for reasonable family demands on his time. In 1914, for instance, he could be present only in spirit at his father's installation as Moderator of the General Assembly of the United Free Church of Scotland; in 1917, with far better excuse, he did not apply for compassionate leave from the United States on learning that his father was gravely ill; and again, at the end of 1919, he did not arrive home from the Ministry of Munitions until after his father's death.

For this final omission, Reith blamed himself somewhat excessively. His admiration for the deep holiness of the man, for his utterly Christian love of others, was tinctured still with awe. Reith more than once informed me of his lasting regret that circumstances prevented him from ever reaching terms of intimate companionship with this remarkable churchman. The shadow of a curious restraint, which persisted between them after their estrangement during John Reith's youth, appeared to rule out close confidence to the very end. Yet how tragic and heart-rending it was for the son to come home from London 'too late for his farewell'. The kind of wise advice he longed to hear from those still lips would never be his, he could merely look on the good man's face, 'benign in the majestic and serene repose of death', and dumbly trust that his father would not desert him in his hour of need.

The comfort of realising, from the contents of an unposted letter addressed to him in 1917, when he was in Philadelphia and his father seriously ill in Glasgow, that 'you have made your mother and me very happy during these last years, and God will reward you for it', could not begin to assuage the grief or remorse of Dr. George Reith's youngest son. There was so much he might have drawn from this fount of unworldly wisdom. Their communication had usually been through correspondence, an unsatisfactory method which often left, or led to, too many unanswered questions. Having failed to reach the death-bed in time, John Reith could only ponder his father's wish for him, expressed in that unposted letter, that he would eventually achieve a 'useful and honourable career'. For the added rider that 'life is for the service of Christ' seemed somehow beyond him, and the admonitory words—'I would rather know that you were a devoted and loving follower of Him than a millionaire'—struck a painful chord.[2] They did not wholly square either with the ambition or the obsession with destiny of the young man. One thing he could promise: if the right moment and opportunity came, he would settle in Glasgow and try to carry on his father's selfless labours as best he might. Had he not said 'without me you can do nothing'? Dr. Reith had been quoting his Master's words, but his superstitious son felt otherwise.

When he returned to the Ministry after the funeral, the emptiness of his role as a winder-up of unwanted arms contracts privately appalled him. He carried on for three more months, to the manifest gratification of his superiors who were surprised and disappointed at his decision to quit. Munitions as a department would, of course, soon be liquidated; but even the firm offer of a permanent post in the War Office did not tempt him to stay. It was true, as Reith publicly acknowledged, that he had 'had enough' of government service. Yet, as he admitted to me, he had privately vowed to go back to Glasgow if the right opening presented itself. His father's memory had to be served, and from beyond the grave his father's influence on him remained uncannily potent indeed. This did not deter him, on the practical and mundane level, from keeping a close eye on property advertisements, approaching estate agents, and hoping to discover a suitable house on the fringes of London, just in case the right opening first presented itself there. After all, he might be getting married shortly; and there was small point in dissipating energy and resources between two contradictory aims which no man, however noble or able, could simultaneously pursue.

So finely did he calculate, and remember the calculations, that he could say without a hint of self-deceit that he missed the house in London that would have suited him 'by half an hour'. The habit of putting out feelers in several directions was already firmly fixed; and before another desirable property could be viewed, Reith had accepted the delayed offer of a position as general manager of Beardmore's, then a large and varied engineering company at Coatbridge, near Glasgow. Like an expert juggler keeping several balls in the air at once, he let London and its alluring but unrealised hopes drop to the floor for the present. Packing his possessions again, John Reith moved north to the city where he had spent the bigger and unhappier part of his life.

For twenty-two months, in the teeth of obstruction from directors and executives who took exception to his forceful methods, Reith drew on all his powers of blunt persuasion, sharp reasoning and hard bargaining to shake the firm out of its torpor. The transition from war to peace conditions was no smoother on the Clyde than elsewhere, and yet most of Beardmore's senior executives seemed indifferent to the muddle and confusion of their once prosperous business. The profits from steady military contracts had all but dried up. Markets for the traditional products of the firm were still very slack and uncertain. Among the workers on the shop floor discipline was lax, partly because the foremen lacked authority. Here was one problem which Reith, entirely careless of his own popularity as usual, grasped and solved with speed. What he had picked up by observing American industrial methods in the big Remington arms factory now began to serve him well, though it proved an uphill task trying to carry the Beardmore board with him in his repeated pleas for a systematic overhaul of planning policy:

'Had I realized the true state of affairs when I met Sir William Beardmore, the chairman, I'd never have taken on the job', Reith once stressed to me. 'I thought I could do it through having immediate access to him and always being responsible directly to him, but I saw far too little of Sir William for my comfort.'[1]

Instead of concentrating resources on one or two highly profitable goods, the firm had spread its capital on the production of several complex articles including motor cars, rotary pumps and oil engines.

This process could not now be reversed, whatever might be said by an argumentative general manager whose influence with the head of the concern existed only on paper. The frustrations of having to deal with directors who appeared quite content to let things drift, regardless of the business risks, caused Reith to regret his overhasty return from London. For the sake of his widowed mother, however, he persevered in the thankless role which he had accepted with such high hopes. At least he was living near enough to console her by his presence—and by his bleak and characteristically forthright tirades against the incompetent individuals who were the bane of his long days at Beardmore's.

The usual determination not to be thwarted or sidetracked, and to persevere until he had instilled professional pride into a dispirited firm, had recently been strengthened by his decision to ask Muriel Odhams to marry him. The one girl in the whole world who seemed to represent his ideal of womanhood, combining charm, tact and common sense with good looks and a self-effacing modesty, Muriel had accepted his somewhat stiff and awkward proposal with joy. For she understood, without yet being able to measure, the force of those tumultuous undercurrents that drove the perfectionist half of him. He was so different from any young man she had known, so simple and unconceited in his convictions yet at the same time so utterly sure of himself, that she found herself irresistibly attracted to him. She privately vowed to protect and comfort the man she loved, to bring warmth into a life that had been largely bereft of human affection, and gradually to teach this rather melancholic partner of hers the true meaning of happiness. They had a quiet, family wedding on July 14 1921; and for several months more domestic felicity provided John Reith with a blessed distraction from his deepening troubles at the Coatbridge factory.

Beardmore's, he had begun to realise, was probably not the place earmarked for him by fate. Yet he was no longer in such a hurry to throw up a well paid job. The impulsiveness which, in other circumstances, would probably have led to a head-on collision with the firm's directors was offset now by the weight he was anxious to allow for his wife's feelings. As he had saved enough from his army service not to be unduly worried about money, considerations of security did not yet enter into his calculations. He would remain at Beardmore's until he found the atmosphere and the difficulties quite unendurable.

Reith remained for nearly nine months more. He was reasonably pleased with his successful efforts to 'get things properly moving' in the plant and on the business side. Industrial unrest was widespread at that time, and the infection reached Beardmore's. It might easily have resulted in a paralysing strike if Reith had not handled the men with firmness and frankness. He left them in no doubt as to what he expected: a full day's work for a full day's pay. The foremen, who at his insistence were obliged to resume wearing the traditional bowler hats which the majority had discarded, were under an equal obligation to keep a strict account of the quality of workmanship quite apart from mere quantity. If he succeeded in curing the bad spirit that prevailed when he joined the firm, Reith attributed his achievement to 'elementary common sense'. His experience, often painful, confirmed him in his somewhat jaundiced view that the industrial unrest, from which Beardmore's had been suffering before he arrived, could largely be explained by the incompetence and short-sightedness of the management. At least he had put that right; and the firm's progress and costing systems were also overhauled by Reith to eliminate what he regarded as the 'haphazard methods of the past'.

The main sales force, unfortunately, was based in London. He depended for ultimate success on the accuracy of the demand estimates they sent in, but accuracy did not appear to be their strong suit. Vague promises were hardly the same matter as solid, firm orders. Reith's frustrations rose to such a pitch that by early 1922 he informed Sir William Beardmore personally that there was little point in his striving further to teach the unteachable. When he resigned at last in March 1922 the concern had fallen on hard times. As Reith put it, 'the factory was virtually closed down'.[1,3]

Surveying his arduous yet mainly fruitless endeavours Reith could not suppress an explosion of impatience as he counted the wasted months behind him. He had failed to save Beardmore's because the decisive power and authority which might have lifted the company out of the morass of its troubles had been concentrated in the wrong hands. Had it not been for a 'modest satisfaction' in what he himself had done, apart from a new-found contentment that had come with marriage, Reith would certainly have been beside himself with remorse at ever having left London. He consulted earnestly with Muriel before taking his next step. With wise forbearance his wife did not oppose the oddly fatalistic reason he gave for contending that this step was one which he must take alone. Since he had committed a serious error of judgment in leaving London two years earlier, to London he must return without her and start hunting for work all over again. She marvelled to herself at his unshakable self-confidence. For he travelled south with no prospects and without the first glimmering of a plan, buoyed up now against the cruel sea of doubt by the inner assurance that this time he would find what he had been seeking since first hearing a message as a boy in the sighing of the wind among the dark fir trees of the Cairngorms.

2

The strain on John Reith's consistently lively faith in himself almost reached breaking point as the weeks of empty job-hunting stretched into months. He scanned the newspapers for likely openings, applied for post after post, attended interview after interview. Yet invariably, when it seemed that his luck was bound to turn at last and hope momentarily burned high in him the postman would deliver another letter of polite regret, cursorily rejecting him. Then he would be plunged into gloom again. Like many a younger man at the outset of a writing career, Reith was absorbing the salutary if hard lesson that until he could paper a room with rejection notes the only sensible course was to ignore the mounting odds on failure, and persevere. Despair crept close enough once or twice to induce the feeling that it might be better to pack up and emigrate. Reith nearly did so when an American colleague from his Philadelphia days wrote with a genuine offer of work in the United States. He replied by return of post, indicating his readiness to come at once; but while feverishly planning to cut his losses and leave Britain for ever, the wholly unforeseen happened. A brief message came to say that his American would-be rescuer had suddenly died. No clearer or sadder sign could have been flashed by destiny to warn Reith against leaving. The logic hit him like a body blow; it was cruel and crushing but definitive.

Partly for want of anything better to try his hand at, he trifled with the idea of entering politics. His father had not been favourably disposed to John Reith's intermittent yet positive interest in pursuing a parliamentary career. The question was first raised seriously in letters that passed between them in 1915. Then the young man's ardour had met with a corresponding coolness. This had been a period of anxiously marking time, before his transfer to the Royal Engineers, and as a break from tedium Reith had elaborated on his post-war ambitions in a letter sixteen pages long. He would like, he said, to 'go to Oxford or Cambridge' after the war, just to surprise his father by demonstrating an authentic capacity for scholarship, after which he hoped to fulfil the ambition held since schooldays of becoming a politician.

'He had said', Reith wrote, 'that it was a wretched occupation. I knew all that could be said against it, and about those who went that way, but that did not affect me. I wanted to use to maximum effect the gifts I had and to do the greatest good I could. No influence was comparable to that which a cabinet minister could exercise and I should be in the cabinet within ten years. . . .'[4]

Dr. Reith had tactfully refrained from committing himself on his son's challenge over Oxford or Cambridge, preferring to deflate his idealistic simplicity about the means and ends of political life. His misgivings on the subject were not unfamiliar to John Reith. They were repeated now in a 'sympathetic and kindly' fashion which had, nonetheless, left little margin for doubt. Again, while Reith was coasting downhill towards his long delayed release from military service, they had a final exchange in which his father reaffirmed his convictions with a serene but incisive objectivity:

'Parliamentary life', he wrote, 'is not the desirable thing you seem to think, and a talk with some of the men already in the House would surprise you. To do as much good to your fellowmen as possible and to serve God in your generation—that *may* be attained by going into Parliament, but only by the *very* few. . . .'

In the same letter, Dr. Reith had urged his son to reflect on the example of exceptional parliamentarians like Cobden and Bright, to 'get hold' of their lives and read them. For such men politics had never been an end in itself, only the means to 'that great end for which they devoted their lives'. What John Reith must ask himself was the pertinent question of the committed Christian: have I a 'burning enthusiasm for some great cause or reform' to lighten the lot of my fellow-countrymen?[2] It was not easy to answer that question with the unreserved detachment required by his father in the confused, isolated and somewhat desperate circumstances in which he found himself in 1922; yet the lure of politics still drew him like a magnet, and there seemed to be no harm in putting his father's treasured rules to the test as an experiment.

So in April 1922, after a careful scrutiny of the three main parties and what they claimed to stand for, Reith took his courage in both hands and sent a lengthy letter to J. R. Clynes, a prominent Labour MP, saying why he believed, despite the fact that he had no party affiliations, that he could best serve his country by going into politics as a socialist. Clynes wrote back and fixed an appointment to see him, but the meeting proved something of an anticlimax. They talked casually and in a desultory fashion that led nowhere. If Reith had been seeking a man to inspire or captivate him, he could scarcely have chosen a less likely person than the woolly and dully pedestrian Clynes. Had he approached Ramsay MacDonald, Philip Snowden or even the pugnacious Emanuel Shinwell instead, his future might have taken an altogether different course. As it was, the noncommittal and guarded reaction of Clynes persuaded Reith that there was no place for him in the ranks of the Labour Party.

Somehow, during the long, desolate summer months that followed, he succeeded in keeping his head above water; financially by living frugally on his savings, spiritually, by wrestling off the demons of doubt and recurring depression, above all, emotionally, by constant reminders through correspondence and through occasional, fleeting visits to Scotland that Muriel, his wife, was content to endure this enforced separation because she believed in him almost as passionately as he believed in himself. London, he discovered, was like a vast, unfriendly desert. He made acquaintances but no lasting friends, yet his self-sufficiency was by now so sure that he needed neither. He had joined the Cavendish Club in Mayfair as a convenient centre where letters could be written to his rapidly shrinking list of prospective employers, and where appointments could, in theory, be kept with them. He became an avid newspaper reader, too, following the declining fortunes of Lloyd George and his coalition government with an interest less personal but no less compulsive than that he lavished on the columns headed 'situations vacant'. It was not an advertisement, however, which finally lifted the clouds of uncertainty and pointed the way ahead: it was a chance visit to his old school in Norfolk. He could recognise few old faces among the teaching staff at Gresham's, yet the warmth of his reception was touching as well as stimulating after so much recent discouragement. When the headmaster persuaded him to address the literary society, Reith responded with an alacrity and fluency which appeared to captivate his young audience. He talked about his wartime experiences, mentioned in passing that he had since joined the army of unemployed but might soon get into politics if his luck turned, and was surprised afterwards at the eagerness of a sixth-form boy to learn more about his political leanings.

'You see', said Stephen Bull, 'it so happens that my father's a politician, and I know he'd be glad to see you.'[4]

Reith delayed taking any precipitate action, but kept in touch with Stephen, the eldest of Sir William Bull's three sons, who was going up to Oxford after the summer holidays. In September 1922, while John Reith himself was enjoying a respite from the arid monotony of London at Dunardoch, his conjugal home in Dunblane, Perthshire, Stephen Bull paid him a visit. As a result, Reith wrote at last to Sir William. The core of this letter, dated September 28th, throws significant light on the desperate state of mind of the writer:

'The position, briefly, is that for many years I have had the greatest desire to take up a parliamentary career, and have felt that this is what I should be doing, but the difficulties are considerable, and I should be glad to have your advice on the matter. If the idea is to materialise at all, it must be soon as I am thirty-three. So far I have been very busy in executive work in commercial and engineering lines. If you would be good enough to have a talk with me, perhaps you would send a line to await me at the Cavendish Club, 119 Piccadilly, where I arrive early on Sunday morning.'[2]

When Reith arrived in London, a note from the accommodating Sir William Bull was awaiting him. Later that week he met the man whose willingness to lend a helping hand profoundly altered the course of John Reith's life. It is an astonishing fact that at no time in his future public career did Reith ever admit how much he owed for his start to the assistance of this long-forgotten politician. At their first encounter Bull asked him a few pertinent questions, seemed quite satisfied with the answers, and concluded the interview by offering Reith a position as his 'honorary political secretary' at a nominal salary. As an admirer and supporter of Lloyd George, though a life-long Conservative, Sir William admitted that he would probably be very busy all through the summer and autumn with political matters. If John Reith was really interested in learning, he could obtain a lot of first-hand knowledge not only of the major issues then confronting the nation but of the leading personalities who backed the Prime Minister all the way in his difficult struggle to hold together an already badly divided coalition government.

What seemed to have softened Bull's normally businesslike attitude to a total stranger in search of temporary work was a letter from the headmaster of Gresham's, which bore out in judicious terms his eldest son's extremely glowing account of the merits of the unknown Reith. Mr. J. R. Eccles, who had replaced Howson as headmaster of Gresham's several years previously, had at John Reith's request, written with polished enthusiasm:

'He is undoubtedly a man of strong personality. As you probably heard from Stephen, he impressed the senior members of the school very much last term when he gave them an address on "Vocation". I had the privilege of hearing it myself and I certainly thought it quite excellent. It was full of sound and practical advice and pitched in a fine key. He talked of going to America, but I have done my best to dissuade him. I don't think we can afford to lose men of character and earnestness like Reith, and, if you can do anything to give him scope for his undoubted powers, I think you will be doing something you will never regret. I understand that, for several years, he has had the desire to enter parliament and I hope he will be able to do so. . . .'[2]

Any residual doubts in the mind of Bull, a seasoned politician who had represented Hammersmith for the Conservatives without interruption since the turn of the century, were dissolved by Reith's broad grasp of public affairs. The current troubles of the Lloyd George government, notably in the Middle East, did not entirely commend themselves to his sympathies. Having too much leisure on his hands, he had absorbed a good deal of information from the newspapers, but he was shrewd enough not to blurt out his personal opinion of the Prime Minister's reckless involvement in the disastrous Middle East adventures of Greece at a moment when Sir William Bull appeared keen to employ him. Instead, he accepted Bull's kindly offer, then was caught up, willy-nilly, in the political consequences of the so-called 'Chanak crisis'.

The first cracks in the foundations of the Lloyd George coalition had, in fact, been exposed to the public gaze for some weeks. As a consequence of the impetuous pro-Greek policy of the Prime Minister, a very reluctant Britain had been dragged to the brink of war with Turkey. The final routing of the Greek Army by the revolutionary forces of Kemal Ataturk meant that only token detachments of the British, French and Italian occupation forces on the Dardanelles stood between the advancing Turks and Constantinople.

The Treaty of Sèvres, which peace delegates of the old Ottoman Empire had signed just two years previously, now lay in tatters; no diplomatic finesse could be expected to ease a perilous situation; the Parliament at Westminster was still in its long summer recess; so Lloyd George, foolishly miscalculating the mood of disillusionment at home, had decided boldly that Britain must fight the Turks, if necessary alone. Orders to that effect went to the three armed services. General 'Tim' Harrington, in command of a single British battalion behind its barbed wire perimeter on the demilitarised Asiatic shore of the Gallipoli straits at Chanak, received instructions to resist any advance by the Turkish troops already surrounding his beleagured position.

Churchill, the Colonial Secretary, strongly approved of a policy of direct confrontation: so did Birkenhead, the Lord Chancellor, whose antipathy to French intrigues with the upstart leaders of the new Turkey led him to speak of 'a probability of a war against the Turks, and possibly France too'. The despatch of ill-considered telegrams to the Dominions, inviting their physical and moral support, marked an irreversible step towards the fall of the coalition government. All but one of the Dominions prayed to be excused participation in an unnecessary war, and opposition to the Chanak adventure quite naturally grew in Britain itself, especially when France and Italy had announced the withdrawal of their token detachments from Chanak on September 18th. The strains on Conservative elements in the government, whose loyalty to the coalition had been weakening well before this crisis, became insupportable when Bonar Law, who had retired from active politics in March 1921, suddenly entered the lists against the war party of Lloyd George. His first sally was an anonymous, forthright letter to *The Times* published on October 7th. In it he declared that Britain must no longer act alone as the 'policeman of the world'; if she could not collaborate with France and Italy, then the only proper policy for her was to withdraw from Europe and safeguard the interests of the Empire.

The effect of this letter, the authorship of which at once became an open secret, was instant and electrifying. It made the unwilling Bonar Law a rallying point for the expressive body of Conservative opinion which supported the break-up of the coalition itself. It also helped to frustrate the Prime Minister's unpopular war policy, gravely undermining his prestige and obliging him, in self-defence, to consider the fateful step of appealing to the electorate for a fresh mandate.

Reith was unaware of these finer points, though he realised that Sir William Bull remained steadfast in his support of Lloyd George who still hesitated to call a general election, just as Bonar Law still hesitated about leading his party out of the coalition. For the main difficulty lay in the stubborn loyalty to Lloyd George of Austen Chamberlain, the leader of the Conservative Party ever since Bonar Law's retirement more than eighteen months before. Chamberlain had no intention of allowing the Government to disintegrate in order to indulge Tory purists bent on committing political suicide. Beaverbrook shrewdly noted, 'quite apart from the question of personal loyalty to the Premier, Austen Chamberlain and his friends had a totally exaggerated view of the value of Lloyd George's assistance as an electioneering asset to the constituencies'.[4] Now Reith discovered that Sir William Bull ranked high among Austen Chamberlain's most stalwart supporters.

The famous Carlton Club meeting on Thursday, October 19th, became 'the arena' in which 'the matador', Bonar Law, reluctantly decided to kill 'the Conservative Cabinet Ministers who favoured the coalition'.[6] If he had let Beaverbrook down by failing to turn up, the coalition might have survived. Bonar Law, however, overcame his unwillingness to appear and spoke out against Austen Chamberlain's unpopular advice that the Coalition Government should go to the country as a united government.

By 187 votes to 87, the Carlton Club meeting of the Conservative Party decided to ignore Austen Chamberlain and support Bonar Law.

On the afternoon of October 19th, Lloyd George resigned and counselled the King to send for Bonar Law. A political era had ended but the erstwhile Premier and his loyal associates were not disheartened.

The caretaker administration of anti-coalition Tories would, they believed, be shortlived. The result of the forthcoming general election would vindicate their faith, sweeping back to power Austen Chamberlain, Birkenhead, Churchill and all those who had put loyalty to Lloyd George and the coalition above party interest. One of the most important backbench associates of the outgoing Prime Minister was Bull, whose position as chairman of all Unionist MPs in the London area since 1910 made him an important tactical influence behind the scenes. The director of several companies, including Siemans, one of the electrical firms then experimenting like a few larger concerns with new-fangled contraptions called wireless receiving sets, Bull had his work cut out. He was pleased with himself for having John Reith at his beck and call as his honorary secretary. The young man had shown great willingness and efficiency in organising the detailed planning of the Conservative coalitionists' electoral campaign. Nor had Bull minded Reith's open admission that he himself was no Tory. For many a Bonar Law supporter would no doubt have denied Sir William the title of a true Tory too. What the job certainly offered Reith was an unrivalled insight into the intricate workings of a party machine.

'An odd political set-up', was his own description of the Bull organisation. 'I did not much like the position into which I had drifted but had nothing else to do.'[1] Reith accompanied Bull on his visits to men who hitherto had been only famous names. Birkenhead, Austen Chamberlain, Robert Horne, and Lloyd George were among the prominent politicians he met, usually in Bull's company. There is an amusing note in Frances Stevenson's diary about Reith's activities and his reflections on them.

'What has been puzzling me', she said to him, 'is what you were doing in that *galère*.' 'It's a queer story,' said Reith. 'I had some amazing experiences. The machinations that went on behind the scenes—the working of the political machine—these things were a revelation to me.' He did not add, but I guessed, though neither of us voiced it in front of D. [Lloyd George], that his experiences then decided him not to go in for a political career.'

The eyes of John Reith were only half opened to the deft wire-pulling, place-seeking and 'general skullduggery' in which he had voluntarily immersed himself when he encountered Lloyd George for the first time in person, evidently catching the Welsh wizard in one of his friendly and charming moods. Yes, the maestro had certainly heard of Dr. George Reith; he even admitted having once shaken his hand in Glasgow. Before they parted, Reith offered the great man a small, symbolic token of his respect and esteem—'a certain quaint little picture of St. George and the Dragon', as Frances Stevenson described it.[1]

Sir William Bull seemed grateful for Reith's tactful handling of the numerous arrangements that had to be made, often at short notice: a visit, for instance, to Birmingham and to an Austen Chamberlain torn between his loyalty to Lloyd George and his embarrassment at having unwittingly split the party he loved. Chamberlain had prepared a message urging all Tory coalitionists to stick together and yet avoid causing further dissension.

There were repeated telephone calls to Chamberlainite candidates in their constituencies, enquiring how campaigning was going and whether they required the aid of prominent speakers to ram home the coalitionist message. A big London meeting addressed by Lloyd George, Chamberlain and Birkenhead took place at the Stoll Theatre in Kingsway, with Bull himself in the chair. Such happenings, and they were many, obviously cost money; and ready money, which it was part of Reith's function to dispense, was ever available. Bull began by letting Reith have 'an open cheque for £3000', assuring him that 'there would be a great deal more coming from the same source'. By the time the campaigning had ended and the big guns had sounded their last salvoes, £15,000 had passed through Reith's hands, 'often in cash'. The eyes of the political innocent were wide now with unedified astonishment, especially when Sir William Bull one day confided his concern at the 'meticulous book-keeping' of his aide. 'It seemed', Reith noted, 'that he would have preferred to have had no records kept at all.'[1]

The lavish stage-management of Conservatives campaigning on the Lloyd George ticket proved a vain as well as an extravagant enterprise. Austen Chamberlain's men mostly survived, but Lloyd George's Liberal cohorts were massacred. Some of the ex-Premier's closest colleagues, including Frederick Kelloway, the former Postmaster-General, Frederick Guest, the former Air Minister, Sir Hamar Greenwood, and Winston Churchill were defeated at the polls on November 15th, and Churchill, who underwent an emergency operation before polling day, did not like suddenly finding himself 'without office, without a seat and without an appendix'. Bonar Law had reversed the odds and scored a notable triumph, with a majority of more than seventy seats, he had also effectively laid the spectre of his alleged dependence on Lloyd George. The Labour Party, benefiting from the double split in the leadership and the ranks of its

Liberal and Tory rivals, meanwhile cashed in handsomely to the tune of over 140 seats for the first time and became the official Opposition.

A John Reith somewhat disenchanted by the expediency of politics, as seen from his unusually privileged vantage point, was still at Bull's right hand during the electoral post-mortems. Dinner parties had to be fixed, urgent long-distance calls put through, inviting celebrated guests to turn up at the London homes of Sir Philip Sassoon and of Birkenhead. Then Bull presided at a Commons' dinner on the last night of November to entertain sixty supporters of Austen Chamberlain who heard their leader define his policy aims. The last occasion of all, on the evening of December 13th, was a business meeting in the group's provisional headquarters at St. Stephen's House, on the Thames Embankment across the road from Parliament, where a handful of prominent coalition Tories, including Reith's Glasgow schoolboy acquaintance, Walter Elliot, unanimously accepted Chamberlain's proposal that, while refusing to accept portfolios from Bonar Law, none of them would rock the Conservative boat unnecessarily. If these exercises in time-wasting and facing-saving were an essential part of political life, then Reith had already sampled more than enough of it. Besides, at an earlier hour that very day, December 13th, 1922, he had kept a much more pressing appointment long fixed, as he persuaded himself, by a kindlier destiny.

3

Reith was still fresh to his unexacting but enthralling duties as Sir William Bull's honorary secretary when he received an unmistakable intimation that something portentous and worthwhile lay in store for him. On the first Sunday of October, fifteen days before King George V earnestly expressed to Lloyd George 'my hope that the result [of the Carlton House meeting] will not cause the break up of my government for many reasons, especially when questions like Ireland and the Near East are still unsettled', Reith followed his customary practice of going to the evening service at the Presbyterian Church in Regent Square. The preacher, as he more than once informed this writer, was a 'good man of majestic eloquence who often put me in mind of my father'.[1] The minister's name was Dr. Ivor Roberton, and that evening he surpassed himself, holding Reith spellbound. The sermon was based on the following text from Ezekiel: 'Thus saith the Lord. . . . I sought for a man among them, that should make up the hedge, and stand in the gap before me for the land that I should not destroy it, but I found none.' Dr. Roberton assured his congregation that God was looking then, as always, for someone to fill the gap as an outstanding example to others. Perhaps there was one person listening to him at that moment who had both the ability and the will to perform mighty deeds for the nation in its new hour of need. The preacher's words sounded like celestial music in Reith's ears. This, he felt, was a marvellously direct sign from above that the unknown task on which his heart and mind were set would not now be long delayed. Who could tell? It might even be that what he had been awaiting for so long might turn up with Sir William Bull's assistance. In his diary that night he wrote with apocalyptic defiance:

'I still believe that there is some great work for me to do in the world.'[1]

Reith's labours in Bull's service provided no great leisure. According to his own account, he was sifting the newspapers less than a week after Dr. Roberton's uplifting sermon when a most interesting yet puzzling advertisement attracted his eye. Listed among the public appointments, it carried the heading, 'The British Broadcasting Company (in formation)'. Broadcasting? What was meant by that, he wondered. He must obviously find out the industrial connotations of the strange word, but meanwhile he had nothing to lose by submitting a formal application. Whatever this broadcasting business might be, the firm which planned to run it had vacancies in all the top positions. They were short of a director of programmes, a chief engineer, a company secretary and a general manager. For this last post Reith immediately decided to apply, underterred by the conventional rider at the end of the advertisement that 'only applicants having first-class qualifications' need bother. He had already folded his carefully worded letter to Sir William Noble, whom the notice described as 'Chairman of the Broadcasting Committee', sealed the envelope and placed it in the mail-box of the Cavendish Club when it occurred to him that he might have done better first to look up Noble's name in *Who's Who*. He now did so. Then he rescued the letter with difficulty and relief, and rewrote it hoping that the additional allusion to his own 'Aberdonian ancestry' might appeal to Noble's sense of local patriotism. Reith then became so preoccupied and bemused in the political toils of Sir William Bull that he admitted to having 'half forgotten' about his quest for a job in broadcasting some weeks before he got a reply from Noble on December 7th, 1922. The note was brief and to the point. It asked him to attend for interview at Magnet House, Kingsway, the following Thursday.

December 13th was the day; and, as we have noted, it was a day already crowded with incident. Little more than a mile separated Reith's offices in Westminster, where Chamberlain and the other members of Bull's small circle of prominent Tory outsiders had gathered together to concert their policy ideas, and Magnet House in Kingsway, where Noble and three of his fellow-directors had summoned the candidates for interview. According to Professor Asa Briggs in his comprehensive study of broadcasting in the United Kingdom, 'there is not even a short list of the six people seriously considered for what was to be a strategic post in twentieth-century history. One prominent journalist who enjoyed a distinguished later career is said to have been approached and to have turned down the offer on the grounds that the post was not big enough. Another person who is said to have been considered is Kellaway, who had not been returned to parliament at the general election of 1922. Instead, to the annoyance of some of the BBC directors, he became a director of the Marconi company.'[1]

There were other hopefuls, apart from Reith, who did not withdraw; but he felt utterly confident, despite past failures and his continuing ignorance as to the bare meaning of the word broadcasting, that the post of general manager would be his. For while he was sitting outside the interview room, Noble emerged, came up, introduced himself and 'greeted me with the cordiality of an old friend'. The questions put to Reith inside were few and none too searching. Could he handle correspondence, one of his interlocuters enquired, after raising a rather puzzling point about letters of complaint. Did he realise, another director asked, that the general manager, 'would, within a short time, know everybody worth knowing in the country?' Reith disguised any uncertainty he felt; and, as he informed this writer, when he rose to take his leave Noble 'gave me a broad wink which seemed to be his method of signalling that all would be well'.[1]

At no time did Reith mention to me the undoubtedly helpful part played by Sir William Bull behind the scenes in smoothing the way for him weeks before that all important selection board.* For Bull, according to his family, had pointed out the advertisement to John Reith in the first place. Bull was certainly aware that his aide had applied for the job, and Bull, though politically very busy, did not lose touch with Noble, a colleague who like himself had a vested interest in the new business of making wireless sets. In the unlikely event that Reith remained blissfully unaware of Bull's personal and financial interest in broadcasting, he undoubtedly unearthed that fact later. To put it no higher, Reith owed far more to Sir William Bull than an intensive short course in the mechanics of electoral politics. For Bull, a kindly and generous man, knew of Reith's anxiety for regular work

* Nor did Reith mention it to Professor Asa Briggs.

and was only too willing to put himself out on behalf of a competent if rather serious young man who had proved his worth. Besides, as the current employer who could and did confirm the candidate's efficiency and good organising ability, Sir William Bull deserves belated credit at the very least for drawing the attention of Noble to Reith's qualities. Quite apart from that, Reith might never have applied for the job at all if Bull had not advised him to do so in the first place.[5]

On December 18th Reith received a telephone call from Noble, who broke the good news that the board had unanimously agreed to offer him the post. The sole question left to be decided was that of salary. Reith had asked for £2000 per annum: a majority of the board was ready to settle for £1750; but Sir Godfrey Isaacs of the Marconi Company insisted on seeing Reith personally before he would agree even to this lower figure. The meeting with Isaacs passed without a hitch. On December 20th the successful applicant wrote formally accepting his appointment, noting that 'the general manager will have the full control of the company and its staff, and will be responsible to the directors'. A brand-new opening was his for the taking after many months of searching and innumerable setbacks. This, as he knew, mystified as he still was about its precise nature, must be that grand opportunity destiny had been reserving for him.

'I am profoundly grateful to God', he noted in his diary, 'for His goodness in this matter. It is all His doing.'[1]

There was no reference, even obliquely, to the human instrumentality of Sir William Bull as a collaborator in the designs of the Almighty. Whatever the reasons for Reith's extraordinary reluctance to recognise the helpfulness of Bull, he did not acknowledge it then or later. The oversight was deliberate. For no man like Reith, possessed by the messianic certainty of being predestined for a role of immeasurable significance, can ever let the intervention of an ordinary mortal come between himself and the winning of that coveted role. If Sir William Bull's mistake lay in his own casual indifference to the whole business, Reith's lay in discounting altogether what Bull did for him—and exaggerating the influence of Sir William Noble. A former Post Office engineer, who was still a comparative newcomer to the business world, Noble appears on the contrary to have been considerably influenced by the personal recommendation of Reith by Bull, who was also an active member of the Board of the new British Broadcasting Company. Besides, Bull happened to be into the bargain a prominent public figure for whose sound judgment and experience Noble had genuine respect. Since Reith measured up in

Noble's eyes to Bull's high opinion of him, and no other strong candidates were in the offing, the appointment of John Reith to the vacancy of general manager could hardly be described with fairness as being directly due to the providence of God.

It was, all the same, a cheerful John Reith who travelled to his Scottish home in Dunblane before Christmas 1922 and was reunited with Muriel. Relief at this happy ending to their long ordeal of enforced separation was crowned by the sweet satisfaction of knowing that soon they would be moving south together. The last area of darkness had meanwhile dissolved itself. For where two of Reith's future colleagues, A. R. Burrows and C. A. Lewis, would throw no light, an acquaintance of his Glasgow schooldays, now an accountant with an amateur's grasp of the mysterious marvels of wireless, described to him the nature of broadcasting and enabled Reith to see what the British Broadcasting Company had been established to carry through. That chance conversation filled Reith with a renewed sense of thankfulness at having been singled out from a multitude of technically able men who might easily have been selected for this providential task. The possibilities it presented were enormous; and he looked forward with the unfeigned calm of a man who had kept his ears studiously open for the inevitable call from on high to the pitfalls as well as the possibilities which undoubtedly awaited him in London. He was ready for anything. His faith in his future had never wavered, so why should he question it now?

Being a practical person as well as a man of faith, Reith went into the offices of the BBC earlier than anyone else except the commissionaire at the enquiry desk and the lift attendant. He chose to appear at nine o'clock on the last Saturday morning of 1922, a year which, for him, had proved harder than most others in the past but which in the end had justified his unrelenting struggle against self-doubt and adversity. He was now well into his thirty-fourth year. He had acquired through his war service some knowledge of men and how best to handle them; through his American experience a familiarity with business and management techniques which would, he believed, have paid off spectacularly in any other firm but a Beardmore's ineptly striving to adapt itself to a changed post-war world. These were vital private assets; and taken in conjunction with his vaguely messianic feelings regarding the unlimited powers of this strange, new thing called broadcasting, Reith seemed uniquely equipped. On the debit side, however, there had to be set a basic immaturity of mind which still warred against the sublime if occasionally subdued belief in his own destiny. He had shed few of his early prejudices. His temper remained unpredictably volcanic. He was a conformist at heart, not strictly a religious man by conviction, and his Christian attitudes had been mostly borrowed from his dead father whose influence on him now was yet unquestionably stronger than it had ever been. So, at this major crossroads in his fortunes, John Reith could not expect any lasting respite from those primitive forces of the spirit which had plagued him steadily since his youth.

The office at Magnet House was small. His one ritual gesture that first Saturday morning was to test the telephone, if only to let any random caller realise that 'the BBC was on the job'. When, at half past nine, a well-dressed man entered wearing a silk hat, Reith said to himself, 'Ah, the secretary, I presume', while the top-hatted stranger, Major Anderson, said to himself as he espied Reith, 'Ah, the general manager, I presume.' Then they introduced themselves. A day or two before, Reith had broken his journey from Scotland at Newcastle. There he had met a small group of local wireless pioneers who, on Christmas Eve, had transmitted their first broadcast through a microphone perched on the back of a truck in a goods yard. Their enthusiasm impressed him, as did that of Burrows and Lewis, the director and deputy director of programmes, relative veterans in the rudimentary arts of broadcasting on whom he proposed to lean heavily from now on. Ever responsive to the challenge of 'being in at the start of a venture', a phrase he was fond of using, Reith quickly assimilated and stored away for future reference all that he could learn from the company's files and from conversations with his colleagues about the most complex and challenging job he had yet undertaken.

4

It was plain, for instance, why the Postmaster-General had appropriated the legal rights that went with his title of 'policeman' and 'political master' of the air waves. The Telegraph Act of 1869 had given him the exclusive privilege to send telegrams inside the United Kingdom. Within a year the Post Office had taken over the telegraph system. Then, in 1904, the powers of the Postmaster-General were augmented by the Wireless Telegraphy Act, the first measure of its kind in the world. This forbade any person 'to instal or work any apparatus for wireless telegraphy' without first obtaining a licence. Such licences, of course, were limited in duration and subject to many other restrictions laid down by the Post Office. The subsequent development of wireless telephony enabled the same department to extend its area of control without legal questioning so that broadcasting itself now fell within its undisputed province.

The bickering over individual freedom arose in 1920–1 when the Postmaster-General had to make up his mind as to the most orderly method of granting licences to the would-be broadcasting firms. Should he hand them out indiscriminately to every bidder as had been blithely done in the United States? The post-war boom in American broadcasting had been largely due to the three years' head start gained by the American radio industry over all European and other rivals between 1914 and 1917. The breathtaking pace of American life, the antipathy of the public there to any notion of paying licence money to the State or Federal authority for the privilege of listening to radio, the sacred tradition of private enterprise which was enshrined in the national outlook: these three factors had ruled out in advance the possibility of direct interference by Washington with the mushroom growth of the new medium of mass communication. Advertising and sponsorship became the automatic props of this American free-for-all; and protests went unheard. For even if, to begin with, visionary broadcasting tycoons like David Sarnoff, or seasoned politicians like Herbert Hoover, deplored the dominance of the commercial element, their words impressed few because no simple alternative method of raising revenue for running stations or networks could be suggested.

As early as the summer of 1922, when the muted debate in Britain still roamed a little uncertainly over the precise shape of any future broadcasting system here, Hoover was crying over spilt milk in declaring it 'inconceivable that we should allow so great a possibility for service . . . to be drowned in advertising chatter'. The voices of such critics could no longer command serious attention above the clamour of the market-place. Radio in the United States was already lost to the advertising industry. The lessons of the American experience left an uneasy impression on the mind of the deputy secretary of the British Post Office, Mr. F. J. Brown, who spent the winter of 1921–2 in the United States observing the jungle-like conditions of the broadcasting business. He reported his findings when he returned to Frederick Kellaway, the Postmaster-General in the Lloyd George government. In due course, on May 4th, 1922, Kellaway had informed the House of Commons:

'It is impossible and it would not be in the interests of wireless if I granted all the applications that have been made to me for the rights of transmission. What I am going to do is to ask all those who apply —the various firms who have applied—to come together at the Post Office and co-operate so that an efficient service may be rendered and that there may be no danger of monopoly and that each service shall not be interfering with the efficient working of the other.'

The burden of this misty message was nevertheless unmistakable. So as to avoid 'the chaos' which had so quickly overtaken the experiment in the United States, Kellaway proposed to give licences to 'a limited number of radio-telephone broadcasting stations'. Britain would be 'divided into areas' based on London, Cardiff, Glasgow, Edinburgh, Aberdeen, Birmingham, Manchester, Newcastle, Plymouth or Bournemouth, with one or more stations in each place. Only British firms which were *bona-fide* wireless manufacturers would receive broadcasting licences. The government would be happier if the successful applicants co-operated instead of competing with each other; but licence-holders in any event would not be allowed to advertise, and there would also be a ban on transmitting news which had not been previously published. These and a number of technical restrictions were not entirely the outcome of negative and ultra-cautious Post Office thinking. It would be wrong to blame that department alone for seeking to put broadcasting into a strait-jacket. Behind the scenes, the Committee of Imperial Defence objected to the granting of concessions that would conflict with the technical facilities enjoyed since war days by the three armed forces of the Crown. The Post Office was not the sole or the main agent concerned.

Reith discovered, for instance, that in 1920, while he still wore army uniform, the Marconi company's experimental transmissions had met with vehement criticism from the RAF. On one occasion a Vickers Vimy pilot, trying to pick up local weather information in dense fog, had to console himself with an intrusive broadcast concert; on another occasion a colonel complained that a recital by Melchior had 'jammed aircraft communication'. The Wireless Telegraph Board, representing the official views of Army, Navy and Air Force, stoutly maintained that any broadcasting by civilians would hamper 'genuine experimenters' and could not be regarded as being 'in the best interests of imperial defence'.

Since the press and the big news agencies already looked askance at the medium as an equally unwelcome threat to their narrow vested interests, it was painfully obvious to Reith as he studied the tangled story of the recent past that the British Broadcasting Company's future had to some extent been pre-empted by the envy or the ill-informed apprehensions of critics inside and outside the government. A single grouping of interests had finally sunk their differences and merged together from an instinct of self-preservation. That much became plain to Reith when he considered with mild astonishment unedifying accounts of the fractious rivalries, the heated negotiations, the recurring deadlocks and the reluctant agreements which the larger commercial claimants for licences were in the end obliged to concoct among themselves as a result of indirect Post Office pressure.

The Postmaster-General's language had been originally tentative and vague because in May 1922 the government had no positive plans of its own and remarkably little interest in the problems of broadcasting. The mercurial brain of Lloyd George was focused on other things; and, as we have seen, the nation was dragged unwillingly behind him. Only the producers of wireless equipment knew, or thought they knew, what public demand would be within the technical limits already prescribed.The wrangling that had followed among these would-be broadcasters was understandable because they had been left to themselves as if the whole ether were their oyster. Then common sense and healthy doubts began to reassert themselves. Compromises were slowly hammered out where none had seemed possible before and the semblance of a united front had painfully been arranged. The BBC was hardly the sturdy, natural business venture it purported to be. A creature of circumstance and of unnatural bargaining, its birthright appeared to bear the faint taint of illegitimacy to the extent that nobody except the lately disputatious partners would admit full responsibility for siring the unwanted child.

The birthright of the company was for that reason a thing of uncertainty from the moment of its conception. Like the infant Royal Air Force in the muddled difficulties of 1917, the BBC came into existence almost by stealth and was therefore frowned upon as something highly suspect. And if the birthright reflected the peculiar, not to say dubious, origins of the creature itself, then the going, Reith realised, promised to be exceedingly rough. The general manager of the British Broadcasting Company could, he knew, count on having to earn the hard way every penny of the salary which, in his canny fashion, he had tried to scale up by £250 per annum. That the prospect did not daunt or displease Reith should cause small surprise to anyone. Because he throve on difficulty and still loved the thought of combat for its own sake, because he wholeheartedly accepted his own God-given faculty for striving and prevailing, Reith reacted like a medieval knight summoned to trial by ordeal. He was only too happy to mount his white charger, gallop headlong into the fray, and emerge victorious if not exactly chivalrous.

Any reservations he entertained about the short, oddly chequered emergence of the new company he had agreed to serve John Reith wisely locked up inside himself. He was sure in any event that the BBC's many critics would soon make their reservations known, and he had no intention yet of volunteering as a hostage to fate. The time for that might come; but to force the hour prematurely would do no good to anyone. As Reith read the tactical situation, the 'big six' wireless manufacturers constituting the solid backbone of the company were now at peace with each other, despite the fact that until forced to recognise the odds against them they had been heedlessly clawing at one another's throats. At one stage during the previous summer it had seemed as if two competing groups would be allowed to go their separate ways. So hesitant was the Post Office that such a division of the available spoils of broadcasting could easily have been reconciled with official policy; and this might well have satisfied suspicious onlookers in Fleet Street and elsewhere who distrusted any government-backed concern which looked for all the world like a pampered monopoly.

That word had been used with an implication of disapproval by the Postmaster-General himself when first outlining the bargaining processes through which a rudimentary broadcasting system should be created. The same word had been hurled like a brickbat during the protracted negotiations between the various interests, big and small, and the Marconi Company was the obvious target. For the small manufacturers feared the potentially excessive influence of this firm with its established expertise, its numerous patents, its capital wealth, and its high international reputation; and so, for that matter, did two or three of the bigger and better placed concerns, jealous of the unequal power of Marconi's in doing down its rivals. The smear, of course, was rejected. Indeed Marconi spokesmen, notably Sir Godfrey Isaacs, had levelled the shrewd counter-charge that three of the firms so busily engaged in name-calling were merely seeking to benefit from Marconi inventions without having contributed anything to them. It was a case of the pots on the stove trying to call the kettle black; and fortunately for all of the protagonists, common interest prevented irreparable breaches and finally produced a self-protective alliance. As Asa Briggs has aptly noted:

'The general public might know little about broadcasting and some of the newspapers and some members of parliament might be chafing at the unwarrantable delay, but behind the scenes there was a dramatic confrontation of points of view and debate about drafting that would have done justice to a committee of the League of Nations.'[9]

So the common interest of the competitors, by now looking somewhat nervously over their shoulders, persuaded the biggest to put away ambition, reject the 'two companies' scheme, and unite. Isaacs of Marconi's and Archibald McKinstry of Metropolitan Vickers shook hands on the deal. They were joined on the board of the single British Broadcasting Company by Sir William Noble, once a leading

Post Office engineer and a director of General Electric, by Major Basil Binyon of Radio Communications, by John Gray, the chairman of the Hotpoint Electric Appliance concern, and by an American, Henry Mark Pease, of Western Electric. As a skilful inducement to the smaller interests, it was decided to elect two of their representatives to the board before the company's formation on November 15th, 1922. These were W. W. Burnham, the managing director of the electrical firm of Burndept; and from the British offshoot of the original German organisation, Siemens, Sir William Bull, who at the time was still acting as John Reith's mentor and tutor in the arts of political management.

The 'big six', by letting in the 'small two', could at least contend that theirs was no privileged monopoly. Besides, every radio producer in the land could join the company by taking up a £1 ordinary share, secure in the knowledge that Bull and Burnham would ably represent their interests on the board. By the standards of the day, the capital outlay of £100,000, all of it underwritten by the giants, was a fairly substantial investment; and the official limitation of dividends to a fixed 7½ per cent could hardly be condemned as an exercise in barefaced profit-taking. The Post Office found no fault with the scheme in its final shape. The lawyers on both sides seemed relatively happy with the compromise in its various aspects. Nevertheless, since all other sections of the business community had been sedulously excluded by the government from participating in the broadcasting game, it would have been wholly unnatural if those interests, reinforced by a powerful press which appreciated on which side its bread was buttered, had chosen to ignore the sudden arrival of a broadcasting authority thinly disguised as an arm of private enterprise yet bearing a curious resemblance to an officially blessed monopoly. The activities of the company would certainly be scrutinised, seldom in a friendly spirit, by forces which disliked on principle the sight of a mixed economy licensed by the State to corner an exclusive market. Nor would the British press be backward in its denunciation. Reith felt in his bones that he would not have long to wait for the storm to break.

5

Meanwhile, all his energies were caught up in the practical, day-to-day details of reorganising the merger from scratch. Magnet House, Kingsway, proved to be a cramped unsuitable headquarters. Six telephone lines connected the office with the outside world. From his desk Reith maintained a close watch on the small staff, on the programmes and on their contents. The first broadcasts had gone out on the air in mid-November when the company came into being. To quote the evocative words of A. R. Burrows:

'In three different parts of Britain (Manchester and Birmingham as well as London) there were functioning nightly three groups of men who had never met, who had no precedent to work upon, and not the faintest idea of what the future would bring forth in the matter of a balance sheet. They had, however, a common enthusiasm for their work (and) a desire to demonstrate to the public the extraordinary, but in the majority of cases unsuspected, possibilities of broadcasting.'[11]

To Burrows and his assistant director of programmes, Reith was glad to delegate responsibility to begin with. Both men were experienced in the still rough-and-ready craft of visualising and producing material acceptable to an invisible audience whose precise composition and size could only be guessed at; both men had much to give, and Reith had so much more to learn and so little time to learn it in. Many years later, he told this witness:

'Left to myself, I'd have dispensed with some of the people who got big jobs in the organisation when I was appointed.'[1]

This sounded rather like a piece of retrospective wisdom. Set in place against the extremely chaotic and experimental background of work at BBC headquarters during the early weeks of 1923, it is a comment which does less than justice to Reith's closest collaborators. Determined as he was to assert his own authority, early opportunities to flaunt it were denied him by an overwhelming mass of unfamiliar problems requiring the instant attention of the general manager alone:

'We're leaving it all to you', Noble informed him before Reith went to the first formal session of the board on January 4th, 1923. 'You'll be reporting at our monthly meetings and we'll see how you're getting on.'[1]

In truth, Reith revelled as thoroughly as everyone else on the operational side of broadcasting in the excitement of sheer improvisation that characterised the earliest phase of the BBC's infancy, when 'the telephone never stopped ringing' and there was so little space in the overcrowded main office that it became necessary 'to place one's hat on the top of one's walking-stick against a wall in order to find room for it'. Besides, the distinction between the people who performed on the air and those selected as administrators could not be finely drawn in such conditions. Programmes began at 5 p.m. and the Marconi House studio in the Strand was fortunately near enough at hand for Reith and others not directly involved in programme-making to savour the singular tension and disciplined confusion of the original staff members who were. He did not disdain the slight effort of leaving the heap of papers cluttering his desk, momentarily mingling with the homeward-bound crowds of office workers outside, and partaking in the indefinable thrills of live broadcasting as a solemn onlooker already stirring imaginatively to its incredible potentialities as a positive instrument for good.

The complexity of his difficulties only spurred him on to work longer hours. He believed, as ever, in showing an example to colleagues who were also his subordinates. If they refused to leave until they had put in an intensive twelve-hour day, Reith would outstay the most zealous of them—and often did. His light in the second-floor room burned late as he tried to digest countless questions 'of which I'd had no experience. Copyright and performing rights; Marconi patents; associations of concert artists, authors, playwrights, composers, music publishers, theatre managers, wireless manufacturers'.[1] Nor did he commit the elementary error of failing to sound others for opinions and expert information, always reserving to himself the ultimate right of judging and of learning from his own mistakes. The strain of all this unremitting endeavour did not affect a man whom nature had blessed with the constitution of an ox and whose spirit responded with majestic resilience to the inner call-signs of destiny. This business, he recognised with prayerful thankfulness, was one which could not be allowed to fail.

A few days after attending his second board meeting in February, however, Reith had to face his first major crisis. A new station was opened in Cardiff on February 13th, 1923. Exactly one month previously, the press had served notice on the BBC through the Newspaper Proprietors' Association that in future the company would have to pay at normal advertising rates for the printing of daily programmes in their columns. Reith had not been wrong in his surmise that those who disliked the monopolistic appearance of the institution would quickly bring their grudges into the open. The alleged reason for the press demand was couched in slightly more reasoned terms:

'The Broadcasting Company', read the ultimatum, 'is a commercial institution with, it is understood, favourable financial prospects.' That being so, it could scarcely expect not to pay at standard rates for the privilege of advertising its wares to the public. There was an emergency BBC board meeting when the press owners threatened to ban all future publication of BBC programmes on February 15th. Reith urged his directors not to yield. The BBC had a public duty to inform, and the press must therefore be resisted in its crude attempts to impose a levy on public information. The logic and tenacity of his argument rallied the board, some of whose members felt that the BBC had troubles enough without trailing its coat in the provocative style suggested by the general manager.

They voted, nonetheless, in favour of ignoring the threatened press embargo, and there were no details about broadcasting arrangements in the morning newspapers that appeared in London on February 15th. But the BBC's answering bluff quickly called that of the press barons and ended the embargo, to the deep relief of all BBC directors and of the general manager himself. For on the afternoon of February 15th Gordon Selfridge, the millionaire London store magnate, offered free space to the BBC and enabled its programmes to appear in his own advertising columns in the *Pall Mall Gazette*, one of the capital's evening journals. So steep and sudden was the rise in the circulation of the *Pall Mall Gazette* in the course of the next few days that the Newspaper Proprietors' Association, in self-defence, caved in. They agreed to let members decide individually whether to print BBC programmes or not during the next six months. That clinched the issue. Nothing more was heard of it again, though Reith's quite separate brainwave of proposing to publish an independent preview of BBC programmes (the germinal concept of the future *Radio Times*) did apparently strike him while the ill-starred embargo was on and 'plans for (printing it) I had already put in hand'.

The honours in this opening skirmish were unquestionably Reith's, but the press campaign against the BBC on grounds not so easily defended by bluff and firm management had not yet been fully mounted. For the company had meanwhile run into trouble with a Post Office ruled by a minister who appeared to be quite unimpressed by the BBC's claim that too many ordinary listeners were evading payment of the statutory licence fee. It had been laid down that bona-fide amateurs with a scientific interest should be entitled to experimental licences at a cost of ten shillings, and recently the number of applications for such licences had risen alarmingly.

The company contended that 'the bulk of applications' were from people who built their own radio sets because these were cheaper to piece together at home 'with the aid of a diagram and a screwdriver' than the ready-made but expensive receivers put on sale by British manufacturers, all stamped with the officially approved BBC trade-mark. Since the previous autumn, in fact, there had been a boom in the importation of foreign components. Small firms purchased these in bulk. In selling them to the growing army of handymen customers, they reaped a double harvest that cost the BBC dear. Not only did the traders avoid having to stock up with the officially approved sets, but the quick turnover enabled their customers by the thousand to pose as amateur radio enthusiasts and apply successfully for the ten-shilling experimental licence.

By December 1922, when Reith joined the company, the situation had deteriorated to such a degree that Noble vigorously complained to the Post Office, recommending that 'except in very special cases they should refuse all amateur licences and advise the applicants to take out BBC licences'. But the Post Office preferred to ignore so drastic a proposal, just as they turned down a suggestion endorsed by the Radio Society of Great Britain, the most influential body representing scientific amateurs, that experimental licences should be raised to a pound. So, on February 5th, Reith accompanied Noble to Birmingham for an informal discussion with Neville Chamberlain, the Postmaster-General. It was a useless journey. Reith could not understand Chamberlain's cool indifference and described his attitude as 'entirely unhelpful'. Indeed Chamberlain 'scoffed at it being worthwhile to enforce licences', an attitude which induced Reith to scoff in turn much later that 'when Chancellor of the Exchequer with eight million licences in force, he [Chamberlain] thought differently'.[1]

Questioned in the Commons two weeks afterwards about the irritating delays experienced by applicants for amateur licences, Chamberlain admitted that the explanation lay in the very large demand from people who did not appear to be bona-fide experimenters. Anxious to cause no further inconvenience to the public or embarrassment to itself, the Post Office refused to 'enforce its own system' by organising 'a large-scale national drive' against licence-evaders, 'backed by the full resources of the police'.[1]

By March 1922 only 80,000 members of the public had bothered to take out normal BBC licences which guaranteed payment of the small additional royalty for the purchase of a BBC-stamped receiver. Deadlock had been reached with the Post Office and its presiding minister. The company's continued existence depended on royalties as well as licence money, yet the drawbacks in the original agreements became only too clear to Reith as he examined with the directors alternative methods of trying to square a vicious circle.

The reluctance of the Post Office to adopt strong, supporting measures was not lessened by the fierce attacks against the BBC which appeared in the *Daily Express* during March and April. The propaganda campaign focused public attention on the company's central dilemma: the acute difficulty of collecting the money due to it without making unnecessary enemies in the process. The solution proposed by Lord Beaverbrook, wearing his crusader's armour as champion of the 'little men' whose privacy was being invaded by organised commercial interests, had the merit of shining simplicity. Radio should be freed from its restricting chains. The so-called licence-dodgers, stigmatised as 'pirates' by the BBC, could just as easily be regarded as heroes of private enterprise fighting the evil forces of monopoly.

Reith wondered what kind of person this Beaverbrook was. They had never met: for at the time Reith had been acting as Bull's political secretary, Beaverbrook was conducting his own successful manœuvres to restore Bonar Law to the leadership of those orthodox Conservatives determined to topple the discredited government of Lloyd George. Though other newspapers, notably the *London Evening News*, were joining in the campaign, the mischief-maker-in-chief was obviously the redoubtable Beaverbrook. Having already talked with a number of press representatives, including the editor of the *Daily Mail*, Reith arranged an appointment to see the man who seemed so determined to destroy the BBC.

'I was not a bit afraid of him as I imagined he expected me to be', Reith wrote in his diary on April 10th after their encounter. 'He said I had impressed him very much. He said all he was out against was the manufacturers taking control of broadcasting.'[1]

Beaverbrook was attracted, in spite of himself, by his plain-spoken unsmiling Scot visitor, a son of the manse like himself, but doubly impressive for his lack of self-interest in the BBC venture. The distinction drawn by the Canadian press magnate between Reith the man and Reith the paid official of a contemptible organisation was genuine and lasting. They met at intervals from that day forward, exchanged friendly letters until the time of Beaverbrook's death, and helped one another with advice and small favours. In all probability Reith disarmed a potentially lethal foe by remarking that though he had 'nothing to do with the BBC or with licence conditions', he still believed that 'broadcasting itself and a policy of broadcasting depended on the survival of the BBC'.[1]

It was not a question of Beaverbrook rashly promising to desist from future attacks on a hateful profit-making monopoly; that would hardly have been his style. It was a matter rather of his letting Reith understand implicitly that he could count on personal support from Beaverbrook if the need arose. Some readers may discern an odd irony in this encounter and its improbable result. For, as Reith learnt within six months, his powerful new friend in Fleet Street 'had made up his mind that there must be monopoly in broadcasting'.[1,9] To what extent the strident but subtle Beaverbrook influenced the ideas of John Reith about the future shape of broadcasting remains a mystery because of regrettable gaps in the former's private papers during the second half of 1925; but it would be unjust to play down the importance of Beaverbrook's personal pledge to back the general manager of the BBC. This was a factor which encouraged Reith to develop his own thoughts about the anomalous constitutional status of the company. If he could alter that by straightforward means, then Beaverbrook would help not hinder him.

However the critical relations between the company and the Post Office had meanwhile worsened with the appointment of another Postmaster-General. Sir William Joynson-Hicks had a remarkable talent for expediency. He refused to be bound by any decisions or agreement entered into by his predecessors with which he happened to disagree; and from the day he took office early in March until his somewhat abrupt transfer to less contentious spheres barely three months later, 'Jix', as he was always called by fellow-politicians, led the BBC a merry dance which kept Reith on his toes. At Joynson-Hicks's request, Reith forwarded him a massive screed early in April, spelling out with clarity and precision the company's grievances and urging on him 'the formulation and enforcement of new regulations'. 'Jix's' own department did not escape its share of blame since 'every condition and regulation is being infringed and evaded, and from past experience the BBC feel they must ask the Post Office to give greater support to the broadcasting enterprise. . . . They feel that they are entitled to expect that the Post Office will give them the promised protection (consequent upon which the capital was guaranteed and the company formed) for the definite period arranged by the preservation of the term of the broadcast licence applicable to BBC sets only, and that it is this class of licence and sets which should predominate.'

Reith referred to the spurious denunciation of the company's rights and noted that 'four thousand firms are said to be clamouring for a drastic revision of the terms under which the BBC is constituted and revenue collected. It is doubtful if any of them had any interest in wireless six months ago, and, apart from this, there is no monopoly, as is alleged, as membership of the BBC is open to any bona-fide manufacturer. Five hundred and forty-seven have already applied. Some wholly unreasonable criticism of the programmes is made by those with their own axe to grind. One newspaper offers to undertake broadcasting free, and states there should be neither licence fee nor tariff. The programmes are not as good as the BBC would like, but are improving in all stations. . . . More rapid improvement is handicapped by antagonism of parties who consider their own interests would be prejudiced, and by the loss of adequate and expected revenue.'[11]

This letter, despatched by Reith to Joynson-Hicks in Norwich, wholly failed to win over a Postmaster-General inclined to swim with the tide of popular opinion. If the public wanted amateur licences, then the public should get them, whatever the BBC might argue to the contrary. Complete deadlock followed when the company warned him off issuing 40,000 constructors' licences at ten shillings each. Reith reported to Joynson-Hicks the unanimous resolve of the BBC board to stand by its rights, and the minister indicated that his formal reply to the lengthy letter Reith had sent him would be his last word on the subject. The press, of course, had wind of these sharp but sterile exchanges. In particular, Joynson-Hicks's 'last word' induced the *Daily Express* to shout gleefully that 'an immense stride has already been made towards clarification of the wireless muddle, and the freedom of the air is almost achieved'.

For 'Jix', while thanking Reith personally for handling his end of the negotiations 'with firmness and courtesy beyond praise', warned in his turn on April 13th that, unless the company came to heel and accepted his plan for a constructor's ten-shilling licence, 'I shall have no alternative but to grant experimental licences to those applicants who have filled up the necessary forms stating that they desire to use wireless telegraphy for experimental purposes.' As the backlog of such applications was formidable, the BBC had good reason to wonder whether the Postmaster-General understood where the logic of his ultimatum would leave him and the company, if pressed to its bitter conclusion. There had already been too many leaks to the press for anyone's comfort, leaks which seldom presented the BBC case in a fair light. So on April 17th the board issued a statement of its own, pointing out that 'since the Postmaster-General had granted interviews and stated his opinions unreservedly', the moment had come to let the public decide between them.

They were not prepared to accede to Mr. Joynson-Hicks's demand for the simple reason that it would 'rob the British radio industry of its protection' and undermine broadcasting standards. 'The protection promised to the company is for a limited period expiring at the end of next year (1924). Having regard to the risks which the members were taking, this period is not excessive. The guaranteeing and the subsequent subscribing of capital to the company by the British manufacturers was on the strength of Mr. Neville Chamberlain's signature; likewise the subsequent large commitments in manufacture. The public can judge the seriousness of the situation which will arise if, by departmental action, the agreement in spirit or letter be violated.'[11]

The fat was in the fire at last. On April 19th Joynson-Hicks rose in the Commons to deliver a statement riddled with sceptical allusions to the BBC's claims. Was it right, he asked, that the Post Office should collect 'what are in effect compulsory taxes' only to hand over half of them to the broadcasters? When Sir William Bull, the sole BBC director who was also an MP, reminded him that the Post Office itself had proposed this arrangement, Joynson-Hicks hedged slightly. Yet he begged leave to doubt whether the company had been granted what amounted to a monopoly licence, adding: 'I am not at all sure whether it is not open to myself to grant a licence, if I so desire, to someone else.' As to the claim that the BBC could prevent other British manufacturers from producing equipment for sale, he did not like it. 'I am not going to be a party to compelling any British manufacturer to join any particular combine. Finally he proposed to establish 'the strongest committee I can get in order to consider the whole question of broadcasting—not merely the question of licences, but the desirability of existing contracts and the questions that have arisen on contracts. . . . I can assure the House that I have devoted days, and almost nights, to try to find a solution, fair on the one side, and without inflicting, what I do not want to inflict, a real monopoly against the would-be manufacturers in this country'.

It was, on balance, a curiously partisan utterance which again stung the BBC into publicly inviting people not to be misled by Joynson-Hicks's damaging innuendoes. The nub of the riposte was a blunt rebuttal of the most glaring of them:

'There has never been any thought or attempt to protect one British manufacturer against another, and nothing in the agreement justifies the suggestion. The whole object of the BBC mark was to make broadcasting possible. . . . There would have been no broadcasting without that agreement. Under it broadcasting has made amazing progress, and if it were capable of being destroyed, the broadcasting wireless industry and broadcasting must be destroyed with it'.[11]

Four days later, on April 24th, the names of the newly appointed members of the Postmaster-General's committee of enquiry were duly announced. The chairman was Major-General Sir Frederick Sykes, who had served briefly as Chief of the Air Staff after Trenchard's wartime resignation from that post. The ten members represented parliament, the press, the public, the Post Office and the BBC; and, as Joynson-Hicks had promised, they looked a very sound team on paper. In addition to the Hon. J. J. Astor, Sir Henry Norman, a keen radio amateur, and Sir Charles Trevelyan from the Commons, there was Lord Burnham, the chairman of the Newspaper Proprietors' Association, two senior Post Office men, including F. J.

Brown whose strictures on American free-for-all broadcasting had led to the formation of the BBC, one impartial but distinguished delegate of the general public in Field Marshal Sir William Robertson, and lastly Reith himself.

'Fortunately I had made some impression on (Joynson-Hicks)', noted the general manager of the BBC. 'I asked him to put me on the committee. As the BBC was in the dock, he might have declined. I was grateful to him for agreeing—and much relieved'.[1] The opportunist in Reith, dubious as he remained about some of the company's pretensions but resolved that broadcasting should not suffer, had begun to flex his muscles in the knowledge that others had begun to respect him as a strong man in his own right.

Perhaps nobody was better aware of this than Muriel, his wife. They had taken a small, elegant town house in Burton Street, Westminster, tucked away behind the Abbey and within walking distance of the office; and John Reith's terse if frequently corrosive observations on men and matters at the end of the hardest day could not deceive her shrewd ear for the gruff undertone of contentment. She was pleased for his sake as well as her own that he had judged so well the grandeur of his opportunity, though a sympathetic intuition more than anything else hinted to her that his judgment was sharpened at times by weird religious impulses that seemed to strike at the most intractable problems like forked lightning. A conventional Anglican herself, Muriel did not pretend to understand the doctrinal differences between the Christian Churches. She had admired and loved Dr. George Reith as a person of exceptional goodness and virtue who happened to be a Presbyterian minister; she loved his son for other reasons, but was conscious also that John's religious impulses were more primitive than his father's. They probably found more happiness together during those early months of acclimatization and slow blossoming in London than would ever be theirs again. For John Reith, not yet having tasted power, could slake his thirst on simpler and better things.

6
The Visionary

1

No sooner had the broadcasting enquiry begun than its work was interrupted by a political tragedy, the outcome of which had far-reaching consequences for the nation, for the BBC and for Reith himself. Yet, quite understandably, his immediate reaction on learning that Andrew Bonar Law had contracted an incurable disease and would be resigning as Prime Minister was one of impatience. Some days earlier, on May 1st, 1923, the secretary of the company, P. F. Anderson, had informed the Post Office that 'owing to the agitation and the statements which have been made to the press', member firms were left 'with large stocks . . . on their hands and a most serious falling off in sales. Many report that they have not sold a single BBC set since the agitation commenced.' Any undue delay could only aggravate the crisis of confidence. Reith had to wait three weeks before he thought it discreet to tell Sir Frederick Sykes, the enquiry chairman, on May 23rd, when the larger political problem of choosing a new Premier had been finally solved: 'It is no exaggeration to say that the wireless trade is practically at a standstill.'[1]

The trouble was that Bonar Law, on giving up office, had refrained from making any recommendation to the King about his successor. Relieved to be out of harness, he fully expected Curzon to become Prime Minister but 'was glad that it would be none of his doing'.[2] The subsequent consultations between the Palace and those elder statesmen whose advice it sought were naturally complicated by Bonar Law's departing gesture of indecision. The King was led to believe, rightly or wrongly, that the retiring Conservative leader favoured the comparatively unknown Baldwin whom Curzon, a man of surpassing arrogance, despised as a 'man of the utmost insignificance'. In the resulting confusion it was thought right and proper to sound out opinion in the family circle; and as a son-in-law of the ailing ex-Prime Minister, Sykes played a part in this rare constitutional drama.

Sir Frederick had to take time off from his broadcasting enquiry to appear at the Palace as the honest broker, telling the King in effect that, whatever impression others might have gained to the contrary, Bonar Law's attitude to the business of choosing the next leader remained studiously negative. The impartiality of Sykes, who could be punctilious to a fault, failed, however, to tip the balance in Curzon's favour. The King sent for Stanley Baldwin instead and invited him to form a government. In the ensuing reshuffle of portfolios Sir William Joynson-Hicks was replaced at the Post Office by a former Secretary of State for War, Sir Laming Worthington-Evans.

Few tears seem to have been shed over the shattered hopes of Curzon. Reith certainly had none now for Joynson-Hicks: almost anyone, in his opinion, would have been preferable to that slippery customer as Postmaster-General. On June 4th, a week after Worthington-Evans's arrival, Reith expressed his belief that the newcomer 'will be very friendly and helpful to us'.[3] By then the broadcasting enquiry, in the tortuous and long-winded fashion of such bodies, had uncovered step by step many of the vicissitudes preceding and following the birth of the company, which went far towards explaining the present parlous position. In his privileged dual role as a member of the committee who could also bear witness when asked to the BBC's policy and intentions, Reith proved himself throughout a loyal servant of the directors. It was an unpleasant revelation to him how deep-rooted lay the suspicions of several eminent representatives of the press, who declared again and again that a private monopoly which might compete with Fleet Street and the provincial newspapers had to be curbed for everyone's sake. They foresaw, though in a different way from Reith himself, the threat to their own interests of an institution that was bound to extend its technical scope and public influence. On behalf of Britain's provincial press, Sir James Owen of the Newspaper Society stated that the BBC should be debarred from disseminating 'certain social, political and religious ideas which suited the company and which could not be answered'.

Offering a back-handed compliment to the company's growing hold on the British public, Owen also stated that any broadcasting of outside events would be 'the thin end of the wedge: before we knew where we were, knowing the enterprise of the BBC, we might find that you had driven a coach-and-four through the agreement'. Lord Riddell of the Newspaper Proprietors' Association, the body representing the National Press, fully supported him; and when Reith asked whether their opposition applied to the relaying of parliamentary debates as well Riddell assured him that it did: 'You are trying to take the bread out of our mouths', he added. He denied that the press was primarily concerned to stunt the growth of radio. 'We recognise that this is a great invention, with great possibilities, but in dealing with new things you have got to consider existing things.'

It was true, Riddell admitted, that the news agencies of Fleet Street were a combine; it was not true that this combine simply wanted to perpetuate its monopoly as a purveyor of news. 'You call it a monopoly', he said, 'I call it a privilege'—which was precisely how Reith felt about his job as the front-man of the broadcasting monopoly. 'This was language', as Asa Briggs has justly remarked 'that Reith at least could understand.'[4]

There was a certain incoherence of thought in the press witnesses' attempts, under cross-examination, to define what exactly they objected to in the broadcasting of outside events. Were they against the transmitting of any account of such events, or did they merely oppose putting on the air the voices of the people involved? Reith joined in and pressed them for an answer once it became plain to him that they had not seriously considered the alternative option at all. Owen, 'speaking on the spur of the moment', as he acknowledged, said that 'there would be no objection to broadcasts of the actual voice', if the Prince of Wales, for instance, talked into a microphone. The decision to put a microphone in front of such a speaker, Riddell confirmed, must be 'a matter for the broadcasting company. . . . An occasional speech here and there is not a matter to worry about. But no more.'

The press insisted on retaining the pound of flesh it had extracted from the BBC when the company was formed. The 'fourth estate' in the early twenties exerted immeasurably more power than it does today, and it had been relatively easy to hobble the company severely once Noble assured Riddell and his fellow-representatives in October 1922 that 'the BBC did not contemplate the collection of news'. The agencies had then agreed to supply a daily summary of the world's news between 6 pm and 11 pm 'solely for the purpose of distribution within the British Isles'. This summary would 'constitute a broadcasted message of half an hour's duration and approximating to between 1200 and 2400 words', and bulletins must start with the acknowledgment: 'Copyright News from Reuter, Press Association,

Exchange Telegraph and Central News'. Beyond obstructing any new proposals which might enable the company to blur the edges of this original narrow compromise, the press representatives were not prepared to budge.

They appeared to be wholly at a loss when one of the Post Office nominees on the committee, Sir Henry Bunbury, asked whether the news policy of the BBC should be still restricted if broadcasting were controlled, not by the radio manufacturers, but 'by a body representing the people who receive the news'. The idea of broadcasting 'in the public interest' was still so novel and alien that Owen confessed that he did not understand the question; though it should be added that Bunbury had expressed himself none too clearly anyway. But when its significance dawned fully on Owen, he said that 'a monopoly under any guise whatsoever' would be resisted. Riddell at once concurred. Then the chairman, Sykes, urged Riddell to reflect whether the public ought not to get what it wanted, if the public, under whatever new auspices, actually controlled broadcasting.

'You say,' Riddell replied, 'you can conceive that the time may come when broadcasting will be controlled not by the manufacturers but by the public. Well, I gather the fact that you gentlemen are sitting here today indicates that the public indirectly controls broadcasting, if a government can be said to represent the public, as I suppose it ought to do. The government obviously control the whole business, and if they grant a licence they do so because they think that it is the best way to make use of their powers.'

It was a clever retort as far as it went, but it carefully avoided a conclusion still as unpalatable to Reith's directors as it was politically unthinkable to Riddell and many others. A broadcasting system divorced from the control both of the trade and of the Post Office seemed to smack unpleasantly of socialism. Only Herbert Morrison of the London Labour Party was bold enough to advocate a thoroughgoing socialist solution to the Company's dilemma in his evidence to the Sykes' committee. Sir Charles Trevelyan, the landowner Labour MP and a great-nephew of Macaulay's refused to venture so far away from the beaten track of experience. He would have liked to see the Post Office assume complete responsibility for broadcasting, an honour which that department declined on the highly practical grounds that 'a minister might shrink from the prospect of having to defend in parliament the various items in government concerts', to quote the words used in the committee's final report. Reith tended in retrospect to exaggerate his own prescience as champion of the public service ideal. The exchanges undoubtedly opened his mind to it. And, since he was the chief prompter, he had good grounds for welcoming it,' as Briggs has noted.[4] But Reith's claims to have coined both the concept and the phrase 'public service broadcasting', and to have offered these to Sykes as 'a personal opinion' at the first meeting of the committee, is not confirmed by the facts. The BBC's general manager would have been unwise in any event to push his personal opinion so rashly. For, as he admitted himself: 'It was an anxious time and one of some embarrassment lest there be a conflict of interest between the interests of broadcasting and the interests of the wireless trade as the trade then saw them'.[5] His dominating mood was one of anxiety, its acuteness being reflected in a diary entry towards the enquiry's half-way mark:

'It is a dreadful struggle', he wrote on June 10th, 'and I have to watch everything that is said and every word of evidence afterwards'.[4]

Reith's sense of moral responsibility was further heightened by his daily contact with the company's directors who relied on him to protect their interests at each turn in the maze of exchanges with witnesses. He did not let them down. For Reith evolved a formula which conveniently squared this circle; 'I had discerned something of the inestimable benefit which courageous and broad-visioned development of this new medium would yield', as he stated years later. 'There lay one's commission, and there need be no conflict of loyalties. Whatever was in the interests of broadcasting must eventually be in the interests of the trade.'[1] The directors were gratified by his firm handling of the BBC case; they would unquestionably have been considerably less enchanted with Reith had he been the first to voice the paradoxical vision of a public service broadcasting service as the perfect answer to all difficulties. Just as inventors or writers sometimes hit almost simultaneously on the same ingenious conception, or plot, remaining fixedly convinced of their own originality, so Reith seems to have deluded himself in this matter. Possibly the only true discoverer in this world is the man who lights upon something which nobody else at the time happens to be looking for; given the hothouse conditions of 1923, with so much hostility focused on a business in distress, Reith was in no position as general manager to pose as the true discoverer and 'onlie begetter' of the public service ideal.

The Sykes committee preserved an open mind about future developments, emphasising that 'subject to existing rights, the government should keep its hands free to grant additional licences, and should consider various alternatives for the question . . . (either by company or by other authorities) of local or relay stations in addition to larger stations'. In other words, so incomplete was BBC coverage in the summer of 1923, so insecure also was the company's tenure, that the enquiry refused to look too far ahead.

The majority of the committee did, however, conclude that 'a broadcasting board should be established by statute to assist the Postmaster-General in the administration of broadcasting and to advise him on important questions concerning the service'. More experience was wanted, more experiment required, before anyone in the seats of power bothered his head too much about long-term questions of status and tenure. The unwanted child of compromise had first to educate itself and pay for the privilege. An inordinate amount of time had been wasted on repetitive arguments over the riddle 'when is a monopoly not a monopoly'; and to Reith's enduring credit, he avoided the trap by underlining instead the benefits of unified control in the day-to-day direction of any broadcasting service worthy of the name.

'There is a very great advantage in having a uniform policy for what can or cannot be done in broadcasting', he said. That much at least could be demonstrated; and Reith knew better than anyone how the process of co-ordinating the once fragmented stations of the company had begun. While the BBC's directors had remained almost totally preoccupied with justifying their financial and business aims, the general manager gratefully accepted *carte-blanche* to overhaul the elements of the rudimentary broadcasting service as he thought fit. Nobody possessed of Reith's high moral drive, astounding energy, and messianic outlook could have done less when presented with such a heaven-sent opportunity. How he tackled the initial difficulties, human and technical, will be explored below, but Sykes and his committee had nothing but praise for the 'enterprise and ability' of the BBC and wanted to see 'substantially greater freedom' in the conditions of broadcasting.

The major drawback, alas, was that the committee could not accept the company's demand for continued protection of the British radio industry. They therefore rejected any further royalty payments on the sale of receiving sets. Licences sold to the listening public should provide the BBC with all the money it needed. The possibility of collecting extra revenue by commercial advertising had been examined and dismissed, not because of the head-on conflict this would have entailed with jealous press interests but because, in the words of the report, 'it would lower the standard' of the broadcasting service. That, then, was that; but the BBC prepared to dig in and defend its precious royalty system, 'the cardinal principle on which broadcasting was established'. The uncompromising attitude of Sykes struck consternation into the BBC board when the directors studied the draft findings towards the end of August. It looked as though they had lost the decisive battle. Their glum conclusion can well be appreciated. Despite the flattering tributes heaped on themselves and the general manager, their contention that survival was bound up with continued royalty protection had cut no ice: and the committee's proposals were already in the hands of the new Postmaster-General, Sir Laming Worthington-Evans.

Reith was despatched at once to ask the Postmaster-General that publication of the report should be held up since the BBC could not accept it as it stood. On August 28th, a Saturday, he spent most of the day at Worthington-Evans's country home, and partly succeeded in his unlikely quest. This latest 'policeman of the ether' was a distinct improvement on his predecessors. Reasonable, dispassionate and generous, he told Reith that he would gladly look at other proposals that upheld the company's claims so long as these could be harmonised with what Sykes had recommended. At a second meeting with the minister three days later, Reith found him still 'very friendly indeed'.[3] The BBC now had to decide whether 'to stand fast' and fight for their demands or to 'adopt a policy of compromise'. Since Worthington Evans could hardly ignore the guidance of his own officials, some of whom disapproved of the company's stubbornness, and since the Baldwin Cabinet itself had to be consulted, the path of compromise seemed the only safe way out. With some reluctance, the company agreed to take it.

In the light of hindsight, the terms of the compromise settlement worked out in September 1923 with the Post Office were better than the BBC had any reason to expect. Trade interests would be protected against foreign competitors until December 31st, 1924, when the Company's original licence was due to expire in any case. After that date the uniform ten-shilling licence proposed by Sykes would come into force, and only from 1925 onwards would the use of foreign-made radio equipment be permitted. Meanwhile, the BBC could go on collecting its cut on British sets and salve its monopolistic pride. The introduction of a fifteen-shilling constructor's licence, side by side with the existing experimental and listener's licences, would make doubly sure that the company could only gain money on the deal. For the extra five shillings on each constructor's licence would compensate handsomely for the eventual discontinuance of royalties. And any doubts entertained by the company's directors were soon dispelled by the public's prompt response to a revised tariff which seemed to cater imaginatively for all types of listener. Within ten days of the joint publication of the Sykes' committee's report and of the new scheme, there was a sensational jump in the demand for licences from 180,000 to 414,000. Nearly half of the increased total comprised the 'interim' licences taken out by handymen constructors who had never troubled about paying up in the past because no previous Postmaster-General had shown the willingness of Worthington-Evans to enforce his own rules against evasion.

The tightening-up of several loose sections in the original BBC agreement with the Post Office stilled the last fears of the directors. The period of the company's amended licence to broadcast was extended to the end of 1926, the Postmaster-General reserving his formal right to call in additional broadcasting authorities should the BBC fail in its prime duty. No licence revenue would go to these mythical rivals, however, unless the BBC refused to provide adequate broadcasting facilities for listeners. Direct advertising was ruled out, in keeping with Sykes' proposal; yet the company was given specific permission to transmit 'sponsored programmes and commercial information' of which the Postmaster-General approved. In fact nine concerts sponsored by various newspapers, including the *News of the World*, the *Evening Standard*, *Titbits* and the *Daily Herald*, went on the air in the course of the next two years; and the practice caused no recriminations or difficulties on either side. The BBC had not yet the resources to organise such events by itself. On a wider plane, the Baldwin government's make-shift philosophy of safeguarding home industries may be glimpsed behind the reason offered by Worthington-Evans for qualified acceptance of the company's claim to royalty protection: it deserved support because of 'the unemployment which at present exists and which would be accentuated by the importation on any considerable scale of wireless receiving apparatus from abroad'.

Parliament had not yet returned from the summer recess, so there was less outcry than expected about the evils of monopoly. Press comment on the compromise tended to be lukewarm and merely to damn with faint praise. Only the *Daily Express* sustained an impenitently hostile tone. Spurning the deal as 'a surrender' and predicting that the Postmaster-General would regret it, Beaverbrook, whose ambivalent logic had heartened and inspired Reith at the start of the controversy, had personally withdrawn from 'the wireless muddle', at least for the present. Bonar Law, his close friend, was approaching a painful end. So grief-stricken was Beaverbrook that he had little stomach even for politics. His newspapers might make a fuss, but they lacked real bite because their master's voice was mute. For this brief respite from the active enmity of the press baron *par excellence* with whom Stanley Baldwin enjoyed no compatibility whatever, there was cause to be thankful in Downing Street and Whitehall. The BBC had still greater cause to be grateful for such small mercies. For Worthington-Evans proved more accurate than the *Daily Express* in his insistence that people could be trusted 'to put themselves right with the law', and at the same time 'contribute their quota towards the cost of a service which is affording them so much enjoyment'. By the last day of December 1923, indeed nearly 600,000 radio licences had been issued. A year later that figure had almost doubled to 1,129,578.

2

Lord Gainford, the chairman of the BBC Board and himself an ex-Postmaster-General, was not overstating the case in describing the company as 'a going concern' at the first annual gathering of shareholders in October 1923. If he lingered too much on 'the complications and troubles' that had been lived through, Gainford also acknowledged the efforts of the men who had instilled vigour into the service:

'I don't suppose that any of you can have much idea,' he said, 'of the amount of work this has involved in the general administration, the perfecting of engineering arrangements, and in the compiling and transmitting of programmes.' This was as much a compliment to Reith as the unanimous verdict of the board that their case 'could not have been in better hands' than his during the recent enquiry.[3] In token of their confidence, they appointed him managing director of the company in November. By then Reith had resumed what he regarded as his primary task of integrating the service and moulding it to fit his own rough yet practical vision of what such a service might become. As has already been explained, Reith inherited from the Marconi firm his director and deputy director of programmes, Burrows and C. A. Lewis, who brought with them L. Stanton-Jeffries as director of music. Perhaps the most important recruit, hired by Reith himself in February 1923, was Peter Eckersley, the chief engineer and one of the genuinely versatile survivors of the pre-BBC experimental station at Writtle, near Chelmsford. W. C. Smith, a journalistic acquaintance from Glasgow who had once been a missionary, arrived on a day's visit in the same month, was promptly offered a contract as publicity officer, and stayed. Assisted by these five men and a private secretary, Miss F. I. Shields, who had been recommended by Frances Stevenson, the personal assistant of Lloyd George, Reith had struggled to breathe some semblance of order into the uncontrolled individualism of broadcasting during the late spring and summer months of 1923.

This called for patience as well as determination. After all, the stations at Birmingham, Manchester, Newcastle and Cardiff were manned by engineers and officials in touch with local needs and difficulties. They were in no hurry to comply with impersonal directions from London. When the BBC moved in April from its cramped headquarters in Kingsway to the west wing of the building occupied by the Institute of Electrical Engineers at 2 Savoy Hill, Reith looked forward to a steady improvement in efficiency; but his continual dissatisfaction with the uneven quality of programmes sprang from an inability to be in several places at once. He had long believed that what broadcasting needed was a touch of the authoritarian to moderate and discipline the fertile exuberance of the broadcasters who, when all was said and done, were still comparative novices at the game. So he set about creating the central machinery of control.

He found his ideal deputy in Rear-Admiral C. A. Carpendale, an experienced man-handler 'with a magnificent record' of naval service who came to his notice in May 1923, through F. J. Brown of the Post Office. After a lengthy grilling Reith took him on that summer, convinced that this taciturn individual would faithfully interpret his plans and mete out justice evenly. Carpendale became Reith's indispensable ally; and in the small inner circle of key organisers the influence of this new aide to the general manager was matched by his dry common sense:

'He came fresh to everything', C. A. Lewis remarked, 'and was able to throw a new light on all problems.'[6]

As a trouble-shooter and a judge, Carpendale repeatedly proved himself a fearsome figure—'almost as overwhelming as Reith himself', to quote another contemporary. Yet the disciplinarian with the brusque quarter-deck manner seldom had to assume the role: the very thought of his shadowy presence at Savoy Hill, the probability that nothing would escape in the end his eagle eye, was usually sufficient to imbue the wayward with discretion and persuade the headstrong to climb down. In a sense Carpendale so quickly acquired the reputation of a beloved ogre that it is not easy now to separate the myth from the man. For always behind him, ready to pounce if retribution should become necessary, hovered the much grimmer and more inscrutable giant, John Reith, whose lightest word carried the force of divine law.

Because in the autumn of 1923 the BBC still employed relatively few people, the success of Reith's move in putting Carpendale in as his deputy and alter ego was virtually guaranteed. Effective control soon passed in all but name from the provincial centres to Savoy Hill where the loyalty to Reith of the central core of half a dozen leading officials was absolute. If bad feeling or intractable disputes cropped up here and there in the regional centres, a lightning visit by Carpendale or sometimes Reith himself seldom failed to root out the trouble. And, remembering how superiors had dealt with his unco-operative self as a soldier, Reith had little compunction in transferring senior officials to other places or different posts. The tactic was useful not only as a means of asserting his authority but as a short-cut to the goal of an integrated organisation. It also broadened the experience of those who had to move; alternatively it exposed the incompetent or the unruly as no other measures could have done.

About ten-thirty one night in the late winter of 1923, the enquiry bell rang in an attic office above the ground-floor studio of the BBC's Glasgow premises.

'I went down the rickety wooden stairs', recalled the man who answered the door. 'There stood the tallest man I'd ever seen. He introduced himself as John Reith, general manager, and then said, "Who are you?" I replied: "Mungo Dewar, assistant station director". He humphed a bit, asked me into the studio and invited me to join him on a small settee which I expected to collapse at any moment. He outlined his thoughts: "Work up publicity in such a way that you make the man-in-the-street turn automatically to the wireless programme as soon as he buys his paper. . . ." Suddenly he changed the subject: "What do you think of the licence question?" he demanded. I promptly said: "Not much". Reith rose swiftly from the settee, stood up to his full height, and roared down at me: "Why?" I replied: "Simply because I've not received any wages for several weeks. I've to spend all my own money on stamps and items of petty cash". Reith melted at once and became contrite, almost gentle. By the next week I got all my back-pay and a refund of what I'd paid out of my own pocket.'

On such occasions the softer, more tolerant side of the hard, strong yet basically shy personality of Reith became manifest. 'On very personal matters', declared another pioneer, 'the shyness he always showed initially could be embarrassing—until he got to know you better. I remember how, twelve months after my wife had borne our first child, an operation was necessary which might have restricted the baby's activities in later life. Reith heard of our worry and wrote a friendly note of sympathy. Fortunately, everything turned out well. Imagine my astonishment when in February, 1971, over forty years later, Reith wrote out of the blue asking after our daughter. He seemed incapable of forgetting a face or a private problem that caused anguish to any of those who worked with him.'

A colleague who had been with Reith at the old Munitions Ministry at the end of 1919 was Ralph Wade. When Reith left to join

Beardmore's, Wade stayed on. But one morning in the unsettled early weeks of the BBC's existence, a telegram landed on Wade's desk. The message said laconically: 'Ring me up immediately at this number. Reith.' Wade did so and the cryptic manner of Reith mystified him still more: 'Come and see me tonight and I'll explain,' was all he said. They met in Reith's small office on the top floor at No. 2 Savoy Hill. The general manager came to the point at once: 'You are joining me in the broadcasting business next week,' he declared with a smile. 'What as?' asked the puzzled Wade. 'I don't even know what broadcasting is.' Reith was unimpressed. 'I knew nothing about it when they appointed me,' he said. 'I'll expect to see you next Monday morning.' Wade managed 'to get a release from my job and did in fact go to the BBC which I'd never heard of until Reith re-entered my life without warning to revive an old friendship.'[7]

Asa Briggs has written that Reith was fortunate in the 'full backing' he could invariably rely on from the BBC Board which 'remained a fixed point in a moving world'.[4] The broadcasting staff clearly had to expand; but expansion in the meticulously controlled fashion prescribed by Reith meant that virtually every recruit was handpicked. From a total of four in December 1922, the numbers rose to nearly four hundred before the end of 1924. The engineering sphere, where Eckersley ruled, enjoyed a nostalgic place apart in the managing director's heart. For Reith, without any detailed grasp of the technical complexities, liked the chief engineer as an individual and admired his infectious ingenuity and enthusiasm. Besides, had not Noble in the earliest days been persuaded to consider Reith himself for the vacant job of general manager because, as Sir William Bull stressed, the man had engineering qualifications? The mystique that enveloped the BBC's engineering department from then onwards owed much to the unusually protective attitude which Reith adopted towards it and to its first outstanding head.

'Our enthusiasm', Eckersley wrote, 'was maintained by a competition with ourselves: we were on trial against the measure of our ambitions and so we never became complacent.'[1]

That was undoubtedly true of everything in those early days, while the writ of the company still ran; and a similar if more easily criticised verve stimulated the larger number engaged in programme-making. Reith listened to broadcasts with a sharp ear when he went home in the evening. A direct telephone link connected his study to the control room at Savoy Hill, and he installed a set which caused more than one visitor to marvel at his method of easy initiation to the miraculous novelty of radio. When, for instance, he had been introduced in March 1923, to the Archbishop of Canterbury, Dr.

Randall Davidson, through Dean G. K. A. Bell (the controversial Bishop Bell of Chichester during the Second World War), Reith was so taken by the Archbishop's curiosity that he invited him and his wife to dinner at No. 6 Barton Street. It would be an informal way of letting them hear what broadcasting sounded like.

'In the course of conversation before dinner', Reith recalled, 'I pressed, unseen, the switch of the wireless set. In a few seconds the room was filled with music.' Dr. Davidson 'was entirely amazed' by it, and his wife wondered aloud whether the window should be left open when the set was on. The Archbishop's conversion to radio was instantaneous and lasting. On March 17th, the very next day, he summoned a few church leaders to his room in the House of Lords, inviting them to say whether there 'ought to be a religious element in broadcasting: if so what, and by whom arranged?' It was the beginning of the BBC's religious advisory committee, and Dr. Davidson was warm in his praise for 'the officers of the broadcasting company whose aim is obviously a high one and who are anxious to have wise advice'.[4,9]

The support of this central pillar of the establishment for the lofty moral aims of broadcasting was, Reith felt, as important as his dialogue with Beaverbrook, which took place soon afterwards. It was symbolic, maybe, though unsurprising, that this advisory committee on religion (the 'Sunday committee' as it was known at the outset) became the prototype of others set up at Reith's instigation not only in London but in the provincial centres. Their intrinsic and incidental value was vital to his cause. Such expert offshoots as the advisory committee on spoken English, on which sat men like Robert Bridges, the poet laureate, George Bernard Shaw, Rudyard Kipling and the phonetics specialist, A. Lloyd James, indicated Reith's resolve never to put a foot wrong. The same desire for excellence prompted him to seek the best available brains when it came to working out a balanced music policy for broadcasting, so that a safe course might be steered between the extremes of the 'highbrow' classics and non-stop light music or jazz. Here again he drew on the services of leading musicians such as Walford Davies, Professor Tovey, Hugh Allen, and even J. A. C. Somerville of the Royal Military School of Music, who willingly formed their own advisory committee in 1925. Education, with an eye to the needs of schools, ranked almost equal with religion; and a widely representative central body, with local branches to ensure quality programmes, had already begun work the previous year, 1924.

If anything, John Reith carried to a fault this keen method of compensating for his own cultural deficiencies in the interests of the company, of the listener, and of the uncertain future. His avowed aim being 'to bring the best of everything into the greatest number of homes', he had good sense and humility enough not to impose producers' tastes or his own outlandish notions of what constituted 'the best', though these inevitably crept in. Nor did he merely ape or slavishly copy the experts, letting them dictate content to his programme planners. Far higher standards were no doubt thus obtained from the often cosy yet expert recommendations of the advisers. Nevertheless, the advisory structure can be criticised for not being broad and democratically deep enough to impress the man in the street and the woman in the home. Only the authoritative guidance of a true élite could satisfy Reith where broadcasting to an unlimited audience was concerned. The masses, he believed, would learn in time to enjoy what was good. To offer them what *they* wanted would have turned the BBC into a spiritual whore-house, himself into a cultural pimp.

'It would have been extremely difficult', Asa Briggs has stressed, 'in the circumstances of the 1920s—with a divided community, divided by age and social class—to have gone further than the BBC actually did. The temptation to exploit large numbers of people has grown as it has become abundantly clear that effective technical means lie at the disposal of would-be exploiters and that the profits of exploitation are huge.'[4]

Reith thought of himself as already performing a public service, regardless of company profits; and his directors admired the careful, clever way he went about securing the finest minds in the land to help him, though by no means all of them shared his uncompromising view that 'the corruption of the best is the worst'.

Reith did not mind confronting men of calibre on their own territory: his earnestness and singlemindedness enabled him to stand his ground fearlessly, and if it came to disagreement he was seldom at a loss for words. He relished the aura of reflected power which seemed to invest him when face to face with men who had long grown accustomed to exercising it naturally. As a young lieutenant, chafing at the shortcomings of less gifted superiors in the military hierarchy, Reith had believed himself capable of running a battalion, a brigade or an army. Now, no longer willing to admit his relative immaturity even in secret, Reith assumed an air of engaging mastery which sprang from the same indomitable self-confidence. Very limited power had been entrusted to him, he knew, for a mighty end. Davidson and Beaverbrook were among the many human means to that end. So were Eckersley and all his collaborators inside the BBC.

Being also one of nature's born conformists, Reith saw to it that in its general outlook the BBC should cultivate 'a definite though restrained association with religion in general and with the Christian religion in particular'.[4] He imposed the stamp of his own conservative tastes on early programme schedules; yet as these were still confined to the evening hours, he prudently allowed young men with ideas to experiment and learn from their mistakes in fields that were unfamiliar to him. He was good at delegating work to subordinates; and he depended on his small circle of chief advisers to criticise constructively and correct errors. An instinctive devotee of hierarchical values, Reith thus made sure that he kept a steady grip on a system which would otherwise have probably led him and others into deep pitfalls. Once, many years after these events, he spent a whole hour relating to this witness how 'nearly all men in high office have to put on an act, using unconsidered mannerisms, looks and attributes as accessories to enhance their authority'. We had been discussing Montagu Norman, on whose life-story I was then engaged; and after declaring that 'no other man I knew could be so positively attractive if he wished, few could be colder or remoter if that suited his purpose', Reith admitted that his own towering height, his bushy eyebrows, and the scar which often lent his sombre countenance a hint of ferocity had served well as conscious props until at last 'sheer habit took over'.[18]

From the start his personal secretary alone cherished the secret of Reith's fantastic memory for detail which took aback many interviewers. For only she knew of the notes spread out flat on top of the filing cabinet. Inclining his head slightly as he paused in his 'caged tiger act' of pacing up and down across the floor, he would assimilate another set of facts or figures before turning round, striding back, and holding forth to startle yet another visitor. Occasionally, and almost always at unexpected moments, Reith's face would light up in a wide smile as though he had just recollected some deep, private joke which could never be shared. Seldom did anyone hear him laugh aloud at any time. His sense of humour, such as it was, tended to be rarefied and strained. Indeed it may be argued that he had a rudimentary sense of wit only, being addicted to puns and practical jokes; to anything that could be construed as lewd, risqué or vulgar he was impenitently averse. Yet within himself there were traits of the bad actor struggling for release, some of which he put to ready purpose in his manifold daily activities.

'One can tell something of the personality of a manager from his office boy', he was fond of saying. The phrase appeared first in 'Broadcast over Britain', Reith's simple yet almost oracular appraisal of the principles that underlay his direction of the BBC during the first critical eighteen months. If any seeker after truth wishes to learn why Reith deliberately set out to concentrate power in the hands of a few chosen people he will find in the pages of this book an answer which both satisfied the company's board (the members of which had persuaded him in the first place to put his thoughts down on paper) and attracted a small but influential segment of the public to his narrow but high-minded ideals as a decision-maker. Some prominent people were edified by his aspirations, if somewhat less sure about the methods he used to carry them into practice. Sir Frederick Sykes was not alone in doubting their validity during the formative period between 1923 and 1926, while Sykes sat on the special Broadcasting Board which his own committee of enquiry had recommended.

'Personally,' he admitted, 'I would say that his weakness is towards trying to create a monopoly—and a government monopoly at that. . . .' Yet Sykes, uneasy though he was about the end, gave Reith the benefit of the doubt on the means employed:

'There are some critics who think that he brought with him too much of the atmosphere of the manse in which he was reared, but few realised the heavy weight of responsibility which rested on his shoulders.'[10]

The Broadcasting Board was the only attempt in the days of the company to 'express the conception of public service through public representation', as Asa Briggs put it.[4] The trade unions, the press, the radio trade and the radio enthusiasts had their spokesmen on it, but the chance to speak came their way only half a dozen times in three whole years. The Post Office did not care for or encourage the board; Reith characteristically ignored it. To him it was a futile and superfluous body far best forgotten. This may strike the modern reader as odd, given that Reith, in his heart of hearts, was already groping for some alternative to the contradictory and unpopular organisational concept of the original company. Any monopoly run by the trade primarily for the trade would in time alienate the public. So Reith's silent resolve to grow in stature and consolidate his own position was not simply explained by 'an accident of management'. Like the rising reputation of broadcasting, it was also due to the ruthless, dynamic thrust of an exceptional individualist with a taste for public service, who had found his predestined role in life.

The 'heavy weight of responsibility', to which Sykes had also alluded, was no burden to Reith. The atmosphere of his father's manse, oppressive though it might lie at times on BBC subordinates, had merely radiated into the wider world and blended well with the changed political climate. Indeed, when we consider the desire for tranquillity which Baldwin seemed to epitomise as Prime Minister, the arrival of Reith as the prophet and practical mystic of broadcasting may be seen as a singularly fortunate conjunction indeed. It will be indicated later how much the BBC owed not just to Baldwin the Prime Minister or to Baldwin the man, but to the soothing, elevating if sometimes tenuous spirit of reconciliation which he seemed to exude like precious balm. There was room in the new world of Baldwin for individuals of the most contrasting types, always provided that their hearts were in the right place. For a strong reaction had set in against the unprincipled expediency and corrupting chicanery of the Lloyd George era. Just as Baldwin had displayed a flash of courage in risking his own political neck to speed the downfall of 'the goat', so now he offered the hand of fellowship to any man of goodwill and potential consequence who would grasp it. The opportunity to reciprocate would come Reith's way in time, but not before the Prime Minister decided to fight the ill-chosen, inconclusive election of December 1923, which enabled the Labour Party to form their own first, short-lived administration.

Reith wrote in *Broadcast over Britain* that men and women 'of every social class' were listening to radio even 'in the most inaccessible and remote regions of the country. . . . Broadcasting is much too big a thing to be ignored for long. Sooner or later it will cross all paths. It has crossed most already. It will eventually force itself on the attention of any who may have succeeded for a time in overlooking it.' As for the broadcaster, under him they were acquiring 'a high conception of the inherent possibilities of the service'. Not for them the easy and contemptible temptation of catering for the lowest common denominator of the unseen audience. 'Incalculable harm' only would have resulted if the controllers of the medium had been 'content with mediocrity, with providing a service which was just sufficiently good to avoid complaint'. And in an illuminating passage about the care and thought devoted to this pursuit of the best, Reith remarked:

'The responsibility weighs heavily with us. Let there be no misunderstanding on that score. It is realised to the full; it is apt to become an obsession. It is a burden such as few have been called upon to carry. Whether we are fit or not is for reasoned judgment only, but at any rate it is relevant and advisable that our recognition of the responsibility should be known. Pronouncement may be reserved till the proofs of the effort are established.'[11]

It must be said that Reith was less at ease with directors absorbed in the purely business side of the company's affairs than with his small nucleus of controllers concerned exclusively with planning and judging day-to-day programmes. Here, despite what he wrote, the mantle of responsibility sat very lightly on him: all too quickly he had begun to enjoy the taste of authority, and with it the appetite for power grew steadily by what it fed on. His logical eye for detail told him that increasingly centralised control was as essential now to raise broadcasting standards as the combine of interested companies had originally been to avert the waste and anarchy of factional business rivalries. The directors' unqualified confidence in his judgment and good management thus permitted John Reith systematically to stamp his own stern personality on programme output; and because his fellow-controllers at Savoy Hill and in the regional centres tended to be overawed by him, the dominance he exerted over every aspect of broadcasting policy and philosophy remained unchallenged until the company itself withered away almost without a whimper of protest at the end of 1926, having by then served its purpose as a means to the higher end meanwhile formulated and willed by Reith.

Control from the centre made it possible for Peter Eckersley 'to decide the claims of relay stations in relation to a national plan (without which) there would have been chaos'. The distinctive talents of producers were not flattened or levelled down by surveillance from on high. Good producers were too few. Only as the staff increased were the personal credentials and background of applicants for posts in education and talks, for example, carefully scrutinised. Asa Briggs did not exaggerate in stating that 'a newcomer to the BBC in 1924 or 1925 could not fail to note the existence of a "core" or "stratum" of authority within the organisation. There was as yet no clear-cut or even gossipy distinction between "them" and "us", but there was an immediately apparent and definable leadership and direction. The BBC was not just a collection of individuals; it had a genuine corporate existence.'[4]

Lord Gainford had assured the company's shareholders in the autumn of 1923 that 'we intend that local individuality shall be preserved, being of paramount importance. . . . It is not our intention to dispense with the local station.'[3] Reith took care to honour this pledge in the letter without, however, relaxing his grip on policy which applied equally to local stations and to 2LO in London. He approved of excellence and individuality in regional programmes, but insisted on conformity with the same broad principles and rules he laid down for broadcasting practice. When simultaneous transmissions began in August 1923, with land-lines linking all stations to the voice of John Reith as news-reader behind a single microphone in London, the output of the BBC at last 'went national'. Reith took a further step to eliminate any flaws in the quality of what was broadcast by establishing a policy control board. This held its first meeting in January 1924.

It was confined to five men: Carpendale, Eckersley, Burrows and

Rice, who had replaced Anderson as secretary of the company the previous summer, in addition to the managing director. The new supervisory apparatus proved extremely effective, soon fulfilling its master's intention of creating 'a real management committee'. Meanwhile, by keeping his fingers on the pulse of station directors in the provinces, Reith usually working through Carpendale or Burrows, succeeded in forestalling avoidable lapses in judgment and taste. The machinery of control was completed in May 1924, with the institution of a programme board. It included such specialists as the directors of music and education; it met weekly, and it superseded the informal, personal contacts which Reith and his aides had tried to maintain with the regions. By continuing his deliberate practice of posting trusted and capable men to strategic points, Reith gradually achieved the uniformity he desired while strengthening the small pyramid of power he had devised. It was no mean feat.

The broadcasters did not necessarily chafe under his firm rule. Most of them were so busy and so keen that they accepted Reith's methods as they accepted his manner, in a reasonably constructive spirit of resignation. For, however rigidly he controlled it, the system worked. Reith also knew how to administer wisely; the pay was good if the hours were long, and opportunities for the industrious as well as the talented abounded. From his alarming height the architect and driving force of this well-ordered, semi-creative establishment looked down and missed little that went on beneath him. 'The marvellous thing about him', as one of his younger lieutenants confessed, 'was that he never became complacent. There were always improvements to be tried, and he'd come down like a ton of bricks on the self-satisfied or the idle. Perhaps this was inevitable because Reith seemed to radiate a definite sense of mission denied to the ordinary run of mortals. We took his whims like his leadership for granted; but we were careful not to incur his anger which could be terrible.'[7]

Almost pathologically averse to the flattery of publicity, Reith reacted firmly when C. A. Lewis, for one, tried to hold up for popular adulation a character sketch he had written of the masterful John Reith. The managing director of the BBC 'sternly refused' permission to print; and Carpendale, whose personality had been similarly dissected, dutifully followed Reith's lead. The latter preferred to read criticism of broadcasting itself from ordinary listeners, and he retained all his life a belief in the value of such criticism, regarding it obstinately as more relevant and significant than the modern, 'pseudo-scientific fetish for percentages and audience ratings'.[18] The mere counting of listeners heads seemed to him a hollow sham and a delusion: it said nothing about the quality of broadcasting, leaving that on a par with soap or newspapers or anything else dependent for its so-called respectability on mass selling. An unnamed Birmingham listener was given space to complain about BBC output in the first issue of the *Radio Times* on September 28th, 1923:

'Do you really think', he wrote, 'that the majority of their "listeners" are really interested in such lectures as the Decrease of Malaria in Great Britain, How to Become a Veterinary Surgeon, etc? Why is it apparently not thought advisable to repeat the "Request Nights" which are now so popular? Would it not be sufficient to have only one thoroughly classical night a week? . . . Frankly it seems to me that the BBC are mainly catering for the "listeners" who own expensive sets and pretend to appreciate and understand only high-brow music and educational "sob-stuff". Surely like a theatre manager they must put up programmes which will appeal to the majority, and we must remember that it is the latter who provide the main bulk of their income.'

An editorial note was appended to the article. It said:

'The BBC is untiring in its efforts to judge the requirements of the majority. Every "listener" is invited to express his opinions freely and the comments are carefully collated.'

Without an editor as experienced as Leonard Crocombe, who came to the BBC from *Titbits*, it is doubtful if the first issue of the *Radio Times* could have been produced in a single week. A quarter of a million copies were sold, the circulation figure rising steadily year by year until it reached the million mark by the end of 1928. To Reith the weekly magazine was 'the connecting link' between the broadcasters and their public. Less immediately concerned than the company's directors with its instant success as a journalistic and financial venture, Reith was too involved in fighting off opposition from Fleet Street and in foraging for suitable readable material. A message to all BBC station directors on October 27th, 1923, requested 'a regular supply of photographs, anecdotes, talks and any other material to make the magazine of the greatest value'. There was a sound tactical reason for his appeal. As Asa Briggs noted: 'The provincial stations did not need to be appeased, but they had to be encouraged.'[4]

Burdensome conditions were attached to the early contracting-out of the *Radio Times* to the publishing house of Newnes. Profits were shared on a sliding scale, with a minimum guarantee to the BBC of £1000 a year whether there were profits or not. The directors of the broadcasting company urged Reith to accept a small percentage of the profits, pointing out that he had not been 'hired to run a magazine'.

He thought about it, then said no. To have accepted would have been 'hardly proper'. And there was no firmer stickler for business propriety than John Reith.

3

Except when the urgent and paramount needs of broadcasting required it, Reith was quite content to insulate himself in his Savoy Hill citadel against the fickle winds of politics that disturbed the world outside. He stood aloof, reserved and proud, unashamed of being what Mr. Babbitt would have called a poor 'mixer' with the great of that world, until necessity steeled him to venture out alone for occasional appointments with leaders of Church, State or press. Yet sudden squalls blowing up at Westminster were watched by Reith with a distant and discerning eye. He was becoming with practice quite adept at interpreting political portents. So when Baldwin, who had hardly stirred since his unexpected move from No. 11 Downing Street to the house next door, rose to his feet in Plymouth one October night in 1923 and horrified most of his colleagues by publicly declaring that 'he could fight unemployment only if he had a free hand to introduce protection', Reith was mentally prepared for another time-wasting political upheaval. The Conservative leader would plainly have to go to the country for support. Reith, having been marginally embroiled in the previous election, which led to the eclipse of Lloyd George, appreciated how badly Baldwin had 'put his foot in it'. The Prime Minister's motives for rescinding the clear pledge of Bonar Law that there should be no fiscal changes were obscure. Only the consequences were crystal clear: since Baldwin would need a fresh mandate for his newly-adopted policy of protection, another election would have to be held.

Reith was sorry at the prospect of Worthington-Evans leaving the Post Office. It would amount to losing a friendly ally who always said what he meant. Baldwin was someone whom Reith still looked forward to meeting, but his second-hand impressions of the Tory leader were good. An attempt to persuade him, as well as Asquith and Ramsay MacDonald, that a single broadcast during the electoral campaign would have more impact than any amount of shouting from the hustings turned out to be premature. Political leaders might speculate airily about the long-term uses and misuses of radio. They had no wish yet to test its drawing power for themselves, no matter how much it would redound to their advantage. When campaigning finished and the votes were counted at last in December, no single party commanded a sufficient majority to form a government. The Conservatives had 258 seats to Labour's 191, the Liberals under Asquith won 159. It was obvious that Baldwin would be defeated and forced to surrender power soon after the new parliament met; and various wild schemes were meanwhile canvassed for averting the awful calamity of letting in the socialists by default.

Possibly the most extravagant plan was one which would have brought in Reginald McKenna, who had refused the Exchequer under Bonar Law because he deemed it less secure than his exalted position at the Midland Bank, to become the head of an interim government of 'public trustees'. This, like several other fantastic ideas, came to nothing. For George V sensibly decided that Labour should receive 'a fair chance' if and when Baldwin suffered his expected setback in the Commons. On January 22nd, 1924, the morning after that happened, Ramsay MacDonald went to Buckingham Palace, kissed hands with the King, and emerged as Britain's first socialist Prime Minister.

'Today twenty-three years ago dear Grandmamma died', George V wrote in his diary. 'I wonder what she would have thought of a Labour Government!'[12]

Queen Victoria's probable inability to be amused by the phenomenon would nevertheless have been more dignified and correct than the foolish reactions of many public figures. Montagu Norman, the mysterious and powerful Governor of the Bank of England, responded in a fashion which typified the instinctive alarm of the City, perhaps the least vulnerable part of the entire establishment:

'This means the beginning of the end of all the work we have been doing,' he said.[13]

Unlike the orthodox bulk of the alarmists, Reith was privately pleased at the Labour leader's unexpected elevation. He had a fellow-feeling for this unpopular man of obscure origins, self-schooled like himself and not lacking in courage or vision, who had graduated into politics after a period (also reminiscent of Reith's own) as secretary to Thomas Lough, one of the pre-war Liberal members for Islington. MacDonald had been the inspired founder of the group from which the parliamentary Labour Party eventually emerged; only six or seven years before, his pacifist opinions had been reviled, he had lost his seat in the Commons, and he was virtually written off as an unpatriotic failure. Writing with the benefit of hindsight, Reith adopted a drier, more dispassionate attitude to the arrival of MacDonald, merely noting that 'the political cast of the government did not matter much, then or at any time'. But his natural sympathy went out at the time to the unfashionable Labour leader and his associates. On the practical plane, he wondered who the Postmaster-General would be and how this newcomer would compare with his predecessors. For while the cast or colour of an administration 'did not matter much—the personality of the PMG did—his attitude to the BBC, his position and influence with his colleagues'.[5] Vernon Hartshorn, when appointed, caused Reith no sleepless nights. Their paths, as it happened, seldom crossed in the months that followed. For Hartshorn showed no serious interest in broadcasting and its problems, and 'there were very few dealings with him'. That relief was very welcome.

Reith had enough to do consolidating his early gains without having to worry about unnecessary political intrusion into BBC business; and Hartshorn, in common with others in MacDonald's inexperienced team, had his work cut out learning the unfamiliar processes of ministerial responsibility. It offended the new Prime Minister's proud nature to realise that he held office rather than power and this largely on sufferance like a head waiter on probation. His every decision was studied and judged by Asquith who seemed disposed to wait on events until the hour of his own political come-back struck. Nevertheless, the Labour Government took its numerous judges and opponents by surprise, demonstrating a capacity for dull, straightforward rule which upheld the *status quo* and silenced those soothsayers who had warned of impending revolutionary changes. John Wheatley, the Minister of Health, improved on the performance of Neville Chamberlain, his forerunner in that post, with a Housing Bill which 'recognised that the housing shortage was a long-term problem' and 'put the main responsibility back on the local authorities'.[2] The Bill became law, despite its rough passage through the Commons, an institution despised by Wheatley as 'a second- or third-rate debating society'. Snowden at the Exchequer rapidly astounded Montagu Norman by his unswerving Gladstonian orthodoxy; in Snowden's view a balanced budget was the prerequisite to even the smallest social reforms.

Unemployment figures in early 1924 still ran well over the million mark, and nobody in the Labour Government had any patent remedy to suggest. The army of workless remained workless. When industrial disputes led to awkward strikes by dockers and London tramwaymen, MacDonald boldly invoked the detested Emergency Powers Act, introduced by Lloyd George, which every socialist had denounced then without reserve. A Labour Government had to prove that it would not flinch from governing, and MacDonald's willingness to deal as firmly with recalcitrant strikers as any true-blue Tory leader convinced the sceptics that he was at any rate on the side of law and order. The Prime Minister, who acted also as his own Foreign Secretary, spent much time and thought on international relations, winning a deserved reputation for his initiative as a conciliator between France and Germany. Reith met him only once or twice, yet the two men took to one another on sight, as Scots sometimes do when accidentally drawn together like self-conscious fellow-conspirators among the alien English.

Two broadcasting events stood out like sunlit landmarks during the spring and early summer of 1924. The first was the Wembley Exhibition in April, an ostentatious but not unsuccessful effort to prove that Britain as a nation still believed in herself. Reith invited King George V to broadcast and secretly crowed with delight when the invitation was promptly accepted by a monarch who prided himself on being old-fashioned enough to dislike flying. The Wembley triumph indicated not merely how smooth was the relationship between the Labour Prime Minister and the BBC's managing director but how swiftly the accolade of respectability had descended on them both. The second event also shone like gold, not the fairy-gold of dreams and hopes but the kind that could be converted into hard cash. The abolition of the fifteen-shilling licence for home-made radio sets on July 1st meant that the company's financial position was at last really sound. Reith, who had fought and planned well for the time needed to tide the BBC over its early teething troubles had 'established myself with the board and the trade', thereby reinforcing his claim to be allowed greater freedom to go on developing broadcasting as he saw fit. Gainford, the company's chairman, appeared to be somewhat discomfited by Reith's sharp annoyance at being passed over for an honour after the triumph of the Wembley Exhibition:

'The BBC *ought* to have had recognition', he wrote. 'It has done an incalculable amount of good service to people—apart from its growth and success being considered remarkable. Perhaps it may be more easy to believe it when I say that, had I been offered a CB or anything of that grade, I should have asked to be excused and suggested Eckersley for it. The company is worth a great deal more than that and yet is kept out when masses of civil servants and service officers are handed out things. . . . It would be infinitely better if the thing came from the King himself instead of from any political party. I don't know if He knows the amount of work we have accomplished—probably not. I do think, however, that if you enlightened him he would deal with the matter and that it would be immensely popular. . . . To be ultra-veracious it's about 5 per cent personal and 95 per cent for the great benefit that would accrue to the BBC. . . .'[14]

Gainford ignored the plea. After all, as a Whip in Asquith's government during John Reith's youth, this Liberal ex-minister had acquired inside knowledge of the intricacies of the honours system. Besides, he genuinely felt that the BBC had done enough already for its zealous managing director. In a note to Sir William Bull of the BBC board, dated April 5th, 1924, Gainford had stated:

'Reith should have his value to us more adequately recognised and I think £2500 per annum, excluding directors' fees and his entertainment allowance, is not too much.'[15]

The comment scrawled on the top of Reith's lengthy letter of complaint to Gainford at not being singled out for recognition by the monarch said pithily:

'John Reith wants an honour!'

MacDonald was just as unlucky when it came to asserting his negligible power over political opponents who gradually grew tired of Labour's paradoxical fitness to govern. It was Lloyd George, not Asquith or Baldwin, who contrived to speed the end of MacDonald's administration after official recognition was granted to the Soviet Union and negotiations for a commercial treaty with the Russians had begun that summer. 'A thoroughly grotesque agreement', was Lloyd George's description of this abortive initiative; and Liberals responded to his charge that even to consider lending money to Communists was a shocking state of affairs. With public attention now fixed on the unseemly flirtation of the Prime Minister with the unspeakable Russians, the Conservative opposition decided to censure the government on a parallel matter, once it became known that a prosecution against a member of the British Communist Party for alleged incitement to mutiny had been hastily dropped on MacDonald's instructions to his own Attorney-General. The so-called 'Campbell case' seemed to expose the irresolute mind of a Prime Minister on the retreat. The Liberals sided with the Conservatives, and MacDonald asked for a dissolution of parliament.

To compound the Labour Party's difficulties, a letter was published in the press and by the Foreign Office just before polling day, purporting to have been sent by Zinoviev, the president of the Communist International, to the British Communist Party. It contained all kinds of seditious orders, and it caused a major scandal. Could MacDonald, so moderate in his policies and their execution, really be trusted? Many voters wondered; and they went out one day in late October 1924, to vote Baldwin back as Prime Minister, unimpressed by Labour's belated counter-claim that the Zinoviev letter was fradulent. Reith had in the meantime tried to interest Asquith and MacDonald in the merits of broadcasting to the electorate from a BBC studio. Each of them preferred to be seen as well as heard by the people. Only Baldwin accepted Reith's advice, in response to Ramsay MacDonald's reluctant agreement that 'the three party leaders could broadcast once'. Through his secretary, MacDonald stipulated that a speech he would deliver from a public hall in Glasgow might be relayed over the BBC. Reith did his best to reason with him. 'I told him it was a mistake to append an invisible audience of millions to a visible audience of two or three thousands. He replied that that was what had been decided.'[5] With defeat already staring him in the face, MacDonald had little regard for such technical niceties. His period of living on time reluctantly borrowed from Asquith had expired, but Asquith reaped no benefit whatever from it. The imperious and abrupt style in which the Labour leader had defied the Commons and his own fate by seeking an early election reminded one seasoned observer of 'Samson pulling down the pillars of the temple'.[16]

Asquith was haughtily indifferent to Reith's offer for reasons of his own. Having suggested a select committee to look into the inept handling of the Campbell case, a big majority of MPs favouring such a move, he had not expected the Prime Minister's contemptuous decision to ignore it. MacDonald had suffered enough, so for that matter had Asquith. An old man of seventy-two, the Liberal leader travelled north to Paisley, allowing Reith to relay only one of his noisy campaign meetings. The election was a costly one for the Liberals and for Asquith personally: he lost his seat to a Labour opponent, and only forty of his followers were returned.

It was the Conservatives who scooped up votes and seats, and with 419 victorious candidates behind him, Stanley Baldwin became Prime Minister again. Somewhat naïvely, Reith attributed Baldwin's triumph largely to the broadcast talk he gave in the closing stages of the campaign:

'Wiser than either (MacDonald or Asquith)', he commented, 'he took the opportunity seriously, came to Savoy Hill to see exactly what he had to do, asked many intelligent questions, spoke a week later from a studio.'[5] Far more significant than the broadcast itself was this casual meeting of minds. If, as A. J. P. Taylor has declared, 'it is hard to decide whether Baldwin or MacDonald did more to fit Labour into constitutional life',[2] since the two leaders held remarkably similar views on political problems, there can be no question that it was Baldwin more than anyone else who enabled the BBC to gain total respectability. For it was Baldwin who had both warmed to Reith and assured for him a coveted place in the establishment. When Reith wrote to the Prime Minister, requesting that the speech from the throne at the opening of the new parliament should be broadcast, Baldwin asked him to call at No. 10 Downing Street one morning for a talk.

'We last met on a rather momentous occasion', the Prime Minister said, as if Reith needed any reminder of the fact. Then, in the cabinet room, they sat down and conversed at length about broadcasting and its special problems.

'He seemed to be genuinely interested', Reith said. 'I delighted at the opportunity of telling him about the BBC, its policy and intentions.'[5]

This discussion with Baldwin in such informal and congenial circumstances was to be the first of many. The two men 'clicked' at once for reasons that merit closer examination. Like Ramsay MacDonald, if in a slightly more paradoxical way, Stanley Baldwin shared with Reith something of the romantic vision and imaginative aspirations of the Celt. He was as proud of the MacDonald blood in his own veins as he was of his better known literary connections. The Scottish strain was a legacy from his mother's side of the family, and though he cultivated the popular image of a simple English country gentleman, fonder of pigs and his pipe than of anything else in life, except people, the real man was altogether less ordinary. He loved Britain. He wanted to be loved by the British, regardless of divisive irrelevancies like distinctions of class and wealth. The rich son of an ironmaster, who had anonymously contributed a considerable sum of money to the national coffers after the war as 'conscience money', Baldwin believed that his mission in public life was to break down barriers and build social bridges instead between rich and poor, duke and dustman.

It was an intuitive, colourful if nebulous creed. Yet in his ponderous, almost indolent way he acted on it with consistency. Montagu Norman, a subtle friend who had penetrated a layer or two of the Baldwin charm, once remarked admiringly that this 'quiet homely' fellow who 'thinks there is no place in the world quite like Worcestershire . . . seems to be where he is more from duty or necessity than from real choice'. Norman hedged his bet by adding sententiously: 'But here again appearances may well be deceivable.' Reith, who tried not to judge too much by appearances, was more captivated by the warmth and the 'spiritual cheerfulness' of the Prime Minister. Each man was attracted to the other, regardless of their dissimilarities, by the magnetism of 'a common interest in improving the moral climate of Britian'.[9] Reith quickly recognised that he found his strongest and most improbable ally yet in the quiet Stanley Baldwin. Dim as Baldwin's idealism might be beside the white hot flame of Reith's, it was nevertheless the authentic and selfless light of a reformer.

'I find the study of the varying types in the House of Commons a very interesting occupation', Baldwin once declared. 'I find there, especially among the Labour Party, many men who fifty years ago would inevitably have gone into the Christian ministry. They have been drawn into political life from a deep desire to help the people. Such men are common in all parties today. These are facts which relieve the darkness of the outlook. Things will change again. We must not let ourselves imagine, amidst the changes of the day, though the very foundations are cracking, that the things we hold most precious are going to pass away. I certainly agree with many observers that since the war the manifest forces of Satan have been more conspicuously at large. But the very manifestation of these forces is calling other forces into the field.'

The tongue was the tongue of Baldwin. The sentiments were also his. Yet they could easily have been mistaken for Reith's without anyone, except a purist with an eye for individual style and an ear for tell-tale rhythm, being able to tell the basic difference. Take another example:

'Political work is of enormous importance at this time. We do not all realise in what a changed world we are living. Superficially it is a frivolous world, full of "jazzing" and preoccupation with pleasure, but under the surface it is intensely serious. I believe the electórate is intensely anxious to listen to men who have sincerely at heart the uplifting of the nation. . . .'

Of Scotland and the drive of the moral imperative in some Scotsmen, including his new friend Reith, Baldwin professed unqualified approval:

'There is nothing that fills me with more admiration than the way in which your people for generations have held up that standard of plain living and high thinking—a lesson which today a world that would, if it could, be a world of high living and plain thinking, needs more than ever before.'[17]

Instances of Baldwin's virtuosity as a moralist for all occasions could be multiplied. The three given here suffice to show why Reith and the Prime Minister took so quickly to one another. As fellow-idealists, fired with the same moral convictions about the needs of the nation and the postwar world, each accepted the other as a fellow-crusader in the same lofty cause. Baldwin did not condemn David Lloyd George as being solely responsible for the degradation of public life during his six years in charge of the coalition regime. Being a mercurial and less than scrupulous leader, Lloyd George had simply let moral standards and values slip by ignoring their very existence. The sale and profanation of honours had been just one glaring symbol of an amoral outlook which had encouraged the growth of corruption and dishonourable ways. Now Baldwin, in his unassuming but honest fashion, proposed to restore virtue to its traditional place; and he regarded Reith and the BBC as natural confederates in his high-minded campaign to reinstate peace, beauty and goodness in the hearts of his fellow-countrymen. With good reason, the BBC's managing director welcomed both the trust reposed in him and the unofficial conferment of a predestined commission which he prized.

Whether Baldwin or anyone else had become Prime Minister, Reith would have carried on as zealously as before; now, however, he did so in the knowledge that, like the King's grocer or hatter but not in a grovelling, mercenary way, he had been singled out 'By Appointment' as a kind of unofficial standard-bearer to the nation's leader. It is not difficult to surmise what precisely Baldwin found attractive in the new broadcasting instrument, apart from its practical use to a consummate politician like himself. To reach out through a microphone into the homes and ears and hearts of a million people was an astounding, exciting responsibility, as he saw it. He was happy that the control rested in such responsible hands. The first modern political figure to understand the extraordinary changes for good or ill that radio could bring, Baldwin also accepted the necessity of letting the British experiment develop quietly and naturally.

He liked what he knew of Reith and refrained from pre-judging the existing BBC; he admired the visionary ideals of the former, but as yet could not quite make out how these squared with the business aims of the latter. The company, a public utility in private hands, had been granted an extension of its limited franchise until the end of 1926 only. Before that date, the government would have to choose a permanent constitutional pattern for broadcasting, preferably one into which Reith's lofty principles and ideals would fit. No proposal to that effect, either spoken or tacit, ever passed between the Prime Minister and the BBC's managing director, but Reith already felt as sure about the future as if Baldwin had spelt out his intentions. In this Prime Minister broadcasting had at any rate discovered its shrewdest and wisest friend so far.

Reconciliation was in the air. The three diehards who had gone into the political wilderness with Lloyd George had returned like prodigal sons to Baldwin's side: Austen Chamberlain, as Foreign Secretary, Birkenhead as Secretary of State for India, Winston Churchill as Chancellor of the Exchequer. Their roles would have been better reshuffled, since Chamberlain had once proved a sound man at the Treasury whereas Churchill had no head or flair for finance. As for Birkenhead, the India Office attracted him hardly at all. Nevertheless, hatchets had been buried, old scores forgiven, through the diplomatic dexterity of a Prime Minister who had mastered the arts of flattery. When Churchill, for instance, heard Baldwin mumbling that he wanted to offer him the job of Chancellor, he had jumped to the instant conclusion that the Duchy of Lancaster must be vacant. The offer of the Exchequer had seemed almost too good to be true.

The broadening of the government strengthened its base, even if Churchill at the Exchequer could never by any charitable stretch of imagination be described as a success, just as Birkenhead hardly shone at the India Office. Only Austen Chamberlain both justified and enjoyed himself—producing in the Locarno Pact an earnest of Britain's desire to live and let live, as an off-shore island of Europe with an Empire of her own, by guaranteeing the frontiers of France, Belgium and Germany. Political powerlessness had become the lot of the vanishing Liberals at home. Political power from now on would lie between Baldwin and MacDonald who, despite superficial differences in emphasis and policy, seemed as hard to distinguish from one another as Tweedledum and Tweedledee.

The facility for enveloping everything he touched in a kind of unifying ectoplasm let Baldwin down rarely. His sincerity was as contagious as his amiability. The illusions he fathered or fostered took in only a few men who should have known better; and if the national harm these illusions did was ultimately grave, this was certainly not true of them in the short term. The ten-year rule laid down in Lloyd George's day, for instance, was based on the hypothesis that there would be no war for a decade. This was reinterpreted by Churchill in such a way that a fresh decade started every morning, so that the heads of the armed services found themselves pinned down helplessly by a Chancellor who would have behaved differently in his natural element back at the War Office. On such an endlessly moving escalator of economic thrift, no solid defences could be built or even planned. Baldwin did not believe in interfering with the business of colleagues whom he trusted. He did not enjoy browsing through despatch boxes stuffed with official papers, preferring to sniff rather than read them. Fortunately his intuition was preternaturally keen. He could scent trouble miles or months ahead so that it seldom caught him wholly unprepared, despite the almost irresistible inclination whenever he felt energetic to lie down until the disagreeable feeling had passed off.

The return of Britain to the gold standard in 1925 realised an old dream of the alchemist who ruled the Court of the Bank of England,

Montagu Norman. The effect on the national economy was neither direct nor immediate. Food and other imports became cheaper to buy, but exports of old-style goods, which would have been hard enough to sell at the old, lower prices, suffered a check. Churchill maintained afterwards that he had been hoodwinked over the gold standard by Norman and others. Not to put too fine a point on it, this was dubious wisdom long after the event.

Baldwin's own desire for a quiet life was shared, for the most part, by his colleagues. The government gave an impression of being older and staider than the actual ages of its members warranted, the Prime Minister himself displaying the spirit in which he meant to rule when a back-bench Conservative introduced a private members' Bill in March 1925 to abolish the political levy in the trade unions, on which the financial solvency of the Labour movement depended. Baldwin thrust the measure aside, his speech ending with the significant and typical phrase: 'Give peace in our time, O Lord.' The omens suggested that his prayer might perhaps be heard. For the matters which divided Labour from Conservative thinking were smaller and less important than those which united them. The controversial questions of recent years, Ireland and protection included, had been settled. There were no fundamental disagreements on unemployment assistance or national health insurance; each side accepted the principle, disputing only the methods and the amounts.

But one dark shadow loomed over the land. It was the shadow of unemployment on a massive and growing scale. Its effect was most harshly felt in the traditional heavy industries on which Britain's prosperity had once depended. Nearly three men out of every four unemployed had once earned a livelihood in textiles, in iron and steel plants or in the coalfields. It was perhaps axiomatic of the economically irrational condition of things as they were that Britain's coal industry alone still provided jobs for more than a million men in 1925. The coal owners were thus the largest single group of employers, despite the fact that many of their pits had begun to run at a loss. Ironically, Gainford of the BBC, with family interests in Durham, was one of these hard-pressed, coal-owning magnates. The fat years between 1921 and 1924, when British coal had been in such demand that supplies kept continental industrialists going, were over. The interlude had shed a deceptive cheerfulness. For it sustained too many uneconomic mines. The workers had meanwhile secured from MacDonald's government a favourable wage settlement. Then the reviving German and Polish coal industries, with cheaper products to sell, stole the market and forced the British mine owners to cut back. Stanley Baldwin wanted peace, but not necessarily at any price.

He did not consider it any part of his government's business to assist the reorganisation of the coal industry by means of an immediate subsidy. Nor had his government any intention of dissuading the coal owners against widespread reductions in wages and working hours, the only remedy they recognised. The miners naturally responded in kind. Led by tough and uncompromising men, they soon confounded even the conciliatory spirit of Baldwin.

4

John Reith had no high opinion of Sir William Mitchell-Thomson, the fourth Postmaster-General with whom he now had dealings. The feeling was, to some extent, mutual. For Mitchell-Thomson disliked Reith's suspicious air of always being hard done by almost as much as Reith disapproved of Mitchell-Thomson's heavy aura of pomposity. When the new minister, therefore, introduced a Bill in February 1925 to reinforce his own status as 'policeman of the ether', the BBC's managing director could not put hand on heart and wish its promoter well. Reith had not been consulted; otherwise he would have certainly advised the Postmaster-General to tone it down. For if its general purpose was innocuous enough, namely the removal of all doubts about the ministerial right to collect licence fees from the public, the methods proposed by Mitchell-Thomson pleased nobody. As he also threw in as a sop a proposal to reduce licence fees, Reith was in fact livid with rage. MPs normally critical of the BBC linked up with forces outside parliament to condemn the 'inquisitorial' features of the measure, particularly those concerned with searching premises and with punishing offenders.

The Bill was thrown out. Baldwin's policy did not run to defending what almost everyone else opposed; and Reith found himself in wholehearted agreement with the Labour Party whose spokesman, Tom Johnston, told him privately that if the Postmaster-General got the 'arbitrary powers' he wanted, the position of the BBC itself would have to be reconsidered. In Johnston's view, the company had probably outstayed its welcome anyway, and some institution with 'a greater measure of public control' would be more acceptable in its place. Reith hoped that this double thrust at the Post Office and at the BBC might help to bring Mitchell-Thomson and the company's directors to their senses. The board seldom peered beyond its collective nose at the monthly meetings. It was almost as if the gross inferiority complex under which the directors laboured, because of the BBC's unhappy start in life, inhibited any sensible discussion about the future. Yet time was no longer on the BBC's side. The directors had less than ten months to go before their monopolistic rights, that constant source of self-consciousness if not of guilt, ceased to have further validity. At the first opportunity, John Reith decided that he would confront the board with its inescapable obligation: he would say as tactfully as he could that, unless the BBC acted on its own behalf, the politicians would probably seize the initiative.

This was the origin of the Crawford Committee, the second enquiry into the BBC since its birth and by far the more decisive one of the two. For if the intervention of Sykes had ensured the company's survival in the teeth of financial embarrassment and much adverse criticism, the intervention of Crawford would ensure the company's extinction and its replacement, amidst much favourable comment, by a public corporation. That Reith deliberately became the prime mover in the affair should shock or surprise nobody who has followed his career up to its present stage: sheer variety and pressure of work had not deflected his mind and obdurate will from *their* prime purpose of making the BBC a worthy instrument for the fulfilment of his personal destiny. It may sound offensive, especially in pious ears, to describe the directors of the company in early 1925 as convenient stepping stones over a turbulent river which Reith could not have crossed unaided; but such was his aplomb, so complete his single-mindedness, that most of the directors, who were mainly interested in selling wireless sets, bore him no ill will in consequence. There were no accusations of treachery or insincerity because he behaved boldly, fairly and openly throughout. Nor could his iron determination fail, while fate or providence stood beside him, to prevent Reith from sinning against Napoleon's cardinal rule of good luck. His nerves held, as did his luck, until the company died at the end of 1926.

It was on March 19th, 1925, that John Reith raised the question of the BBC's future status at a special meeting of the board. Apart from the critical interest of politicians, two further reasons prompted his action. Press representatives, Lord Riddell being the worst offender, invariably talked about broadcasting as if it were a commercial rival, and that slur would not be removed until the company reconsidered its own anomalous standing. Then there was the royalty factor. A half-hearted attempt had been made soon after Baldwin's victory at the polls to prolong the agreed period of royalty earnings from BBC sets and parts; but as this had been turned down flat by Mitchell-Thomson, there seemed to Reith no point in maintaining any further the pretence that the radio trade influenced broadcasting policy. Why not take the straightforward step of letting the Post Office see that the directors appreciated their own dilemma? The proposal evidently bewildered some and slightly scandalised other members of the BBC board. 'There was a considerable amount of drama', as Asa Briggs has recorded, 'everybody talking at once.' Reith, having adopted the unexpected stance of a managing director prepared to bite the hand that fed him, now felt torn by conflicting loyalties:

'I tried to make them see', he noted, 'how anomalous and absurd the present constitution is, but, of course, they have their own position to think about and mine is one of great difficulty and embarrassment.'[4]

The exchanges went on for some time in a charged atmosphere. Finally this bald, unemotional statement was put down on paper: 'The managing director explained that the meeting had been called to discuss the advisability of making recommendations to the Postmaster-General in regard to the future constitution of the company. After considerable discussion it was agreed that the managing director should write to the Postmaster-General to ascertain if he had any views and to indicate that the board was prepared to discuss the matter if desired.' Next day, March 20th, Reith wrote the letter. It was brief, formal and businesslike. No member of the board could conceivably have taken exception to it. Yet, because his connections with senior Post Office representatives as well as with politicians happened to be far more intimate and frequent than could have been claimed for the bulk of the BBC's directors, Reith was already confident that this letter to Mitchell-Thomson amounted to a virtual surrender on the company's part. In due course it would be held to the bargain.

The Post Office, he knew, broadly shared his view that broadcasting needed some form of direction to enlarge its public service character; and if the existing directors could hardly be expected to abdicate forthwith of their own accord, they did not appear to mind letting Reith take official soundings on their behalf. The irony of the situation was not entirely lost on Bull and Kellaway, the two members of the board with long experience of political manœuvring. Yet, as both men knew, there may sometimes be diametrically opposite ways of looking at the same problem. In the uncertain spring of 1925 the BBC board could arguably have sat back, basking in the reflected glory of the broadcasters who ultimately owed their success and increasing popular influence to the benevolent patronage of directors like Bull, Kellaway, McKinstry and Pease under the chairmanship of Gainford. Reith, the firm link between board and broadcasters, had always justified their unreserved confidence in him. The high standards he had set, the degree of respectability he had gained as a result for the broadcasting business in Britain, represented a better return on that confidence than monetary profits alone, but this was no less than their due. Complacency may sometimes co-exist with suspicion. The adroitness of John Reith lay in refusing to humour the complacent or provoke the suspicious members of the board.

Besides, he usually had too much else on his mind for unnecessary luxuries like worrying. His immediate aims were to obtain press approval for broadcasting cleverly coded running commentaries on a few national sporting fixtures—the Derby, the Boat Race, and the FA Cup Final—and to persuade a cautious Postmaster-General to drop the embargo on transmitting topics of a controversial nature. In neither case was he successful. Mitchell-Thomson would not commit himself to introducing changes which, he admitted, would certainly have to be considered soon when the future of the BBC came under official scrutiny. Acting on the belief that freedom from the fetters imposed by the newspapers could be won only step by step, Reith would not accept 'no' for an answer from Riddell and his associates. So he insisted on a further meeting. The complaint from Riddell that he had been 'dragged to St Martin-le-Grand by Mr. Reith' prefaced a definite refusal to be bound by anything which might be decided by the Postmaster-General, who took the chair at the discussion. In any case as Mitchell-Thomson was there only to listen, he did not try to arbitrate:

'Even at the time the last broadcasting agreement was entered into', he said, 'neither Mr. Reith nor the Government, I think, foresaw what a giant this baby was going to grow into, and I do not know what size it will be in December 1926.'[3]

In expressing his personal regret that the press would not yield even to the extent of allowing the first half of an important rugby match to be broadcast, the Postmaster-General stung Riddell into an unintentionally revealing reply. It was the wrong moment, said the press lord, for fresh experiments. The achievement of Reith during the past two years had been 'a bit of wizardry', and to let the wizardry stop where it stood would surely be in everyone's interest. The BBC could not disown the fact that it was a commercial company—and therefore a rival—and that was why the newspaper industry had to resist the attempts of broadcasting to poach on its preserves.

The 'seven o'clock rule', under which no news could be transmitted before that hour in the evening, remained fixed and immutable, though the BBC was not debarred from broadcasting speeches, official functions and what passed under the loose heading of 'ceremonies'. The appetite of the company might increase with its engineering facilities, but Fleet Street saw the dangers in allowing

Reith more scope than was needed for the BBC's minimum bare subsistence. In consequence the BBC went blithely through 1925 and into 1926 without a professional news set-up of its own. When the General Strike came, and most of the big printing presses ground to a halt, the company was singularly ill-equipped to step into the breach. The fault was not directly Reith's, of course. The press lords zealously protected their vested interests against an intruder which, in terms of sheer speed and cheapness of production, might well have rapidly undermined those interests. But, as will be shown in the next chapter, Reith was less prepared than he should have been for the crisis that temporarily shut down most of Fleet Street because of his own allergy to the gathering and processing of news as such. The prejudice was not uncommon at the time, especially among those who mistrusted the political ambitions of the press lords.

He was far more interested in the dissemination of straight talks, of educational matter, of religion, even of controversial social and political topics which would enable listeners to form their own judgments. Because he loathed and despised organs of opinion which sought to manipulate facts and mould false values, he was far slower in establishing the embryo of a professional news-service at Savoy Hill than a person with a subtler appreciation of public taste might have been.

Among his central core of advisers he had, by now, recruited only one ex-Fleet Street journalist, W. S. Gladstone Murray. This former air correspondent of the *Daily Express* had been recommended to Reith by Basil Binyon, a BBC director, and by Beaverbrook himself. But Murray's responsibilities were strictly confined to publicity and public relations from the time he joined Reith in 1924, and if he deserves credit for his energetic and skilful promotion of the general interests of broadcasting he might have done much more, with Reith's backing, to organise a news department as well.

As indicated in an earlier chapter, Beaverbrook's original friendliness had consciously stiffened Reith's resolve to shape the BBC in his own individualistic way. Through Murray, in the spring of 1925, Reith was delighted to discover that Beaverbrook genuinely approved of what he had done. The sons of the manse met again, and Reith was highly flattered by his Canadian host's insistence that 'there must be monopoly in broadcasting'.

Evidence of the managing director's eagerness to air matters of controversy abound. Here he was hedged in by the restrictive rules applied by the Post Office, which proved more frustrating than the restrictive practices imposed by the press. The charge sometimes levelled against Reith that he strove to play safe by banning difficult topics could not have been less well founded.

In the Postmaster-General's book, the broadcasting of political speeches was forbidden along with the Derby. It was not through lack of persistent lobbying that Reith failed to get the bans raised, especially after the engineering break-through of simultaneous broadcasting. When, for instance, he approached Mitchell-Thomson for permission to broadcast part of a debate on the King's speech from the Oxford Union in March 1925, the request was summarily rejected. 'As the speeches to be made would be of an essentially political character', ran the reply, 'he regrets that he is unable to agree to the debate, or any portion of it being broadcast.' Returning with further requests for arranging BBC debates on topics like unemployment and free trade, Reith encountered another reason for Mitchell-Thomson's reluctance to give ground:

'The question of the broadcasting of speeches or pronouncements on political and other controversial questions will no doubt be one of the aspects of the subject to be considered by the committee which the government propose to appoint to undertake a general enquiry into broadcasting towards the end of the year; and in the meantime the Postmaster-General does not consider it advisable to make a fundamental alteration of the present policy on the lines you suggest.'[3]

At least a crumb of comfort was contained in this negative response. Reith longed for the enquiry to start. He had no lasting regrets about his tactical handling of the BBC board to pre-empt its agreement on such an enquiry: the directors, who were content to let him run the service, could scarcely deny him this official chance of permanently improving it. Their sympathetic nods were as unavailing as their shrugs of indifference at occasional board meetings when Reith informed them of his continued frustrations and those of his programme planners. 'We find', the BBC control board had minuted as long ago as March 1924, 'that restrictions are depriving us of many eminent men—men who have achieved a national position by the strong line they have taken in various movements.' If the BBC's directors were helpless and the Postmaster-General remained studiously deaf to all appeals, then Reith stood to gain more than he could ever lose by a full-scale investigation of broadcasting, its needs, its strengths as well as its deficiencies.

On the few basic questions, he would budge for nobody. The rock on which the BBC stood was the rock of Christianity and the moral code that flowed from it. In his view, it needed no justification because 'Christianity happens to be the stated and official religion of this country. . . . This is a fact which those who have criticised our right to broadcast the Christian religion would do well to bear in mind'. Yet equally he had decided that Christianity on the air 'should be non-controversial';[11] and there were many who disagreed with the decision, bearing in mind the innumerable and often fine shades of difference in preaching and practice between the various denominations. Reith boldly set aside these shades of difference, convinced that it would be scandalous and wrong to allow religious sects time to advertise them on the air. The truths taught by Christ were, he held, beyond dispute. The BBC's role was to broadcast these fundamental tenets in a manner detached from the predilections of every church, so that religion would do the least harm to the greatest number of listeners. 'This was an assumption which not everyone shared', to quote Asa Briggs, 'nor did everyone agree with him that "the secularising of Sunday is one of the most significant and unfortunate trends of modern life".'[4] George Bernard Shaw, who had a good opinion of the BBC's work as a whole, is reputed to have described its approach to religion as little better than 'atheisim tempered by hymns'. And A J P Taylor, writing as a responsible historian of the inter-war years, noted how Reith 'used what he called "the brute force of monopoly" to stamp Christian morality on the British people. He stamped it also on his employees.'[2]

Monopoly as he exercised it was already, on Reith's repeated admission, nine points of the law:

'Without monopoly', he declared impenitently, 'many things might not have been so easily done that were done. The Christian religion and the Sabbath might not have had the place and protection they had; the place and protection which it was right to give them, the giving of which seemed to be approved. The Christian religion, not just as a sectional activity but as a fundamental. And as to the Sabbath, one day in the week clear of jazz and variety and such like: an effort to preserve the inestimable benefit of a day different from other days. . . . Almost everything might have been different. The BBC might have had to play for safety, prosecute the obviously popular lines, count its clients, study and meet their reactions, curry favour, subordinate itself to the vote. *Might* have had to, it probably would not, but its road would have been far harder. . . . In magnifying office and responsibility the BBC made itself a target for all manner of acrimony and abuse. It came from the pinheaded—press correspondents among them—who were incapable of seeing more in broadcasting than an agency which should cater for their own particular and limited predilections. Their puny spleens and gibes fell on an impervious and indifferent BBC. It came also from those who . . . imagined their own prerogatives and preserves to be threatened. It was indeed royal to do good and be abused.'[5]

This testament of his own unflinching, despotic outlook omits any reference to Reith's personal religious faith. By late 1925 he was so embroiled in the fascinating task for which destiny had earmarked him that the BBC and its consolidation had become for him a substitute-religion, a surrogate faith in its own right. He still attended church services, the selfless example of his dead father still sustained and inspired him; he even swore to a few of his closest friends that he had met his father's ghost one glorious if improbable summer's day on Cairngorm; and his ageing mother, with whom he corresponded regularly, helped to keep alive in him his youthful resolve to do good in the world. In his home life occasions for relaxation were few and fleeting because he could never leave the problems of the office behind him. He was doubly fortunate in having an exceptionally understanding wife who proved a sympathetic listener as well as a careful housekeeper. Among his feminine admirers he had none more devoted than Muriel. She always knew how to make allowances for his displays of petulance or outbursts of temper. If she tended to spoil him by her excessive meekness, she had the perfect excuse in her unselfish devotion and affection for John Reith.

One night in March 1925 the Reiths were dining with the Baldwins at No. 10 Downing Street. The Prime Minister's wife was to broadcast an appeal later on behalf of the YMCA, but talk at the table was general. At one point Baldwin remarked on the uncovenanted privileges that were the lot of Prime Ministers and offered a topical example. He had been held up on his way to a ceremony a few days before, and to save time the police had cleared the road so that he could be driven 'down the wrong side of Piccadilly'. When Baldwin suggested casually that there could be no comparable power attached to Reith's job in broadcasting, the Prime Minister was clearly asking for trouble. He got it.

'I said I could lift up the private telephone in my study, give two simple orders—"SB", which would connect me with the control room; the second, "All transmitters". Then I could talk to several million people'.

Baldwin handsomely, if weakly, acknowledged defeat.

'He agreed that that was more impressive than his car exploit.'[5]

Two events that summer filled Reith with momentary elation. The first was the official opening in July of the new Daventry long-range transmitter which at last brought the whole country within range of the BBC on sets of cheap and simple design. If proof were needed that the trade respected Reith's prototype of public service broadcasting, here was evidence indeed. As for Mitchell-Thomson, gushing with wordy praise for the broadcasters at the inaugural ceremony, Reith would have liked to remind the public that this was the same Postmaster-General who had tried to cut down the BBC's income not many weeks before. The second event, in the same month, was the long deferred announcement that a new government committee would shortly reconsider the whole position of broadcasting in Britain.

Reith would naturally have preferred a royal commission. An enquiry under the aegis of the Post Office was a disappointment because his low estimate of that department's influence and general wisdom persisted. He thought it 'absurd that broadcasting should be subject to the overriding direction of a junior minister'; but relief banished initial doubts when the names of the committee members were announced during the first week of August. The choice of the Earl of Crawford as chairman seemed a favourable augury of the government's good intentions. An ageing ex-Cabinet minister, with a lively interest in the arts, Crawford would at any rate lend the committee the desired weight of authority and gravity. The accidental distinction of being a Scot was one he shared with several others: Captain Ian Fraser, William Graham, Ian Macpherson and Lord Blanesburgh, who represented both houses of parliament. The varied qualifications of the remainder seemed a guarantee in advance that the enquiry would be conducted with thoroughness, fairness and independence. In addition to Sir Henry Hadow, the musical expert, and Lord Rayleigh, a leading physicist, there were Rudyard Kipling, a cousin of Baldwin's, and Dame Meriel Talbot. . . .

It is conceivable that broadcasting might have got the royal commission Reith desired, had it not been for an ominous cloud which darkened the distant industrial horizon in the middle of July 1925, forcing a reluctant Cabinet to take preventive action.

The bitterness in the coal industry had been allowed to persist, unsolved, for months. The Trades Union Congress, anxious for a compromise, had espoused the miners' case against pit closures and longer hours of work for reduced pay packets; but the owners would not moderate their line, and the government was in no ready position or frame of mind to impose a negotiated settlement. Yet matters could not be allowed to drift on towards a national coal strike. For sympathetic stoppages by railway workers and others who handled or used coal would very probably spread and cause grievous damage to the economy. On June 30th, 1925, the mine-owners unilaterally issued a month's notice to terminate the existing and (to them) unacceptable arrangements. It was an ultimatum which no government could afford to ignore as both sides made ready for a long fight with no holds barred.

Baldwin hesitated until the end. At first he refused point-blank to offer a subsidy and buy precious time. Then second thoughts prevailed only twenty-six hours before the mine owners' ultimatum expired. The Prime Minister decided that for the next nine months, until the end of April 1926, the government would underwrite wages and profits at prevailing rates, while a royal commission spent the winter and spring seeking practical ways of promoting efficiency, productivity and peace in the coal industry. So Sir Herbert Samuel and his three wise men, one an economist the other two industrialists uncontaminated by any first-hand experience of that industry's problems, started work almost at the same time as the much less publicised team led by Lord Crawford was preparing to reconsider the arrangements of broadcasting. Reith failed to get the royal commission he wanted for overriding reasons of state. Reith also failed to appreciate the full significance of these until the impact of the General Strike, in May 1926, shook the structure of the existing BBC to its very foundations, subjecting the broadcasting instrument he had fashioned almost single-handed to the sternest test imaginable of its fitness to survive.

7
The Hostage

1

PERHAPS BECAUSE there were too many other matters of immediate interest or importance to distract it, the public attitude towards the BBC had softened into a mood of uncritical acceptance by the final quarter of 1925. A period of quiet growth, unspectacular but systematic, was precisely what the company had needed after the early struggle for survival against the combined forces of jealous press proprietors and largely indifferent politicians. As a result of the Sykes' enquiry, such a respite was guaranteed; and John Reith, making the very most of it, now had good reason to thank his stars for the docility of an audience which appeared to thrive on the spiritual and mental fare provided by the broadcasters. The government, and in particular Baldwin, looked on him with favour. He had undoubtedly arrived as the effective spokesman and recognisable trustee of an institution which was no longer a novelty and could stake its claim to being treated as a kind of fifth estate of the realm. But anyone who knew him as well as Carpendale and his closest aides at Savoy Hill must have realised why the same John Reith was still far from satisfied with this spectacularly rapid achievement.

If active hostility to the hybrid company he represented had practically died away, that in itself offered him no grounds for complacency. On the contrary, it caused him some anxiety. The business conduct of the BBC had been faultless, silencing those who had feared that a licensed monopoly, even one so limited as the BBC in its scope and profits, might be tempted to run amok. The once-suspect combine of radio manufacturers had disarmed reasoned criticism by putting broadcasting above its own acquisitive instincts, falling in behind Reith's idealistic prescription for survival and steady progress. The glory properly belonged to the board as much as to its dynamic managing director, but the latter did not greatly like this. For the real power was the board's too, and Reith genuinely felt that the actual development of broadcasting had already outstripped the control of a public monopoly in private hands.

The press and parliament, the two sounding boards of opinion, seemed to have developed much too soft a spot for the company and its good works. Their animus was reserved for the Post Office, a convenient whipping boy which could not cry out or answer back. John Reith, too, perversely shared something of this easy-going prejudice, yet his was leavened with experience. He had agreed wholeheartedly with the view expressed, for instance, by the *Daily Telegraph* on March 25th, 1925, that 'the attitude of the Post Office towards wireless in its imperial as well as its domestic aspects illustrates very effectively the dangers associated with the nationalisation of industry, and especially an industry of scientific character still in process of development'. The thought that the Post Office or any new State Board might eventually become the authority in permanent charge of broadcasting was anathema to Reith. In fact, there was little serious prospect of that. So heedless and quiescent had the public mood become that what Reith had more reason to fear was the confirmation of the company in its stewardship. It was still on the cards that this inadequate body, as he now judged it, might receive an extended lease of life from the Crawford committee; and that, excluding only a State-run broadcasting service, was about the last thing on earth Reith wanted.

As has already been demonstrated, the BBC board trusted him entirely to look after their interests while leaving him alone to expand and improve the service. A minority of the directors, notably Kellaway and Binyon, had recently become a little querulous if not openly suspicious about his aims and ulterior motives. The wonder is that the board as a whole continued to pay out more and more rope to a managing director who, whatever else he did, would certainly not hang himself. Asa Briggs has suggested in passing that under a tougher, more self-centred board, Reith might have fared less well and 'the story of broadcasting might have been very different'.[1] Undoubtedly the status of the company would have been far more secure in late 1925, its future less in jeopardy. For despite Reith's inspired self-confidence, and the cat-like agility he displayed in handling an extremely delicate situation without incurring the displeasure of the board, he did admit to Mitchell-Thomson many months after the decease of the old company: 'Perhaps I alone can realise how differently things might have been.'[2] The lonely visionary, steering an adroit course between the narrow concerns of the board and the unlimited ideas of the broadcasters, had convinced himself that their interests were no longer complementary but contradictory. He therefore, in a sense, was now prepared to turn King's evidence on a firm which had, in his view, outlived its usefulness and its rights to run the service.

If that verdict sounds callous and uncomplimentary, consider Reith's sharp reply to a letter he received from the Post Office on October 19th, 1925, shortly before the Crawford committee settled down to its hearings. W. E. Weston, the official who wrote the letter, assumed that the BBC as a company would wish to submit evidence on its own behalf. He suggested various subject headings, a reasonable procedure for a senior man who had recently been nominated as secretary of the forthcoming enquiry. Weston was naturally disconcerted when Reith wrote back to tell him that he had got hold of completely the wrong end of the stick. The company, he said, would not be offering any recommendations about a future constitution, 'believing in view of the manner in which public obligations have been discharged' that their interests would be respected. Reith proposed instead, Weston learned, to send a personal memorandum on 'the scope and conduct of the service'. In plain language, Reith had decided in advance that anything the board of the BBC might care to state about the future of radio in Britain would be inadmissible evidence.[3]

The board were shown Reith's personal memorandum at their November meeting, and several directors felt distinctly uneasy about its tone and contents. It left them wholly out of consideration. For its single aim was 'to show the desirability for the conduct of broadcasting as a public service, for the adoption and maintenance of definite policies and standards in all its activities, and for unity of control'. Reith boldly stated that the public had almost forgotten the circumstances in which the 'quasi-commercial constitution' of the company had been framed, adding that since, in practice, the BBC was run as a public service its existing status had become illogical and anomalous. What he had striven to express was 'submitted in the interests of broadcasting, not of the British Broadcasting Company'. As it was hardly Reith's business to draft an alternative constitution, he wisely resisted the temptation of provoking the board needlessly. All he did was to outline big pitfalls worth pointing out to Crawford and his colleagues who alone had the right to judge the standing of the company and how, if at all, this should be altered:

'Bureaucratic methods, liable under central control and in monopolies, should be avoided in the future as they have been in the past. . . . The service must, however, have a national conception before either a local or a personal one. Greater financial backing would be vital and the community should be encouraged to recognise the opportunities as well as the responsibilities of broadcasting which would establish itself in the end as part of the permanent and essential machinery of civilisation.'[3]

Reith had no doubts about himself or his commanding position. Such prestige as the BBC had incidentally gained was, as he saw it, largely the fruit of his own organising ability and missionary spirit. The board acknowledged the truth of this perhaps less fervently than he did, but even a qualified acknowledgment of his contribution to success strengthened his hand. If they had ever considered dispensing with his services, the chance had long passed them by; but there is no evidence that any such resolve existed now, except in the recesses of one or two directors' minds. The feeling that they had been outwitted certainly persisted, yet it remained a feeling of impotent frustration. It resulted in no biting and surprisingly little barking. Once Reith had taken a decision, he was impervious to criticism and transitory misunderstandings from any quarter: in the words of an old Arab proverb that enshrined his seer-like outlook, 'the dogs may bark but the caravan moves on'. The board did not attempt to resist him or to press their own views for submission to Crawford who could in any case call any of them before him to testify if he so desired.

When Reith gave evidence for the first time on December 3rd, 1925, the chairman listened carefully to his account of the policy which the company had consistently pursued. It was an imposing record of public service broadcasting; and the suspicion seemed to cross Crawford's mind that if a nominally private-enterprise concern could have achieved so much, why should its managing director be so anxious to chop and change. What sort of constitution, he asked, would Reith like to see in place of the existing one?

'I do not think it would be quite right for me', Reith answered, 'to give my opinion.'

'We will make up your mind for you', said Crawford.

'I do not imply that it is not already made up', was Reith's swift and revealing retort.[4]

What he would describe years later as 'the brute force of monopoly' was tacitly accepted without demur as the correct working basis for broadcasting in Britain. The progressive achievements of the BBC since 1922, in the teeth of great difficulties, were not in dispute. There could be no putting the clock back to the distracted period when commercial competition between rival broadcasting companies had still appeared a natural and feasible alternative. Under a Conservative government as supine as Baldwin's, the extreme solution of a system managed by the State was equally inconceivable. So Crawford's room for devising some novel form of authority somewhere between those two poles virtually marked itself out in advance. Reith's personal views were not for public show. Nevertheless, his mildly socialist sympathies, sharpened by a keen distaste for the unimaginative, impersonal and often wrong-headed methods employed by State-run bureaucracies like the Post Office, favoured a system of public control which would incorporate all the best features of private enterprise. He had proved by deeds that the messianic touch could be an effective substitute for the profit motive, so Crawford and his colleagues could hardly fail to propose the necessary new constitutional basis without untimely prompting from him.

Reith nursed no false illusions. He was well ahead of the game. His self-assurance rested on firm ground which, as usual, he had taken good care to reconnoitre unobserved. If the Postmaster-General could scarcely be called one of Reith's bosom friends, Mitchell-Thomson's deputy, Lord Wolmer, was on excellent terms with him; and Wolmer did not hesitate to pass on Reith's clear-cut views to the permanent officials in the department. Sir Evelyn Murray in particular was not unresponsive, respecting Reith for his common sense as well as his drive. The latter learnt with delight from Wolmer that the Post Office had sent written evidence to Crawford which thoroughly endorsed the personal belief, derived from his BBC experiences, in the merits of 'unified control'. Far more significantly, the Post Office's evidence proclaimed positively what Reith could not proclaim himself—that 'the best solution might be the setting up of a corporation with a widely representative governing body'. In fact Murray was the author of this key document; and, to quote Asa Briggs, 'it was Murray and not Reith who stated categorically that "the Corporation should enjoy a large measure of independence and should not be subject either in its general policy or its choice of programmes to the detailed control and supervision of the Postmaster-General, from which would follow the corollary that the Postmaster-General would not be expected to accept responsibility or to defend the proceedings of the Corporation to Parliament" '.[1] As the first witness to be called, Murray amplified his written statement; and the importance of this testimony can scarcely be overestimated. Had the Post Office decided to head off in a different direction, the course of the enquiry and its outcome might well have been more hazardous for

Reith's high hopes. Yet it must be said to his credit that, through Wolmer, he had shrewdly anticipated the danger. This was the explanation of the smooth, straight line followed from an assumption which went almost unquestioned to a conclusion which vindicated John Reith's long-held aspirations. No determined challenge came to the accepted proposition that what Britain wanted and needed for the future was a single, national broadcasting authority under public control. Only Reith could have sidetracked the Crawford enquiry; but as his one desire was to speed Crawford on his way, the result was never in doubt.

'I am quite sure', Reith wrote in a mood of somewhat perverse pride on February 4th, 1926, 'that if I had been categorically in favour of a continuation of the company, this would have been achieved.'[5]

Nobody on the board had the nerve or inclination to demand a hearing and state the company's case for carrying on as before. The dice, they felt, were loaded against them. They also happened to be busy men whose chief interests lay in manufacturing and selling radio equipment. A minority of them resented the lofty detachment of the managing director to whom they had confided the task of running in tandem the broadcasting service and their interlocking relationship with it. Two or three of them may have gone so far as to suspect that Reith was biting the hands that fed him without voicing that accusation, yet the board as a collective whole did not fail to realise that the initiative had irreversibly passed from them through to Reith and the Crawford committee. They could do nothing now but await its verdict, conscious already that the verdict would almost certainly go against them.

Besides, after Baldwin's brief and clumsy flirtation with the protection issue which had led to his rejection by the electorate in 1923, no Conservative leader or government could be any longer expected to bestow uncovenanted blessings on the radio manufacturing and retail industry. The legal honeymoon had lasted until the end of 1924. The BBC's strong plea in the November of that year for an extension of the ban on foreign-made radio sets and parts, supported though it was by the vast bulk of the trade, did not sway a new Tory administration which had learnt from the earliest of Baldwin's political blunders. When King George V had delivered his first broadcast at the opening of the Wembley Exhibition on April 23rd, 1924, an estimated audience of ten million people heard him speak. As listeners grew in numbers, the demand for sets, including the latest and more elaborate ones with valves, had more than kept pace with the supply. This, in addition to the fresh factor of imported sets, helped to pull down prices without unduly cutting back trade profits. Radio had since become a booming industry; and while it would be invidious to overlook the unquestionable altruism of the Big Six manufacturers, who still stood at the heart of the British Broadcasting Company, the economic reasons for their original protective monopoly had all but lost their validity. Reith knew this. Hence his eagerness to unloose the apron strings which still bound broadcasting like a child to the industry which had fostered it. Why should he, the real father, share the glory of this the most enlightened and powerful instrument of mass communications yet invented by man with a 'mere consortium of traders?'[2] If Crawford decided to set him free, Reith would seize the chance of freedom without a shred of false regret.

In his written memorandum, which had caused qualms to some of his directors, Reith declared that broadcasting 'rightly developed and controlled will become a world influence with immense potentialities for good—equally for harm, if its function is wrongly or loosely conceived.' And in a ringing reaffirmation of the faith which had animated his every move since Sir William Noble, nudged by Sir William Bull, had offered him the vacant general manager's job in the infant company at the end of 1922, he warned that 'he who prides himself on giving what he thinks the public wants is often creating a fictitious demand for lower standards which he will then satisfy'. A company which had shielded the broadcasters from the wind and rain for three gruelling years had earned the public's gratitude. Yet 'even those who are most definite in their appreciation of the company's attitude, recognise the desirability of its being a public service not only in deed but in constitution. . . .'[3]

On February 4th, 1926, Reith appeared again to give oral evidence. Captain Ian (later Lord) Fraser asked him pointedly:

'Might there not be a very definite advantage from the administrative point of view, and more especially from a research point of view, if you were a little freer of trade control?'

'I can answer the question to this extent', he replied, 'that I consider it certainly an entirely pertinent question. Perhaps I would rather say nothing further than that.'[4]

Embarrassing as Reith found his situation, the Crawford committee members had no need to press him. For the overwhelming bulk of evidence from outside groups, notably the various wireless associations, presented testimony in a fashion which he could not have improved on himself. The Wireless League, for instance, an organisation significantly founded by Beaverbrook's *Daily Express* a few months previously, opted for a broadcasting commission on the grounds that 'it is undesirable to continue a monopoly service in the hands of a company which is in the nature of a private enterprise. We are agreed that the service must be a monopoly, but monopolies in private hands are always an object of suspicion. . . .' The voice was indeed that of the Wireless League. The language and underlying philosophy were those of Lord Beaverbrook who since his first meeting with Reith in the spring of 1923, had directly and indirectly encouraged the unworldly general manager of the BBC to 'think more of your own future' and less of the company's.[2] The exclusive claims of the latter still conflicted violently with the Canadian press magnate's impenitently individualistic business outlook; and during a further encounter with Reith in March 1925, after the birth of the Wireless League, he stressed that 'he had made up his mind that there must be monopoly in broadcasting'.[1]

It was no part of Beaverbrook's philosophy to fight Reith's battles for him. Nevertheless, the spasmodic correspondence between the two, which went on until the middle of the 1960s, reveals the curiously ripening admiration in which one son of the manse held the other, regardless of a wide world of difference between the character and conduct of each.

Both the League and the quite separate and older Wireless Association urged a policy of catering for specialised listening tastes with which Reith, as it happened, privately disagreed. Alternative programmes on different wavelengths to enable 'the listener to tune in to highbrow music if he prefers it or a jazz band if he wishes' were the recipe they advocated. He did not fly in the face of providence by openly flouting it, admitting instead that the BBC did recognise the need and had 'long since prepared a comprehensive scheme involving the abolition of many lower-powered stations and their substitution by fewer stations of much higher power'. What these stations would put out was not for the Crawford committee or for witnesses to debate, in his judgment. Broadcasting, properly planned, would broaden its spectrum of programmes without yielding an inch to such popular and compartmentalised specialisation; that way, he knew, lay the gadarene slope of debased standards. It was his business, not theirs, to decide what radio would do; it was theirs, not his, to set radio free.

Reith played his cards admirably close to the chest. When the Wireless Association suggested that 'there is no doubt a considerable income could be obtained from some kind of advertising without lowering the tone of broadcasting', Reith once more hedged his answer intelligently in supplementary evidence. The main obstacle to advertising on radio, he said, was the intransigent hostility of the press. This was perfectly true. Still fearful that the circulation of their newspapers would decline if the original embargo on BBC advertising were raised, Lord Riddell and Sir James Owen among others embellished the argument from self-interest with a touch of moral rectitude that made Reith inwardly cringe:

'It would be intolerable', they argued, 'if the broadcasters were used to proclaim the merits of so and so's corsets, so and so's pills and so and so's sausages.' The pose of shocked propriety did not deceive Reith who scribbled the following marginal note at the time: 'Nonsense, their own interests affected only.'

He was similarly stung into jotting down his own white-hot reflections when the press representatives declared somewhat sanctimoniously that there were numerous topics, from racing and betting news to birth control, which would be 'highly objectionable to a large section of the community' and which must therefore be classified as intrinsically 'unsuitable' for the broadcasters to handle. Because of his Calvinist code, Reith did not quarrel with their objection to betting and racing; but at their simon-pure renouncing of any broadcast references to birth control he drew the line. Matters of controversy, he believed, were the very stuff of broadcasting, no matter how delicate or dangerous:

'Give both sides', was his brief, illuminating doodle.

Reith's mind was far from closed on the advertising issue. He had no rooted moral loathing of the practice, as is still commonly supposed. He was too good a businessman for that; but he prudently recognised that not even a Conservative government would ride roughshod over press sensibilities just to extol the virtue of a wholly free market in advertising. He would have welcomed the extra source of revenue, to be tapped judiciously, as a buffer against the grasping miserliness of the Post Office which invariably held back more licence revenue than it was strictly entitled to do. In the hard light of practical politics, however, he saw no hope of obtaining this crock of fairy gold. And if, miraculously, the press withdrew their opposition, his own rigorously selective enforcement of advertising standards could well become a disincentive to all but a few of the wealthiest firms:

'Only richer corporations', he said, 'would be able to take advantage of the facilities offered on account of the price required.'

The *Radio Times*, by now a flourishing periodical, was probably the biggest single impediment to any further advance by the BBC into a market-place which the press continued to regard as its exclusive property. The wireless press especially deplored the very existence of this awkwardly thriving offspring; and Lord Iliffe acridly stated that 'monopoly should not be used to enable such a body as the BBC to compete on privileged terms with the interests of any business community, and we base our belief on public policy and common justice'. Behind these periodicals specifically devoted to radio were large combines like Odhams, the Berry group and the Amalgamated Press. The sad picture of a shoal of minnows struggling gallantly for survival in an ocean dominated by a whale called the *Radio Times* struck Reith as rather ludicrous:

'While recognising the hitherto friendly attitude adopted by the wireless press', he retorted, 'and acknowledging the great assistance which it has in many directions rendered the broadcasting service, it must be remembered that the service itself is in large measure responsible for the success of this press.'[4]

Such sharp scoring of points off powerful spokesmen, who were determined not to give up an inch more ground than they had to, tended to jar a little on Crawford and his colleagues. Their wide terms of reference no doubt permitted them to arbitrate between the press and the BBC on disputed boundary issues, but common sense as well as the time factor urged caution. It was left to the protagonists, in their own good time, to settle the contentious details between themselves. But if the press had grievances, these were less serious or well founded than those put forward by representatives from the world of show business. When the BBC had been in process of formation, the newspaper owners had been consulted whereas the moguls of the entertainment business had not; and that oversight still rankled.

The West End theatre managers informed the committee that they had been denied from the outset the chance of seeking some measure of protection for their productions and artistes, and that only after lengthy wrangling had they secured 'limited and temporary' agreement with the BBC. 'Competitive broadcasting programmes', asserted Walter Payne, their spokesman, had helped to cut down theatre audiences, to cast a blight on shows before they reached the provinces, to offer no compensating return for the cheap use on the air of actors and actresses—since the advertising value of broadcasting to performers in radio plays was 'negligible'. Under questioning, Payne would not budge from his view that radio dramas were 'inferior representations' of productions in the living theatre: 'I cannot think it is satisfactory to hear a play without seeing the actors' make-up and their gestures and the scene to make up the performance.' His prejudices were not only artistic. By what reason should a licence costing a few shillings be treated as an 'entertainment dole for the entire population'?

The music publishers were full of dire complaints as well. Broadcasting, it was alleged, harmed the sale of music and therefore 'the earnings of composers and authors'. There were fewer concerts. Orchestras in hotels were being replaced by radio receivers, to the detriment of professional and amateur players. The sale of popular sheet music was suffering 'because a large number of people who listen to broadcasting absolutely neglect the piano to do so'. The Performing Rights Society bewailed the terms offered by the BBC to its members. At one point in this heavy barrage of unfriendly criticism, Captain Ian (later Lord) Fraser intervened. When William Boosey declared that gramophone records were selling badly owing to the competitive nature of broadcasting, Fraser expressed some doubt. Surely, he suggested, some records were being sold by the million now because of, not in spite of, their popularity through repetition on the air. In fact the majority of the gramophone companies at this time were co-operating amicably and profitably with the BBC.

'On all these matters', Asa Briggs has written, 'there was to be scope for further bargaining, much of it hard bargaining. There was also scope for more generous treatment of creative artists by the BBC.'[1]

Perhaps the most incisively perceptive critic of all was not a delegate expounding a case on behalf of one or other of the many vested interests called in evidence, but an individual with an eye for the structural weaknesses as well as the strengths of the Reithian foundation. Filson Young was a former editor of *The Saturday Review* who had become well known as a broadcasting critic and would later be appointed by Reith as a programme adviser. His praise for what the BBC had so far achieved in the broad content and standards of its programmes was warm. Yet he did not shrink from uttering a timely warning. Artistic policy was too precious a thing to be left to the policy-makers. This deserved to be controlled more by artists and less by boards and committees.

'It was a criticism', Asa Briggs has stressed, 'which was echoed later on by Eckersley, and it clearly contained a substantial amount of truth. The bigger the BBC grew, the greater this danger became.'[1]

2

The Crawford committee's report, which eventually appeared in March 1926, attracted disappointingly little attention. Its most important conclusion, accepted unanimously, was that a public service monopoly should replace the private company at the end of the year. Without question this represented a magnificent personal triumph for Reith, yet it could not have happened at a worse moment. Any tendency to celebrate the predestined culmination of his hopes and strivings would have been wildly premature in that month of all months, when Britain was brought face to face with her gravest industrial crisis of the century. For time had run out on the uneasy armistice in the coal industry; Baldwin hesitated fatally again; the coal-owners again prepared for a fight to the finish with the miners, and the public mind had little thought for anything else.

The temporary truce had been dearly bought by the Prime Minister because neither he nor Churchill at the Exchequer understood the underlying causes of the malaise which afflicted the whole economy. The unobtrusive, year-old decision, contrived like a magician's spell by Montagu Norman, the enigmatic Governor of the Bank of England, to restore Britain to the Gold Standard at its pre-war parity, lay at the root of the matter. 'I will make you the golden chancellor', Norman had told a puzzled Churchill, willing only to suspend disbelief. The deed had been done; but only experts like Keynes and McKenna saw through the City alchemist's illusory dream.

'On grounds of social justice', wrote Keynes, 'no case can be made out for reducing the wages of the miners. They are the victims of the economic juggernaut. They represent in the flesh the "fundamental adjustments" engineered by the Treasury and the Bank of England to satisfy the impatience of the City fathers to bridge the "moderate gap" between 4.40 dollars and 4.86 dollars.'[6]

Even before Sir Herbert Samuel had started to investigate conditions in the coal industry, a less weighty tribunal under Lord Macmillan had declared that the miners were entitled to a living wage, though it also indicated that the owners could not continue to pay it at the level fixed by MacDonald's Labour government; and Sir Josiah Stamp had attached a minority report, placing the onus for the deadlock squarely on the shoulders of Churchill and Norman. Now, at last, Samuel's more searching enquiry was complete. The results of the Royal Commission were published in the same month as the findings of Crawford's, thrusting into the shade the less urgent problems and progress of broadcasting. It was not a happy omen, and Reith felt uneasily that the worst had yet to come.

Samuel proposed that mining royalties should be nationalised, smaller pits merged, and better working conditions introduced. As an immediate, practical step, he recommended that miners' pay should be reduced when the subsidy of £10 million, conceded reluctantly by Baldwin nearly nine months previously, had drained away. The reply of the owners was emphatic. Refusing to consider any schemes for reorganisation, they demanded longer working hours as well as smaller pay packets. The miners, through their leaders, countered with the familiar battle-cry: 'Not a penny off the pay, not a minute on the day.' The deadlock persisted through April in an atmosphere of deepening crisis; and when the government subsidy ran out at the end of the month, the coal owners imposed a lock-out. The TUC unanimously called for a national strike on May 3rd, unless Baldwin would intervene again at the eleventh hour and promise to implement the Samuel report as a whole.

The irresolute Prime Minister did try. Talks with the general council began, but suspicions on both sides had gone too far. The futile attempts to restart negotiations broke down at the twelfth hour. Baldwin called them off on the pretext that compositors who refused to set a controversial leading article in the *Daily Mail*, condemning the unions, had been guilty of an 'overt act' of intimidation, though neither the TUC nor the printers' union officials condoned or were even aware of their action. In this ironically muddled fashion, the nation drifted into the General Strike of 1926 which, while not intended to be at once complete, swiftly became so.

Fleet Street had contributed to the troubles of the BBC even before its presses stopped turning. The morning after the unilateral action of the *Daily Mail* compositors had stung Baldwin into breaking off talks with the TUC, several newspapers reported that the government intended to take over broadcasting once the emergency began. This was promptly denied on the air, at Reith's insistence; yet the BBC's statement of the true position included a rather weak sentence explaining that the company could not escape its obligations under the terms of the licence to transmit all official notices and announcements as and when requested. The first of these, in fact, had been put out at ten minutes past midnight on May 3rd, following a hurried telephone call from the deputy chief civil commissioner, J. C. C. Davidson, to John Reith:

'Although discussions are still proceeding,' it ran, 'yet in view of the action of the TUC the country must be prepared for a general strike in many industries and public services.'

This was a plain warning to the people that Baldwin's patience as a peacemaker was temporarily exhausted, and that the nation's trial by ordeal could not be long deferred. At 11.15 pm on the night of May 3rd, the BBC announced:

'All negotiations have failed and the general strike is fixed for midnight.'[3]

The TUC and its members expected no quarter from John Reith. The general council had already blacklisted the BBC on May 1st, blatantly declaring that, as the government had commandeered the company anyway, no attention should be paid to broadcast announcements. It was not too auspicious a start for Reith or the BBC.

Transport and railway workers, together with those in heavy industry, building, gas, electricity and printing, obeyed the strike call in overwhelming numbers. Others were held back, as it were, in the second line until the government's counter-measures took effect. The BBC, willy-nilly, had therefore to move into the front line at once, since all national newspapers except *The Times* immediately ceased publication. Reith was mentally keyed-up for the trouble that followed; yet it is no exaggeration to say that its effect on him personally proved traumatic, just as its consequences for the unborn Corporation, as opposed to the superannuated British Broadcasting Company, were long-lasting and debilitating. If the General Strike of 1926 marked a turning point in Britain's industrial history, it was unquestionably a climacteric in the public career of Reith.

Largely through the efforts of key civil servants like Sir John Anderson, who had served successive administrations since 1918, the Baldwin government was ready for the emergency. Contingency plans were well laid. Anderson, the permanent under-secretary at the Home Office, had already 'had experience of civil war in Ireland and was to have more later in Bengal'.[7] A special transport system, originally devised under Lloyd George, was quickly brought up to date. The whole country was split into areas, each under a civil commissioner who could exercise all administrative and executive power, if necessary, without referring to the chief civil commissioner, his deputy, or the Cabinet strike committee in London. The development of road haulage traffic was an instant asset: it meant that food and other essential supplies could be rapidly carried from place to place, whereas not many years before a total stoppage on the railways had inevitably spelt paralysis for the normal life of the community. The printers' walk-out gave the Prime Minister one of his rare and unexpectedly ingenious ideas. As Baldwin is reputed to have told his biographer G. M. Young, 'the cleverest thing' he had ever done was 'to put Winston into a corner' and tell him to edit the *British Gazette*.

The production of this government newspaper kept the Chancellor at full stretch between No. 11 Downing Street, the offices of the *Morning Post*, his room in the Treasury, and the daily meetings of the Cabinet strike committee. Naturally bellicose and energetic, the Chancellor thus worked off some of his frustrated rage against Montagu Norman and the bad advice which, as he now he believed, this mandarin of high finance had wished on him, with such progressively dire results. Yet Churchill also saw the General Strike as a revolutionary move which had to be resolutely and forcibly defeated. The bogey of militant Communism continued to haunt him; and with the Home Secretary, Joynson-Hicks, he pressed his Cabinet colleagues to display more ardour in the supposed defence of the realm. 'Jix', as the Home Secretary was nicknamed, incurred the displeasure of Montagu Norman at one stage by insisting on 'issuing an order to embargo £100 million from Russia. TUC and Moscow Bank so advised'.[6] The Bank of England did not, of course, much care for subversive foreign aid of the kind. It cared still less, such was Norman's fine detachment, for government interference between bankers and clients. If 'Jix' brought an evangelical ardour to the task of rooting out Reds from under beds, he had lessons still to learn in that direction from Churchill.

It was fortunate indeed that Baldwin, who was not a member of the Cabinet strike committee, knew, liked and implicitly trusted John Reith. The latter's close relations also with J. C. C. (later Viscount) Davidson were equally helpful. Davidson, as deputy to the chief civil commissioner, who happened to be Mitchell-Thomson, the Postmaster-General, had specific overall responsibility for news, official information and all talks broadcast by the BBC. Reith, whose home at 6 Barton Street was a few steps away from Davidson's, had called on him during the week-end before the strike to discuss some explanatory notes he had drafted. These set down Reith's own ideas of what the BBC should be allowed to do in the emergency. The ideas seemed to the general manager sweet reasonableness itself; but Davidson, a deceptively gentle person of tensile strength, did not disguise his doubts as to their practicability. Consultation between the Government and the company, said Reith, was preferable to giving orders. Moreover, if the BBC got the name of being wholly 'partisan' and a mere tool of the State, the strikers could bring broadcasting to a standstill. If, on the other hand, the authorities acted wisely, the BBC could play a constructive role on the right occasion.

'In the end conciliation of some kind must supervene', the notes concluded, 'and the BBC could act as a link to draw together the contending parties by creating an atmosphere of goodwill towards its service on both sides.'[3]

Davidson did not, indeed could not, commit himself. He had been too long in the inner ring, where Prime Ministers either took decisions or had them forced on them, to offer any comforting promises. He admired Reith for his simple idealism, but did not envy him his total inexperience of political in-fighting at such a moment of deep trouble. He understood well enough the distinct polarisation of views within the Cabinet itself. The vigour of men like Birkenhead as well as 'Jix' and Churchill would more than balance the opinions of the more or less moderate majority. Baldwin, a leader who still longed to act as the great conciliator, would not find it easy to hold the ring if the strike lasted long or got out of hand.

In the small hours of May 4th, dance music from the London station, 2LO, was interrupted for a special announcement on all transmitters. Reith broadcast the news himself that the General Strike had begun. Characteristically, when Birkenhead had learnt of the 'overt act', in Baldwin's loose phrase, which precipitated the stoppage, the ex-Lord Chancellor remarked: 'Bloody good job.' With his cavalier wit and keen taste for adventure, Birkenhead, still at the India Office, relished the prospect of a showdown.

Reith set his own crisis plans into train without delay. The BBC had been declared an emergency service by the government, so that no member of the staff could volunteer for other duties. 'Two charabancs and two motor cars' were provided to bring to work forty-six men and women who lived too far away from Savoy Hill to walk, about a fifth of the total number of 247 who otherwise made their own way there. It had now become clear that broadcasting would be the main channel of communication between the government and the people: for the walk-out in Fleet Street had closed down the entire national press, save for *The Times*. Reith sought the co-operation of Riddell and others, then the news agencies agreed temporarily to lift their routine restrictions on the content and timing of BBC news bulletins. An emergency news staff was hastily assembled at Savoy Hill on May 4th and divided into three shifts, covering the entire day. The makeshift newsroom might well have infringed the provisions of the factory acts, being only 15 feet by 20 feet. It was linked to the outside world by five telephones. A pair of these were used to maintain constant touch with Davidson's headquarters at the Admiralty where two direct lines to Savoy Hill had meanwhile been installed. Reith's secretary and one man occupied a small office at the Admiralty to dictate down the line all announcements from the government. They were joined presently by the more experienced Gladstone Murray whose functions were to sift and pass on official information and, at his own suggestion which Reith endorsed, to compose so-called 'editorials', giving nightly appreciations of the strike situation.

At 10 am on May 4th, the first morning of the stoppage, the BBC went on the air with an apologetic preface to its first regular strike bulletin: 'The sudden change from the bulky newspaper to the short bulletin', said the announcer blandly, 'cannot be perfected in an instant. Moreover, the world has been asleep and not active for the last eight or ten hours and therefore there is bound to be comparatively little news . . . The BBC fully realises the gravity of its responsibility to all sections of the public, and will do its best to discharge it in the most impartial spirit that circumstances permit. . . .'[3]

Under the new arrangements, there were to be further bulletins daily at 1 pm, 4 pm, 7 pm and 9.30 pm. Not unnaturally, Reith judged the earliest samples to be 'pretty rotten', partly because the Admiralty information office lacked the necessary speed and efficiency. His wholly untrained news team at Savoy Hill would simply have to learn a new craft by trial and error; yet he drove the few people on whom he felt he could rely as mercilessly as he drove himself in order to eliminate error in advance, censoring most of the news bulletins himself from May 6th onwards. Improvement in the lumpy, indifferently sub-edited material they contained came somewhat slowly, not a few journalists who listened at home in enforced idleness, or at work in the provinces, comparing the result unfavourably with their own far more skilled handiwork.

'The early difficulties showed what a specialised faculty the "news sense" is', the *Manchester Guardian* commented on May 17th, when the emergency had ended, 'and how it could not be mobilised at a moment's notice.'

It was a fair if obvious point. Asa Briggs has since commented aptly:

'The writer did not add that the improvement between May 3rd and May 12th showed what could be done to develop that sense in a remarkably short space of time. The BBC had not been allowed to exercise it before May 4th because of restrictions imposed by the press.'[1]

To be wholly dispassionate, one should also stress that if Reith had been as keenly interested in purveying news as he demonstrably was in developing equally specialised areas of broadcasting, the BBC would have given a better account of itself, in the professional sense, all through the emergency. For as soon as Churchill launched his *British Gazette* on May 6th, the ministerial editor of this unadulterated propaganda sheet began to pick holes in BBC output and sought support for his resolute proposal to take it over. The Chancellor could see no reason why the resources of broadcasting should not be mobilised as another powerful weapon against the strikers. If this were a political and constitutional crisis of the first magnitude, as he regarded it, any strict interpretation of the company's licence would oblige a compliant Cabinet to do so. To that extent Reith was in an exceedingly more vulnerable position than Geoffrey Dawson, the editor of *The Times*, whose newspaper survived an abortive attempt by strikers to burn down the machine room on May 5th and stoutly resisted Churchill's subsequent efforts to curb, harass and even commandeer the paper. A note in Dawson's diary on May 9th said succinctly:

'. . . To Printing House Square for a hard afternoon of pushing and planning and talking and fighting for our paper and indeed for our existence against Winston's wild commandeering raids. . . .'[8]

Dawson was concerned less with the unlikely threat to the independence of his newspaper than with Churchill's avaricious appetite for its stocks of newsprint. On May 10th 'about a quarter of our available paper stocks' were seized on orders of the editor of the *British Gazette*, though this did not prevent the circulation of *The Times* from reaching a phenomenal peak of 400,000 before the printers resumed work. The BBC could not yet compare with this august journal either in prestige or in journalistic expertise. Reith had won for it a commanding place in the sun, which the recent Crawford committee upheld, but the government had still to accept Crawford's proposals for staking out the ground. It did not matter that the BBC was a private company. Any firm enjoying monopoly rights to broadcast could go on doing so during a national emergency only with the blessing of the Postmaster-General; and Mitchell-Thomson, though he lacked the fiery aggressiveness of Churchill, was the chief civil commissioner and inclined to take Churchill's side.

One can only marvel at the strange combination of luck and foresight which had induced Baldwin to appoint as Mitchell-Thomson's deputy a man as sympathetic to Reith as J. C. C. Davidson, whose appointment made him the direct link between the government and the BBC throughout the strike. Reith did not agree with Davidson's laudatory remarks about the first issue of the *British Gazette*, telling him bluntly that 'I did not think much of it'. He was also taken aback by Davidson's initial air of uncertainty about 'what he wants me to do'. Dissatisfied as he was with his own newsroom's early labours, Reith still considered it worthwhile trying to persuade the deputy chief civil commissioner that, even while the BBC was 'for the Government in the crisis', it should 'be allowed to define its position to the country'.[1] Davidson preferred to let well alone, deciding that this walking paragon of independence should cross his own tightrope unassisted. In fact, the BBC managing director would, in all probability, have been unceremoniously dislodged from his precarious foothold by the militant members of the Cabinet if Davidson had been rash enough to let him state outright where the company stood. Reith was at pains to preserve as much independence for the BBC as he could, and Baldwin offered him benevolent moral backing at least.

After a meeting with the Prime Minister early on May 6th, Reith left No. 10 Downing Street convinced that Baldwin 'entirely agreed with me that it was far better to leave the BBC with a considerable measure of autonomy and independence'.

The trouble was that Churchill had already underlined his own opposing attitude in typically forthright terms:

'At the beginning of the strike', Asa Briggs has written, 'the editor of the *Gazette* tried to treat the BBC as an "offshoot". "I told him", Reith wrote in his diary, "that I was not going to have that at all." '[5]

The Cabinet strike committee was fortunately divided on a question which Churchill had taken for granted from the start. When Reith went from his private talk with Baldwin to attend his first meeting of this high-powered committee later on May 6th, Joynson-Hicks, the Home Secretary and the chairman, invited him to speak. Reith said briefly that the Prime Minister's wish, as he understood it, was that the BBC should remain above the battle. Churchill 'emphatically objected and said it was monstrous not to use such an instrument to the best possible advantage'. There was a deathly pause. Reith more than half expected 'Jix', the loquacious ex-Postmaster-General of whom a critical contemporary onlooker said that 'the soil of his mind is meagre and his tongue outruns his judgment', to echo Churchill's uncompromising lead. To his astonishment, 'Jix' did nothing of the kind. Perhaps influenced by Reith's unexpected reference to the opinion of Baldwin, the Home Secretary merely said that since the question stirred strong feelings, it should be discussed by the full Cabinet later. There, for the moment, the decisive issue rested.

During the next seven days, Reith kept an unsleeping vigil over the shaping and presentation of the news. If Churchill had got his way, and the BBC had been requisitioned as an auxiliary propaganda machine at once, the managing director's day-to-day task would have been obviously lightened; but the bitter recognition of personal failure would also have been inescapable, and he might well have resigned. At any rate, a short reprieve was still his to earn the right of a nominal independence by staying out of avoidable trouble. It was a tense and depressing week that followed. The BBC survived on sufferance rather than on the collective goodwill of the Cabinet; and Reith's room for free movement became so restricted that his passionate nature chafed at the tightening bonds. What bruised and hurt his spirit most, perhaps, was the suspension of official trust in the ability of his child to remain impartial. It was an affront to the accepted standards he had laid down. It gave deep offence to his touchy pride.

'Directly the news began', Beatrice Webb noted in her diary, 'it was clear that the BBC had been commandeered by the Government and that the main purpose was to recruit blacklegs for the closed services. Granted that the evidently harassed announcer (we could hear the agonised whispers!) did his level best to seem detached and disinterested. They treated the general council of the TUC as if they were of almost equal importance to the Cabinet and they gave out their communique exactly as they gave out the messages from Downing Street. There was not a word of condemnation in BBC announcements, not even the citation of condemnatory announcements from the foreign press. Also there was a clear distinction made between business announcements from the civil commissioners, and their own news, through press agencies. "We can't help being used by the Government—it is right we should be so used with the newspapers shut down; but when we are on our own we stand above the battle and view the strike as we should a cricket match", was their tone.'[9]

The TUC, as we have seen, had warned its members from the start against believing anything they heard on the BBC because radio would be just another tool in the hands of the government. For its part, the BBC had warned the public that there might be attempts by strikers to jam reception. In fact, as the emergency wore on, the public as a whole, including strikers, listened as never before to the broadcast bulletins. Pejorative slogans like 'The British Falsehood Company' were brickbats in the war of words and nerves, not always or necessarily expressions of honest individual opinion. At Savoy Hill and the regional stations messages of praise and condemnation came in a steady stream. The disembodied voices of the announcers, speaking as prescribed by Reith many months before, on the best advice obtainable, in impeccably formal, well-educated southern accents, were heard all over the land. To what degree the voices themselves, which had been carefully tutored to 'build up in the public mind a sense of the BBC's collective personality',[1] detracted in working-class ears from the reliability of the news will always be a matter for conjecture. Richard Hoggart has offered this searching analysis of the working man's attitude in general:

'When the voices, especially those of the press, really have something important to speak to him about, he gives them the old smile and continues to read the funny bits. They have cried "wolf" too often. The BBC news service is trusted, with the qualifying suspicion that it is the voice of officialdom, and the qualifying conviction that it is dull anyway.'[10]

Hoggart was not talking specifically of the General Strike. For, like myself at the time, he had not yet attained the age of reason.

But with no national newspapers except the *British Worker*, an emasculated *Times*, very unevenly distributed, and the heavily slanted *Gazette* to distract them, the strikers in their millions must have been hard put to it not to disbelieve the BBC, though most of them went on listening. Reith's constant scrutiny of material, his instructions to station directors 'not to exclude items from TUC sources provided they are objective and you are convinced of their truth',[3] and his insistence on a balanced selection of parliamentary speeches, stood out for a week as a brave and honourable attempt at impartiality. Only when Mr. Justice Astbury pronounced his verdict in the High Court on May 11th that 'the so-called General Strike by the TUC is illegal', corroborating Reith's own instinctive feeling that the whole affair was an anarchic irrelevance, did the BBC's managing director grow a little easier in his mind. That judicial decision helped to clarify essentials for him; and the BBC's official attitude to the strikers hardened. 'We were unable', as he reminded his senior staff afterwards, 'to permit anything which was contrary to the spirit of that judgment, and which might have prolonged or sought to justify the strike.'[3]

Much news had to be excluded, on occasion items actually broadcast turned out later to be incorrect or misleading. Accounts of engine drivers and firemen resuming work at Oxford, of the unloading of food ships off Grimsby, of the breakdown of the stoppage at Salisbury—broadcast on May 7th—all proved unfounded. The rule that inaccuracies should not be admitted or corrected on the air was firmly enforced, however, at every stage. Inevitably, Reith's relations with Ramsay MacDonald, Thomas, Snowden and other Labour politicians became increasingly frayed and edgy. Their own situation, as political leaders left far behind by the mass of their supporters in the country, was worse than his. Another note in Beatrice Webb's diary paints a sombre picture of 'Henderson as angry with the miners, of J.R.M. (MacDonald) and J.H.T. (Thomas) as depressed at their powerlessness to bring about a settlement. Philip Snowden, being dead against the trade unions, is philosophical. The inner circle hates the General Strike and sees no good coming out of it.'[9]

Pressure was directly brought to bear on Reith by several prominent Labour men, including MacDonald, Trevelyan, and William Graham who had recently served on the Crawford committee, to enable 'one of their people' to broadcast. Davidson would not hear of it. The pressure increased after permission to speak on the air was granted to the Liberal elder statesman, Earl Grey of Falloden, on May 9th. Instead of delivering the expected homily on the uselessness of industrial strife, Grey threw caution to the winds and attacked trade union irresponsibility with unaccustomed verve. The Labour Party reacted strongly. A formal request was submitted on MacDonald's behalf, stressing the right of the Opposition leader to state his case. Reith sympathised but could promise nothing. He tried to soothe MacDonald on the telephone, admitted that he was not 'entirely a free agent', but undertook to do what he could. The Labour leader said that he would prepare a talk. The manuscript was delivered that evening to Reith's home; he looked at it approvingly and sent it at once to Davidson with a covering note, strongly recommending that the Prime Minister be asked to authorise the proposed broadcast by Ramsay MacDonald. Permission was again refused, and Reith lamented to his diary:

'I do not think they treat me altogether fairly. They will not say we are to a certain extent controlled and they make me take the onus of turning people down'.[5]

Churchill, he suspected, was the prime mover behind all this hideous and humiliating uncertainty. Reith had got embroiled in fairly heated exchanges with the Chancellor and Mrs. Churchill that very morning at No. 11 Downing Street when he went to collect Grey by car and take him on for the broadcast whose acrimony had so antagonised MacDonald. Churchill at first failed to recognise the BBC's managing director, despite the somewhat impersonal encounter on May 6th at the Cabinet's strike committee. Inviting him inside to join the others for coffee, he casually enquired, as though addressing a stranger, whether Reith was connected in any way with the BBC and if so what he did there. 'Yes', said Reith, 'until the strike I ran the place.' Belated recognition suddenly glittered in the Chancellor's eyes:

'Are you Mr. Reith?' he demanded with mock incredulity. 'I am', said Reith. 'Perhaps I had not come up, or rather down, to his expectations', the unexpected visitor commented at a later date. 'He said he was greatly interested to meet me; had been trying to do so all week. I replied that I had been on the job every day and most of the night, and would have been very glad to meet him. As an instance of his indignation he cited an item in the news the day before about Lord Knutsford having arranged with a TUC official to have power maintained at the London Hospital. From this a general argument developed, Mrs. Churchill supporting him, Lord Grey supporting me. He was polite to me. I wished we had had a proper set-to at the beginning of the strike. He came to the car with us, said he was very glad to have met me. He had heard I had been badly wounded in the war. "In the head, wasn't it?" I said yes, but that my present attitude wasn't traceable thereto.'[11] The riposte seemed to catch Churchill bending. Reith could only hope that this flamboyant, intolerant minister felt as non-plussed as he suddenly looked.

He would have liked to continue the argument, mainly to clear the air. For much as Reith resented his powerful adversary's partisan views, some faint understanding might have come if these had been countered by his own dogmatic logic. The chance slipped away, and Churchill was left with an unflattering private impression of the so-called 'strong man' who ruled at Savoy Hill. The impression developed with time into a dismissive contempt for Reith, the master-mind responsible for all the 'anonymous and pontifical mugwumpery' of the BBC.[12] Indeed, we can trace back safely to their original, brief encounter on May 9th, 1926, those warped and twisted sentiments of distant respect and extreme aversion which characterised relations between the pair to the very end. The long-term consequences of misunderstanding were grave and melancholy for Reith personally; as for the BBC, it was bound to suffer also, if vicariously, through him.

By the night of May 9th, less than a week after the outbreak of the General Strike, Reith's spirits had sunk to their lowest ebb. His hopelessness was sedulously masked from his colleagues; yet, in his heart, he knew that any influence and power the BBC might have possessed as an intermediary had shrunk to pathetic proportions in the course of the past twenty-four hours. His own standing had also been cast into doubt. If not disrepute. Only the day before, on May 8th, he had been obliged to write a letter to Dr. Randall Davidson, the Archbishop of Canterbury, explaining in diplomatic terms why the BBC could not risk letting the Primate broadcast an appeal to the nation 'after full conference with leaders of the Christian Churches', for a cessation of the stoppage and the immediate resumption of talks between the government and the unions:

'Although it might appear that we were neglecting to do right in this respect,' wrote Reith, 'I am sure you will see that it would be unfortunate to do right if it led to what we consider a wrong being imposed on us . . .

'We are in a position of considerable delicacy at the moment', he declared. 'We have not been commandeered, but there have been strong representations to the effect that this should be done. . . . It would therefore be inadvisable for us to do anything that was particularly embarrassing to the government, by reason of the fact that it might lead to the other decision that we are hoping to obviate.'

Off his own bat, the Primate had already been in direct touch with Baldwin who, with courteous finesse, informed his caller that, while he would not prevent the broadcast, he would prefer that there should be none. If the Archbishop sounded keen, the Prime Minister was evasively cool:

'A nice position for me to be in', expostulated Reith afterwards, 'between Premier and Primate. Bound mightily to vex one or other, at thirty-six years of age.'[11]

'You will see how serious a matter this is', Davidson wrote in answer to Reith's letter. 'Are we to understand that if the churches desire to put something forth, their grave utterance must be subject to the approval of its wording by the broadcasting committee, and that without such approval we are confined, as we were yesterday, to utilising the scraps of publicity available by means of the few newspapers which have their limited circulation? . . .'[13]

Only when Lloyd George asked in the Commons on May 10th why the Archbishop's appeal had been refused time on the BBC and space in the *British Gazette* was any official reason offered. It was Churchill, much less forceful than usual, who replied:

'I cannot answer any question about broadcasting for which I have not even a general responsibility. . . . As far as the government newspaper is concerned, it is used to give the country information as to what is proceeding in all parts of the country and also to sustain the nation in the difficult period through which we are passing.'

This rather lame answer contained hidden depths: Baldwin had meanwhile had second thoughts. The ban on the Archbishop's broadcast was lifted. Millions heard it at last on May 11th. By skilful evasion of any premature confrontation with diehards belonging to the Churchill faction, Baldwin let time and the tide of influential opinion take their natural course before deciding on which side of the fence to come down. The Prime Minister might have been happier sniffing papers rather than reading them, might even have presented to hard-pressed, impatient men like Reith an image of inperturbable capacity for drift that made the blood turn cold with impotent despair: nobody, however, unless perhaps Lloyd George at his peak, had a sharper ear for the subtler shifts and changes in public feeling. Baldwin's apparent supineness belied the skill of a manager quietly aware that it was better to move late than never, best of all to move with slow but deliberate sureness. It was also on May 11th, the day before the strike petered out, that the full Cabinet at length discussed what should be done about the BBC. They decided collectively against a complete take-over. The decision left Reith in a state of continuing uncertainty. He appeared ungrateful for the incidental knowledge that the Prime Minister, moving at his own pace, had at any rate effectively spiked the destructive guns of Churchill:

'A negative decision', was Reith's sour comment. 'Things to go on as they were. The BBC neither commandeered nor given full liberty. Not quite fair.'[5]

He had fondly hoped for more than this from Baldwin whose political tactics genuinely puzzled and disappointed him. Given the warm geniality of the person, such a compromise seemed to reflect on Baldwin's lack of guile. The Prime Minister, exercising his own prerogative, had broadcast a short message to the nation on May 8th from the study of Reith's home in Barton Street. For once, the managing director of the BBC was able to inject a few drops of his own thwarted inventiveness into the peroration, Baldwin gladly assenting to the addition of these words:

'I am a man of peace. I am longing and working and praying for peace, but I will not surrender the safety and the security of the British Constitution.'[3]

Reith, in this writer's considered judgment, was drawing the long bow of the romantic in stating that 'it would have been better for me, worse for the BBC and the country' if the company had been commandeered. Missionaries as inflexibly monolithic in their outlook as he happened to be, seldom resign without suffering lasting remorse at the betrayal of their trust. If it is impossible to suppose that Reith could have served for any length of time under Churchill, running a *British Gazette* of the air, it is equally inconceivable that the BBC could have survived intact without him, either as a company or as a corporation. It was not in his character to settle for half-measures. He put up with as good a grace as possible with the shadowy condition of semi-independence only because the circumstances were exceptional. Yet to pretend, as many admirers and acolytes still try to do, that the experience left him psychologically unscarred, and the BBC politically unscathed once it won the status of an independent public corporation at the end of 1926, is to both misunderstand the messianic character of John Reith and to oversimplify the nature of British politics.

The harsher lessons of the General Strike were bound to affect the BBC's relations with the political parties for the next half-century. More immediately, the dejected man of destiny, who had undoubtedly expected too much for and from his child as they stumbled together up this last, precipitous slope leading to the peak of his ambition, would never be quite the same again. The General Strike cost Reith his innocence. Henceforth he became less unworldly. His eyes moved towards the establishment, on the sound principle that what a man could not defeat he must join, if only to safeguard the creature he had fostered and reared and moulded in his own image.

Napoleon, looking down from a hill above a Paris handed over to the enemy against his orders, is said to have remarked:

'Where I am not, nothing but folly is committed'.

That thought, laced with an 'exaggerated sense of personal loyalty' which, in Reith's own admission, 'was often to give trouble in future', imbued him on the last day of the General Strike. He had actually prepared a defiant statement on the BBC's position to broadcast himself after the 1 pm news bulletin on May 12th, when Stuart Hibberd tiptoed into the studio with a piece of tape from the nearby teleprinter. Reith glanced at it, motioned to Hibberd for a pencil, and scribbled in his neat handwriting on the paper:

'Get this confirmed from No. 10 Downing Street.'

Ten minutes later Hibberd returned with the necessary confirmation, and Reith announced to the nation:

'At a meeting with the Prime Minister at No. 10 Downing Street, Mr. Pugh announced on behalf of the General Council of the TUC that the General Strike is terminating today'.[3]

So ended the nine days of confusion that shook the small world of John Reith to its foundations. The rudimentary, sometimes clumsy, news service of the BBC had 'broken' the beginning and the end of this tangled and sorry story. It had failed 'to depict the realities of working-class life, the sense of solidarity, struggle and occasional triumph which the strikers felt', to quote Asa Briggs again. Was this really surprising? Hardly. For, to quote the same dispassionate source, there was no doubt that 'the straight facts of working-class life were not well known to most members of the BBC'.[1] Despite a residual bitterness and mistrust affecting a large section of its vast audience, the BBC had nonetheless striven, within its own limits as opposed to those externally imposed on it, to maintain its reputation for truth and impartiality. In the seclusion of her country home at Passfield Corner, Beatrice Webb had proved more accurate in her appraisal of how the crisis would end than many of those closer to the centre of events:

'The net impression left on my mind is that the General Strike will turn out not to be a revolution of any sort but a batch of compulsory bank holidays without any opportunities for recreation and a lot of dreary walking to and fro. When the three million strikers have spent their money they will drift back to work and no one will be any the better and many will be a great deal poorer and everybody will be cross.'[9]

On the evening of May 12th animosities were buried momentarily as Reith went to the microphone again and announced that Stanley Baldwin was beside him with 'a special message' for the British people. It was an appeal to forget and forgive, to look forward instead of back, to close the ranks and unite and build the nation up in a new spirit of harmony. When the Prime Minister finished speaking, Reith paused and intoned in his high, clear burring voice the words of Blake's 'Jerusalem', which were then picked up by massed choir and orchestra in a great crescendo of sound. Such displays of ritual he found irresistible in times of stress. Nor did they ever fail to move him beyond the edge of tears.

3

The post-mortem on the BBC's conduct raged on until the summer. The Labour leaders were particularly critical of Reith's alleged one-sidedness: this once impregnable pillar of impartiality, whom Churchill had castigated for being unable to distinguish 'between the fire and the fire-engine', was upbraided by Ramsay MacDonald for manifestly failing to cater for the opposition. Nor would MacDonald accept the excuse of the Astbury judgment:

'Astbury gave no judgment whatever on the strike', he wrote to Reith on May 17th. 'He referred to it in a most improper way from the bench one day when dealing with a case arising out of trade union law. That, however, I only refer to because you say it influenced your action. I am afraid I am still of the opinion that it (the BBC) was biassed and was an agent in misleading the public. . . . We have become so accustomed to unfair play in publicity that we are beginning to take it as an ordinary experience, but I regret that this new form of publicity seems to have already yielded to tendentious propaganda. . . .'[14]

What chiefly distressed MacDonald was the reluctance of John Reith to defy Davidson, Baldwin and everyone else on behalf of the Labour leader and his natural right, as he conceived it, to broadcast during the strike. William Graham, no admirer of a fellow-Scot who had apparently wanted only to keep in the good books of the government, provoked Reith into retorting:

'If you accuse me of duplicity, the experience has at any rate the merit of novelty.'

He could afford to ignore 'the pain and indignation' of lesser lights like Ellen Wilkinson who said that 'during the strike I travelled by car over 2000 miles and addressed very many meetings. Everywhere the complaints were bitter that a national service subscribed to by every class should have given only one side. . . . Personally I feel like asking for my licence fee back, as I can hear enough fairy-tales in the

House of Commons without paying ten shillings a year to hear more.'

There was, nevertheless, some substance in Reith's boast that the BBC had conceivably contributed to shortening the strike by staying on the air even in a posture of semi-independence. The scholarly Gilbert Murray went even further:

'As soon as I heard of the suppression of the newspapers', he wrote, 'the thing that I feared most was the lying rumour. . . . I certainly heard the beginning of rumours which, if they had once got going, would have done infinite harm and made reconciliation almost impossible. But they never did really get going, at least not among the nation as a whole, and I think that was chiefly due to the BBC. Of course the BBC gave the official messages, marking them as official; and we suspected that other messages had been scrutinised by someone. But, allowing for all that, the BBC has already built up a tradition and a habit of impartiality which in this crisis enabled its listeners to feel that they were listening to friends who had never deceived them before and could be trusted now. . . .'[15]

The licking of wounds continued unobtrusively at Savoy Hill. Utterly fair and straight with his own senior staff, not one of whom could have emulated Reith's singleness of purpose in shrugging off adversity, he told them that 'it was impossible to give the lead which we should have liked, but it is a satisfaction to find an almost universal appreciation and recognition of the services rendered, and it may be only ourselves who feel that we might have done more with a freer hand. The only definite complaint may be that we had no speaker from the Labour side. We asked to be allowed to do so, but the decision was that since the strike had been declared illegal this could not be allowed.' Elsewhere in this 'highly confidential document', the BBC's managing director spoke in praise of the Prime Minister and, more puzzlingly, of the Home Secretary who 'in particular approved of our being left with a considerable measure of independence'.[3]

If the strike had dragged on, the line-up of forces inside the Cabinet would undoubtedly have altered, and Baldwin's belated decision to let the BBC continue serving the community on probation, and under close surveillance, might have been reviewed. Joynson-Hicks, in that event, could hardly have been counted on to resist Churchill's buccaneering persuasiveness, addicted as 'Jix' was himself to harrying the enemies of society who seemed to lurk everywhere. Mitchell-Thomson, the Postmaster-General, would undoubtedly have joined them for different reasons. Having been sidetracked by Baldwin during the emergency into the more responsible position of chief civil commissioner, with his deputy J. C. C. Davidson in charge of information and broadcasting, he had been deprived of the privilege and pleasure of lording it over Reith whom by now he cordially disliked. Quite apart from accepting necessary reasons of state, the opportunity thereby afforded of teaching the arrogant managing director of the BBC a long-overdue lesson in humility would have appealed to him.

Mitchell-Thomson's unfavourable opinion of Reith was fully reciprocated. In March and April, while the storm clouds were thickening and approaching, there had been several minor clashes between the two men over money. The Scrooge-like propensities of the Post Office had never attracted Reith; and, in spite of his current cuckoo-in-the-nest behaviour, this went also for the BBC board. Lord Gainford and his fellow-directors, loyal and altruistic to the last, still backed Reith consistently even after Crawford proposed the equivalent of a suspended death sentence on the old company. The publication of the Crawford report was overshadowed, as has been shown, by the worsening deadlock in the coal industry; the press, for a while, forgot the BBC; and yet by far the most searching analysis of relations between the government and the corporation, especially on the financial side, had appeared in *The Economist* on March 13th, 1926.

Recalling how and why the original combine of manufacturing interests had been prevented from making unlimited profits out of its monopoly holding, the periodical stated that the Corporation from the outset must receive from the State all the cash it needed for development. Surpluses should go to the Treasury only after such needs were met, and the broadcasting authority ought not to fear 'the raids of even the most predatory Chancellor of the Exchequer'. If the bulk of MPs before the General Strike had displayed relatively small interest in the BBC and how it conducted its affairs—the sentiments varying from sweeping demands for lower licence fees because of the 'innocuous inanities suitable only for invalids and imbeciles' that were broadcast to shrewder attacks on the Post Office for retaining a 'preposterous' quarter of each existing fee in the name of so-called administrative expenditure—the unprecedented impact of BBC programmes on the nation when most printing presses were silent had since swept away the apathy of Westminster.

Not that this helped Reith much during the strike aftermath. The Post Office, he knew, was going through the Crawford report with a fine tooth-comb; and Mitchell-Thomson meanwhile used all his authority as chief civil commissioner to cut short editorializing on the air. The miners had refused to accept surrender. They were stubbornly ignoring all overtures to woo them back to work. Only hunger forced them to give up the unequal struggle after seven bleak months. Gladstone-Murray, who had enjoyed writing and broadcasting his daily sermons on the general situation, continued to do so after May 12th. More than once he trod over ground judged by the Post Office to be dangerously controversial. On May 24th, for example, speeches by miners' leaders were analysed by Gladstone Murray in such a way as to suggest that they might be edging towards a settlement.

Mitchell-Thomson reacted at once. He protested indignantly to Reith against the policy of allowing opinions to be expressed on behalf of the BBC. Next day he promised the House of Commons that the reviews would be suppressed if they became too polemical: from then on, as a matter of routine, either Davidson or the chief civil commissioner would insist on passing them first. The press was naturally happy when this hangover from the nine critical days without national papers ended on Reith's instructions. So were many MPs, though Reith adopted a carefully defensive pose. Aware that Gladstone-Murray had been reflecting the unofficial views of Davidson in emphasising the desirability of reconciliation and co-operation, he was equally aware that other members of the government still persisted in advocating a harder line. Mitchell-Thomson was among them:

'The recent emergency proved conclusively, if proof were required, how important a factor broadcasting can be in the life of the community,' Reith wrote to a senior official at the Post Office on May 27th, 'and we have, as you know, long felt that it is much to be regretted that the influence of the service should be so restricted.'[3]

His plea for further broadcast reviews and talks on industrial relations fell upon stony ground. Mitchell-Thomson had clearly had enough, and would not relent:

'The Postmaster-General considers it right that the existing policy of avoiding the broadcasting of controversial matter should be maintained during the remaining period of the company's licence', was the unhelpful reply from the Post Office.

As a straw in the wind, this could not have been more disquieting to Reith at a time when Mitchell-Thomson was considering the permanent future of a new BBC. The premonition proved to be only too well founded: the question of broadcasting controversial issues remained as big a bone of contention between himself and the Post Office as that of finance for ten years to come. The tendency to blame Mitchell-Thomson and his officials for niggardly intransigence runs thread-like through Reith's utterances then and later; and the historian of the BBC has accepted a version of events which may fail to account for the overriding influence of the Treasury, and of the penny-wise Churchill in particular, especially during this period of increasing economic stringency.[1] If the Chancellor had been more kindly disposed to the BBC, as Baldwin had briefly been in that office, there would probably have been less reason to complain of the Postmaster-General's supposed iniquities. Since the return to gold, the staple industries on which Britain's prosperity had once depended continued their steady decline. Well over a million people were now unemployed. The Bank of England was intervening experimentally to 'rationalise' the cotton trade in Lancashire, to amalgamate the sprawling interests of Armstrong with those of Vickers, as well as to streamline a group of iron and steel concerns that were considered worth salvaging. Wages outside the lifeless coalfields remained relatively stable, but prices were rising higher than Churchill liked. And credit, controlled by the enigmatic Montagu Norman whom the Chancellor had begun to treat with venomous contempt, became systematically tighter.[6] Any money that could be saved by trimming expenditure in government departments Churchill quite naturally held back. The plight of the Exchequer had much more bearing on Reith's financial problems than the traditional parsimony of the Post Office.

When Mitchell-Thomson announced the government's acceptance of the Crawford report in July 1926 Reith did not exactly throw his hat in the air. It was one thing to accept the main proposals in principle, quite another to honour that principle in practice: 'By the time the Civil Service has finished drafting a document to give effect to a principle', he wrote, 'there may be little of the principle left.'[11] Priding himself on knowing better than any Postmaster-General what the real monetary needs of the BBC were, he drafted a paper and circulated it to all members of Parliament, greatly to Mitchell-Thomson's annoyance.

'The BBC feels that the service cannot stand still', the paper began. 'If it does not go forward, it must decline. The saturation point of productive and efficient expenditure on broadcasting is not yet within sight. Moreover, if it is desirable to make broadcasting a permanently supplementary source of public revenue, much more satisfactory results may reasonably be anticipated if the service is more fully developed, particularly in research, equipment and improved quality and variety of programmes, before its resources are curtailed.'[3]

Several MPs were impressed by this cogent reasoning. The Post Office was less impressed; and Mitchell-Thomson seemed to take particular exception to Reith's publicity tactics. Quite unmoved by his requests for assurances that more money would be forthcoming, the minister advised him against trying to whip up outside support. Such campaigning would not help the BBC.

A placatory letter from Reith on July 19th hints at the keen resentment felt by Mitchell-Thomson:

'We have all along, as I think you will agree, acted loyally by the Post Office and have never sought to defend ourselves at their expense. I hope you have not felt in our recent discussions that I was in any way obstructive. I am motivated solely by a genuine desire to see the service under the new constitution maintain the same rate of progress that we have maintained, and by a real alarm that the present proposed provisions are absolutely inadequate to take care of its normal developments, still less of the new ones which must come.'

But the Postmaster-General would not be cajoled or pushed into explaining or excusing his tight-fistedness. Hard bargainers like Reith, who tried to wear down opposition by sheer, indefatigable persistence, were not to be encouraged. So Mitchell-Thomson kept him waiting on tenterhooks until October 28th when, at a stormy meeting which lasted for several hours, the minister put forward fresh proposals for financing the future corporation. The essence of the scheme was a guaranteed share of gross licence revenue on a sliding scale, after subtracting 12½ per cent to cover Post Office expenses. On the first million licences the BBC would get 90 per cent, on the second million 80 per cent, on the third 70 per cent, and on the fourth and subsequent millions 60 per cent of the annual total. The Corporation could also borrow up to £500,000, on condition that suitable provisions were made for depreciation and a sinking fund. 'Still inadequate', was Reith's verdict. 'The treatment of finance is abominable'.[5] As these proposals would be incorporated in the draft charter if Mitchell-Thomson had his way, Reith told the minister to his face that they were quite unacceptable.

By this time the names of the first governors-designate of the BBC had been announced: Sir John Gordon Nairne, formerly of the Bank of England, Dr. Montagu Rendall, an ex-headmaster of Winchester, Mrs. Philip Snowden, the wife of the Labour ex-Chancellor, with Lord Gainford the sole survivor of the old board, as vice-chairman. Reith would have been happier if Gainford, whom he admired, had been allowed to carry on as chairman instead of having to make way for Lord Clarendon, then the parliamentary under-secretary at the Dominions office. Gainford and Reith had struck up an excellent working relationship; and through all the internal embarrassments of recent months, when some of the directors had suspected Reith of being a turncoat, that relationship stayed firm and unfrayed. It may well have been that Gainford was passed over for political reasons:

he happened to be a coal-owner and a Liberal. Nevertheless, Clarendon, the chairman-elect, seemed to have too little imagination and sympathy for Reith's taste. He seemed to lack political courage, too; and, in the phrase once used by Haig to describe Lord Derby, 'like the feather pillow he bears the marks of the last person who has sat on him'.[16] This had struck Reith when Clarendon, anxious to demonstrate his willingness to learn, had attended several confrontations with the Postmaster-General without once opening his mouth. Now, at the end of October 1926, furious at the haughty take-it-or-leave-it attitude of Mitchell-Thomson, the managing director of a company already in its death-throes succeeded in persuading the governors of an unborn corporation to protest against the financial terms of its own draft charter.

For two and a half hours on October 29th Reith was locked in further argument at the Post Office with the Postmaster-General and his chief adviser, Sir Evelyn Murray. Neither side would budge. Then Reith pointed out that the new governors shared his misgivings. It was his last card; but if he imagined that Mitchell-Thomson could not trump it, he erred badly. It was a pity, said the Postmaster-General, that the five governors were adopting such an obdurate stance. Perhaps he might have to find another five people who would be more amenable to reason.

'Why?' asked Reith.

'Because it looks as though the present five won't sign the agreement.'

On October 30th Clarendon was sent for by the Postmaster-General who said in so many words that fresh governors would be appointed forthwith unless the draft agreement were signed. The chairman wobbled, then submitted without a murmur. Reith could scarcely contain his scornful indignation: such a display of 'appalling weakness' confirmed his worst fears of being left to fight the Postmaster-General unaided and with both hands tied behind his back.[2] Other points in the draft charter dissatisfied him, but it seemed hopeless to expect a chairman as spineless as Clarendon to insist on reasonable amendments. There was the ban on controversial broadcasting, for instance, which Reith had vainly tried to have lifted in the summer; there was the refusal to insert a specific promise that no other body would be licensed to start a broadcasting service; there was also the clause forbidding all forms of commercial payment for broadcasts, including advertising. This last had appeared to Reith a likely bargaining counter in his protracted dispute with the Post Office over revenue, and an undated note in his handwriting reflected his perversely strong feelings on the subject:

'Should not the Corporation have liberty with regard to advertising as a supplementary source of revenue?'[1]

The decision to establish the new BBC by Royal Charter rather than by special statute or under the Companies Act was also Mitchell-Thomson's. He repudiated the idea of a statutory measure to obviate any risk of the public regarding the corporation as 'in some way a creature of Parliament'. As for the Companies' Act, any body formed under its provisions might not only 'lack a certain amount of status and dignity' but would be confined to doing what its articles entitled it to do and no more. On the other hand, a body incorporated by Royal Charter could do anything which the agreement did not specifically prohibit it from doing. Each of the five governors was appointed for five years: all would be eligible for reappointment; the chairman would receive £3000 a year, the vice-chairman £1000, and the others £700. In Reith's view these salaries were too large. He feared that as a result the recipients would spend excessive time interfering with him and his executive officers.

On November 15th, three days after the charter had been published, the Postmaster-General told the Commons that it was an 'agreed' document. Reith's rage at this misuse of language knew no bounds. He sat down and wrote bitterly to Clarendon:

'I cannot express my opinion of the way that the Post Office has treated us. They have been unfair, arbitrary and quite dishonest. They have printed outside the document that the terms were mutually agreed. . . . The constitution was to be changed to admit more scope and more autonomy, but none of these has materialised.'

He next sent a wire to Gainford, asking whether the statement in the White Paper that the terms had been 'mutually agreed' was really fair. The reply came back:

'No, but acceptance is some justification. Suggest Clarendon might publish letter to PMG remove misunderstanding.'[3]

Reith might derive some mysterious gratification from firing off his paper darts, but Clarendon would not join in that game. He had already seen enough of this solemn, bleak and arrogant man with the explosive temper and proprietorial ways to conceive a thorough dislike for him.[12] The auguries for harmonious co-operation between the Director-General, the new title conferred on Reith, and the first chairman of the new BBC's board of governors thus looked dim indeed as the old company died. In Asa Briggs' words: 'the ringing terms of the charter gave no hint of this last chapter of doubts and disillusions.'[1]

'Whereas', the quaint scroll began, 'it has been made to appear to Us that more than two million persons in Our United Kingdom of

Great Britain and Northern Ireland have applied for and taken out Licences to instal and work apparatus for . . . the purpose of receiving Broadcasting programmes AND WHEREAS in view of the widespread interest which is thereby shown to be taken by Our People in the Broadcasting Service and of the great value of the Service as a means of education and entertainment, We deem it desirable that the Service should be developed and exploited to the best advantage and in the national interest . . . [by] a Corporation charged with these duties . . . [and] created by the exercise of Our Royal Prerogative.'

There were no recriminations from the directors of the expiring company, only the odd gesture of mild discontent and disapproval. Kellaway argued at one of the final board meetings that his firm, Marconi, felt under no obligation to part with its patents, and the price he suggested for selling them off was one which Reith promptly refused to consider paying. Neither Binyon nor Burnham could wholly condone the equivocal tactics pursued by the managing director before and during the Crawford enquiry. Sir William Bull was not exactly enchanted by the conduct of his one-time protégé. The memory of a particular circular to MPs which had appeared blatantly to undervalue their 'stewardship' still stuck sourly in the collective mind of the old board. But it was too late for reproaches. And on December 9th Reith was formally named as liquidator, a title he kept until the last remnants of the British Broadcasting Company were tidied away towards the end of 1929. Meanwhile, he repaid all the shareholders at par.

The closing days of the company's corporate life did not go unmarked. At a farewell dinner on December 16th Reith made conscious amends by praising the board's 'fundamental policy of public service' which had led to the changed constitution. Of his own tribulations of spirit he said little—and that rather obliquely in stilted military metaphors:

'In the past by forced marches we have advanced through unknown and dangerous country, with adversities and conflicts which will never in like degree beset us again; some of us feel the effects of the campaign more than we dare to admit, but we know that the expedition is not yet near fulfilment.'

His own philosophy of letting the light of goodness and wholesome truth shine forth for all to see took up the major part of his speech:

'We have broadcast systematically and increasingly good music; we have developed educational courses for school-children and for adults; we have broadcast the Christian religion and tried to reflect that spirit of common sense Christian ethics which we believe to be a necessary component of citizenship and culture. We have endeavoured to exclude anything which might, directly or indirectly, be harmful. We have proved, as expected, that the supply of good things creates the demand for more. We have tried to found a tradition of public service, and to dedicate the service of broadcasting to humanity in its fullest sense. We believe that a new national asset has been created; not that kind of asset which brings credit entries to the books of the Exchequer, though it happens to be that kind of asset too and to a much greater extent than we had imagined or thought right; the asset referred to is of a moral and not the material order—that which, down the years, brings the compound interest of happier homes, broader culture and truer citizenship.'[3]

Baldwin, between puffs at his pipe, alluded to the 'silent, anonymous, obscure people' who had created the broadcasting business. They were, he said, 'far more distinguished' than the 'darlings of the press', the well-known and the famous who sat with him at the top table. 'We shall follow with immense interest your progress, sympathise with your struggles, and rejoice in all your triumphs.'

It consoled Reith that the old company should have gone out 'in a blaze of glory', as he put it, 'but some of the blaze lit on me—in five hundred telegrams and twelve hundred letters'.[11] Then, on December 20th, he was bowled over by a highly confidential missive containing the offer of a knighthood. Muriel, his wife, who had watched over him anxiously and helplessly during all the tensions and setbacks of the recent past, wishing that she could have done more to placate him, received a separate letter from the Prime Minister's secretary which said that 'Mr. Baldwin has submitted no name to the King with greater satisfaction'. Reith could not make up his mind whether to accept or refuse, and more than a week went by while he wrestled with his doubts.

'I consulted Dean Bell, Woodward, Ramsay MacDonald and Carpendale', he wrote to his ageing mother on the second last day of 1926, 'and they all urged it, so eventually I accepted. I am not happy about it.'[5]

Baldwin, becoming slightly anxious, rang up in the end to find out why Reith had delayed so long in replying and made no secret of his delight at the affirmative decision. If a conventional element of false humility lay behind John Reith's reluctance to enter the establishment on its terms, unquestionably the clinching factor was his naïve belief in the accoutrements of power. He was tired of being a hostage to fate. The honour and glory of knighthood might compensate for the influence which the BBC had undoubtedly forfeited, in his mind, through the General Strike. This, beyond question, was his greatest illusion.

8

The Autocrat

1

WHEN JOHN REITH, unmollified by the superlatives showered on him personally, settled down early in 1927 to the job of running the new corporation, he was obsessed by the restrictions imposed on it by the government of the day. What was only nominally a fifth estate of the realm, possessing the shadow rather than the substance of power and influence, would have to resist, he feared, further encroachments on its vulnerable, open frontiers by the politicians, the press and other vested interests. Still smarting from the setbacks of recent months, he saw this as the predominant peril confronting the BBC, his own reduced role being that of a modern captain-general whose experience and organising skills would hold off outsiders' incursions until someone else was ready to succeed him. His destiny had cheated him: the earlier grandiose design of a model broadcasting service, independent in fact as well as name, had been severely tested and found wanting. So, as Reith surveyed the dangers, his face turned outwards. Yet by the time the BBC celebrated its sixth birthday at the end of 1932 its development was endangered not by external forces, but paradoxically from within the organism itself.

The signs of internal strain appeared on January 4th, 1927, when Reith attended his first meeting with the new board of governors. He sat listening to an unedifying squabble between Clarendon, the chairman, and Mrs. Philip Snowden about the form of the minutes and the appointment of a secretary. Lord Shinwell, the only active survivor of the Labour movement at this time, has described her to this writer as 'the would-be Sarah Bernhardt of the party, small, buxom and fearsome when crossed, with an unerring knack of squeezing the last drop of drama out of the most trivial incident'.[1] The hold exercised on her husband by 'Annikins', the not always complimentary diminutive conferred on Ethel Snowden by party associates, caused some embarrassment to the Labour leadership. Ramsay MacDonald's indignation at the failure of Mitchell-Thomson to consult him before nominating her to the BBC board was a trifling instance of her accident-proneness. At stirring up unnecessary trouble she had few equals. Reith took against her at their first encounter, confessing that he 'could not make her out at all'. Clarendon, of course, was a different sort of cross; but between the chairman's cold, insensitive touch and the unpredictable histrionics of Mrs. Snowden, Reith found difficulty in deciding which was the more distasteful. As individuals they had one thing in common: both showed an equal and disturbing determination to 'poke their noses into mine, and other people's business, as the whim took them'.[2] This led to nearly four years of feuding over the division of power and responsibility inside the BBC; and the long demarcation dispute cost Reith and the corporation much stress and strain.

'There were few weeks without complaints from Mrs. Snowden. Minutes were unsatisfactory', Reith noted. 'The board should meet more frequently. Matters should not be settled between me and the chairman. Newspapers were continually discussing matters of the gravest importance of which she knew nothing; several questions to which answers were overdue; charges about the treatment of staff and artists—salaries and fees too high or too low; objections to new appointments, salary roll being already too heavy for amount of work done. The BBC too prone to give in to the press—someone had only to be hasty in print and the BBC would concede anything. Charges that senior executives and I were discourteous to her: "Not once but time and again I have been treated with great rudeness by all the members of the control board." . . .

'Patient and conciliatory explanations by Clarendon and me. Urgings to come and talk with me about anything that worried or interested her; or with any of the division chiefs if she did not want to talk to me. . . . Several letters from me to her—agreed by chairman and others of the board—trying to get her to a better frame of mind. Each of the other governors was to try to ease her suspicions, bring her to a more rational outlook. Without effect.'[3]

This staccato catalogue of grievances, alleged offences of commission and omission, and repeated if vain attempts to reassure the untiring accuser on the board of governors, is sufficient to indicate what Reith now had to endure. Shy and intolerant at the same time, he did not know how or where to start handling such a domineering woman with so many toy axes to grind. He also stood at a double disadvantage in that, as Director-General, his situation was always the invidious one of the defendant in the dock. The trial bore down cruelly on his once-sure sense of purpose. For Clarendon seemed quite incapable of calling Mrs. Snowden to order or of calming her predilections and doubts about the proper conduct of the BBC's affairs. The long-drawn-out agony of John Reith had its ludicrous and fantastic aspects; but the essential enormity of it lay in Mrs. Snowden's 'insatiable appetite for mischief'.[2]

'Part of the difficulty', Asa Briggs stated, 'was that neither Clarendon nor Mrs. Snowden had great committee experience: they had not sat on a board of this kind before. An even greater difficulty was that while the Postmaster-General had given none of the governors any idea of what they were supposed to do, he had hinted to Clarendon that three-quarters of his time would be needed for his post as chairman and to Mrs. Snowden that she would be "almost fully occupied" by the BBC. She expected to have a room at Savoy Hill and believed that "the board should meet every day".'[4]

The more Reith attempted to disabuse Mrs. Snowden of the idea that she had become a full-time director, the deeper grew her suspicion that he was trying to foist his own rules on the board. She did not like being headed off; and her assertions that the unhelpful attitude of the Director-General proved that he must have 'something to hide' afforded Reith numerous occasions for the exercise of self-control. Admittedly, Reith had always enjoyed taking decisions himself. Gainford and his long-suffering colleagues on the board of the deceased company had spoiled him by leaving too much to a wholly dependable managing director. Now the boot was on the other foot. For the precise functions of corporation governors had never been spelt out on paper; and Reith was not a natural committee-man:

'I have always functioned best', he wrote, 'when responsibility for decision rested wholly and solely on me. Every faculty is then alerted, mobilised. When, as on a committee, others are involved, it has often been otherwise. I can neither explain nor defend; it is certainly not the result of a deliberate decision to sit back and let others do the thinking and deciding. It is at least as likely to indicate respect as disrespect for other people.'[3]

This was not the case, however, when Mrs. Snowden convinced the board and Reith that she meant business. His respect for her good sense dwindled to vanishing point; he was conscious only of her monumental vanity and of her infinite capacity for squandering time and energy in pursuit of pet phantoms. Her nose for smelling out non-existent rats was uncanny. Lord Shinwell may be right in saying that "Annikins wanted the power she couldn't get in the Labour movement and underestimated Reith as she tended to underestimate anyone who stood in her way". There is, nevertheless, a touch of irony in this bizarre duel between a man of action and towering ideals, who had already received a political rebuff in his bid for matching power, and a woman of large conceits whom nothing could divert from invading Sir John Reith's narrow power-base at the drop of a big, flowered hat.

Since Asa Briggs published the first volume of his history of broadcasting, several of Mrs. Snowden's letters have fortunately come to light. These disclose, as nothing else could, her reasons for disliking and distrusting the sometimes arbitrary head of the BBC executive. On May 1st, 1927, for example, she wrote to Gainford:

'It is impossible either to be happy or to contribute one's best if one is bound to the tender mercies of a man whose overwhelming egoism is as distasteful as his character and ability are overestimated. . . . My method of learning about an organisation is perhaps unorthodox but it is satisfying to me. It is perhaps a woman's method. I am less concerned with masses of facts, in the first place, than with personnel. I want to know through personal contact what a person is worth. You can see how little it helps to be told that I can go to the D.G. if I want to know things.'

Reith usually thwarted her by saying that he was too busy to concern himself with the details of problems which happened to prick her curiosity. Mrs. Snowden brightly countered this by urging that the board should acquire its own independent secretary through the Treasury:

'Sir John Reith complains of being overworked', she informed Gainford in July 1927. 'The chairman constantly makes that point. . . . My own view is that Sir John Reith makes unnecessary work for himself by not sufficiently delegating work, by insisting on knowing every detail about everybody's job, and by writing and speaking in wearisome detail and often irrelevantly on matters raised by members of the board. . . .'[5]

The loyalty binding Carpendale and other members of the control board to their chief would have thrown off the scent far tougher inquisitors than Mrs. Snowden. Their corporate sense of interdependence kept the prying lady governor at arm's length. 'By what usurpation of right does she presume to prosecute Sir John?' is a not unreasonable paraphrase of their warily protective point of view. On one occasion, when Mrs. Snowden persuaded Clarendon to gather together at his home all the regional controllers for an informal, working lunch, the doorbell rang as the guests were sipping their cocktails. Reith's deputy had arrived, uninvited, to the stupefaction of everyone else:

'Carpendale brazened it out', said one of those present, 'behaving like a guest who had merely turned up late. It seemed to put Mrs. Snowden off her stroke. At any rate she asked no awkward questions about work and conditions. If Carpendale's intelligence service had functioned less efficiently that day, she might have picked up some useful ammunition for her campaign. The regional controllers tended to be a disaffected lot, believing that London was always pillaging their ideas, their broadcasting time—or both. Those without independent means also felt that Reith underpaid them.'[6]

A person of Ethel Snowden's irrepressibly feline instincts lost no opportunity of preaching to a Director-General whom she thought of as one of nature's disagreeable autocrats. Beneath his outwardly correct manner the chairman of the board shared the same conviction, but Clarendon lacked Mrs. Snowden's enthusiasm for combat and played the would-be peace-maker until 1928. Then, perhaps succumbing to her unabated desire for reforms, Clarendon adopted the same destructive course. Their tactical efforts to infuse more 'democracy' into Reith's individualistic scheme of governance led next to even greater friction:

'Clarendon suddenly wrote that he was concerned about the atmosphere at Savoy Hill as to the listening public and the board; the staff did not appreciate what the board's duties and responsibilities were; the board were kept in the background. . . .'[3]

A divided board was anything but a healthy prescription for progress. Influential people outside the BBC became increasingly aware, through idle gossip in clubs and at dinner parties, of the triangular feud between Clarendon and Mrs. Snowden on the one hand, and the intransigent Director-General on the other. It did Reith's reputation little good. For the chairman was not disposed to make light of his difficulties, and Mrs. Snowden could hardly be expected to take a vow of silence about hers. The two charges commonly levelled against Reith were intolerance of criticism, however constructive, which he appeared to misconstrue as a personal affront, and a corresponding reluctance even to discuss the uses and the limits of his executive power. The new public service, in the considered view of Clarendon and Mrs. Snowdon, had become Reith's private plaything.

They grossly oversimplified their case, of course, because they had no understanding of the man, but rumours of Reith's mania for playing the tyrant spread like wildfire from Savoy Hill and improved with repetition. It was a strangely desolating period for him. Having grown used to exercising unquestioned authority in every area during the days of the old company, referring matters upwards only for formal approval by a board of businessmen beset by other preoccupations, Reith could not easily shed the settled habit. Nor would he compromise himself by drafting any formula that set defined limits on his own rights. The only sure result of that, he feared, would be to tempt Mrs. Snowden further. For the ineffectual Clarendon was mere putty in her hands. So this curious conflict of wills and temperaments, in itself a minor domestic drama with far-reaching implications, rolled on almost without a break until the end of 1930.

It did occur to Reith more than once that by threatening to resign he might succeed in bringing Clarendon to his senses, but that bright idea had its dark, inner lining: how could he be certain that his proferred head on a platter would not be accepted by the board with alacrity? The BBC would, in that case, be the victim, not himself. He decided to 'stick it out' and contrive somehow to promote the best interests of broadcasting, despite the friction and his own desperate frustration. Yet rumours of Reith's impending resignation persisted widespread throughout the greater part of 1928. When Lord Aberdeen, a distant admirer, wrote and asked point-blank whether there was any truth in a new version that had just reached his ears, Reith replied:

'The rumour has had pretty wide circulation, but, as far as I know, there is no foundation in it—unless it be optimism on the part of some individual. I certainly have had offers which, in the financial sense, were extraordinarily attractive. I do not know that I should stay long where I am. I have been delegating more and more, and have an amazingly efficient and loyal staff. At any age one should be in a post which makes an absolutely full demand upon one—but I would not resign if I felt that either the service or the staff would be prejudiced by my so doing.'[7]

Reith's mother, now eighty years of age, was opposed to his leaving the BBC on any pretext; and her influence over him remained exceedingly strong. A formidable, matriarchal figure with a persuasive tongue and pen, she corresponded freely with many eminent people, including Lord Aberdeen and Gainford, whom she had met through her son:

'I remember well', she told Gainford on his eventual retirement, 'how very annoyed and sorry [John] was that you had not been made chairman of the Corporation, and would have made what he called 'a row' about it had you not dissuaded him: though he never talked much about it, I could see that he and the others were having a trying time with your successor . . .'[8]

To be quite dispassionate, Gainford, as well as Rendall and Nairne, found that Reith could be very trying, too:

'I both wrote to Reith and I saw him', ran one laconic note from Rendall to the vice-chairman. 'At first he was terribly stiff and gloomy: but I think he is coming round, and I have fair hope for the future.' Of Mrs. Snowden, whom Rendall had recently sought to appease over the luncheon table, he remarked:

'Poor lady: she is terribly upset and her health has suffered: But all her conduct appears that of a person (almost a child) wholly unversed in public affairs. She is amazed and collapses if we don't agree with her. She really means well but her methods are deplorable.'

It should be stated that, at one time or another, all the governors came to regard the petulance and obstructiveness of the Director-General as equally deplorable and much less excusable.

'Reith is intolerable', Clarendon informed Gainford in July 1929, 'and I am glad you intend to tell him that he has got to behave properly.'

Gainford, whose business concerns pressed hard on him at this time, was less disposed than in the past to side automatically with Reith. When the latter wrote a long, pleading and somewhat flattering note, recalling their ideal co-operation in company days, the vice-chairman would not be drawn:

'I wish you would talk with me', declared Reith. 'I am not to be read as implying or suggesting disloyalty to Clarendon, but we did get on so well. . . . About a month ago I said to you that things weren't satisfactory or comfortable. You replied: "It's not your fault, Reith, it's not your fault." . . . You know that all this sort of thing is unsettling and discouraging, and one cannot do one's proper work. . . .'

Board meetings almost invariably reflected the abiding deadlock of minds. Clarendon in that same month of July 1929 wanted to insert in the minutes an official rebuke to the recalcitrant ways of the Director-General, who seemed intent on impeding progress:

'Of course we do not want to humiliate him', the chairman confided to Gainford, 'but unfortunately he has given us all the impression that he wants—if he does not agree with the board— to override us. That creates an impossible situation and we cannot tolerate it.'[9]

According to Reith, what brought matters to a head on this occasion was a hair-brained idea of Ethel Snowden's:

'The cause of world peace caused a little war at Savoy Hill. Peace messages were to be broadcast by women in other countries addressed to Mrs. Snowden; she was to broadcast replies to them and then take them to the London Naval Conference. . . . It was quite impracticable technically . . . but Mrs. Snowden concluded that I was determined to prevent her from broadcasting—and said so.'[3]

Reith had neither expected nor sought any help from Baldwin in these recurring troubles. He underwent a gradual reversion to the lonely, melancholy moods of his long adolescence as a spiritual prisoner in the College Manse. Bouts of depression, which he had been spared during the exhilarating years of pioneering before the shock of the General Strike, closed in on his spirit like night. What he thought of as 'the fateful stirring to achieve', that inner voice urging him never to lose sight of the goal, faded into an uncertain whisper when accidie, the affliction well known to monks in the middle ages, held him in its grip. The party wrangling at Westminster had never greatly interested him. Except for occasional questions or debates on BBC affairs, the business of politics left him cold. Many others shared Reith's lack of response to the artificial heat generated by esoteric political issues.

Unemployment had replaced poverty as a chronic social ailment for which no instant cure had yet been discovered; and even if a modest trade revival, accompanying the ephemeral hopes of keeping peace between the nations of Europe in the spirit of Austen Chamberlain's Locarno treaty, sustained the appearances of a Britain well governed, the second administration of Stanley Baldwin seemed to die slowly of inanition in that summer of 1929. 'Safety first', a slogan borrowed from current official posters aimed at reducing road accidents, was the Conservative watchword to the electorate before polling day. This advice against any further truck with socialist experiments, coming from a government indicted by some of its followers for resting lethargically on withered laurels, was studiously ignored by voters. Colonel Ivan Moore-Brabazon (later Lord Brabazon of Tara) had complained of his leader from the Tory back benches: 'The snores of the government resound throughout the land', and the people went to the polls in June 1929 and turned the sleeper out of office.

Reith, who as usual abstained from exercising his right to vote, was not comforted at finding 'Mrs. Snowden's position in the country changed'. Her husband was restored to the Exchequer, where Churchill had clung on tenaciously to the last. The new Prime Minister, Ramsay MacDonald, visited Savoy Hill to broadcast his first message. He told Reith what a 'dreadful business' Cabinet-making could be. Most of his colleagues, he said, 'were dissatisfied with what they were given. "Maybe you'll find out for yourself some day what it's like" ', he added sententiously, as though John Reith did not have problems enough already.[3] The governors of the BBC were by now following the custom of lunching together after board meetings at the Savoy Hotel, never inviting the Director-General to join them. They also gathered on occasion at Clarendon's home, as Reith discovered once on ringing through and speaking to the butler. This drove Clarendon to conclude that there must be spies abroad, reporting back to Reith on the governors' every movement.

Another issue that rankled came into the open when Clarendon demanded that the governors should be able to attend sessions of BBC advisory committees if they so wished; to call on heads of departments 'collectively or in pairs' and speak to any member of the staff in the presence of the chief; and to ratify all appointments and resignations. This 'incredible move', as Reith termed it, was approved and passed by the others. He reminded them that from the very beginning there had been a standing invitation to attend advisory committee meetings, just as he had suggested visits to heads of departments when the board first met. As for appointments, was it not enough to inform them of prospective changes in senior staff, as he always did? They had offered no previous hint that they wished to extend the process: how far down the hierarchy were they anxious to carry it?

A long, private discussion with the chairman outside the BBC left Reith still more disheartened. Clarendon asked at one stage why he had hesitated before accepting the board's three points. 'Because they make the governors look ridiculous', Reith replied. Before the chairman could think of a rejoinder, his antagonist raised the unexpected question of salary, reminding Clarendon that as long ago as January 1927 he had suggested for himself an increase of £750 for two successive years, and no more. This had been orally agreed. Nothing had been done, despite two further requests since. What mattered to Reith was not so much the money as the vote of no-confidence in himself which the withholding of the money evidently implied. They parted with nothing solved, the Director-General expressing his personal regret at the strained relationship while the chairman confessed, 'I really don't know what can be done': perhaps Sir John might care to let him have a memorandum of his views.

Nairne, in the main a supporter of Reith but no match for the thrusting and incomparably inventive Mrs. Snowden, tried next to influence the chairman. Charles Carpendale, employing bluffer tactics than the dignified written disclaimers of Nairne, also warned Clarendon independently that the work of the BBC would inevitably suffer if existing difficulties and tensions continued. The senior staff were demoralised, said Reith's deputy, by the chairman's failure to show them any sign of trust. Why should the slightest shift in the whims of Mrs. Snowden blow Clarendon off courses already fixed by agreement? What possible reason had he for insisting that all his letters should be forwarded unopened to his home? Did he imagine that anyone at Savoy Hill would destroy correspondence that criticised BBC practices?

In answer to this last question, Clarendon did admit to the suspicion that certain letters addressed to him had been 'suppressed'. As to the allegation that both he and Mrs. Snowden had been known to act behind Reith's back on staff matters, the chairman repeated that this had been done because 'there's so much discontent on the staff'. Carpendale remarked that rebels and misfits existed in all big organizations; he found it scandalous that complaints from such people should be welcomed and eagerly swallowed by any member of the BBC board, without reference to the Director-General and his fellow executives.

'Yes', retorted Clarendon, 'but Reith is a Mussolini. The staff are afraid of him because he's a hard man.'[3]

Early in October 1929 Reith received a rare personal letter from Clarendon. Nairne had had a talk with him, the chairman wrote; and he would now be happy for another discussion at his home with Reith. The meeting turned out to be a fiasco. It began virtually at first base, Clarendon demanding in a supercilious tone whether the Director-General now accepted his interpretation of the BBC Charter, a copy of which he produced and parts of which he started to quote. Reith could hardly believe his ears when the Chairman put down the document and said:

'The Charter makes absolutely clear the supremacy of the board of governors', he said. Like the commander-in-chief on a battlefield, their status and powers were unquestionable. Reith thought this a poor analogy and contradicted him. Surely, he said, the board held an equivalent authority to the Cabinet, with the chief executive in the position of commander-in-chief. They sparred for a while over the distinction, then Clarendon got down to brass tacks. Why had Reith objected to the governors' private meetings outside the BBC? Why had he indulged in what looked remarkably like spying on their movements? Rejecting as 'either ludicrous or insulting' any suggestion of espionage, Reith stressed that 'if a proper relationship existed between governors and staff, you wouldn't have had to stage these extraordinary sessions at the Savoy Hotel or in your house here'. Clarendon seemed to have a fixation over Reith's undeniably detailed knowledge of these external activities; and when, in self-defence, Reith asked facetiously if the chairman actually believed that detectives had been hired for the purpose, he was confounded by the reply:

'Yes,' said Clarendon, 'either detectives or an agency of that sort.'

'You obviously blame me entirely for the bad situation we're in?'

'Yes, I do.'

Reith reminded him that almost three years before, when the new board had been appointed, they were at one in their unfavourable opinion of Mrs. Snowden. Why had the chairman swung round since in her support? Clarendon vouchsafed no satisfactory reply, simply reiterating that Reith seldom behaved like someone who genuinely accepted the supremacy of the board and its unassailable right to information. Glancing at his watch, he said he must leave at once to keep an appointment, and rose to go:

'I've given you an hour of my time,' he remarked.

Reith somehow managed to choke back a withering retort, and next day rang up to suggest that they should continue their exchanges. Clarendon thought it better for Reith to 'let me have a memorandum. It's all so confusing.' Nairne, on balance, felt that it would be far better 'to let bygones be bygones', and drafted the outline of a memorandum himself, in which regret was expressed for past misunderstandings and the board's unquestioned authority was fully recognised. Consternation followed when the chairman wrote back not to Reith but to Carpendale, saying that a differently worded memorandum of agreement seemed desirable to him and other members of the board. This petty trading in insults might have gone on indefinitely had not Gainford intervened and persuaded the chairman to declare a truce. In a constructive note to Reith, which Clarendon pondered over for two weeks before sending, the chairman declared that he was willing to wipe the slate clean so that the board and chief executive could start afresh 'in happier circumstances'.

According to Reith's account, 'the happier circumstances did not come'. Mrs. Snowden, zealous in her pursuit of real or imagined staff grievances caused by the high-handed, incorrigible Sir John, suddenly flew off at a tangent. She insisted on the instant re-engagement of a temporary assistant who had recently been sacked. Reith, in fact, had no direct hand in this particular dismissal. Then he learnt after careful enquiries that the man had no grievances against anyone, and so informed an incredulous Mrs. Snowden. At the next board meeting in January 1930 Clarendon coolly stated that any member of the staff had the right to approach a governor with a complaint, bypassing the executive. Gainford at once dissociated himself from such unsound doctrine, and there for the moment the matter ended. But Carpendale was so outraged that he took it up personally with the chairman, whom he called on by appointment at the House of Lords. Any person on the BBC staff had the right of appeal to Reith, he said, and only if still not satisfied could he see the chairman if that happened to be his wish. The message seemed to percolate through. For Gainford told Reith before the end of January, 1930, that Clarendon at last accepted as the correct procedure that appeals to governors should pass through the executive first.

It was on February 7th that Reith first heard a whisper that Ramsay MacDonald had other plans in mind for Clarendon:

'I invited confirmation from a friend in Buckingham Palace', he recounted. ' "Yes", he said, "but however did you know? It isn't to be announced for some days yet." '[3]

The Labour Government had persuaded the BBC chairman, a former under-secretary for the Dominions, to go to South Africa as Governor-General, but Reith feared that the appointment might not become effective until the end of 1930. MacDonald set his fears at rest. The BBC's internal turmoil had naturally reached his ears, he told Reith: it was unnecessary to ask the source: 'There's great activity next door at No. 11', he said. 'I think Clarendon should leave at once.' Reith was overjoyed and said so. 'Have you anyone in mind for the chairmanship?' enquired MacDonald. Reith suggested Gainford, but the Prime Minister replied that Gainford 'would not do'. He would think about the matter and consult Lees-Smith, the Postmaster-General. Mrs. Snowden, for her part, protested at the efforts of the Director-General to canvass on behalf of his own candidate:

'It has come to my ears', she informed Gainford on May 15th, 1930, 'that Sir John Reith is working hard to have Lord Burnham made chairman. Reith is, I understand, Lord Burnham's tenant (at Beaconsfield). Verb. sap.'[5]

However, a day or two later, Reith learnt that a former Speaker of the Commons, John Whitley, had been chosen in a highly peculiar fashion; Lees-Smith, unable to think of anyone suitable, had pored over an alphabetical list of Privy Councillors and his eyes had lit up with relief when they came to rest on the final name at the very bottom of it.

2

With Whitley there came to the BBC 'light, understanding and excellent wisdom', according to Reith, after three and a half years of backbiting, bickering and stalemate. Mrs. Snowden remained, but her attitude gradually changed for the better. When Reith paid Clarendon the courtesy, some twenty years later, of letting him see his version of these unhappy years of sterile collaboration, the latter did not dispute its accuracy. He 'was so generous as to say that he accepted responsibility'.[3] Theirs had been a clash of incompatible temperaments; and two minds so differently constituted could hardly have failed to provoke tantrums. Yet it must be added in fairness that Mrs. Snowden's consistent willingness to condemn Reith as an arbitrary and despotic ruler in a house which he regarded as his own did sometimes have foundation in fact.

The qualities which he had consistently demanded of newcomers to the staff were unexceptionable:

'In our work', he had written to station directors as long ago as June 24th, 1924, 'there is demanded a wider range of qualifications than in any other business. Our people should be of social, educational and business standing. In addition to this there are peculiar qualities demanded of them, and the one which is most conspicuously lacking is, I think, imagination.'[10]

The method of recruitment since that time had altered little. Reith's final approval of young men and women earmarked for jobs by controllers and other senior staff could never be taken for granted. His judgment was not always sound, and when would-be applicants came to his personal notice through important members of the establishment, errors could occur all too easily. Cecil Graves, for instance, owed his original appointment partly at least to a word dropped in Reith's ear by Earl Grey of Falloden who happened to be Graves' uncle; yet Graves was an outstanding exception to the rule-of-thumb, possessing the requisite qualities of character and intellect as well as the 'right connections'. What Cecil Graves did lack was the vital attribute of decisiveness. Even so he was commonly regarded from 1927 onwards as the man most likely to succeed Reith as Director-General. Roger Eckersley, the controller of programmes, stood in a different category. His brother, Peter, the dynamic head of the BBC's engineering division, had helped to secure his direct appointment in 1925. Because Reith admired Roger's social gifts and conspicuous charm, promotion to the control board was swift and automatic; at a time when 'programme reorganisation is the biggest thing on hand', as the executive head of the old company had noted, men of Roger Eckersley's calibre had to be 'marked out for "greater responsibility" '[4]

Not a few of Roger Eckersley's contemporaries considered that Reith had overvalued as well as over-promoted him:

'He was a marvellously smooth operator in the field of social and public relations', said one of them. 'He even taught Reith how to fasten a bow tie without turning a hair, and nobody resented his position as one of Reith's favourites for several years. A select town house at No. 21 Thurloe Square was leased, equipped, maintained and run at the expense of the BBC so that Roger could deploy his social graces officially and to the full. Entertaining quite lavishly and presiding at informal soirées, formal dinners and large receptions attended by pillars of society, politicians and other public figures, Roger Eckersley was in his natural element there as he seldom was on the control board.'[6]

The cost of this extraordinary venture into public relations on an elaborate, individualistic scale is almost impossible to assess now with accuracy. The chief accountant of the BBC, Mr. T. Lochhead, a fellow-Scot whose devotion to Reith was absolute, never questioned any move, however exorbitant, which the Director-General had approved. Besides, the Thurloe Square experiment in social lionising did not fall within his direct scrutiny because in April, 1926, a new system of programme expenditure had been introduced. All Lochhead was required to do was 'to allocate annually to the programme department a sum which it was expected would cover the entire programme expenditure for London and the provincial stations. This sum was to be administered by the organiser of programmes, Roger Eckersley, who was given complete control over its allocation.'[4]

Though Reith believed in avoiding 'At Homes' frequented by artistic, social, political and even ecclesiastical celebrities, he thoroughly welcomed and underwrote the scheme. It provided a valuable meeting ground for a wide cross-section of the fashionable world with which the BBC as such had to do business. It produced not a few recruits for the Corporation. As a listening post for picking up useful information it also had incidental advantages. The basic fact, however, that Reith had condoned this quaint exercise in gracious living, which at its height cost the BBC the then considerable sum of £30,000 a year, silenced the censorious among senior members of the staff.

When evidence of this unconventional arrangement eventually reached Mrs. Snowden, the BBC was still in the process of taking over the accounts of the old company.

'The only three points which are not mentioned in the schedule list B,' Reith told Gainford, 'which might not be clear to you are the big item under head office accommodation, which includes the purchase of the house for the programme director [Eckersley], that was mentioned in previous correspondence and was finally settled in October 1926, but which had been discussed earlier. . . .'[8]

Whatever malpractices the old company might have turned a blind eye to, Ethel Snowden refused to condone them in the corporation, displaying the resolve of a high-minded egalitarian with clear views on how public money should be spent:

'I have definitely decided', she informed Gainford, 'to oppose Reith's proposal that Eckersley shall entertain on a large scale in a corporation house. I shall move at the next meeting that, from January 1st, 1928, all entertainment allowances cease, and our station directors, who feel they must invite distinguished visitors to their own, shall send in their bills to headquarters. . . .'

Reith took umbrage at her tone of moral superiority and would not be moved. It is sufficiently plain from the evidence that he did not realise how deeply he had scandalised the lady governor by his defiant attitude:

'It cannot be defended morally as it is an indirect attempt to get something for nothing, or to extract concessions and favours through social pressures or social habits which might not be regarded as right or reasonable on their merits', she noted privately to Gainford. 'I have reason to believe that it is easy to step outside the law in this matter, as it is simply bribery and corruption.' Then, as if she were seeking to out-Reith Reith, Mrs. Snowden declared bleakly:

'It would be disastrous if a reputation for convivial practices became attached to the BBC, and our employees should not be exposed to the danger of constant entertainment of people of artistic temperament. . . . This sort of thing is apt to be two-edged. . . . We should suffer in the end because men and women generally regret in the morning the promises wrung from them overnight, or over the wine. . . .'[5]

Even though Gainford, thus sharply reminded of a public corporation's responsibilities, admitted that Mrs. Snowden had made out a reasonably sound case, the board failed to dent Reith's invincible sense of self-righteousness. Roger Eckersley, naturally, had henceforth to watch his step and justify all official expenditure at home; but only gradually, as he fell out of favour with Reith, did he lose the fine perquisites which he had enjoyed for so long.

It has been well said of Reith that 'he believes in democratic aim, not democratic method'.[11] The tyrannically minded overlord, for ever exacting homage from his lieges, was the conventional image which opponents of Reith like Mrs. Snowden helped to perpetuate; but the truth was far less simple than that. His moral principles had the tensile strength of steel and extended to everybody, high and low alike. When Peter Eckersley had become involved in divorce proceedings in 1929, the downfall of this exceptionally gifted engineer and publicist, who 'knew more about broadcasting than any other man in the country', was settled overnight.[4] It might matter to Reith as a person that an individual in this predicament happened to be the innocent, not the guilty partner: but the stigma on the good name of the corporation could never be overlooked. One of Peter Eckersley's contemporaries has justly remarked that his speeches and writings 'caused him at one period to be almost better known to the public than Reith himself', the latter offering him 'every possible support and latitude'. No latitude, however, could be offered to Eckersley now: his seniority, his general acclaim, above all his knowledge of the Reithian code told conclusively against him. He stood condemned by his own folly.

Lord Boothby, one of Peter Eckersley's close friends, met him immediately afterwards:

'He told me that Reith had wasted few words on him and had spoken as much in sorrow as in anger, like some doom-laden prophet straight out of the pages of the Old Testament. "My son", said the Director-General, "you have strayed from the paths of righteousness. Our ways must part for ever. You are dismissed." And dismissed he was on the spot, though the official statement later said that Eckersley had resigned for personal reasons.'[12]

Yet even in this open-and-shut case the Director-General did not escape criticism from his unfailing persecutor on the board. It was the firm judgment of Mrs. Snowden that Reith, left to himself, would probably have forgiven the unforgivable:

'I have come definitely to the conclusion', she wrote to Gainford, 'that he [Peter Eckersley] should be allowed to go whenever he wishes to leave. I am not sure that his services should be retained even if he desires to stay. I should not support his being retained as consultant engineer to the BBC, nor in any position which gives him room, position or status in connection therewith. The DG's extraordinary desire to retain him explains in a way I had not understood his condonement of the most flagrant offence against decency and discipline of which a responsible individual can be guilty. . . .'[5]

Reith himself certainly repudiated the allegation that 'divorce was inevitably followed by resignation or termination of appointment'. Cases were judged, as in other public bodies, 'on the circumstances of the divorce and of the individual's employment. . . . If the board or I felt their employment must cease, no moral condemnation was thereby implied. One might understand and fully sympathise, but the BBC could not be determined by any such personal views.'[3]

Orthodox Christian conduct was expected and enforced 'only if relevant'.[2] A senior talks producer would be a liability to the BBC if he broke the ten commandments. A conductor or a variety producer would probably do his job just as well if he behaved like a dissolute agnostic. The distinction, unreal and unfair as it was, roused some derision but no mutinies. During a period of massive and growing unemployment, BBC staff had an additional reason of expediency for embracing Reith's moral pragmatism. Jobs were too scarce to be jeopardised too recklessly.

There could also be an element of the totally unexpected in his selection of people for vacancies. Val Gielgud was a junior assistant on the *Radio Times*' staff in 1928 when Reith had singled him out quite arbitrarily for his true vocation in life. To the unfailing amazement of everyone, the Director-General enjoyed taking part in BBC amateur theatrical productions. Once he played the role of the thief in *The Bishop's Candlesticks* with all the relish of the bad actor; and again under Gielgud's direction he took an equally incongruous part in the cast of Ian Hay's comedy, *Tilly of Bloomsbury*. On the day of the first run-through 'some of the actors were missing'; and, 'as a believer in setting an example of punctuality at rehearsals, I decided to go ahead', Gielgud recalled. 'After some minutes the door opened and two figures entered, conversing with animation: one immensely tall, the other lean, greyish and spectacled. I paid little attention to them apart from saying that I expected punctuality, and that people must not talk while others were working. It was only at the end of the read-through that I realised I'd indulged in public rebuke of the Director-General and Carpendale.

'I felt that my prospects of a successful BBC career were at that moment distinctly bleak. As it turned out, however, Sir John in particular seemed immensely to enjoy relief from his official cares implied by playing the part of a drunken broker's man, which he did with great aplomb and success. He made up to the life: bleary-eyed, scruffily-bearded, thoroughly disreputable; and I believe he got as much fun out of acting the part as his slightly bewildered staff got out of watching this reputedly grim and humourless figure letting himself go.'

There was a sequel. The BBC at the time needed a new drama director. Reith suddenly thought of Gielgud and sent for Carpendale.

'I've found just the man for the job', he said. 'This fellow Gielgud will do. If he can be rude to me, he ought to be able to tell a lot of actors what to do.'

The astonished Val Gielgud thus took up early in 1929 the career in radio drama to which he brought distinction for the next thirty-five years, becoming in the process one of Reith's 'unashamedly proud young men'. Gielgud's verdict is not without interest:

'I don't think any man can be categorised as truly Calvinist when he could tell me, as Reith did more than once, that he never expected conventional religious or moral behaviour from one irrevocably tarred with the theatrical brush.'[13]

The ethical values that were Reith's inheritance could not have been whittled down or altered for convenience because they lay buried in the bedrock on which the BBC itself stood, like a tall lighthouse illuminating the surrounding blackness. This ancestral legacy of fixed moral standards lived on in the place; and he knew with the conviction of self-knowledge that those values would also remain his as long as he remained with his child. Stay he must. Stay he would, now that the internal storm had virtually blown itself out with the departure of the unlamented Clarendon. Besides, in his quiet and rather dull domestic life, the seventy-eight months of Reith's trial-by-ordeal at Savoy Hill had added to his private cares, reinforcing his own instinctive resolve against leaving the BBC. He was now a family man. His first-born had come into the world in 1928, and Christopher had since acquired a sister, Marista. He had vowed to rear them by precept and example in the Christian way of his fathers, so that they might share with their mother that natural capacity for happiness which had eluded him since boyhood. As Reith wrote of himself:

'BBC public relations were supremely handled; mine, by my own choice, were non-existent.'[3]

Yet he religiously kept all press cuttings about himself and his alleged shortcomings, not with any wistful hope of learning from them but from a compulsive curiosity about other men's opinions. These formed in time companion volumes to his excessively long diary. He did not minimise the range of Mrs. Snowden's unflattering propaganda, for instance, when Harold Laski wrote a paradoxical piece about the man who had managed, in less than a decade, 'to put a girdle round the earth' and impose himself as a character of sorts on the British public mind. Laski described Reith as 'vehement, determined, aggressive, masterful, capable of thinking and administering on the big scale, driving plans through, fighting hard for what he believed in, making people work with the art of utilising ideas to the maximum value'. But Reith's fanatical quality could be a limitation as well as a gift. 'However big the mind, to be big enough or wise enough to exercise unlimited powers he must learn to take criticism, to be persuaded that opposition was sometimes intelligent and sometimes right, to be less concerned for the country's spiritual health, to realise that the wicked heresies of today are the sober commonplaces of tomorrow. . . .' Respect for his achievements was usually tinctured with abhorrence of his methods. So tightly did he guard his inner thoughts and doubts from everyone, his wife included, that only a few ever discovered that Sir John Reith, far from regarding himself as a man of outstanding achievement, still felt at times like a stranger in a hostile land.

The feeling was by no means novel. It squared with the almost atavistic sense of inadequacy which had possessed him at intervals since adolescence. The remorse grew more intense when he was most frustrated; and, characteristically, he railed against the awful conviction of being a misfit and a failure in the spring of 1929, at the height of the protracted deadlock on the BBC board of mangement. By a strange irony Lord Clarendon and Mrs. Snowden succeeded, by dint of their often clumsy obstructiveness, in persuading the hypercritical and hypersensitive Reith that he himself was 'not at all successful'. However he strove to alter that, he could do nothing now to change the course of destiny.

His spirit cried out for reassurance which nobody could give him. For none of his acquaintances inside or outside the BBC knew his handicaps, just as only a dozen women and perhaps half a dozen men ever claimed to understand why his personality was so deeply flawed. To his wife, his ever-watchful mother, and other relatives he could not begin to unburden himself.

His snobbery lacked the common factor of fawning on dukes and lesser members of the nobility or on the upper classes. His tastes and aspirations did not run that way. With seeming contrariness he doted on the monarch, never failing to ensure that the BBC paid frequent, ritualistic obeisance to the royal family. For Reith stood in almost feudal awe of the crown as the anointed fount of all honours. Snobbery as mere status-seeking was not for him. Reith nevertheless found himself drawn to those rungs of the political establishment where powerful, successful and important people gathered. Yet the alien pride he felt in his Scottish and Calvinist background, which made him contemptuous of all underhand moves in the English power game, ironically prevented him then and later from being welcomed as a natural or wholly credible member of the coldly businesslike end of the establishment where he longed to be accepted. When, for instance, he sent a note, probably through Sir Gordon Nairne, to the Governor of the Bank of England, saying that he had not yet had the good fortune to meet Montagu Norman, and suggesting that this omission should be put right forthwith, Norman's reaction was typically petulant:

'He screwed the letter into a tight little ball, hurled it across his room, and exclaimed that the writer of such a letter was the last person on earth he ever wished to see', said Ronald Norman, the Governor's brother.[6] The mannerisms and quirks of Reith tended to play too easily into the hands of those who held the levers of power. His influence with Ramsay MacDonald, he fondly believed, had induced the Prime Minister to pack Clarendon off, like a character in one of Hilaire Belloc's cautionary verses, to run South Africa and leave the BBC to solve its own problems in peace. Yet when John Whitley called on the Postmaster-General shortly before the replacing of Clarendon, Lees-Smith confounded him by saying:

'I doubt whether you'll be seeing all that much of Sir John Reith. We fear he's off his head and won't be at the BBC for very much longer.'[6]

It may be argued that Lees-Smith, not a particularly effective politician, was probably ventilating his own prejudices. If so, he chose an inappropriate moment and audience. Yet so simple an explanation remains very questionable. Many stories and jokes at the expense of Reith were circulating at that time, and nothing would have surprised Whitley, not even a mad Director-General. Thus he approached his new task as chairman of the BBC board with care and a mild apprehension. It was perhaps a measure of the angular ease with which the Director-General exposed himself to ready caricature that Whitley and Reith came to terms virtually at once and conceived a genuine and lasting affection for one another. The aloofness, the severity, the puritanical dislike of all talk about sex, the tenacity with which Reith imposed his principles and workaday rules on others, such things represented the obvious side of his tangled nature. It was the dominating half, no doubt. Yet those who were privileged to see the other, gentler half felt everlasting gratitude to him. He put himself out to assist anyone who approached him with a personal problem. His tone of voice then took on an unaccustomed softness all the sweeter for its utter contrast with the ferocity of his manner in dealing with a sexual misdemeanour or a professional blunder.

The Max Beerbohm cartoon of Reith recaptures the aloof, mercurial figure whom outsiders so frequently scorned as a throwback to less democratic days. The word-picture drawn by the historian Alan Taylor is pithier and more damning. It depicts the 'Scotch engineer, Calvinist by upbringing, harsh and ruthless in character, [who] turned broadcasting into a mission [using] what he called "the brute force of monoply" to stamp Christian morality on the British people. He stamped it also on his own employees. . . . Broadcasting became a dictatorship, as though Milton and others had never made the case for unlicensed utterance. In no time at all the monopolistic corporation came to be regarded as an essential element in "the British way of life". Like all cultural dictatorships, the BBC was more important for what it silenced than for what it achieved. Controllers ranked higher than producers in its hierarchy. Disturbing views were rarely aired. The English people, if judged by the BBC, were uniformly devout and kept always to the middle of the road. . . .'[14]

Taylor's thumb-nail sketch of the man and his creation is too crudely drawn. Far more finely sensitive is Francis Meynell's description of Reith pacing his office in the Ministry of Works during the Second World War:

'I went to see him, arguing that he needed an information officer and that I was the man for the job. He showed no interest—either in me or in his Ministry. Something else was on his mind. The mounting emphasis of his talk was about his qualifications to be our ambassador in Washington. He strode up and down, showing me what was, in a purely literal sense, his two-facedness. When he passed me in one direction I saw that his expression was sensitive and mild; my hope was a little encouraged. When he went the other way, his profile was stern, set, unmoved; and I felt that I hadn't any chance at all. Slowly I realised that the set expression was due to the facial wound he had suffered in the First War. Finally a gentle and abstracted handshake was my dismissal.'[15]

By then his vaulting ambition had long ago lost its pristine rhythm. The personal crisis confronting Reith in 1930 was a personal crisis of decision: Should he go or stay? There was never much doubt about his answer. For Reith believed, quite correctly, that his child still needed guidance. This practical consideration conformed, at a slight tangent, with his old dream of reaching for the rainbow arched across a horizon from which the local thunder clouds had lifted. In Reith's incorrigibly romantic moments, of which there were many after the arrival of John Whitley as BBC chairman, it seemed that greater power might still lie within easy stretching distance at the rainbow's end.

It was incredible to find Mrs. Snowden behaving like a reformed woman under the courteous control of Whitley. The former Speaker of the Commons, a religious man renowned as the author of the civil service arbitration machinery which still bears his name, asserted his quiet authority without delay, to Reith's intense relief. The mending of fences separating board and executive became a first priority; and though Ethel Snowden mistook the new chairman for an ally in her campaign for staff representation of a permanent kind,

Whitley indicated that he preferred to pursue a deliberate policy of hastening slowly.

The political world receded for a spell. The BBC basked in its new-found calm, indifferent to politicians' concerns. The stock of Stanley Baldwin had meanwhile declined under the vituperative assaults of the 'two rascals', Rothermere and Beaverbrook, the latter 'courting him between insults', on behalf of his latest crusade for Empire Free Trade.[16] Reith, from a distance, retained some fellow-feeling for the kindly Opposition leader. Throughout 1930 Baldwin's continued leadership of the Conservative Party trembled in the balance, especially after the official Tory candidate was defeated in a by-election at the hands of a Beaverbrook nominee. Baldwin seemed to have lost his touch, and so strong ran the current of disaffection among his followers that his overt intention to resign in March 1931 was accepted with something approaching relief. Then Baldwin capriciously changed his mind, moving over to a counter-offensive against the two press lords who were making his life a misery. Borrowing a neat phrase from his cousin, Kipling, Baldwin condemned Rothermere and Beaverbrook for seeking 'power without responsibility, the prerogative of the harlot through the ages'. It was as much a shrewd appeal to public prejudice against the sensational press as anything else, but it paid off handsomely a few days later when Duff Cooper, the official Tory candidate, turned the tables on his Empire Free Trade opponent in the St. George's, Westminster, by-election. Baldwin's last-ditch counter-attack secured his unchallenged hold on the Conservatives until he withdrew from politics in the late thirties. Reith rejoiced in his triumph. Churchill, however, still continued fitfully to goad and irritate him.

The ambivalence of the late Chancellor's view of what was then termed 'access to the microphone' appeared in a brisk exchange of letters with Reith in late December 1929 and the first week of January 1930. Tongue stuck in cheek, Churchill's opening salvo was a 'public offer' to the BBC of '£100 out of my own pocket for the right to speak for half an hour on politics'. Reith declined promptly enough. The American pattern of broadcasting 'on a cash basis' did not operate in Britain, he replied. In the United States the cash system operated 'irrespective of any consideration of content or balance'. His logic left Churchill quite unappeased. He retorted that American methods were preferable to Reith's system of 'debarring public men from access to a public who wish to hear'.

Conveniently forgetting his own energetic efforts to muzzle the BBC in 1926, Churchill declared that Reith had erred in letting the party organisations regulate the BBC's political broadcasts: 'I was not aware that parties had a legal basis at all, or that they had been formally brought into your licence.' Reith's tactful counter-suggestion that Churchill should choose as a radio topic some broad canvas like 'the party system', the pretext being that 'the expression of original and provocative points of view can be done more effectively outside the confines of stereotyped party rota', went unheeded.[10]

Later, if wholly inadvertently, the Director-General succeeded in winning the scornful mistrust of Churchill whose violent disagreement with the Conservative Party over its moderate India policy had lately led to his resignation from the Shadow Cabinet. Churchill was adamant that his views deserved an airing on the BBC:

'He came to see Whitley and me', Reith noted, 'and told us what he wanted to say. . . . He did not mind who else spoke or what they said. I suggested that we might have someone from the left wing as well and finish with a representative of the Round Table point of view. He thought that a good idea. I walked with him to the lift. "I can tell you're a friend", he said. I observed that the same probably applied to Whitley.'

But Churchill quickly modified his opinion of Reith's friendly overtures. The Secretary of State for India, Wedgwood Benn, put his foot down: there was no Churchillian broadcast. Whitley and the Board had to abide by a 'request emphatically made by the minister responsible for dealing with a particularly delicate and critical situation', as Reith put it.[3] The decision incurred the somewhat childish animosity of Churchill who, unable or unwilling to resist his ingrained habit of personalising issues, laid the blame entirely on Reith. There was irony in this official rebuff to the politician who had schemed so hard in 1926 to commandeer the BBC. Nevertheless, the effect was to rekindle Churchill's smouldering distaste for a man who had baulked him twice within five years.* A keen sense of the practical told Reith how far he would ever be allowed to go in delicate political decisions of the kind. The advantages of being immediately accepted as an important member of the establishment weighed more in his scales than any possible personal disadvantages that might accrue later. Many

* 'You see these microphones?', said Churchill to the Royal Society of St. George in April 1934, poking fun at Reith for permitting a live broadcast of the speech. 'They have been placed on our tables by the British Broadcasting Corporation. Think of the risk these eminent men are running. We can almost see them in our mind's eye, gathered together in that very expensive building with the questionable statues on its front. We can picture Sir John Reith, with the perspiration mantling on his lofty brow, with his hand on the control switch, wondering, as I utter every word, whether it will not be his duty to protect his innocent subscribers from some irreverent thing I might say about Mr. Gandhi, or about the Bolsheviks, or even about our peripatetic Prime Minister. But let me reassure him. I have much more serious topics to discuss. I have to speak to you about St. George and the Dragon . . .'.

years afterwards, I questioned Reith on the validity of this view, which apparently nobody had ever had the temerity to question before in his presence. His answer was enlightening, if pompous:

'Perhaps if I had thought more or known more I would have tried to avoid the BBC becoming part of the establishment, but perhaps not. Establishment has a good deal to say for itself. And indeed such a charge was surely a considerable tribute to the BBC—that anything of such recent appearance should have attained to such entitliture [*sic*].'[2]

The main drawback, as he reluctantly acknowledged, was that the BBC sometimes failed at critical turning points in the nation's life to reflect, like a mirror faithfully held up to nature, the ugly, evil, mystifying and perilous problems of the day, along with the beautiful, the good, the intelligible and the safe. The corporation was not always so professionally aware, or equipped with knowledge, as it might have been. It moved obediently at the dignified pace prescribed by Reith himself. Contentious domestic issues such as chronic unemployment, high prices, lower wages and the manifold economic ills inseparable from Britain's return to gold were best avoided altogether or handled with a kid-glove discretion which robbed them of any relationship to reality. Professionalism certainly had a place at Savoy Hill: the inspired techniques of Hilda Matheson, Charles Siepmann and others in the talks department demonstrated what could be done. But technique was one thing, the choice of prickly topics quite another. Moreover Reith preferred producers who became jacks-of-all-trades and masters of none, for the prudent reason that 'committed men with specialised mystiques' would have been far harder to control. The idea of creative producers outpacing his all-important controllers was intolerable to him. That way lay needless anarchy.

By January 1931 the army of British unemployed had swollen to two and a half millions. The Labour Government, hobbled by Snowden's unswerving faith in the financial merits of balanced budgets, had little but goodwill and hope to offer the workless multitudes. Perhaps because the worst-hit areas of depression were remote from London, the problem itself failed to touch the springs of the average conscience. Like poverty in an earlier age, unemployment had become a permanent blight which the rulers and the ruled must learn to live with, since only two or three bold men, whom most of the experts discounted as eccentrics, claimed to know how the blight could be checked. 'We are not on trial', Ramsay MacDonald bleated, 'it is the system under which we live.' Yet rhetorical railings against the legacies of capitalism were hardly calculated to fill empty bellies or reconcile the jobless to their lot. Only Oswald Mosley among

Labour politicians had constructive ideas for trying to curb the disease, but his colleagues disregarded these until Mosley's low fund of patience evaporated. Abandoning the party in disgust to found a new political organisation of his own, he veered rapidly to the extreme right of British politics. Like Churchill, though for radically different reasons, he also met and fell foul of Reith, persuading himself that his name stood high on the 'black list' of public men debarred from broadcasting by the magisterial edict of Sir John. Such a list did not, in fact, officially exist. Controllers and producers alike had no need to consult one. The instinctive working of the Director-General's mind in these matters was well enough known to them already.

There were dozens of influential men and women who believed, rightly or wrongly, that their unfashionable or outré opinions had so offended the susceptibilities of Reith that they, too, would never be allowed to offend the ears of listeners with their blasphemies or impieties. They did him an injustice. For Reith could never keep abreast of all *avant-garde* trends. One of these self-styled victims, the editor of *The New Statesman*, had the good sense to raise the question with him personally. Kingsley Martin called on him by appointment, ostensibly to discuss the whole range of Reith's philosophy of broadcasting, then skilfully drew him out on the BBC's method of selecting speakers whose convictions were out of tune with the respectable common run:

'In other words', teased Kingsley Martin, 'you censor views you don't happen to regard as acceptable. Is that why I'm in your little black book?'

The direct accusation appeared 'to flummox him completely', according to Kingsley Martin. Reith replied evenly, after silently pacing up and down the room a few times, that the BBC operated no positive ban of the kind. As for the so-called 'black book', this was a figment of Kingsley Martin's imagination: if he had a legitimate complaint about not being asked to broadcast, it would certainly be looked into at once. Reith was as good as his word. Within a few days of the interview, Kingsley Martin received a letter inviting him to speak on the air.[6]

It was John Reith's ambition, now that the internal power struggle had ceased, to let the outside world see the corporation as he saw it as the dependable keeper of the nation's conscience. Its rightful position was that of an arbiter standing above the clamour of all political and social factions. As the paragon of impartiality, honesty and respectability, its good name had to be defended at all costs. It hurt him when the BBC, his other self, was pilloried for indulging in vulgar bias or for falling short of its almost unattainable ideals.

When charged personally with unfairness, he scrupulously sought to set the balance straight. Yet he equally accepted it as his bounden duty to prevent 'scandal of the weak'; to protect listeners against anything that could be construed as harmful, contentious or dangerous; and to work untiringly as a promoter of those causes of which the government and the establishment approved without qualification. This policy seemed to have everything in its favour. The fact that he adopted it naturally strained at times the credulity of those who asserted that the BBC was neglecting its chief responsibility: that of claiming something more positive than a pale and nominal independence. What these critics failed to understand, mainly because they possessed no close personal knowledge of the Director-General or his foibles, was that the credibility of the BBC and that of John Reith had by now become inseparably entwined. The suspicion that he had been swallowed by the establishment gained wide currency in the early thirties, especially among the politically well-informed who remembered how vulnerable to political pressure the BBC had proved during the General Strike. The recollection did not encourage them to swallow his credentials or always to welcome his pretensions as an enlightened autocrat.

When the financial crash shattered the second Labour government in the high summer of 1931, Reith was far away in Poland. His fame as a pioneer of broadcasting had gradually spread across the globe. Because John Whitley's presence had restored complete calm at Savoy Hill, there was leisure and opportunity for the Director-General to move about the world at last so that distant admirers could learn of his achievements at first hand. The BBC, he knew, was almost universally trusted. If, as its detractors alleged, the flavour of its offerings was sometimes insipid and colourless, Reith would retort with feeling that democracy could often be colourless, too. He thought of his service as providing what he called 'a tempering factor', enabling democracy for the first time in its history to function as a self-conscious 'living force' among its members.

By strengthening the ordinary citizen's grasp of the institutions that ran the nation's affairs, the BBC's microphones might become in time a more potent influence for harmony than the printing press. For the high-sounding theories of the best political philosophers were seldom the stuff of mundane, everyday existence: only when their maxims became part of the very tissue of men's minds, through the instrumentality of broadcasting, would the art of democracy become as natural and instinctive a process as breathing. Where newspaper owners often abused press freedom by selective presentation of facts and comment, the BBC would complement their deficiencies by speaking out dispassionately to the entire public.

The ultimate challenge as Reith saw it, was 'one of integration', since 'the key to unity of the nervous system of the body politic' had yet to be discovered. The key was in the possession of John Reith, or so he deluded himself. The BBC, he felt, could alone supply that unity as a corporate citizen in its own right, not just as a technical agency subservient to the needs of government ministers. Too few of them, too few civil servants, too few people of distinction and influence yet appreciated this basic Reithian truth. His task must be to convert them gradually to his realistic mode of thinking. Then the rough way upwards to the rarefied heights of 'supreme responsibility', where destiny still beckoned him fitfully, could be made smoother. The old, fractured vision of grandeur still returned like a friendly ghost to haunt him thus at intervals, especially when he compared other broadcasting networks with his own. For these reasons, among others, Reith gladly accepted a number of invitations from foreign broadcasting authorities in 1930 and 1931.

Like a modern Wesley, but travelling in the style befitting a modern celebrity, he drew swift and usually unfavourable conclusions about other systems in use elsewhere. The experience reinforced his ludicrous conviction that somehow the past could be undone and that he still might piece together again the fragments of his youthful dream of greatness. He spent several happy days in Germany during the summer of 1930. The visit was clouded only by fears for the future of that weak and divided country, which his hosts freely expressed to him. A lengthy tour with Lady Reith across the United States then followed in the spring of 1931.

Despite the laconic contrariness of President Hoover, who told him that the American people disliked monopolies in radio as in all else, Reith spoke up in defence of the public service ideal. Herbert Hoover offered him little encouragement: a special Federal Commission existed to protect the public interest, he said; if the commissioners tamely submitted to political or other pressures, then they had only themselves to blame. Reith revived nostalgic wartime memories during a weekend in Philadelphia and Swarthmore, where old friends gave him the welcome of a homecoming hero. It touched him that the ageing Presbyterian minister even 'remembered some of my favourite hymns'. Then they crossed to Chicago, the middle west, and the Pacific coast; travelling north again to Portland, Oregon, re-crossing the continental divide to the east, and finally reaching Canada. The impressions left on his mind were kaleidoscopic, but nothing could shake the belief now that in the BBC he had founded a service without an equal anywhere. A brief stay in Vienna during August 1931 further embellished his mystical crown of glory. And nothing he noticed or heard on the rail journey east to Poland disturbed his self-congratulatory mood. Then the wholly unexpected happened.

In the restaurant car of the train steaming from Cracow to Warsaw, Reith caught sight of a startling headline. One word, 'ENGLAND', stood out in ominously black type among the indecipherable foreign phrases splashed across the front page of a newspaper held up by a stranger at the next table. Reith's Polish host craned his neck for a closer look:

'It seems', he said, 'that there's a political crisis in England.'

That was how John Reith first became aware of the second Labour government's catastrophic downfall. The consequences for Britain and all Europe were to be bitter and long-lasting; yet Reith's superficial impression that this was simply another stage in the mismanagement of the nation's finances reflected both his abstracted mood of euphoria and his detachment from stark reality. Indeed it was in Vienna, a bare three months earlier, that the failure of the Credit Anstalt Bank had touched off a tidal wave of panic which had finally engulfed Britain; and Reith had recently been in Vienna, quite impervious to the dangerous onrush of events.

'At Warsaw a telegram informed me that the Labour Government had resigned. MacDonald was Prime Minister of a coalition. The names of the new Cabinet were given. I absorbed all I could about Polish broadcasting at its headquarters. . . .'[3]

Single-minded as ever, he decided not to cut short his stay. Neither in the elegant, agreeable company he kept in Poland, nor later in Berlin on his leisurely, homeward journey, did Reith awaken to the uncomfortable fact that the inter-war period had crashed to its ruinous end. He was far more out of touch with the facts of everyday life than a person of his position and aspirations had any title to be; yet it should be said in his favour that here he did not stand alone:

'We are sitting on top of a volcano', Sir Clive Wigram had warned the King privately as long before as July 11th, 'and the curious thing is that the press and the City have not really understood the critical situation. The governor of the Bank of England is very pessimistic and depressed. . . . A minority government will hardly be able to deal with the situation, and it is quite possible that Your Majesty might be asked to approve a national government.'[17]

The intensely secretive Montagu Norman had anticipated the hurricane more than six weeks before it struck; but Norman, too, was abroad recovering from a nervous collapse by August 24th, when MacDonald hesitantly accepted the King's commission to carry on as leader of an emergency coalition, which included the few colleagues who left the splintered Labour Party at his side. Events had certainly moved too fast for Reith to follow on his excursions overseas. His political antennae were much poorer than he supposed. Winston Churchill, basking in the sun at Biarritz, had nevertheless correctly read the storm signals at a distance with a flash of typically self-righteous anger:

'Everybody I meet seems vaguely alarmed that something terrible is going to happen', he wrote to his friend and former private secretary, Eddie Marsh. 'I hope we shall hang Montagu Norman if it does. I shall certainly turn King's evidence against him.'[18]

Churchill was not asked to turn King's evidence nor to join the new government, while Reith resumed his duties at Savoy Hill a sadder and slightly wiser man. The baffling sequence of calamities since the early summer had at least taught him once more not to bank too much on unearned expectations. He contented himself with holding on stubbornly to the ground that was indisputably his, sallying out only to resist the Exchequer's demand for a voluntary saving from the BBC of £100,000 and whittling that down by half. Technically, the broadcasting system had kept an uncertain nation fairly well informed and entertained; but professionally the service had not risen to the nuances of the financial crisis any better than its absentee Director-General had done.

The so-called naval mutiny at Invergordon in September 1931 was duly reported by the press and the BBC. It caused a sensation, one which Britain could ill afford. Units of the Home Fleet were preparing to put to sea on routine manœuvres when discontented ratings, who had learned of prospective cuts in their pay only from the newspapers, deliberately refused to obey orders. Faulty public relations and incredibly bad communications inside the Admiralty had partly provoked this embarrassing response from the lower deck. Its effect undid the new government's early attempts to stabilise confidence in sterling. The nerves of foreign investors cracked. Funds began to flow rapidly from London. If the Royal Navy, an institution thought to be no less secure than the British Crown itself, could no longer be trusted to introduce essential economies, there might be no end to the revolutionary possibilities. The fears of the foreign investors were understandable if grossly distorted by sensational reporting and panicky rumour. The absentee Norman's lieutenants at the Bank of England warned the government that the run on gold was so heavy that, unless it could be stemmed, Britain would be impoverished by the end of the month. The Bank then formally requested that it should be relieved at once of its obligation to sell bullion on demand under the Gold Standard Act of 1925. The requisite Bill suspending such payments was passed in a single day, Monday, September 21st, 1931, while Montagu Norman sailed peacefully across the Atlantic towards Liverpool, quite oblivious that the curtain had come down on his epoch of fairy gold.

One man's attempt to restore the old order in Europe on a new financial basis had foundered. Many will endorse the retrospective view of Lord Salter that 'June, 1931 was the watershed of the inter-war period. The gathering forces of financial chaos and economic distress gave Hitler his chance and precipitated the Second World War.'[19]

The aftermath of that disastrous summer of 1931 clearly was not the most propitious time for John Reith to think of throwing up the sponge. The BBC needed him as much as ever; and he was just as glad of the security it gave him in what promised now to become a long grey period of economic difficulty for the nation and the individual alike. Intimations of 'equal discontent' from all sections of the emergency Coalition Government came his way in the campaigning before the 1931 autumn election. The only broadcast that impressed Reith was that of Lloyd George whose 'bardic note' had its own magnetic appeal for him. Churchill protested in a letter to *The Times* that inviting a solitary Tory speaker, Stanley Baldwin, 'was carrying the suppression of Conservative opinion beyond the bounds of reason and fair play'.[4] Reith spent some time talking freely to Lloyd George after his virtuoso performance on the air:

'Very depressed about unemployment', he noted. 'He could cure it in a year if I were seconded to work with him.'[3]

It was an empty recipe for recovery. Lloyd George had long shot his bolt politically; any flattering if empty allusions to Reith's considerable gifts as an organiser would have come better from the true source of power in Whitehall, but there nobody seriously considered his candidature. Ministers asked voters for 'a doctor's mandate', and got it, the Conservatives and their allies winning 521 seats to Labour's 52 and the Liberals 33. Snowden went to the House of Lords as a Viscount, Neville Chamberlain to the Exchequer in his place. Nobody suggested bringing back Lloyd George. Austen Chamberlain was gently passed over. Nor could room be found in the Cabinet for the 'pugnacious imperialists, Amery and Churchill'.[14]

Britain bent its patriotic back to the slow haul uphill towards economic recovery. There was nothing better Reith wished to do than speed that process with the means still at his disposal. Only when the nation, which had saved itself by its efforts, managed at last to rise again to its full stature, would the time be ripe for him to think of handing over to a younger man. Yet there was a suspicious if subconscious hint of a swansong in one decisive step he took, in conjunction with Whitley, before the BBC (obliged like all government departments and all citizens to put a cheerful face on temporary cuts in its income and delays in its plans for growth) said goodbye to its old home at Savoy Hill. Together they agreed to draw up a simple formula, defining the rights and duties of the board of governors so that there would be no repetition of the friction and misunderstandings which had bedevilled the conduct of corporation business in the arid period preceding Whitley's arrival. The chairman urged Reith to draft a document setting down his own ideas, while he tried his hand separately: they could then compare notes and amend accordingly. When the chairman read Reith's version, he admitted spontaneously that it was preferable in its succinctness to the Whitley version. Its text runs:

'The governors of the BBC act primarily as trustees to safeguard the broadcasting service in the national interest. Their functions are not executive. Their responsibilities are general and not particular. They are not divided up for purposes of departmental supervision. The suggestion sometimes made that governors should be appointed as experts or specialists in any of the activities covered by the broadcasting service is not regarded as desirable. The governors should as far as possible be persons of wide outlook and considerable experience of men and affairs, preferably with previous public service of one kind or another; and there should be included also a person or persons with financial and commercial experience. They are, subject to the duties laid upon the Postmaster-General by Parliament in the Royal Charter, responsible for seeing that the many purposes for which broadcasting was established, and which in 1926 were reviewed by the Royal Charter, are carried out. With the Director-General they discuss and (then) decide on major matters of policy and finance, but they leave the execution of that policy and the general administration of the service in all its branches to the Director-General and his competent officers. The governors should be able to judge of the general effect of the service upon the public, and subject as before mentioned, are finally responsible for the conduct of it.'[10,3]

Whitley took this exceptionally important paper, a kind of insurance policy against future hazards, to the new Postmaster-General, Kingsley Wood, and to the Prime Minister—'both of whom approved it'. The only change suggested by Ramsay MacDonald was the insertion of the word 'then', which can be seen bracketed in the second last sentence of the text.

This clear brief was to be read by the responsible minister to every future governor on appointment. It seemed to Reith a necessary and valuable reminder that power had limits and imposed its own obligations. Anyone less addicted to detailed preoccupations with future plans might have judged this to be the cue for leaving. Alas, Reith had no close or wise friends to consult: and even if there had been, he would not have welcomed the advice that outside the BBC there were fresh fields to conquer. For, in his innermost soul, he knew that he would feel utterly lost by deliberately separating himself from his child. What Reith overlooked, what any good friend would certainly have pointed out if there had been one fully to confide in, was that the child had imperceptibly reached young manhood. It had therefore earned the inalienable privilege of learning from its own mistakes. Perhaps it was only to be expected that so strong a personality, who had been deprived of his own youth, would never be genuinely swayed by that argument. Yet John Reith's complacent belief that the BBC still needed him turned out in time to be the worst mistake he ever made.

9
The Paternalist

1

Only eighteen of the original band of thirty-one men and women who had accompanied Reith to Savoy Hill in 1923 were left to join him in the shining new concert hall of Broadcasting House on May 2nd, 1932. Most of them, significantly, were people in the lower grades of the hierarchy. At nine o'clock that morning the Union Jack and the BBC flag were run up and broken at their mastheads above the dazzling white cliff face of the building. But if his taste for ritualistic touches died hard, Reith felt inwardly uneasy. He did not care for the size, the shape or some of the principal features of these otherwise desirable premises:

'It was really too early', he mused later, 'to contemplate a comprehensive headquarters for British broadcasting, and I did not like the building. . . . I had persuaded the governors to agree to buy the adjacent houses, feeling sure that before long the whole island site would be needed. There it was, however, and most of the staff were quite pleased. It was a great improvement on the improvisations and congestions of Savoy Hill.'[1]

His uneasiness quickly proved well founded, just as his reluctance during the months of preliminary planning not to urge 'my own view against those of others' had held a deeper meaning. But for the catastrophic events of August 1931, Reith might well have decided to look around for a fresh opening commensurate with his talents. He was only forty-two; the world was full of unsolved problems and splendid opportunities befitting a man of messianic drive and unrequited ambition; foreign travel, particularly his American visit, had unsettled him; and he judged correctly that the pioneering days of the BBC were over. His misfortune was that an inveterate shyness kept him on the outer ring of an establishment which, while taking good care of its own, tended to nourish well-bred reservations about John Reith's candour, solemnity and other less clubbable traits. Not unlike Trenchard or Churchill, but lacking the latter's connections, flair and guile, the Director-General of the BBC had no option now but to wait upon events and make the most of his unexacting task.

There may be some readers who will quarrel with the word 'unexacting'. Undeniably, the Corporation had not yet secured all the legal rights to which Reith believed it was entitled. Nor had it developed its fullest potentialities, professional and technical, in a way that would enhance its prestige as the one model which the whole world might justly envy. Yet there were younger men in the wings who had grown up with Reith in broadcasting. They shared his ideals and, perhaps somewhat imitatively, his sharp sense of the practical. Their grief at his departure then would no doubt have been assuaged by the knowledge that he was handing down an inheritance which even the most irresponsible prodigal among them could neither disentangle nor wantonly squander. For the plain truth is that between 1932 and 1938 a different set of problems confronted the governors and the executive of the BBC, and an august father-figure was not necessarily the most suitable person to tackle them. Reith rarely failed to plunge straight to the heart of any issue; but the issues of the thirties demanded something less spectacular than the individualism of the frontiersman bent on heroic survival. In any case, a faint impatience had begun to stir in him. The longing to be 'fully stretched' grew steadily with the advancing years. It turned a man of unexampled vigour into the crotchetiness of late middle age well before his time. The effect on the establishment was to mar his already hesitant relationship with it, still further dimming his once bright prospects of gaining enviable preferment when the huge, bronze doors of Broadcasting House closed behind him for ever.

On that May morning in 1932, however, Reith's manner betrayed no hint of uneasiness. Addressing some 700 members of the London staff in the concert hall, he reiterated his pristine beliefs with evangelical fervour: he would remain, he said, 'to repel attacks on the BBC and to secure more freedom for it, to look out for new avenues of development and progress, and to ensure, if possible, the satisfaction and happiness of each one of you. . . .'[2] Like a mystical body of which he happened to be the undisputed head, the corporation thrived as a living organism. It was not just any public organisation. No division, branch, department or section could work to itself alone without damaging the whole. . . . They could depend on him, Reith, to hold them. Alas, natural adaptation to these new surroundings was not so simple.

The move from Savoy Hill marked a distinct watershed in the life of the BBC. Before, all was 'intimacy and harmony'; after, all was 'bureaucracy and conflict'.[3] This oversimplification, quoted by Asa Briggs, quickly became common currency, especially among the older hands. The new premises set their heavy, impersonal mould on high and low alike. Broadcasting House was not the place for instant psychological adjustment: 'that damned monolithic imitation of a battleship in Portland Place', as one wit described it, seemed to cast its cold, functional spell on all without regard to rank. The veterans looked back wistfully to the cramped discomforts of Savoy Hill, recalling that the very inconveniences of that rabbit warren had cut right across most demarcation lines, forcing senior staff to mix, freely in a more human and easy manner. 'A leviathan of a building', another critic wailed. 'Not the dove or the eagle but the white elephant should be its crest. Savoy Hill was suitable for the pioneering stage of the BBC, and maybe Broadcasting House is suitable for its bureaucratic stage.'[4]

The portentous dedication in classical Latin, adorning a pillar in the wide, marbled entrance hall, appeared to enshrine the stony formality of 'this temple of arts and muses'. The rotund phrasing was Dr. Rendall's, the mild, classical scholar from Winchester. It was he who had been nominated as 'the ultimate authority' on all questions of taste and décor; and he it was who interpolated the name of John Reith in the dedication without thinking to consult him. Too late to alter the lettering of the sculptor, Eric Gill, Reith comforted himself that the sentiments at any rate were 'magnificent'. He suspected that much of the outside gossip evoked by this and other salient features had a disagreeably sarcastic ring, but chose as usual to ignore it. In fact some external trimmings evoked unseemly mirth inside as well. The fastidious were of the opinion that if a talks studio, economically lined with bogus book-backs, showed execrably bad taste, a new religious studio, which could never be consecrated as Reith desired, deserved to take the proverbial biscuit. Men versed in the arcane rubrics of these things had counselled the Director-General, to his distress, that hallowing was out of the question. They could find no precedent, so he was assured, to justify the act of solemnly consecrating a single room on the seventh floor of a multi-storey modern building. Whether such liturgical squeamishness owed anything to the location, several floors directly below, of another studio devoted to variety and similar profanities, was not recorded. Nor did Reith trouble to enquire.

There was general approval of Gill's expressively symbolic figures which, nevertheless, brought a flinty look to the faces of many prudish bystanders.

One MP, Mr. G. G. Mitcheson, questioned the Home Secretary on the propriety of the sculptor's design. Would Sir John Gilmour, he asked as late as March 1933, instruct the removal by the metropolitan police of the statue above the main entrance to Broadcasting House, since it was offensive to public morals and decency? The Home Secretary declined. Yet the staff already accepted without a blush that the concrete battleship hard by the Queen's Hall had as its figurehead a work of art which the philistines condemned as lewd. What Mr. Mitcheson possibly did not realise was that less than two years previously, while Eric Gill was completing his handiwork behind a tarpaulin, the governors had mounted the ladder to the platform for a closer inspection of the nude figures of Prospero and Ariel. Apparently disquieted by the generous proportions of Ariel's pudenda, they climbed down to convene a hasty meeting, in the course of which Dr. Rendall admitted:

'I can only say, from personal observation, that the lad is uncommonly well hung.'

The spare phrase of another collector of such anecdotes must be cited for the sequel:

'Like Michelangelo before him, Gill was tactfully asked to remount the ladder and cut the things down to size.'[5]

This, with tetchy grace, the sculptor did.

In other departments it proved less easy to 'cut things down to size'. For the new milieu lent itself at once to the sturdy growth of bureaucratic practices and proclivities. Reith's resolve to preserve his usual single eye for essentials was emulated by his aides, not always without internal friction and disharmony. The record of the previous nine years had been fairly free of rancour, discounting the recent wrangling for power with Clarendon and Mrs. Snowden, of course. The BBC's uphill struggle for existence, recognition, and an assured place in the sun had extended Reith to the limits of his versatility and panache. Even the severest tests of status and stamina, as in the awkward days of the General Strike, had yielded some small compensating sense of exhilaration, however badly they shook Reith's self-confidence and sapped the BBC's nominal independence. Now these nine lean years were giving place to seven relatively fat years: and long before their close John Reith, for all his apocalyptic fervour and unchallenged leadership, began to feel like a man lost in a maze.

Up to a point, of course, the maze was of his own making; for the inexorable laws of growth operating within the structure itself required careful handling, and Reith had neither the patience nor the delicacy to check the insidious growth of bureaucratic formalities. His genius for self-justification enabled him to fob off most external criticism as evidence of jealousy, ignorance or sheer malignancy, while critical voices from within were either muted or tactfully modulated out of fear or respect for the master-builder himself:

'The BBC might be considered autocratic or arbitrary in attitude or procedure', Reith wrote in a characteristic passage. 'It had the courage of its convictions; it did what it believed was in the public interest. Ought not that to apply to any body vested with authority and responsibility? There was no electoral process anywhere in BBC constitution and procedure. The governing body was nominated, not elected; the programmes were compiled not to meet but to antedate the popular vote. One knew of what sort they would otherwise have been. Here was a lesson for other public bodies from Parliament down.'[1]

The BBC now had permanent roots. The danger in the early and middle thirties, a grey political period of introspection and of agonisingly slow recovery from the blight of the depression, was Reith's waywardness in resisting any internal pressures for change which conflicted with his preconceived, élitiste ideals. The brave outrider of the twenties, who had been repeatedly forced to improvise brilliantly in the interests of self-preservation, betrayed an increasing inflexibility that systematically worked to the detriment of the BBC as a whole. This fatal tendency can be seen most clearly in the plans he drew up and executed in 1933 for modernising the machinery of control. Reorganisation was overdue owing to the rapid increase in staff before and after the move to Broadcasting House. Between 1927 and 1931, when Clarendon and Mrs. Snowden were at his throat, recruitment had slowed down: only 298 men and women in all categories were added to the strength in those five years, against fully 157 who either resigned or suffered dismissal. The staff totalled 1287 members in 1931 when expansion began again in earnest. By 1935 it had doubled in size to over 2500; before Reith left it had practically doubled again. As the promised developments of Empire broadcasting and experimental television loomed up, more men and women of ability were needed, together with an adequate system of operational and administrative control. And it was precisely here that Reith went badly astray.

His practical views on the methods of devolving authority and responsibility inside the BBC remained unchallenged for years to come:

'Controllers can give their subordinates no more than they themselves get from above, but increasingly they too are devolving authority and responsibility on their departmental directors', he told the recently inaugurated staff training school in October 1936. 'There are therefore a great many people party to and concerned in management at the BBC. What the BBC does, therefore, is more and more *not* what one individual thinks; more and more it comes from a consensus of opinion and experience.'[2]

In theory, the consensus theory of control was admirable. In day-to-day practice, the difficulties of applying it proved to be almost insuperable. Controllers were key men; but their abiding instinct was to play for safety and interpret the rules of devolution strictly in accordance with Reith's lights rather than their own. So down the chain of command the spirit of a dutiful conformity descended with sluggish predictability. It caused shudders of frustration among more discerning producers and not a few senior staff members at departmental level, if not higher. Any closed society, but especially one enjoying monopoly privileges and untouched by the profit motive in its mainly creative endeavours, cannot escape the risks of stagnation once decision-making has to 'emerge' like ectoplasm from above, and when good programme-making ultimately depends on the uncertain whim of departmental bosses nervously peering over their shoulders. This trend had already set in during the last months at Savoy Hill. By 1933, when Reith's master plan was ready, the trend had become the rule at Broadcasting House.

The producers in shirt-sleeves on the studio floor, whose work a later governor loftily described as 'the kitchen-end of broadcasting', felt most of all the deadweight of such unimaginative and often counter-productive methods of interpreting and passing down the Reithian philosophy of broadcasting. Forgetting for a moment their resentment, which might be rejected by the orthodox as ill-informed and irresponsible, we cannot, however, ignore the evidence of those senior staff members who had served with Reith from the beginning and were probably in the best position to judge. One of them, Ralph Wade, ascribed the trouble in part to the BBC's excessive reliance on committees instead of on the exercise of individual commonsense. According to Wade, who had joined the old company at the express invitation of Reith and became an administrator in 1924, even the central control board had to be treated with sceptical care: 'as a shield against outside, or even government, criticism', it had its purpose, but as the begetter of speedy, intelligent, or original decisions on programmes it left very much to be desired:

'The members', said Wade, 'are at best exercising a remote

control over what their executive staff are in fact doing and many of the decisions reached are really quite wrong ones. . . . You can't sack a control board *en bloc*, but you can sack an individual director or head of department. To my mind the best test of suitability for headship of any group or activity is the willingness to accept responsibility. Once you have a board or committee which is technically responsible for *your* opinions, either you despair of getting things done *as you know they should be done* or, if you are that type, you nestle snugly down behind the protective screen of high level decision and become a "Yes" man.'[6]

The new Archbishop of Canterbury, Dr. Cosmo Lang, told Reith on one occasion that the job of Primate would never have suited the Director-General of the BBC. 'Why?' demanded Reith. Because, Dr. Lang replied, the clergy invariably 'trot out their consciences' and 'frustrate the best-laid schemes at every turn'. BBC controllers and producers were not encouraged to flaunt their consciences or to demonstrate their powers of initiative. The most sensible course, especially for newcomers in the early thirties, was to dispense outright with such luxuries. For the fiat of Reith and his small group of trusted aides could occasionally be anticipated but never questioned. When, for instance, the unusually independent-minded programme head of North Region, Archie Harding, allowed the corrosive opinions of some hunger-marchers to go out in interview-form on the air, the Director-General warned him that there must be no repetition of so grave an 'error of judgment'! The broadcasting of such anti-government sentiments was scandalous and damaging to the corporation. Unwilling to incur another reprimand too soon, Harding decided not to transmit an allegorical verse-play by D. G. Bridson, *Prometheus the Engineer*, before submitting the script to head office. By then Colonel Alan Dawnay had been recruited by Reith from the War Office as chief programme controller of the BBC. Written in the form of a classical tragedy, with passing references to social credit as a utopian panacea for mankinds economic ills, the play was summarily banned by Dawnay as being 'dangerously seditious'. The *Radio Times*, however, had already billed it in advance; its cancellation led to some press enquiries. Moreover, a copy of the work had been sent by someone in Broadcasting House to T. S. Eliot, together with a premature invitation to come along and hear the actual transmission. Eliot duly arrived on the day. He was greeted with profuse apologies, and went away still somewhat bemused by the inadequate explanations for the BBC's odd decision not to broadcast a play he liked. When the poet subsequently learnt the true reason, he was so amused that he agreed to print *Prometheus the Engineer* precisely as it stood in his highly conservative literary review, *The Criterion*.

Val Gielgud had been luckier, at an earlier date, in obtaining Carpendale's sanction for a radio adaptation of Ibsen's *Ghosts*. The admiral admitted that he had not read or seen the play; but what he had heard of it by reputation roused his darkest suspicions:

'In some way *Ghosts* had become associated in the admiral's mind', said Gielgud, 'with the friskier type of Paris boulevard comedy of sexual entanglements and marital infidelity. I failed to disabuse him of this notion.'

Nevertheless, Carpendale promised to scrutinise the text on the train to Cardiff next day, the one recompense in prospect being that it 'might enliven a dull journey'. His advice to Gielgud meanwhile was: 'Don't waste your time, just drop the whole idea of this production.' On Carpendale's return, Gielgud was sent for. One glance at the admiral's glum face convinced the director of drama that *Ghosts* would never be heard on the air. He was wrong, as it happened:

'I don't see why you should want to do the thing', grumbled Carpendale. 'It's very long—and very dull.'[7]

The increased sensitivity of government ministers and MPs to alleged lapses in good taste or editorial judgment often lay at the heart of the censorship problem. Reith's closeness to MacDonald and Baldwin, coupled with an overreadiness at times to humour them, intensified the control difficulties at Broadcasting House. The Cabinet seemed to have an excessive regard for the mischief-making potential of the corporation, particularly in the sphere of news and controversial talks, despite the fact that only in 1932 did the BBC create its own rudimentary news department of four subeditors, directed by John Coatman, an ex-chief of the Indian Police who had vast experience of the world but none as a professional journalist. Coatman's name, it seemed, had been obligingly mentioned to Reith by Lord Willingdon, the Viceroy, who both knew and admired this excellent, one-time Indian civil servant. The small news staff, however, came under the control of the flourishing talks department, an area of dangerous unpredictability, in ministerial eyes, which needed watching and consistently firm handling. Engineers were different. These backroom boys in the Peter Eckersley tradition could be invariably relied on for such triumphantly dignified coups as the first Christmas Day transmission by King George V.

Talks producers, by contrast, had to mind their step after a projected broadcast by the ex-commander of a German U-boat was cancelled by the board on the unanimous advice of the Cabinet. To be fair, Reith hated this weak-kneed decision and strongly dissented from it, genuinely considering that the talk would have been 'a serious contribution to the elimination of war'. The dangerous sleep-walking phase of British diplomacy had begun, and its impact on the chartered freedom of the BBC continued to be felt intermittently until 1938.

2

The selection of Colonel Alan Dawnay in 1933 as Reith's 'new broom' mystified many people, including one or two internal aspirants for the job who considered themselves far better qualified. Asa Briggs has pointed out that Reith would have liked the Oxford don, Sir John Masterman, as his first choice; but the careful Masterman turned the offer down, claiming that he lacked 'the missionary impulse to do something great which you would be entitled to expect from your second-in-command',[8] so Reith concurred reluctantly in his decision. As Dawnay was mentioned by Masterman as a likelier candidate, and some of the Director-General's more influential acquaintances at the Athenaeum and elsewhere thought well of this former friend and associate of T. E. Lawrence, Reith sought out the man himself and took to him on sight. It was a grave misjudgment. For it must be said that the appointment of Dawnay inserted a square peg into a round hole. The effect was to stunt the proper development of the BBC until the outbreak of war at least.

Apart from his credentials as a scrupulously conventional and well-connected staff officer, Dawnay possessed neither the training, the taste nor the strength of personality necessary to lubricate and manipulate the topheavy machinery of management which the Director-General now thought it expedient to introduce as a means of easing his own load. Within eighteen months of Dawnay's appearance in October 1933, the ranker weeds of bureaucracy were flourishing like orchids in the hothouse atmosphere of Broadcasting House.

Under the reorganisation Dawnay was entrusted with the control of all 'output' and required to work in tandem with Sir Charles Carpendale, the recently knighted new controller of administration.

'It is dreadful to have been in the position of having so magnificent a job in one's gift', Reith noted of Dawnay's appointment. 'I could not help taking account of the fact that an incalculable amount depends on this decision, to me personally, to the BBC, and to the country generally.'[9]

Two men only were now directly accountable to the Director-General, instead of four or five as in the past. The object was 'to secure the better co-ordination of authority and responsibility; the clearer definition and separation of administrative and creative functions; and the freeing of the Director-General from much of the detail with which he is at present dealing'. Under Dawnay's division came four main 'creative' branches: programmes, talks, publicity and publications, as well as the rudimentary foreign service of Empire broadcasting which had started at the end of 1932. Carpendale's command comprised finance, internal administration, business relations, and engineering: but as an earnest of Reith's special regard for the last-named branch, Noel Ashbridge, who had replaced Peter Eckersley as chief engineer, continued to enjoy untrammelled personal access to the Director-General. Undoubtedly the most radical change was the infiltration of Carpendale's army of administrators into the sensitive areas of programmes as a deliberate act of policy:

'The transferred administrative staff', Reith's blueprint proclaimed, 'will work, under their administrative chief, to the requirements of the creative staff who will be relieved of all immediate and direct responsibility in administrative matters. It is intended that the transferred administrative staff shall form something in the nature of an Output Secretariat, carrying out the smallest administrative functions on behalf of the creative staff, e.g. taking the minutes of and making all arrangements for their meetings. The system implies that Heads of Branches, Departments and Sections in the Output Division will work direct to their corresponding Executives and through them to the Director of Internal Administration and Controller (Administration), the referring of administrative questions to their creative superiors not being contemplated as part of the normal procedure.'[2]

On paper, the scheme looked rational enough, though there were no doubt less cumbrous ways of unscrambling and reconstituting an omelette. What it did ensure first and foremost was the concentration of power in the hands of the top triumvirate of Reith, Dawnay and Carpendale. Unfortunately, Dawnay was quickly carried out of his depth. He lacked the innate ability to inspire confidence and become the leader and mentor of the so-called 'creative' staff. His duty, as he saw it, was to discourage any manifestations of originality or inventiveness that might be construed by the administrators, Reith or the politicians as wayward or controversial. He evoked increasing disapproval from below as a remote and none too discriminating censor, who duplicated the administrative labours of Carpendale's men in a plodding manner that frequently caused even his own departmental chiefs to wonder 'whether he knows whose side he's on'. Disharmony spread steadily like an infection. The plain, unadventurous diet on which Dawnay insisted became as unpalatable as prison fare to men and women lower down the scale. Who could blame producers for distinguishing between 'them', the bosses who cultivated the virtues of prudence and temperance, and 'us', the underlings who discovered that initiative and originality seldom paid? The hierarchical clamps bore down on their spirits, and as if Dawnay's negativism were not enough, the indignity of having Carpendale's strong guard of administrators intruding into their private griefs seemed to add needless confusion and humiliation to resentment.

'An attitude of guarded suspicion on both sides', Asa Briggs pointed out, 'made for a division of outlook between "output" and "administration". It became an article of faith that programme people should not be bothered with administration—they certainly did not fully free themselves from it—and this could lead all too easily into irresponsibility. On the other side, administrative staff could all too easily come to regard themselves—and even more easily come to be regarded—as the "policemen" of the system.'[3]

Ossification might still have been avoided if Dawnay had been less shy, less remote, more willing to admit ownership of a pedestrian mind. Content to let sleeping dogs lie, he normally shut his ears to the snarling and yelping of the puppies chained up in the cellars below. He had his own dismissive way of handling complaints, of meting out advice to senior staff who dared so much as to hint that the system itself was leading to absurd demarcation disputes. Loyalty was his strong suit; and in his loyalty to Reith he never shrank from sitting heavily on anyone whose attitude smacked of disloyalty. Clashes frequently occurred between programme staff and administrators on matters of detail which, under the revised order of precedence, had to be referred upwards for the decision of a Carpendale man, when common sense suggested that it was really the concern of a Dawnay man. The process caused frequent sparks to fly. It also slowed down the elaborate machinery of decision-making, offending the sensibilities of seasoned programme heads like Cecil Graves of the new Empire Service, Charles Siepmann of the Talks Department, Gladstone Murray of publicity, and Roger Eckersley, now in charge of programmes, who propably felt his demotion most keenly of all.

Reith refused to intervene or to be influenced by special pleading. Dawnay, his 'new broom', would sweep aside all selfish doubts of discomfited empire-builders. A stickler for the rules of deference, the colonel went meticulously out of his way to ensure that an almost unworkable system was obeyed to the letter. Dawnay's rejection out of hand of a play already billed in the *Radio Times*, on the pretext that it was 'seditious', has been mentioned previously. It was one instance of excessive caution among scores that could be cited. The talks department was probably the worst affected; less so those highly specialised areas like drama, light entertainment and music, where administrators seldom dared to tread heavily for fear of making complete fools of themselves. Yet one day a momentous decision, the source of much unnecessary delay and embarrassment to the director of music, Adrian Boult, went upstairs for resolution by the highest authority. The vexed question of employing two piccolo players for the performance of a certain composition scored for two piccolos had reduced the normally placid Boult to a state of frenzy with several thick-headed administrators lower down the scale, who were adamant that a single piccolo player would suffice. Carpendale was anxious to oblige Boult, but reluctant to overrule his own subordinates. Suddenly smitten by a brainwave, he offered this Solomon's judgment:

'Why not use one piccolo, Boult, and place it closer to the microphone?'[10]

The director of music controlled an impulse to burst out laughing, assured Carpendale that this simply would not do, and retired with permission to use the two piccolos. Of such derisory trifles was the conduct of Reith's model control system too often compounded. The writing of memos developed into an abstruse art-form as the rivalry between the feudal kingdoms of administration and production intensified. Long before Northcote Parkinson hit upon the precise functioning of the law which bears his name, the BBC was unnecessarily afflicted by its pre-natal pangs. Falling back on the line of least resistance, submitting to control from above, saved time as well as tempers, so the less adventurous usually sat back waiting for decisions, allowing the ambitious, the mettlesome and the trouble-seekers on both sides to fight themselves to a standstill.

It was hardly what Reith had intended when he chose Alan Dawnay. His disappointment grew at the disturbing evidence of muddle and turmoil below. The man on whom he had relied to inspire trust in the revolutionary possibilities of dual control had mysteriously failed him. With characteristic obstinacy, however, Reith refused to admit that the system itself might be as much at fault as Dawnay. No fundamental alterations took place after Dawnay resigned in 1935. Carpendale was promptly moved upstairs as deputy Director-General; and Basil Nicholls took his place. The administrators were thus allowed to entrench themselves further. Engineering under Ashbridge enhanced its own dim mystique as a separate division. Graves became the new programme controller, with Eckersley and Gladstone Murray to assist him: and within twelve months, acting on the advice of the governors, Reith brought in another outsider to handle public relations. Sir Stephen Tallents, whose name had been suggested among others by Kingsley Wood, the Postmaster-General, came direct from the Empire marketing board with the rank of a full controller.

Experimental television and overseas broadcasting formed part of the vast domain now ruled by Cecil Graves. Fifth wheels had been added to coaches, loose nails and bolts tightened up, but the ill-conceived reforms devised by Reith stayed virtually unchanged. We may be tempted to ask: why did the staff remain so mute and compliant under conditions which increasingly militated against efficiency, speed and the creative quality of work? Were the controllers themselves so blindly loyal to Reith that they either refused to accept constructive criticisms or heed the rumbling discontent of subordinates? There is no simple answer to these questions. The normal channels of communication were often clogged as a result of the wrangling, at all levels, between administrators and programme makers over points of protocol. An atrophying sense of fatalism, very unnatural in an institution so young and potentially dynamic, pervaded the artificially cellular structure of Broadcasting House. Yet there was almost no willingness at the top to recognise the root cause. The veneration of the entire staff for the Director-General matched the profound awe he continued to inspire at a distance. Nobody but the controllers were conscious of Reith's ultimate culpability in the matter, and their allegiance to him was absolute. Poor Dawnay, for all his weaknesses, scarcely deserved the odium of total failure: his end was tragic; his one big blunder had surely been to leave the War Office at all.

'No good would have come from complaining', said one fairly senior member of the London staff, who after the Second World War occupied one of the most coveted and important jobs in the BBC. 'We had either to accept the situation and make the best of it—or get out. There was something abnormal about "Reith Worship". It seemed to be at its most intense when things were clearly going wrong. I've sometimes wondered since how far this was subconsciously bound up with the terror he could rouse in each of us. I suppose we all had reason to fear him. Jobs were scarce during that period of mass unemployment and there was still no court of appeal against summary dismissal by Sir John. . . .'[10]

On Saturday, October 14th, 1933, Germany left the disarmament conference. The nine o'clock news that evening contained an extract from the speech of Sir John Simon at Geneva, as well as the rantings of the new German Chancellor, Hitler, who had been addressing his supporters in Berlin. Then a talk by Vernon Bartlett, a friend of the BBC's Talks controller, Charles Siepmann, was broadcast. Reith received a letter of protest from the Prime Minister on the Monday morning. It looked as though the BBC, said MacDonald, 'were determined to get Europe into a war'. As a result of subsequent to'ings-and-fro'ings between Broadcasting House and No. 10 Downing Street, three non-controversial talks by leading politicians were arranged by the Director-General to redress the balance.

'You are turning my hair grey', MacDonald told Reith, adding that sometimes he wondered which was the government, 'we or you'.[1]

Proximity to MacDonald, Baldwin and other political figures had an understandable psychological effect on Reith. He was outwardly flattered by their attentions, inwardly dismayed by their customary pusillanimity. They admired him for his tremendous panache but feared, quite needlessly as it happened, that the BBC shared and emulated it. A less shy and fastidious man would have ventured to open his mind to them about his hankering for some other post: but such soliciting for favours was beneath him. The establishment's indirect and almost oblique ways of arranging deals and 'fixing' coveted appointments he theoretically frowned upon, so that when the well-disposed John Buchan approached him one day, on the cue of 'the awful shortage of men for positions of great responsibility', then asked casually whether he would be interested in 'a governor-generalship or the Washington embassy', Reith choked him off. Buchan admitted that MacDonald and Baldwin had been talking to him; but he shrugged aside Reith's blunt enquiry whether the two leaders had authorised this approach.[11] Nothing further came of that or other overtures, presumably because Reith offered to such envoys the paradoxical impression of a person wholly contented with his lot and therefore playing impossibly 'hard to get'.

Certainly Reith derived satisfaction from the public as well as the patronising aspects of his job. It delighted him, for instance, to draw like an aristocratic benefactor on BBC reserves to subsidise the composer, Elgar. George Bernard Shaw had written out of the blue at the end of September 1932, with this tantalising suggestion:

'You could bring the Third Symphony into existence and obtain the performing rights, for, say, ten years, for a few thousand pounds. The kudos would be stupendous and the value for money ample; in fact if Elgar were a good man of business instead of a great artist, who throws his commercial opportunities about *en grand seigneur*, he would open his mouth much wider.'[8]

Reith set Boult and others to work. Elgar, astounded by Reith's 'kind and generous attitude in the inception of the idea', called at Broadcasting House before Christmas 1932, and signed 'the momentous agreement'. The composer did not live to complete the masterpiece, yet the kudos for trying to extract it was deservedly Reith's. A contrasting impishness, never spontaneous but usually good for a headline, occasionally stirred him into delivering restrained broadsides against British modes and conventions. There were three classes of people speaking three types of English, he told a London University conference on the subject, 'the educated, the uneducated, and the clergy'. He was also talking from the heart, rather than with tongue in cheek, at a luncheon club whose members seemed amazed to hear Sir John Reith, of all men, suggest that the British took their pleasures too sadly and that London ought to 'go carnival' and stage its own kind of continental saturnalia. Again, to the same gathering, he expressed satisfaction at indiscriminate accusations of bias against the BBC from each of the political parties. His appetite for the incongruous added to his notoriety; such an outsize character, with so many quirks, did not thereby endear himself to the politicians or their friends. 'A good egg—if a little cracked', was the general verdict of objective admirers.

The BBC, compared with many other institutions, was an outstandingly good employer in nearly all other respects but the representation of staff grievances. Any other governor than Ethel Snowden might have managed long before, by less histrionic tactics, to make Reith reconsider his instinctive aversion, which Carpendale shared, to any form of staff association. Yet Sir Horace Wilson, the Ministry of Labour's permanent secretary in 1930 and a potent grey eminence behind the scenes at No. 10 Downing Street for the remainder of the thirties, felt that something more was required than the traditional 'personal approach' by BBC employees to the awesome presence of the Director-General. The question hung fire during John Whitley's term as chairman, however, because Whitley's word on such issues carried rare authority; and he agreed with Reith that it would be premature to inaugurate a representative staff council. So the jockeying for position, the disputes between administrators and programme-makers over the minutiae of procedure, and the unlovely plots and counter-plots inseparable from office politics, continued to ruffle the deceptively smooth surface of life below stairs at Broadcasting House.

It was a measure of the exalted and growing detachment of Reith from reality that he heard of the restiveness only when reprehensible incidents, or head-on collisions between identifiable individuals, plainly affected morale or work. This had once happened when a disedifying squabble broke surface and led to the departure of Hilda Matheson from the talks department: and that was before Alan Dawnay's overlordship even began. There was nothing so spectacular under Dawnay to induce Jove's intervention with one of his lethal thunderbolts. For more and more Sir John seemed content to hover like some half-legendary if still menacing presence in the background.

It was not a happy or healthy state of affairs. Bottled-up disaffection among producers could not contain itself indefinitely; and while the lid never blew itself off the pressure cooker, exaggerated tales of internal unrest and intrigue on a byzantine scale eventually leaked out to the press, and Reith's concentration on rebutting them too readily diverted him from problems under his own roof. The anti-BBC campaign of 1934 was conducted by Jonah Barrington, who had lately left the Corporation, with the lively backing of Oliver Baldwin, the Tory leader's eldest son and the then film critic of the BBC.

There were several points of attack, the lack of proper staff representation being only one. Hostile MP's echoed the charges in the House of Commons, obliging Reith to leap up indignantly in defence of his child. His motives, of course, were mixed. Since the 'sustained' onslaught 'seemed to be as much against me personally as against the BBC', his bristling talent for self-justification was naturally called into play. Just as he had recently bearded the editor of the *Morning Post*, H. A. Gwynne, and successfully demolished his obsessive view that the BBC must be a tool of socialism because Reith himself was a socialist in disguise, so one afternoon in March, he accepted an invitation from the Conservative 1922 committee to let him beard them at the Commons:

'I spoke for five minutes', he wrote of this meeting, 'said I would answer any question at all, even personal ones. I had hardly sat down when one of them rapped out a carefully compiled, comprehensive, complicated question on financial control. For nearly an hour it went on, question and answer—thoroughly enjoyable. . . . The meeting ended in much cordiality and acclaim.'

Reith had contrived this with a touch of the theatrical. He had been handed a sheaf of papers by a secretary on his way out of Broadcasting House. A glance at the contents had shown him how acutely distressed the staff were at the gratuitous press attacks on their chief. It was an unusual roundrobin, signed by 800 people, testifying their 'loyalty and gratitude to the Director-General' and denouncing the 'false and malignant statements' about him in the popular papers. On being pressed by one MP to explain whether the condition of staff morale was as low as had been alleged, Reith handed the roundrobin to William Morrison, in the chair, who saw its relevance and read it aloud. The press headlines next morning vindicated his single-handed counter-attack. Labour Party critics were similarly silenced a few weeks later 'in the same room, with Attlee in the chair'.[1]

He was wise, none the less, in his reckoning that 'another hare would have to be hunted before long'. Certain high Tories like Hailsham could not rid their minds of the groundless fear that the BBC under Reith was a subtle and disruptive agency of socialism, while some Labour men like Cripps held that the corporation had developed into a propaganda engine of the establishment, despite vigorous assertions to the contrary by its founding father. Meanwhile, the muffled sound and fury of the minor power-game at headquarters did not abate, the contestants having called a momentary truce only to declare their unabated affection for the great Sir John. How earnestly some of the more thoughtful among them wished that he were not so withdrawn. The reputation of their leader could be more easily defended than many of the muddled or spineless decisions perpetrated in his name by men of straw whom he had unaccountably chosen for high office.

The Listener, launched in 1928, provided a relatively sheltered backwater for a minute staff of rare versatility. Janet Adam Smith, whose parents had been on polite visiting terms with Reith's in his boyhood, was the weekly's gifted assistant editor when 'the bell rang one July day in 1933 and I was summoned to the presence of the Director-General'. She had been responsible for the recent publication of a four-page supplement of modern poetry, with woodcut illustrations by Gwen Raverat. Verses by Charles Madge, C. Day Lewis, Herbert Read and John Lehmann were included, and spread across the middle pages was the unabridged version of W. H. Auden's poem, *The Witnesses*.

'Why is there so much that's odd, uncouth and puzzling in modern poems?' Reith demanded. Janet Adam Smith tried to explain.

'He wasn't objecting to modern poetry as such any more than to modern music broadcast by the BBC. He made that plain. Nor was he choleric like the outraged pundits who frequently wrote in from the Athenaeum. He genuinely wanted assurance that anything which appeared in *The Listener* should be recognised as having merit by responsible and informed people beyond the paper.'

When she mentioned the name of T. S. Eliot, Reith said that it would be interesting to have *his* opinion, possibly having in mind 'Mr. Eliot the critic, the director of Fabers, indeed the member of the Athenaeum, rather than the poet of *The Waste Land.*' In due course Eliot's expert advice was sought officially. His comments were long, measured and closely reasoned. At first they left Janet Adam Smith feeling distinctly deflated. Only younger poets, he wrote, would wish to advertise their wares in a weekly, given the paltry payments they could expect. As to the works of younger poets published in *The Listener* 'the great majority is mediocre and conventional; it reveals the occasional influence of myself, Mr. Yeats, Mr. Pound and Gerard Hopkins, and some other more discredited originals'. But it was the conclusion that Reith seized upon: 'While not very encouraging for poetry, the selection is on the whole creditable for *The Listener.*' After that he interfered no more, though Dawnay and others tiresomely tried on occasion. And a discreet reminder from T. S. Eliot many weeks later enabled Janet Adam Smith to light a touch-paper under her own administrators for overlooking his ten-guinea consulting fee.[10]

Regional directors felt doubly cut off. The policy of centralisation had been formulated towards the close of the Savoy Hill era; and as bigger transmitters came into use, the centralised direction of output from the oldest clusters of local stations had proceeded apace without serious protestation. The Dawnay interregnum, however, did not pass so peacefully. Reith's earlier promise of 'a genuine attempt to make the transmissions on the regional wavelengths genuinely regional'[3] seemed to go by the board. The victims believed that they had been left high and dry by the high-handed, blundering Dawnay. The cultural boundaries of the North, Midland and West regions were less easily drawn than those of Scotland, Wales and Northern Ireland. Resources, too, were universally short; and ingenuity seldom overcame the rigid obstructiveness manifested at nearly every turn by administrative moguls at head office. Repeated questions of hierarchy arose, regional directors usually having to withdraw defeated. When West region applied to broadcast a Rubinstein concert from Dartington at the end of 1933, the proposal was turned down flat 'on the score that Rubinstein has not yet broadcast at all and that his first broadcast should be National rather than West Regional'. Cases had to be treated individually and on merit. Yet Lindsay Wellington, who had been commissioned to smooth over such awkward problems, encountered an entirely different one when Harding in Manchester refused to carry a Sunday symphony concert conducted by Cassals because North Region wanted to broadcast their own programme—a less prestigious performance by a Merseyside orchestra of unemployed musicians. Wellington's notes on his verbal duel with Harding offer a nice insight into the contradictory workings of two well-matched and unusually flexible minds:

'Surely', said the man from London, 'you ought not to drop the Cassals programme, a very important one, and substitute a lesser programme of the same kind.'

'Yes, I think it's right', said Harding. 'To give a platform to this Merseyside orchestra is of great social importance.'

'I quite see that—but not on this date. Give them a special studio date or take another of their public concerts on a date when you don't have to pay such a price.'

Special pleading of the sort left Harding unmoved:

'I'm most unwilling to change. I see the force of what you say but I very much do not want to disappoint them.'

'All right: if you have committed yourself to them, go ahead, but you know you ought not to have done so without knowing what you would have been dropping. Now you will have to keep faith with them but only at the cost of disappointing all the listeners in the North of England who would want to hear Cassals conducting. I really do feel this is wrong.'[3]

Men big enough, as in this instance, to bend the rules or allow the rules to be bent under protest, were exceptional in the BBC of the mid-thirties. Independence of spirit had sunk to a lower level than John Reith, dazzled by the hero-worship of his staff and distracted now by long-term personal and strategic considerations, would have tolerated if only he had been kept better informed.

3

The first strategic aim, conceived by the Director-General in December 1933, before Dawnay had time enough to demonstrate how ineffectual he could really be, was to prepare the ground for battle when the BBC Charter ran out at the end of 1936. Reith cleared his lines by broaching the subject formally with Kingsley Wood, a Postmaster-General whom he ardently and rightly distrusted, and by next stepping aside to discuss informally with Sir Warren Fisher, the secretary to the Treasury, and Sir Donald Banks, the new head of the Post Office, the 'best tactics for getting our new Charter and Licence'. The three men met several times and covered much ground. But Reith's hope of frustrating Kingsley Wood's express wish for another full-scale public trial of the BBC quickly came to nought.

The draft agreement reached by Fisher, Banks and Reith cut no ice whatever with a Minister who 'obviously did not intend to leave Reith free to determine national broadcasting policy after discussing matters with them'.[3] That emerged plainly from a sterile encounter between the pair in Kingsley Wood's office on June 25th, 1934. Though Reith had taken the precaution of getting Ramsay MacDonald's advance approval for informal exchanges with the influential Warren Fisher, the Postmaster-General smelled an intrigue and reacted haughtily. Whether the BBC and its leader liked it or not, a public committee, not a private cabal, would scrutinise its affairs and determine its future needs. This was, fumed Reith, 'most unsatisfactory'.

Just as unsatisfactory, in his view, were certain members of the committee itself when the official announcement of the names followed at Easter, 1935. The chairman, Lord Ullswater, like Whitley a former Speaker of the House but now in his eightieth year, seemed a most improbable choice: Reith had vainly suggested the nomination of Lord McKenna or Ernest Barker. The last-minute inclusion of Lord Selsdon, with whom as Sir William Mitchell-Thomson he had so often quarrelled in earlier days, annoyed him still more. The membership appeared to be packed: 'Everything that bothers us in the Charter and licence he is responsible for.' There was, he complained to Banks, 'far too much of the Post Office about it—appointed by the PMG, two Postmaster-Generals [Selsdon and Attlee] and one Assistant Postmaster-General [Graham White]'.[2] He was slightly happier about the other politicians, J. J. Astor, Clement Davies, and Lord Elton. He equally approved of Sir William McClintock, the financial expert; but he feared that the whole business might be beyond the grasp of a chairman in his dotage. It was a mild relief to learn from Banks that Ullswater was 'not in the least inclined to turn the world upside down'. For the committee's far-reaching terms of reference were 'to consider the constitution, control, and finance of the broadcasting service in this country and advise generally on the conditions under which the service, including broadcasting to the Empire, television broadcasting, and the system of wireless exchanges, should be conducted after December 31st, 1936'. And what Reith specially wanted to avoid was any turning over of the past, in the unnecessary graveyard style of the Crawford enquiry ten years earlier. The future mattered most.

Unfortunately, the baleful mistrust he felt for Kingsley Wood's 'political expediency' was reciprocated in full as the hour of reckoning approached. The Postmaster-General had an ingrained dislike of Reith's arbitrary methods. The thwarting of the Director-General thus became one of his deliberate sports. Ernest Barker no doubt would have made a better chairman, but Barker had virtually ruled himself out. Was he not, in any case, a creature of Reith's? Had the professor not served with D. B. Mair, the retired civil service commissioner, on the so-called independent enquiry which the corporation had conducted towards the end of 1933 into the paternalistic procedures for staff recruitment and promotion? They had set the seal of their approbation on the BBC's method of 'collecting candidates'. Kingsley Wood was not deceived. Their proposals that in future there should be selection boards with an official present from 'the particular branch of the service concerned', and that vacancies should be advertised 'as widely as possible', seemed hollow. No word of condemnation had been uttered against the time-honoured tradition of personal recommendation favoured by Reith. Hence Kingsley Wood's determination that exemplary justice should at last be done to the BBC for all its detractors and admirers to see.

A graphic description of this Reithian tradition in action has been furnished by Harman Grisewood who had joined the staff as an announcer in 1933:

'The interview with Reith took the course which had been foretold, but I was unprepared for the personality of the man. He asked me to pronounce certain words. "Fire" was one of them. He grasped the poker and pointed to the flames as though he could extinguish them by a frown. "What am I pointing to?" he asked. "What is this?" he said next shaking his cuff-links at me. I knew I should say "gold" and I knew, too, that he would then correct me by pronouncing the word "goold". "Goold, goold!" he cried testily. "You've a southern accent—like your cousin". If he had been playing the part of an ogre I think the Children's Hour producer would have told him to tone it down a bit. . . . He seemed more an eccentric than a bully. The end of the interview was positively feeble. "We have one Grisewood on the staff", he said, referring again to my southern accent, "and that's enough". Well, that's that, I thought. I couldn't imitate a Scotsman any more than I imagined Reith could imitate an Englishman. Poor cousin Freddie. I had not seen him lately. Perhaps he had been frowned into obscurity because of his accent. Then came the feeble last sentence—spoken with a sigh—"but they say they want you. That's what they tell me". . . . I have never lost a sense of perplexity which started at this strange first meeting; he has never lost his power to surprise.'[12]

Though the Ullswater committee, which began its hearings in May 1935, was held in secret, the evidence of the many witnesses and interested parties has been preserved in the archives of the Post

Office and the BBC. Reith ensured that the corporation's well-prepared memorandum was concise yet comprehensive. Programme and engineering policy, financial control and constitutional status were explained in simple, unvarnished terms. Stressing that the expanding income from radio licences must eventually reach its peak, the statement warned that when that happened the BBC would have no ready surplus for capital expenditure. More financial provision must therefore be forthcoming both for the Empire service and for the start of television transmissions. The BBC proposed that the Postmaster-General ought not to alter the licence fee without agreement; that the fixed percentage of licence revenue retained by the Postmaster-General as a collection charge ought to cease; that the entire income from licences should be payable to the BBC, only the true cost of collecting being deducted; that the corporation ought, as a non-profit-making body, to pay no income tax; and that its borrowing powers should be stepped up to £2 million.

Perhaps the most contentious point, and the one which seemed to confirm Kingsley Wood's suspicions about the Director-General's megalomania, was a new constitutional proposal. This suggested that in future the BBC should be answerable not to the Postmaster-General but to the Lord President of the Council, a minister of Cabinet rank, on all questions of policy and direction under the Charter. Only on finance, wavelengths and other technical matters covered by its licence should the corporation have dealings with the Postmaster-General. The then incumbent of that office was well aware, through his chief adviser, that this unpleasant pill had been concocted in the private agreement Reith had previously reached with Warren Fisher and Banks. The sugaring did not take in the slighted Kingsley Wood:

'The Lord President's control should be so expressed as to ensure that the Corporation gives an adequate and satisfactory service, and to prevent its whole character being changed to the sponsored system of the United States', explained the BBC memorandum.[2]

Since January 1933, when Gainford had finally retired from the board, the BBC had had as its vice-chairman Ronald Norman, a younger brother of the Governor of the Bank of England. Reith, who had occasionally wondered afterwards at receiving no reply to the self-introductory note which the fastidious high priest of the City had discarded so scornfully, eventually met Montagu Norman socially; and this oddly assorted pair struck up a ripening if guarded friendship. Reith did not hesitate to recommend the brother's name to Whitley who, in turn, had recommended his appointment to the

Prime Minister; and when ill health forced Lord Bridgeman to retire prematurely as BBC chairman in the course of 1935, Ronald Norman succeeded him. His long administrative experience with the London County Council and the National Trust attracted Reith, and though neither a forceful nor a magnetic personality like Montagu, Ronald obviously had excellent connections and was a sound judge of men. Where Clarendon had brought discord and Whitley balm, Ronald Norman now injected his own blend of charm and realism. It is impossible to overrate the crucial importance of the part this BBC chairman would increasingly take in these declining years of Reith's once-supreme hegemony. First as a willing partner, then as a more critical counsellor, finally as a devious schemer regretfully contriving the removal of a Director-General who had clearly outstayed his usefulness, Ronald Norman would prove himself a chairman capable of the big decision. We shall unravel before the end of this chapter the tangled mystery of precisely how Norman managed to dispose of Reith. Meanwhile, with Ullswater and his committee embarked on their detailed investigation of the BBC's business, he seemed as anxious as the Director-General to wring the best terms obtainable out of a cautious, thrifty government.

Hitler by now had consolidated his dictatorial hold on Germany. Vansittart, at the Foreign Office, Hankey of the Cabinet Secretariat and the Committee of Imperial Defence, as well as the ubiquitous Warren Fisher, confided their fears for the future to Reith, whose mind began to turn on the unforeseen problems of broadcasting in the possible event of war. They all shared reservations about the leadership of the ailing Ramsay MacDonald and of the gently abstracted Baldwin; but reservations of the kind were empty gestures indeed. Reith still had energy enough to control the BBC's destiny and to plan its future without entirely losing sight of the wider world and the three or four places of power for which he secretly yearned. A ten-week visit to South Africa the previous autumn had unsettled him more than ever. He had gone with Lady Reith to draft a broadcasting constitution for the Union Government, but in Cape Town one night the telephone rang and Whitley came unexpectedly on the line from London to read out a letter from Willingdon, the Viceroy, who urgently needed a 'superman' to put Indian broadcasting on its feet:

'I'd like to take on the job—for good', Reith had said.

Whitley quietly dissuaded him. The Director-General was more than ever needed at home, what with the forthcoming enquiry into the BBC:

'Your duty is to come back and see that through', said Whitley, and with some reluctance Reith had complied.[1]

His really burning ambition was to become Viceroy of India, and that broadcasting post might have been a useful stepping stone. Yet now, looking about him at home where drift and bare-faced expediency passed for official policy, Reith at certain moments of self-doubt would have gladly exchanged his increasingly isolated BBC eyrie for a key position in one of the service ministries. He envied the amused benevolence of new acquaintances like Major-General Jack Dill of the War Office; it comforted him only slightly to learn that such different men as the R.A.F.'s founder, Lord Trenchard, and the ex-proconsul, Lord Lloyd, endorsed his own sharp indictments of the timidity, mediocrity and bumbling self-satisfaction of most of the policy-makers in Whitehall. Individuals of independent vision appeared to be an embarrassment to the bulk of politicians and their attendant civil servants; the National Government backed away from strong men; and the thought of settling for bold decisions appeared to petrify them.

Reith thought of himself as 'a lightning conductor', attracting to his own person the calumnies of the weak. Yet the observant among his well-wishers did not doubt that Reith's own injudicious tongue led critics either to leave him be or to blast back at him, sometimes viciously. The Ullswater hearings offered a fair chance to a few of them. Familiar charges were levelled against his tyrannical conduct; and his massive indifference to those who mouthed them did not necessarily help the BBC's case. Reith disliked the petty sniping of Selsdon and Attlee. The former harried him on the issue of letting the Lord President of the Council, rather than the Postmaster General, lord it over the BBC:

It was 'the voice of Kingsley Wood as well as of Mitchell-Thomson', he noted acidly. 'He is against our having Wireless Exchanges and is playing a dirty game about Luxembourg and advertising generally.'[1,3]

When Attlee, no admirer of autocratic behaviour in the discharge of public business, raised the bogeys of staff representation and the non-publication of detailed BBC accounts, the Director-General was unreasonably incensed. He sent a note to the man who had barely learnt how to run the Post Office for the five months preceding the 1931 crash, reminding him that public bodies had the right to 'full freedom' in the efficient handling of their affairs. 'The staff', Attlee had also said, 'should be given full opportunities for ventilating any grievances collectively. . . . The BBC should definitely recognise the right of every employee to join an appropriate union and a proper system of consultation and collective agreement should be instituted.' Labour's continued scepticism about the BBC's professed political impartiality also emerged. Attempts to hold the balance evenly between the parties had been inconsistent, it was alleged. During the General Strike, for instance, broadcasting had been 'used' by the Baldwin government to propagate its cause, an abuse surely of its licensed freedom. In Attlee's view the BBC needed both to assert 'sufficient independence to resist being made the instrument of one side in a national controversy'.[13]

It was a cornerstone of Reith's broadcasting philosophy that an 'ethical policy cannot stand competition'. What he thought of as 'the brute force of monopoly' could alone protect it against 'force and money—unfortunately the only two unfailing powers'. Demands for limited sponsoring appeared in the evidence submitted by Philco, one of the big radio manufacturers; an even stranger demand for a separate wavelength devoted exclusively to advertising came from the International Broadcasting Company. This stung Reith into retorting that the committee would be well advised to examine the firm's programme schedules. Such an examination might convince them that commercial competition of the kind, whatever else it did, would certainly not 'raise the standard'. The IBC was the creation of a colourful entrepreneur, the appropriately named Captain L. F. Plugge, who as early as 1925 had induced Selfridges, the London store, to sponsor a fashion talk for British listeners from the Eiffel Tower station in Paris. By the early thirties, when Radio Luxembourg and Radio Normandie had begun to catch the ears of a disturbingly large part of the BBC's audience on Sundays, Plugge's agency was busy selling air time on behalf of toothpaste, cigarettes and other consumer interests based in the United Kingdom.

Reith's somewhat austere and unalterable sabbatarian concepts had continued to play into the hands of the IBC since then, despite ineffective protests by the corporation to the International Broadcasting Union which tried to regulate the activities of its members without, however, possessing any power to command them. Piracy of the ether in defiance of agreements could neither be controlled nor simply wished out of existence. Even more ominous from the BBC's point of view was the growing popularity of relayed programmes through the rediffusion service of the expanding wireless exchanges. By the end of 1935 there were 343 of these operating up and down Britain, with over a quarter of a million registered subscribers. Specially licensed by the Post Office, the exchanges provided good reception on relatively advantageous terms. 'They were bound', as Asa Briggs has pointed out, 'to be used, in a free market, for the rediffusion of foreign commercial programmes, if these programmes genuinely made an appeal to large numbers of listeners'.

It is ironical, perhaps, and not without relevance that Sir William Noble, who had appointed Reith in 1922, was now one of the major protagonists of this system. He sat on the board of Rediffusion Ltd., along with Peter Eckersley, the former head of BBC engineering. The attitude of the Post Office had a weird ambivalence. While defending the rights of the BBC on the international front, it refused to restrict the rights of relay service listeners on the home front. The press broadly supported the BBC because its own advertising interests were not exactly served by the intrusion of commercial radio programmes from abroad. In 1933, the corporation had retaliated by extending its hours of Sunday broadcasting. The once empty time between 12.30 and 3 pm was now filled, but Reith would still not allow jazz, variety or dance band music. Well-known artistes like Tommy Handley, Vic Oliver, Jack Warner, Anne Ziegler and Webster Booth could be heard on Radio Normandie—but over the BBC, never on Sundays. A commercial survey conducted towards the end of 1935 showed that 'one out of two of the British listeners interviewed listened to Radio Luxembourg regularly on Sundays: on weekdays the figure dropped to 11 per cent'.[3] Figures produced by the BBC itself about this time were even gloomier. Among 2,000 people addicted to light entertainment, 66 per cent listened regularly to foreign broadcasts on Sundays against 22 per cent on week days.

The Ullswater committee rejected Captain Plugge's attempt to breach the monopoly, declaring that 'we are most anxious that the intellectual and ethical integrity which the broadcasting system in this country has attained should be preserved'. Selsdon, however, dissented. He favoured wireless exchanges and could not see why subscribers should be denied the freedom already enjoyed by any owner of a private set. Why should the Post Office or the BBC seek to control it? 'After all', he argued, 'the relay companies, if they are to succeed, must give their public what that public wants.' It was the voice of a former Postmaster-General, no doubt, but its vibrant sentiments should have been taken more seriously as belonging to that small but not insignificant section of the establishment already seized in the mid-thirties with the lucrative possibilities of commercial competition against a monolithic BBC.

Direct advertising, Ullswater insisted, should continue to be banned. Sponsored programmes should be permitted, so long as sponsoring was used 'discreetly'. The committee recognised the fact that the coming of television would impose a heavy financial burden, but hoped that sponsoring 'will be limited to the initial stages'. Accepting the BBC's case for more money, they recommended that television should be adequately financed out of public funds.

Three members, Astor, Elton and Graham White, warned that unless sponsorship disappeared there was a 'real danger that advertisement may intrude itself over the whole range of BBC programmes'.

Discordant notes were sounded by other witnesses grinding axes on behalf of several vested interests. Publishers contended wildly that the Children's Hour had damaged the sale of books for the young; the trade press opposed the BBC's claim that its publications were an integral part of the broadcasting service, urging that the corporation should be confined to the spoken word; critics from the musical world, Sir Thomas Beecham prominent among them, deployed arguments firmly rebutted by Adrian Boult that the BBC's activities made that world less secure for musicians; and Fleet Street, supported by the Empire Press Union, resurrected some hoary objections to the broadcasting of news bulletins containing 'last minute items' as well as material of 'human interest'. The Ullswater committee in all these instances upheld the case of the BBC.

'Our recommendations are directed towards the further strengthening and securing the position which the broadcasting service of Great Britain has happily attained in the few years of its history', said the final report. The Charter should be extended for ten years; governors should be neither specialists nor the representatives of particular interests and localities, their function being to exercise a joint responsibility for policy and leave its execution to the BBC's own officials; existing methods of recruitment were generally approved, but in future all vacancies should be advertised and candidates judged on merit by selection boards. The committee also accepted that 'a senior member of the government', not the Postmaster-General, should become the overlord of broadcasting. On finance, they proposed that 75 per cent of licence revenue should go to the BBC for purposes other than television, after deducting Post Office costs, and the balance should be made available if needed. Only then should any surplus be taken by the Exchequer. The past practice of finding all capital expenditure out of revenue was sound and ought to continue; but the BBC should be allowed borrowing powers up to £1 million.

The balance of programmes was judged to be good; but while the BBC deserved more freedom to broadcast news, 'a strong and impartial editorial staff' would be 'vital' for this. The committee's firm support was offered for the airing of controversial subjects: 'if broadcasting is to present a reflection of its time, it must include matters which are in dispute. If it is to hold public interest, it must express living thought. If it is to educate public opinion, it must look upon the questions of the hour from many angles'. As regards overseas broadcasting, the small but developing Empire service in

English received Ullswater's blessing, and 'in the interests of British prestige and influence in world affairs, the appropriate use of languages other than English should be encouraged'.[13] The BBC emerged from its ordeal unscathed and shining with reflected virtue. Even the moot point of the wireless exchanges was adjudicated in the corporation's favour, the committee proposing that the Post Office should take them over and that programmes should be controlled by the BBC. On the face of it, Reith had again scored off his numerous critics almost at every point. Only on the question of providing facilities for staff representation was he implicitly rebuked. Yet, as he realized, from past experience, committees could only propose. It was the privilege of governments to dispose.

4

There was hardly a hint of festive cheer in the Reith family during the Christmas break of 1935. They had long left behind the compact town house in Barton Street, Westminster, for a bigger if less central residence on the leafy fringes of Beaconsfield. The two children needed room to spread themselves without having to be banished upstairs, or otherwise stifled, whenever an important guest or caller looked in to see their father; but neighbours as well as visitors to their country home often felt a sense of pity for Christopher and Marista, young as they were, under the control of a taskmaster alternatively so sternly exacting and so distantly abstracted as the formidable Sir John. Total abstraction was his mood that Christmas when he received an advance copy of Ullswater's findings and retired to his book-lined study from which he rarely emerged except for meals, under the 'reproachful eyes' of his family.

'I went through it critically, hypercritically; made a hundred notes where the wording might have been different, eliminated ninety and wrote a memorandum for the governors about the residual ten. If, despite my comments, they were pleased with the report it would mean much more than if they had not realised in what respects it might have been better. . . . Children of seven and three could not be expected to understand why, even at Christmas time, their father had so little time or thought for them. They and their mother have much to forgive all down these years.'[1]

The severance of two secure and sacred links with the past deepened Reith's gloom during the oppressive days that followed. Before the old year ended, the abrupt news came of his aged mother's death. Again he had been cheated by his own preoccupations of the chance to attend the departure from this vale of tears of an enviably serene soul: his father's spirit, like hers, could not tarry until their youngest son arrived. Then, after what proved to be his final Christmas message through the BBC's microphones to the peoples of the Commonwealth, illness struck down King George V, whose life drew peacefully to its close in January. 'How's the Empire', he had whispered in a last, lucid moment. Had Reith realised how poor the health of the monarch really was, he might have moderated his private wrath on January 1st, 1936, after scanning the Honours List with his usual jaundiced eye. He thought it 'monstrous' that the King had neglected to confer on him the Grand Cross of the Victorian Order as a merited embellishment of his knighthood. For his work in South Africa alone, on that country's broadcasting report, he should have been made a Knight Commander of the Order of St. Michael and St. George into the bargain. Reith adored honours and held strong private views on the arbitrary and sometimes incomprehensible way they were distributed to the unworthy.

The Ullswater affair, of crucial interest to the BBC as it was, seemed to have hacked a huge, improvident slice out of John Reith's existence, so much of wider and more lasting importance had meanwhile passed him by.

Baldwin, offhanded now to the point of genial absent-mindedness or evasiveness, had been caught up against his will in the unfashionable Churchillian clamour for rearmament. Hoist with the petard of his own unguarded remark that 'the bomber will always get through', and accepting Hitler's unreliable claim to have achieved parity with Britain in the air, the man who had returned as Prime Minister in June 1935 ratified an immediate expansion of RAF strength that looked all very well on paper but which was hopelessly impracticable in a period of industrial dislocation, continuing mass-unemployment, and economic stagnancy. Trenchard, free at last to speak his mind after four energetic years reforming the Metropolitan Police, proclaimed to Reith and to any other sympathisers who would listen to his booming indiscretions, that nothing could be more fatal for the nation than 'a contented old man at the head of affairs'.[14] Churchill had still been offered no place in the Cabinet reshuffle that followed the general election of November 1935. The almost coincidental invasion of Abyssinia by Mussolini had unmasked the chronic and long-suspected weakness of the League of Nations: the hesitant imposition of economic sanctions scrupulously drew the line at the oil required by Italy for modern war-making in East Africa. And with more than half the voters blithely or dumbly acquiescing in Labour's abjuring of any action, except collective security condoned by the impotent League, the time had come for rousing the nation to a new sense of awareness.[15]

Reith felt the old uneasiness stirring again in his veins. The government were at least acting in the realistic belief that defence rated higher than broadcasting on their list of housekeeping priorities; and in occasional dispassionate moods he could not honestly blame them. Rumours circulated widely that Reith's name was one of several being canvassed for a new post: that of minister in charge of the co-ordinating of defence. Then, shortly before the incredible appointment to that potentially vital ministry of the ineffectual Sir Thomas Inskip, fresh rumours suggested that Reith might be asked to take Hankey's place as secretary to the Committee of Imperial Defence. The momentary flattering of his ego by such canards was a poor substitute for the revitalising offer of a real, solid job in the national interest. Nothing of the kind happened.

When Hankey and other members of the C.I.D. 'offered me the director-generalship of the ministry [of information] in the event of war' so that he, Reith, could 'shape the whole organisation in advance of need', he declined as gracefully as he could. 'I said I had other ideas for employment in time of war—greater or lesser, I was not sure which.'[1] If he could have combined the chairmanship of the BBC with any outside task of full responsibility, Reith would not have hung on longer at Broadcasting House. By no means an inverted Micawber waiting for something to turn down, he accepted with private reservations the board's view that 'it would be disastrous if I left'. Contrarily he held, against their unspoken doubts, that the BBC's administrative system, the running of its programmes, its relationship with the public, and its constitutional status, were safe enough to be handed over to another director-general. 'Perhaps I am still useful', he consoled himself when no offers came from Whitehall. After all, lightning conductors still had their uses; and this apt, original remark of Ramsay MacDonald continued to impress him, despite nagging uncertainties about his genuine usefulness to the BBC except as a figurehead and the defender of the faith.

This unsettled mood, a compound of self-justification and the restlessness of a man with too little to do, did not greatly help the corporation during the intermittent squalls that broke about Reith's head when the Ullswater report was debated by Parliament, then implemented in large measure by the Baldwin government. The process was protracted: not until the end of 1936 did Reith feel that he had extracted enough of his pound of flesh, in defiance of the grotesquely heightened odds against him. There were enemies in the government, self-declared antagonists like Kingsley Wood, whose exertions at the Ministry of Health did little to deflect his anti-Reithian pique, and cold critics like Neville Chamberlain who cared less than ever for Reith's peculiar ability to supplement fervour with intimations of infallibility. There were vehement if less dangerous enemies on the opposition front and backbenches at Westminster. There were as yet no enemies within, though Ronald Norman tended to brood increasingly over the Director-General's defiant indifference to criticism from any quarter. The BBC had difficulties enough without unnecessarily provoking more, the chairman considered; yet Reith obstinately insisted that the BBC was old enough to look after itself. When parliamentary snipers likened the corporation to 'an autocracy which had outgrown the original autocrat', Reith might fume in private at their 'incredible credulity' and their 'serene malignity', but that did not ease Ronald Norman's disquiet.

The internal machinery of control functioned far less smoothly than he or the other governors had been led to expect. Dawnay's resignation, which provided an ideal moment for correcting the drift towards avoidable bureaucracy, had not stirred Reith into any positive reaction. Power was redistributed between four controllers instead of two. Like four separate beanstalks rearing upwards to the cloudy lair of Sir John the Giantkiller, the control structure tended to foster four distinctive and separate areas of loyalty and latent antagonisms, without lessening the confusion of mutual antipathies at lower levels where administrators and programme-makers still clashed. Gerald Cock, for instance, had many harder if pettier problems on his hands than the inherently exciting one of launching the world's first television service. Apart from the fact that the new, untried medium was not popular among the policy-makers at Broadcasting House, the hierarchical pattern of authority itself became an unnatural brake on orderly progress. Cock 'was handicapped by his place in the hierarchy. He was responsible to the controller (programmes), his executive officer, Leonard Schuster, was responsible to the controller (administration), and the engineer-in-charge of television, Douglas Birkenshaw, was responsible through a chain of higher officials to the controller (engineering). . . . Anything concrete that was done—for instance in negotiation with newsreels and sports promoters—was due to his short-circuiting all the authorities and doing it himself'.

More interested 'in order than creation', the rule-bound operators of the BBC's unwieldy control system often had to be bypassed thus. Fortunately for everyone, 'there were always plenty of obscure people on the production side who did their jobs according to their lights and not according to the book'.[16] The most serious long-term danger, as Ronald Norman now belatedly realised, was that no controller chose to risk his own neck by working against a system originated and blessed by Reith.

So reticent was he about his personal hopes that neither Norman nor any other governor, let alone the controllers, had the slightest inkling of his true dilemma. Caught between two stools, he stayed on because there was nowhere else he could go. Business did not interest him. The offer of a job at between £15,000 and £20,000 a year by a city financier 'to launch an English associate of a big American corporation' did not tempt him away. He had passed beyond pecuniary self-interest of that sort. What he wanted was a political job, but the politicians steadfastly ignored him. Lord Dawson of Penn, the eminent physician, was mortified one evening at the Athenaeum by Reith's puzzling response to his casual greeting.

'How are you?' enquired Dawson.

'Not at all well. I've a serious disease.'

'Disease? What's the trouble then, Reith?'

'I'm suffering from *accidie*.'

'*Accidie?*'

'Yes, surely you must have heard of *accidie*. It's a well-known complaint.'

Dawson confessed his ignorance and broke off the conversation, saying that he must go away 'to look it up'.[11] Many others would have been still more put out by Reith's deeply held conviction that this medieval malady of the spirit was 'perhaps more of a sin than a disease'. It weighed him down unbearably when the tempo of life slackened and he could find insufficient work or distractions to slough it off. He did not mind being likened to a terrible Tsar or to the head of a powerful new chartered company in which 'the diseases of the old chartered companies' were fast incubating: Baldwin's advice that public figures should 'avoid logic at all costs and cultivate the hide of a rhinoceros' was advice that appealed to Reith. No advice, no ready prescriptions, could be sought in any event for *accidie*. Nor would Reith have thanked anyone for suggesting that the disease might have been a form of spiritual hypochondria, if not of corrosive self-pity. He knew otherwise. And with the searing knowledge of the self-condemned, he knew also that there was no earthly cure for it.

5

Possibly no other single episode attracted more notoriety, roused more hilarity, and did graver indirect damage to Reith and the

BBC's good name than the case of the so-called 'talking mongoose' in November 1936. It all began the previous February when Sir Cecil Levita, a prominent figure in London local politics, made some disparaging remarks about R. S. Lambert, the editor of *The Listener*. Lambert, while inclined to take himself rather seriously, had a somewhat rarefied sense of the absurd. In the 'silly season' of the summer, when there were few interesting talks to reprint, he would often run original articles. Some of these displayed a taste for psychic stunts; and one of his colleagues, Maurice Gorham, had once accompanied him 'to the famous laboratory where Harry Price, his collaborator in these experiments, measured alleged psychic phenomena, planned ghost-hunting expeditions, and laid traps for *soi-disant* mediums. I used to rally Lambert on these silly season stunts of his, and perhaps that is why I got a preview of the Talking Mongoose from his own mouth'.[16] Price and Lambert even worked together on a small book entitled *The Haunting of Cashen's Gap*. This told the whole tale of Gef, the mongoose from the Isle of Man, with a nice blend of belief and repudiation. But the British public came to accept Gef as a household word through Lambert's subsequent legal action against Levita. Through the lengthy court reports in the press Gef achieved transient fame of a ludicrous kind.

Levita, who had become acquainted with Lambert through their association with the British Film Institute where the original dispute between them arose, was alleged to have used some offensive words about the editor of *The Listener* over lunch one day at the Carlton, in the hearing of Murray Gladstone of the BBC. The words were duly reported back to Lambert who demanded a retraction and an unqualified apology. What he particularly objected to was the slur on his character and professional standing implied in his 'belief in the occult, notably the talking mongoose answering to the name of Gef'. When Sir Cecil refused to apologise, Lambert took recourse to the law. An extraordinary sequence of events, each trifling in itself but all linking up to expose the BBC in an accidentally lurid and ridiculous light, filled the next ten months of 1936.

Sir Stephen Tallents, by now controller of the key post of public relations, warned Lambert that if he proceeded with his case he would not only lead the corporation to doubt his good judgment, but he would be 'placing his own interests in priority to those of the corporation'. The chairman, Norman, whom Levita had meanwhile approached direct, saw Lambert and issued a similar warning. The strange fact was that Reith, whom outsiders naturally branded as the prime mover behind official attempts to silence Lambert, hardly came into the matter. He came to hear of it, of course; but, greatly irritated that Lambert had failed to confide in him first, Reith deliberately chose to stay out of it. The teacup tempest soon spilled over into the public sphere, and for bad timing alone the BBC's heavy-handed method of trying to check an unco-operative Lambert could scarcely have been matched. Rumours multiplied. Suspicions were stirred. Surely the BBC must have many other skeletons to hide? Even members of the government, still deliberating over Ullswater's proposals, wondered a little. 'What right have they', asked Sir Stafford Cripps during the debate on the Ullswater report on April 29th, 'to use their economic power over Lambert to make him discontinue an action against Mr. X?'

The BBC background came into full view when the charge against Sir Cecil Levita was pressed and finally heard in open court. In Asa Briggs' phrase, the whole case 'undoubtedly did the BBC harm. Lambert, who was awarded heavy damages, £7500, had appeared as a solitary individual fighting for his reputation and his rights not only against Levita but against the BBC, the Big Corporation'.[3] To interfere with the private conduct of employees was one thing; to tamper with a man's civil liberties was quite another. So the imputation ran, and in an effort to restore public confidence, Norman, on his own initiative, asked Baldwin to institute an independent investigation into the BBC's handling of the affair. The three-man enquiry produced a report which exonerated the corporation from the imputation of exerting undue pressure, but also demonstrated that formal warnings to Lambert had been crudely expressed without sufficient regard to the strength of his case:

'A tradition and technique in dealing with staff matters has to be established in controlling authorities', the inquisitors concluded. 'On the staff side, a code to determine how far individual freedom of opinion and action are consistent with the paramount responsibilities of the governing body must be built up and accepted *ex animo* by the staff.'

The government, working through the unobtrusive Sir Horace Wilson, were now determined to press for reforms so that all temptations to paternalistic abuse should end and proper staff representation begin. This was an overt dig at Reith; and in the light of his almost entirely passive concern with the Lambert-Levita fracas, it was quaintly ironic. His response to the board was characteristic. Let the question of staff representation be put to the vote, he suggested:

'I had no objection whatever to staff associations . . . but I came on great opposition to the idea. They [the staff] felt it would be taken as a reflection on myself, particularly if imposed from outside. Eventually it was decided to put the matter to a free vote of all the staff. Nine per cent were in favour of an association of some sort; 11 per cent thought it might be considered; 80 per cent were categorically opposed.'[1]

That, for the time being, clinched the question as far as Reith was concerned. But Sir Horace Wilson, with whom Ronald Norman had begun to cultivate a close if discreet understanding, had other views. Wilson came to regard Reith as tiresomely obdurate; but so long as Baldwin remained at No. 10 there was little Wilson could do but bide his time.

On great royal or state occasions, the BBC still strove to surpass itself, in keeping with the worshipful attitude to the monarchy of Sir John himself. Whether it was the death of a king, a jubilee celebration, or a coronation, the national mood of mourning or rejoicing would not merely be vividly reflected but partly shaped by the technical forethought lavished on every ceremonial detail and on the strategic positioning of every microphone. Yet undoubtedly the abdication drama of December 1936 enabled Reith finally to fulfil himself in a walking-on part of the utmost personal and even constitutional significance. Paradoxically his attitude, his actions and reactions, his intensely acute sense of involvement in the affair were not unworthy of a Roundhead on guard when Charles I faced his executioners in Whitehall.

The friendly liaison of Edward VIII with Mrs. Ernest Simpson had not passed unnoticed inside Broadcasting House. The young monarch, who looked upon his ministers as stuffy 'old men' and ignored their tacit disapprobation of his own unconventional behaviour, had seemed all set on creating a new style of modern kingship. He was, perhaps on that very account, a highly popular figure in the country; but his desire to marry a commoner, who had already divorced one husband and was meanwhile on the point of divorcing a second, inevitably led him into a head-on collision with the Anglican Church in particular and with the establishment as a whole. For the monarchy was an inextricable part, the anointed head indeed, of the Church itself; and though British moral standards had become laxer in recent years, the Anglican view of divorce had grown if anything more rigorous, not less.

'It was commonly supposed by the staff at my lowly level', Harman Grisewood has written, 'that the Director-General's sympathies were aligned against the King and so with Mr. Baldwin and the Anglican establishment. . . . The announcers in the 1930s had far more responsibility than nowadays. They were in control of transmissions . . . They had an operational autonomy, rather as a commander in the field. . . . It was one thing to turn off a speaker who was drunk or to decide to cancel a concert because the orchestra was late. But supposing the King suddenly and unexpectedly wished to broadcast? Or—worse still—if Mrs. Simpson wished to say a few words? The position had already declared itself whereby the seat of constitutional power was not the Palace but Downing Street. There was no king's party but there were the King's supporters. Were they to ask leave of Mr. Baldwin before they could break silence?'

Grisewood's dilemma was real if rare. Both as a Roman Catholic and as an intellectual who contrived to see such problems in a European rather than in an exclusively British context, he believed that much more than the fate of a king was at stake. With a rare upsurge of romantic defiance, comparable in its smaller intensity with the romantic conformism animating Reith, he made up his mind to disobey any edicts from on high which conflicted with his personal allegiance to the crown.

'The King, we gathered, was not to broadcast without the previous knowledge of the Government and the Director-General. No one seemed to be troubled about this at Broadcasting House. But I felt quite clear that the King should be able to broadcast whenever he liked and did not need to consult Mr. Baldwin or the Director-General of the BBC. I resolved that if I were on duty and it fell to me to deal with any telephone request for a broadcast by the King, I would give the facilities. . . .'[12]

It was an empty resolve. Reith's preparations left no loopholes for mistakes, accidental or deliberate. For months he had been grimly aware of the King's dilemma through reports and casual gossip, all emanating originally from the United States. For once he admired the tight restraint displayed by the British press. Not a hint of the unsavoury truth besmirched its columns. A form of voluntary self-censorship was imposed to which the BBC was party through Reith's instinctive rather than conspiratorial rejection of the scurrilous, sensational and even perilous facts: 'It's too horrible, and it's serious and sad beyond calculation', he noted as early as May, 1936. The dam suddenly cracked and broke. On October 27th, at Ipswich, Mrs. Simpson obtained a decree of divorce *nisi* from her husband. In the words of the historian, Alan Taylor, 'the cohorts of morality now mobilised'. The editor of *The Times*, Geoffrey Dawson, among others, prodded the Prime Minister into belated action. Baldwin 'posed a stern choice: renunciation of Mrs. Simpson or abdication. Mrs. Simpson posed an equally stern choice on the other side: marriage, 'whatever the price'.

The King himself wavered like a man longing to have his cake and eat it. He wanted to marry the woman he loved—and still to keep the throne. He wanted also to present his case to the people in a radio broadcast, and here he fell foul of a BBC board naturally anxious to fall in with the wishes of the government. As for Reith himself, every fibre of his being revolted at the flabby, irresolute conduct of a king unable or unwilling to admit where his true responsibilities lay. When on December 1st a relatively obscure, provincial bishop, apparently without any personal knowledge of the Mrs. Simpson affair, declared that Edward VIII stood in urgent need of divine grace, several local newspapers grasped this as an excuse to break the long silence of the press. The national dailies duly followed next morning, but by then the King had lost the virtually single-handed struggle to share his throne with a twice-divorced commoner unacceptable to the ecclesiastical and political élite.

It was on December 3rd that Reith heard direct from Warren Fisher at the Treasury that the Dominions had been consulted and were unequivocally in favour of abdication, having turned down the alternatives of a morganatic marriage or of recognising Mrs. Simpson as queen. There were further telephone calls on December 4th from Fisher and Horace Wilson, each being disturbed to learn that Windsor Castle had been provisionally wired for broadcasting: 'Yes,' said Reith, 'but Sir Godfrey Thomas rang me at midnight to say that Mr. Baldwin had agreed to the King's broadcasting on December 4th from Windsor.' Warren Fisher denied the truth of: 'You can't believe anything the King says.' Reith reassured them: the King's voice would not be heard on the BBC until Baldwin gave the signal. As far as the Director-General was concerned, the procedures laid down weeks before with the Prime Minister's approval would be followed to the letter. In what he regarded as a 'constitutional crisis of the utmost gravity', the correct protocol prescribed by Downing Street for the emergency could no more be set aside than the eternal moral law. It would have scandalized him if any suggestion of Harman Grisewood's traitorous trueness to the King's cause had ever reached him. What turned out to be a distinguished BBC career would no doubt have been abruptly terminated:

'Alas', wrote Grisewood, 'the abdicationists had an easy time of it. The broadcast of the King was notable only for the pathos. Sir John Reith was there at Windsor. Any outbreak of Stuart feeling would surely have withered under that stern Knoxian gaze.'[12]

Reith's immensely detailed account of the minutiae of that abdication broadcast provides a fascinating footnote to one of the shortest and uneasiest reigns in British history. It also reveals, between the lines, his stern pride and extraordinary sense of theatre.

A man obsessed with the consummate importance of his small yet important role, Reith could never condone the folly of a king who sought to exchange an incorruptible for a corruptible crown.

'The former king seemed to be in a different mood from usual "Good evening, Reith", hesaid. "Very nice of you to make all these arrangements and to come over yourself." He introduced his companion—Walter Monckton. I knew how much he had meant to his master in recent weeks. On the way upstairs he asked if all were in order. Yes, I said, and no chance of anything going wrong; everything had been duplicated; and the civil war in Spain had not prevented Madrid ringing up to ask permission to relay his talk. That amused him. . . . In a little sitting room the microphone had been installed. Next door the engineers had their apparatus. . . . At half a minute to ten I sat before the microphone at the table waiting for the signal—the tiny red light that would bring the ears of the whole world into that little room. A thousand million people were there to hear what the man standing beside me was about to say. I thought with quiet satisfaction of the vast and flawless efficiency of the organisation behind the now dull circle of glass . . . "This is Windsor Castle. His Royal Highness the Prince Edward."

'I slipped out of the chair to the left; he was to slip into it from the right. So slipping he gave an almighty kick to the table leg. And that was inevitably and faithfully transmitted to the attendant multitudes. Some days afterwards I was invited to confirm or deny a report that, having made the announcement, I had left the room, slamming the door. It was even suggested that, by so doing, I was not just forgetful of microphone sensitivity, but was indicating disapproval of what was to follow. I had left the room, but no microphone would have noted it . . . . The Prince came to the head of the stairs with me. He referred to his visits to Broadcasting House; he had always enjoyed coming there. He had made great use of broadcasting; it had helped him in many ways; he hoped he would be able to use it again. I could only say I hoped so too. "Good luck, sir", I said, coming to attention; bowed, shook hands. He looked up at me and smiled; seemed to be going to say something more. For two or three seconds no movements; then I bowed again, turned and went down the stairs. I felt there was something I ought to have said, wanted to say, could not. . . .'[1]

The stiffness of that solemn leave-taking, with the legal formalities of the Abdication Bill well and truly disposed of, and a new king already proclaimed, stood out starkly in Reith's memory. The last and probably the hardest peak looming up in an unduly protracted career of mountaineering had been scaled with something of the old, ferocious aplomb by this strange man, once predestined for a greatness which continued to elude him like a will o' the wisp.

6

The abdication left its mark on the political world. It restored the fading prestige of Baldwin who departed in a blaze of glory when George VI was crowned in Edward's place the following summer. The stock of Churchill and of others who had openly sided with the former king seemed to have been irretrievably broken. It occurred to Reith, musing over the ritualistic splendours inseparable from a coronation, that the BBC chairman might have been allowed to 'present a golden microphone symbolic of the ears of all his peoples attendant on the utterances of the King'. A long evening with the Baldwins at Chequers shortly before the mantle of power descended on Neville Chamberlain enabled Reith to share confidences with the retiring Prime Minister:

'I said I was personally sorry that he was dropping out. I had had little or no contact with his successor: and for the Prime Minister as head of His Majesty's Government, as distinct from the leader of a party, I preferred to have both liking and respect. I had felt that way to him even though he had not taken nearly as much interest as he might. I could hardly feel it to his successor . . .'[1]

Reith had never found it easy or agreeable to communicate with Chamberlain who kissed hands as Prime Minister on May 28th, 1937. They had been snappy and testy with each other at their earliest encounter in 1923. A temperamental barrier still divided them. It had betrayed itself recently while the one-time Postmaster-General was systematically seeking to restore the nation's economic fortunes at the Exchequer. Twenty-two years Reith's senior, and no respecter of persons or pretensions, Chamberlain disliked both the boldness and the reputation for Olympian presumptuousness of this younger man who firmly ruled the BBC. What the new Prime Minister would write later of Leslie Hore-Belisha, on accepting his resignation from the War Office, could just as aptly have been applied by him to the uncomfortable character of John Reith:

'He has very exceptional qualities of courage, imagination and drive. . . . Unfortunately, he has the defects of his qualities—partly from his impatience and eagerness, partly from a self-centredness which makes him careless of other people's feelings.'

From the start, Chamberlain's was effectively a one-man government. He looked to himself alone for decisions; and the Tory Party, while maintaining a high regard for the leader, 'had little for the leading figures about him, above whom he stood head and shoulders, solitary, a natural spearhead and target'.[17] For much of Reith's final year at Broadcasting House, therefore, frustrations multiplied with unfulfilled longings, and the stifling tendency towards corporate inanition grew within the portals of Broadcasting House. The BBC produced several schemes on paper, notably a proposal for introducing foreign broadcasting without delay to counteract the crude but efficient and well-financed propaganda machines of Germany and Italy; but the tight control exercised by Sir John Simon, the Chancellor, over all marginal public spending reflected his own master's strict sense of priorities. The rapid developments Reith wanted were thus held back. In the previous February the Baldwin government had published a new defence White Paper, on which Chamberlain, rightly, claimed to have done 'most of the work'. This had asked the nation to expect, over the next five years, public expenditure on armaments to the tune of £1500 million—'a contribution indispensable to peace, and one which it is the duty of this country to make'.

A depleted, antiquated airforce had to be rebuilt almost from scratch; yet rearmament was expected to expand almost of its own accord, side by side with the steady if slow recovery of general industry. Since neither the necessary machine tools nor the skilled men were available to meet demands, let alone delivery schedules, rearmament could not be rushed except on paper. For this was peacetime; Britain had still not adapted herself to the processes of mass production; and the traditional insistence on individualistic quality of products inevitably spelt long delays. Always provided that in any future war the British could fend off a sudden knock-out blow from the skies, there was no doubt something to be said for Chamberlain's policy of hastening slowly in defence matters. A convinced advocate of financial and economic stability, he stood by his sincere belief that 'wars are won not only now with arms and men, they are won with the reserves of resources and credit.'

The needs and aspirations of the BBC lay on the furthest fringes of official thinking. There were too many bigger bottlenecks calling for more urgent unblocking. Despite the prompting of Foreign Office advisers like Vansittart, the government was in no hurry to extend the scope and direction of overseas broadcasting. Such lack of urgency nettled Reith; and his indiscreet comments did little to improve his personal standing with Chamberlain. The corporation's budgetary position was by no means unhealthy. A clause in the Finance Bill had exempted it from the new and very unpopular national defence contribution; 75 per cent of licence revenue had been allocated for radio; and television costs were to be met for the next two years by means of a short-term Treasury loan.

Funds would not stretch, however, to cover what Reith wishfully thought of as 'the projection of England': broadcasts from London to the world at large in many tongues. He had tried 'periodically and urgently for three years to have this matter taken seriously. Almost every month brought news of extensions of activity in totalitarian lands'. A Cabinet committee under Kingsley Wood was formed in the summer of 1937 to consider what should be done. Again Reith expressed his exasperation, this time because no BBC representative was invited to attend. Not until October did that happen, and then only after Reith and Norman, accompanied by two senior executives (one of whom openly disbelieved in foreign broadcasting on the pretext that the BBC's reputation for impartiality would eventually suffer), had stated their own terms. They stressed that any genuine overseas radio service would demand programmes as well as news; that the corporation should be authorised to undertake it without prejudice to the existing Empire service in English, and with the same freedom from official interference as was enjoyed on the home air; and that further finance must be provided for it. Only an élitiste branch of the BBC would, in Reith's view, be good enough. Any alternative, like that then being considered in Whitehall of letting the Foreign Office build and run its own radio station in Cyprus as the precursor of others, would be self-defeating.

Even Kingsley Wood, the committee chairman, seemed reassured by the firm declaration that the foreign news service of the BBC 'would be based on telling the truth', but that Foreign Office guidance would be sought on all complex issues of policy. Before the end of October, 1937, the BBC's loose prospectus was accepted in principle by the Cabinet, Anthony Eden's qualifying request for written rules on practical working relationships between the Foreign Office and the corporation being overruled. Instead, both parties undertook freely to enter into a 'gentleman's agreement' which, so Kingsley Wood informed an unusually credulous Director-General, could be taken as 'a great tribute' to the BBC. And so the new Arabic service started life on January 3rd, 1938; some four months later it was followed by the Spanish and Portuguese services.

On one cardinal point Reith would have been better advised to disregard Kingsley Wood's glib encomium and refuse anything short of a written guarantee from the government of long-term financial support for the whole operation. Anthony Eden's demand for a written accord might have given rise to problems of interpretation.

Yet an uncovenanted grant-in-aid, in strict accordance with the BBC's actual needs, was probably the greater of two evils. The corporation would, from now on, depend increasingly on the grace and favour of the Treasury and the Foreign Office; and the BBC, as never before, would be held to ransom when economic troubles loomed or when ministers and anonymous advisers took it into their heads to grind political axes at the slightest whim. A man less disorientated than Reith had now become would certainly have anticipated such dangers. He might have been more chary of entering into an informal undertaking which tied the BBC willy nilly to the purse-strings of future governments, subjecting it to pressures unpredictably different from those confronting Neville Chamberlain in the late thirties. The ambiguity of Whitehall's attitude to the BBC as late as in 1938 can be studied in its curiously mixed reaction to the sustained impact on British listeners of programmes from European commercial stations, notably in France and Luxembourg, which mostly came through the medium of the home-based wireless exchanges.

Repeated attempts by the BBC to curb these broadcasts in English, through appeals to successive ministers in the unstable administrations of the Third Republic, were quite unavailing. As a result, Whitehall became interested, fitfully and largely for expedient reasons, in the possible alternative of a sponsored or commercial broadcasting system to which at least a million British households were estimated to be already addicted, if only as an escape from the relative tepidity of the BBC's Sunday offerings. Kingsley Wood was 'not averse to commercial broadcasting from inside Britain; Sir Robert Vansittart of the Foreign Office and Robert Boothby from the Conservative backbenches, conscious of the stormy international scene, thought that Britain might actually sponsor advertising stations abroad from which British programmes could be disseminated; there were voices in the Treasury hinting that the BBC's licence revenue was becoming insufficient to cover the amount required for the future development of television and overseas broadcasting, and that different ways of financing broadcasting might have to be considered'. Such is the detached verdict of Asa Briggs on the state of official thinking in 1939.[3]

These were years of marking time, years of gathering doubts about the performance and status of a corporation which, mainly as a consequence of Reith's alternating moods of disenchantment with his own job, and of his undisguised impatience with a procrastinating government apparently unable to do its own, had for far too long been marking time as well. The Director-General was quick to take offence about small particulars, quicker still in tracking down to source external allegations of bias or contentiousness in BBC programmes and news bulletins. Once, in the summer of 1937, after debating with Lord Halifax at Chevening, the country home of the Stanhopes, how far great wealth and privilege could be reconciled with the practice of Christianity, Reith walked off leaving Halifax idly wondering why on earth the BBC was still under the executive control of a God-fearing socialist. And nobody in the Cabinet, then or later, was closer to the Prime Minister than Halifax.[11]

Unquestionably the BBC itself paid the penalty for Reith's aloof but unabashed paternalism by pulling too many punches in its staid, and often excessively cautious, approach to the unending problem of enlightening its enormous but often bewildered public. The dangerous undercurrents of international trends, speeding the drift towards a second world war which nobody wanted, were by no means always indicated by the broadcasters. The undue sensitiveness of the government to implied criticism of its policies did not help: too many ministers subscribed to the fairly common belief that the hold of the corporation over public opinion had already grown too great under Reith and must somehow be diminished. The proud prisoner of his own virtues and their countervailing defects, the unhappily blinkered Director-General had far more time on his hands than he liked to consort with members of the ruling class. These people seldom enjoyed hearing the unsparing truth, as he saw it, about themselves, their friends and the general incompetence of Britain's leaders in the handling of public affairs.

When, in November 1937, Reith suddenly tendered his resignation to the BBC board, he was touched and also taken aback by the embarrassed assurance of the chairman, Ronald Norman, that he must remain as Director-General 'for everyone's sake'. His reasons for wishing to leave then were clear:

'I was not satisfied with myself, and as long as I was there I knew it would be difficult for the governors to deal as they might have liked with the BBC, its organisation and policy'.[1]

One of the retiring governors, H. A. L. Fisher, wrote to say that the board were unanimous that 'your retirement at this juncture would be a calamity'. Norman, who, left to himself, would have been tempted to accept the resignation with a sigh of relief but still lacked the will to force so unpalatable a decision down the throats of his colleagues, had little option but to wait. In Norman's private judgment, Reith had already outlived his positive usefulness: 'A chief executive whose desk was cleared early enough each day to permit undue and sometimes pointless interferences with the work of senior subordinates can all too easily become an embarrassment.

This, I'm afraid, was the case with Reith before the end of 1937.'[10]

To what degree the presentation of news and talks programmes was inhibited by Reith's hovering and vaguely menacing presence must remain a question for conjecture. Certainly some senior producers felt less free than they would have wished. On such complex and controversial issues as the failure of collective security through the League of Nations, non-intervention in the Spanish civil war, the recognition of Italy's conquest in Abbyssinia, the Austrian *anschluss* in March 1938, and the desirability or otherwise of 'stopping' Hitler before it was too late, the threads of fairness and objectivity were invariably difficult to isolate and illuminate satisfactorily. Nor was the staff yet professionally adept to do so properly. As the BBC was enjoined by licence to eschew all editorialising and opinion-making on its own account, controllers as well as producers tended to act on the wise prescription: 'better be safe than sorry'. The General Advisory Council, an 'ambassadorial' trust of carefully chosen brains, was too general and remote to influence the daily running of programmes from its foundation in 1935 onwards.

'The BBC is almost overburdened with a sense of responsibility', a writer in the *Political Quarterly* had commented in the autumn of that year. 'One sometimes has the impression that because it is not answerable to one particular body it feels itself to be answerable to everyone for its actions'.

On the other hand, relatively few citizens (and these mostly of the type nicknamed the 'ins' by Keynes, because they had either knowledge or informed interest in events) seemed to understand where developments in Europe were leading Britain. Chamberlain, as narrowly rational as he had always been, whether grappling with the problems of the unemployed or complaining that Edward VIII's dithering over Mrs. Simpson was 'holding up business and employment', pursued his own complicated line of rearming while appeasing the dictators, like an anxious housewife tidying up in the middle of a riotous party. The BBC did its level best to follow him with the dustpan; but there were numerous confusions, inhibitions and distractions, probably unavoidable, in that tortuous process. With benefit of hindsight Mrs. Mary Agnes Hamilton, a BBC governor who genuinely admired Reith and was with him until the end of 1937, declared that 'the policy pursued [by the BBC] was evasive. We ought to have given a positive direction—we did not. . . . What the BBC did do was faithfully to reflect a quite general outlook.'[18]

The objection, obviously, was and remains a serious one. Examining it briefly in historical perspective, Asa Briggs has remarked with unwonted sharpness:

'Viewed in this light, the talking mongoose was as much a creature of escape as the Loch Ness monster, and talk about the "prussianism" of the BBC was an excuse for not understanding what was happening in Prussia.'

John Reith could justly have grieved that he was much misunderstood. Perversely, however, he gloried in the fact and persevered in the thankless task of serving as a 'lightning conductor', both inside and outside Broadcasting House, until Ronald Norman's overstretched patience finally snapped. The chairman, having voted with the rest of the board in persuading the Director-General to withdraw his sudden offer to resign, resolved early in 1938 that Reith must go—on the BBC's terms and not on his own. The reasoning was simple. Reith, not unlike the late king, wanted to have his cake and eat it; to give up the now tedious business of chief executive and yet to retain his throne as a member of the board. This, in Norman's private judgment, would be most unfair to everyone, excepting Reith himself. It would never do. But how could the man's unconditional removal be contrived? There seemed at first to be no conceivable method of dislodging the giant without a monumental fuss; yet Norman applied himself assiduously to the problem and at last found outside allies—and an ingeniously elaborate answer.

Reith began to hear disturbing reports outside that the government had another post in mind for him. The earliest whispers reached his ears in November 1937, when the only way of creating work for himself at the BBC appeared to be that of resuming responsibilities he had already devolved on others. To have done so, would, he felt, have been 'monstrously unfair'. According to the gossip in the clubs, a new chairman would soon be needed to straighten out the affairs of Imperial Airways, and the name of John Reith was being knowingly bandied about. It was, he said, 'a peculiar rumour, and I did not like it at all'. A winter cruise to the West Indies in January and February 1938, as the guest of his influential acquaintance, Montagu Norman, left him more depressed and unsettled than ever. For the governor of the Bank of England had told him pointedly that 'I should be fully and urgently occupied' in the event of war. As Kingsley Wood had recently said much the same thing to him, adding that Reith should not think of staying much longer at the BBC, it was clear that moves must be afoot to accommodate him elsewhere. Then, on March 9th, the Cadman report on the parlous state of Imperial Airways was published. Its criticism of maladministration in the concern made Reith less inclined than ever to consider the post of chairman, if it were offered. For the managing director, Woods Humphery, had been a fellow-apprentice of his some thirty years before at the North British locomotive works in Glasgow, and they had since remained casual acquaintances. Nothing untoward happened meanwhile at Broadcasting House, except the progressive enquiry into staff conditions which a recently appointed specialist controller, W. St. John Pym, had been conducting since 1936. Then Horace Wilson took a hand in the machinations to rid the BBC of Reith.

Through Wilson, and again through Mrs. Neville Chamberlain, who happened to be seated next to him at a public lunch early in May, Reith conveyed to the Prime Minister a spirited but untimely impenitence for the BBC's alleged policy of unfriendliness to the government, and in particular to its head. It was no part of the BBC's duty, he declared, to help the Conservative Party 'to put its house in order'. A Cabinet reshuffle took place later in May. It pushed Kingsley Wood into Swinton's place at the Air Ministry, and when the new aviation minister invited Reith to call and see him informally, the conversation went off at a customary, prickly tangent:

'Are you any busier than you were at the BBC?'

'No, I'm not,' said Reith.

'Something must be done about it,' said Kingsley Wood.[11]

Reith retorted that he doubted whether anything would be done because politicians, irrespective of party, disliked him for holding the BBC 'constitutionally clear and politically impartial'. Stating bluntly that Kingsley Wood disliked him, too, Reith got a flustered denial. And there the matter rested, for the moment.

Hore-Belisha, a flashing blade in that dull, prim Cabinet, next offered Reith, without consulting anyone, the hitherto non-existent post of organization director at the War Office. Nothing came of it. Warren Fisher begged Hore-Belisha not to proceed, since Reith had already been earmarked for the Imperial Airways vacancy, and with splendid indiscretion Hore-Belisha duly informed Reith of the fact.

It was on June 3rd that Horace Wilson played the card which clinched the fate of John Reith. A senior BBC official, visiting Broadcasting House from one of the regions that day, shared a taxi with the Director-General from Broadcasting House at lunchtime:

'I'm seeing the Prime Minister this afternoon', said Reith gloomily. 'It looks like the sack.'

Gerald Beadle, who had worked with him for fifteen years, realised that Reith was not joking but could hardly bring himself to believe him. Nor did anyone else, most of the governors included, ever succeed in getting to the bottom of the extraordinarily cumbersome shifts by which the first Director-General was gradually eased out of office. The prime mover, it must be repeated, was the chairman, Ronald Norman, who, unwilling to risk an unpleasant confrontation by employing normal constitutional procedures, worked indirectly on the ingenuous Reith through his brother Montagu, through Kingsley Wood, Warren Fisher, and Horace Wilson, and at the end through the severely practical Neville Chamberlain. The unguarded honesty of Reith in telling any well-placed member of the establishment who cared to listen that he had insufficient work to do at Broadcasting House conveniently played into the hands of them all. For Ronald Norman could and did vouch for the unwelcome difficulties created by an underemployed Director-General who remained a fearsome law unto himself, however hard he might strive to desist.

The preliminary interview with Wilson at No. 10 Downing Street on June 3rd, 1938, confirmed Reith's worst suspicions. The Prime Minister and Kingsley Wood had authorized Wilson 'to instruct me to go to Imperial Airways—tomorrow if possible'. It would be a full-time job with no outside interests, which meant severing every tie with the BBC. Wilson handled the exchanges adroitly. By appealing point-blank to Reith's disinterestedness, to his loyalty, above all to his unshakable reverence for higher authority, he pierced the victim's Achilles' heel. The despondent Reith made a last lunge in self-defence. Since he was still 'utterly reluctant' to take the job, Reith said that he must see the Prime Minister. Obligingly, Wilson rang through at once to the private office:

'He won't take it from me. He insists on seeing the PM', he said.

The meeting with Chamberlain, thus swiftly arranged, was brief. It turned on one ridiculous but decisive question: when is an instruction not an instruction? The Prime Minister told Reith that he would prefer not to use the word 'instruct', but he and his colleagues would be pleased if Reith would take the job offered. That was good enough. Clearly, at such a time of growing international tension, the head of the government left him with no alternative.[11,1]

In a letter to Chamberlain on June 14th, when his imminent departure from the BBC was finally announced in the Commons, Reith asked whether in due course the 'no other interests' stipulation attaching to the Imperial Airways post might be waived. Before the Prime Minister could reply, the Director-General rang through to No. 10 and cancelled the request. The long agony of self-recrimination was fast setting in. The 'monstrous pusillaninimity' which had betrayed him at No. 10 yielded to an impulse of petulance when an extremely embarrassed Ronald Norman entered his room on June 29th and suggested that Reith should not attend the board meeting that day. Apparently one or two of the governors considered that 'it would not be fair to my successor if I were on the board'. The suspicion of no longer being wanted, even of being jettisoned like a corpse at sea, hardened into a knot of bitterness which would torment him for the rest of his life. Reith's love for the child which had long ago outgrown him curdled overnight into antipathy approaching hatred. On June 30th, before turning his back on Broadcasting House, he gave orders for his radio and television sets to be recovered from his home and had his name struck off the subscription list for BBC publications. A short farewell message to the staff hinted obscurely at the awful pain he felt. To turn his back on these devoted men and women, some of whom had served his predestined cause from the beginning, without a formal word of thanks would have been unthinkable. So, too, would have been the sickening nostalgia inseparable from a leave-taking party, the very notion of which he refused to entertain. Had he submitted to the ordeal of the sentimental speeches and the hasty presentations amidst the clink and clatter of tea-cups, his choked emotions might for once have got the better of his judgment.

'A sad day for the BBC', Stuart Hibberd wrote in his private diary that night, 'to lose the man who has been mainly responsible for its creation: a man of vision, a fair man, a man who knew what he wanted and knew how to get it; a statesman of the first order; a disciplinarian with a sense of humour; a shy man who combined a stern expression with a leaven of sweet reasonableness; a much misunderstood man; a born leader of men; a doughty fighter; a man with an iron will, but a lonely man—at least that was my impression—but a human being and a most loyal friend. The country and Empire will never forget how much they owe to him for his public service conception of the BBC.'[19]

It was of panegyrics like that that John Reith, in this darkest hour of betrayal and frustration, was most afraid; he had good reason to spew out the thought of farewell celebrations. He chose to suspend belief in his overrated virtuousness when his whole world had turned upside down and he was at last being hurled off into the unknown. Of the first Director-General of the BBC Reith would continue to say sceptically until the very end:

'I once knew him very well but never cared for him much.'

There were a few of his earliest colleagues in the entrance hall of Broadcasting House that last evening as he walked out with his wife. One of them was Ralph Wade who noticed that 'tears were literally pouring down his cheeks. And Lady Reith, anxious to show the staff how much they disliked leaving them, kissed the commissionaire on duty at the door.' John Reith's last semi-public act was symbolic and wholly in character:

'With three or four others I drove to Droitwich high-power transmitter, myself closed down the big oil engines at midnight—and it was not necessary for the engineers to tell me what to do. They asked me to sign the visitors' book, J. C. W. Reith, late BBC.'[1]

10

The Outsider

1

IF LADY REITH's reflexes as a driver had been a trifle slower, the big lorry bearing down on her car at a blind cross-roads in Cornwall would almost certainly have killed her, her husband, and their two children, instead of merely bruising and shaking them. The father of the BBC, still within a year of his enforced retirement, would then have posed a much more enigmatic problem to the biographer than the embittered, haunted yet marvellously injudicious and tactless octogenarian who had lived on to rue his narrow escape from death that summer's day in 1937, and much else besides. Legend is notoriously difficult to disentangle from the fragile gossamer of truth. In the case of a man like John Reith, who was revered by his staff as a minor deity, and subsequently acclaimed or reviled by opinion-makers in Britain as a freakish master builder of consummate if rigid genius, the very singleness of an achievement cut short almost at its pinnacle by a tragic road accident might well have guaranteed him a legendary footnote in the short roll-call of leading twentieth-century pioneers. But fate, once so kind to a son with such a preternaturally fine ear for its subtler messages, had crueller designs in store for him.

From 1923 to 1938 his public reputation seemed to soar upwards on thrusting eagle's wings. If the establishment, of which he wrongly felt himself to be a natural member, feared his sharp eye and merciless talons more than Reith in his innocence would ever allow, the degree of his influence was relatively greater as long as he remained at the BBC. Only when he took his reluctant leave, riven by unspoken doubts and suspicions as to the actual manner of its contrivance, did he have to reckon with the slow vengeance of time and his many outside enemies. From 1938 until death finally claimed him in June 1971 he accomplished remarkably little of lasting value. Gradually the shadows of near-oblivion closed about him. The story of these closing thirty-three years is one of accelerating anticlimax. To recount it in detail would not only be a gratuitous insult to his memory; it would serve also to foreshorten and distort the perspective of his true attainments in the prime of life, while destiny still bore him upwards. It must be treated episodically and with a becoming brevity, excluding all that is redundant but nothing that is genuinely significant. To do otherwise would be to falsify the effect of his increasingly neglible impact on men and events, as well as to court the risk of overlooking the far more momentous spiritual struggle he had to wage with the last enemy of all—the living death prescribed for an unworldly man infatuated by the tinsel glories that seduce the worldly.

When Chamberlain, needing little persuasion from Kingsley Wood, Horace Wilson or the brothers Ronald and Montagu Norman, finally decided, as we saw, that Reith's long reign at the BBC must end, the Prime Minister had directly appealed to the victim's overmastering sense of duty. Obstinate and determined as he was by nature, Reith could never disregard a call from higher authority; a request from the King's first minister was, in his book, as irresistible as a royal command. In selecting him for the chairmanship of Imperial Airways the Government were thus consciously killing two birds with one stone. The airline business had fallen on evil days, and only a fearless trouble-shooter of Reith's thoroughness seemed capable of disentangling the muddle of its affairs. With a heavy heart, the late Director-General of the BBC set to work in July 1938.

'In BBC days', he recalled, 'I had travelled to town on an 8.51 train (from Beaconsfield) fetching up at the office at 9.30. On joining Imperial Airways it was an 8.20 train and a 9.00 arrival at the furniture depository (in Buckingham Palace Road).'[1]

The trouble-shooting process helped to distract him from the newly festering wound, inflicted by men he thought of as insensitive, on his pride and self-esteem. He had always been good at tidying up and clearing out the debris of the past. Sometimes this orderliness had gone to excess. When the old BBC had faded out to make way for the new corporation, the bonfire he formed of its papers was so big that one day it would be regretted as the social historian's loss. And when visitors went to lunch or dine at his country home, the observant among them noticed a small shelf in the entrance hall. There were always books on it, books to which departing guests were invited by their host to 'help yourselves—take two each. I've no further use for them.'[2] At the former furniture depository near Victoria Station the thicket of airline problems defied such ruthless and simple disposal. All his gifts of persuasiveness, firmness and far-sightedness were in immediate demand. He had, for a start, to 'waste much time investigating the various charges, some of them absurd, which had been made against Imperial Airways under Geddes and Woods Humphery'.

He felt sorry for the retiring managing director, Woods Humphery, that old acquaintance of his Glasgow days who had taken too much on his own shoulders. He had less regard for Sir Eric Geddes, Sir Hardman Lever and Sir George Beharrell, all of whom evidently had put profits and the narrow interests of their shareholders above the larger considerations. The three men were at least as deeply immersed in the activities of the Dunlop company's boardroom, a dual allegiance which Reith found distasteful if not quite improper. The public service motive of an airline partly dependent on the tax-payers' money had been permitted to wither, a sin of neglect in the fastidious eyes of John Reith. That was why he swiftly decided that a constitutional change in the character of Imperial Airways must be authorised to eliminate any future possibility of conflict between private and public interest. An airline which carried the name, the flag and the prestige of Britain 'across the seven skies' deserved no less.

To assist him in amalgamating Imperial with British Airways, and in conferring on the merger of these separately run units the new dignity of a public corporation, Reith secured the services of Leslie (now Viscount) Runciman whom Cecil Graves had privately recommended to him as an eminently suitable managing director. Despite the counter-pull of his family shipping business as well as banking and railway directorships, Runciman readily agreed to put these temporarily aside for the experience of collaborating with Reith. From December 1938 onwards the two men caught the same morning train to London and became ideal partners in an enterprise which as yet existed mainly in the mind's eye of its vigorously imaginative chairman:

'It was an extraordinary interlude in my life', Lord Runciman told me. 'Reith drew on his BBC background instinctively in deciding that I shouldn't have a seat on the board, but would none the less be informed of every move he planned as a matter of course. I was sceptical at first whether the arrangement would work. It did—and we never exchanged a cross word.'

It startled Runciman to learn, in passing, 'how deeply and passionately Reith felt' about his unseemly and abrupt departure from

Broadcasting House. Through a handful of former colleagues, including Graves, the ex-Director-General watched the BBC's hesitant progress balefully from afar. These confidantes were as clearly aware as Runciman of an inconsolably bitter edge to his unhappiness. Yet self-respect inhibited Reith then and later from trying to discover precisely how his enemies had outwitted, outmanœuvred and displaced him, just as a basic if repressed affection for the child he had nurtured always prevented him from turning openly against it. He had a soft spot for Graves, the kinsman of Earl Grey, whom the BBC board had passed over (partly because of his adopted Roman Catholic beliefs) in favour of F.J. Ogilvie, the mild and cultured academic whom Reith had naturally pronounced as being wholly unfitted for the job of usurping his own once unchallenged authority. Time vindicated that typically unsparing judgment. But time utterly failed to heal Reith's shattered pride.

'From April 1939', he noted of his henchman at Imperial Airways, 'Runciman took the chair at the weekly meetings of the management committee. Following BBC precedent, with the boot on the other foot, I attended them.' By midsummer that year the last objections of British Airways to the merger had been overcome amicably and without loss of face. Rates of pay, staff conditions, the machinery of control had been overhauled to Reith's specifications; terms that were 'fair to generous' had been calculated to recompense former shareholders for their trouble; and clause by clause, line by line, the statute empowering the State to establish a public corporation in place of the two former companies was agreed with the Treasury solicitors and Sir Arthur Street of the Air Ministry.

Reith also dreamed of a rich and promising long-term growth which would have transformed the new British Overseas Airways Corporation, his own title, into a huge international business partnership spanning the entire Commonwealth. Representatives of every member country, not excluding South Africa, Southern Rhodesia and Eire, would have become joint-owners and joint-operators of BOAC. He was already engaged in taking the first, hopeful soundings before the corporation came formally into being on August 4th, 1939. By then Reith knew that this fugitive dream, like so much else, had evaporated like morning dew. Within a month, Neville Chamberlain dolefully broke the news to an expectant if unprepared nation that the evil of war, which he had striven to exorcise by the twin policies of appeasement and slow rearmament, had broken out at last.

Until the end of the year, Reith and Runciman chafed at the inevitable though slow disintegration of their recent handiwork.

BOAC languished: any thought of postwar planning, even of immediate practicalities like developing emergency routes for British civil aviation across neutral and non-belligerent lands, had to be abandoned for the duration. Worse still, no sign appeared of the 'really big job' on which the late Director-General of the BBC had been counting when a prearranged, coded message from Horace Wilson recalled him and his family from a touring summer holiday in Canada. Acting on the unanimous advice of American friends and well-wishers, Reith left his wife and children behind—'a harrowing decision', as he called it. He had often given Runciman to understand that, when war came, the protective relationship he had enjoyed with the BBC would probably be renewed on a different footing: 'he firmly hoped and believed that Chamberlain would send him to the Ministry of Information, the post he really wanted.' But such eager hopes were dashed; and for the first four months of the phoney war Reith sat restlessly poised by a telephone which somehow failed to ring. As he put it himself:

'The first news on landing from New York was that Lord Macmillan was Minister of Information. . . . With all his brilliance of intellect and integrity of character I could not imagine his being happy or successful in that office. No experience of the tortuous ways of propaganda, press procedure, public relations; and too much of a gentleman for what would be entailed. No message (for me) from anyone. I was not required.'[1]

He would have done better to heed Beaverbrook's friendly warning in June 1939: 'I hope very much that you will be made minister when the time comes. But I don't think so. If (Sir Samuel) Hoare had the appointment in his hands you would be put in at once.'[3]

2

According to Horace Wilson, Reith's name had been suggested for various ministerial appointments at the outbreak of hostilities, but 'they wouldn't have it'. Only the Lord Mayor of London was kind enough to float the uninviting suggestion that Reith might like to take charge of a campaign to raise Red Cross funds by the sale of jewellery and other precious stones. Trenchard, also unemployed and discontented with idleness, commiserated with him: 'Not using you', he said, 'is the most glaring and scandalous example of unemployment in the country. You and Churchill are so alike in temperament that you would do well together'.[4] But sympathy was not enough. He had to act, however tangential the action. So, at the end of

November, Reith embarked on a transatlantic liner at Southampton, sailed for New York and arrived, unannounced, to surprise his family in Swarthmore and bring them home for Christmas. It was a measure of the desperate lengths he would go to in the exercise of killing time and relieving dark despondency born of tedium. At length, while dressing for dinner on the night of January 5th, 1940, he heard the telephone ring. The Prime Minister's private secretary came on the line and invited Reith to call at No. 10 the following morning at eleven o'clock.

He had been there only once since the fateful interview with Chamberlain preceding the severance of his umbilical ties with the BBC. A business associate had half heartedly accompanied him on that more recent occasion to a small, gloomy annexe where the official who dispensed ecclesiastical patronage listened in stunned silence to an importunate request. Reith said that he wanted 'instant preferment' for an older brother, the Church of England clergyman; and he did not take too kindly to the pained refusal of the functionary behind the desk to promise anything. Wholly unembarrassed, Reith walked out, commenting unfavourably to his silently thoughtful companion on the slothful and dubious ways of the patronage office.[5] On this latest and more important visit to No. 10, he was ushered straight into the Cabinet room where, in the past, he had often sat in pleasant conversation with Ramsay MacDonald and Baldwin. Chamberlain's manner was, as usual, businesslike and cold. He explained why he now wished Reith to go to the Ministry of Information.

'I imagine it's incumbent on me to do whatever I'm asked by you to do at such a time', said the unwilling minister-designate. That was broadly correct, said Chamberlain, who, however, would not commit himself when asked how much support Reith could expect in trying to re-establish the authority and influence of a department which had fallen low in public esteem in the four months since the outbreak of war. The Cabinet, Chamberlain intimated, would be happier if all 'brawling' could be avoided. Reith was advised to 'have a look round', then come back in a month or two and let the Prime Minister hear what needed to be done:

'As to the BBC, it would to some extent come under my direction. There was a great deal of dissatisfaction with it, but he hoped I would be gentle with it, and not use my knowledge of it to do things that another minister could not do.'[6]

Lord Macmillan's short tenure of office had been calamitous, his relations with the press, the BBC, and the Foreign Office (which, under Sir Campbell Stuart, had assumed control of propaganda to enemy countries) had been fumbling and inept. The newspapers stood up and fought together for their own interests. The BBC in its isolation and uncertainty became a popular whipping boy. The immediate dispersal of its key departments to country centres for security reasons, and the switching over of all programmes to a single channel, had tended to lower both the standard and quality of broadcasting in those empty months of phoney war, yet neither Macmillan nor any other minister had considered it right so much as to hint at the real difficulties which dutiful compliance with short-sighted government edicts had meanwhile imposed on the BBC. Evasiveness and great caution characterised all official allusions to such problems. Many had agreed with George Bernard Shaw's denunciation of the premature closing down of theatres, cinemas and concert halls as 'a master stroke of unimaginative stupidity'; many more now agreed that the BBC's efforts to compensate were somewhat less than inspired. A sustained and clamorous press campaign against the insipid programme policy of the corporation was supplemented by criticism in parliament where Attlee, among others, had complained: 'I am not a habitual listener, but I must say that at times I feel depressed when I listen in.' Yet what few critics appeared to understand was that the BBC, under a chief executive as mild and unsure of himself as Ogilvie, could neither explain its own technical handicaps in public nor do anything else in general but emulate the timorous and mediocre attitudes of Whitehall.

'I believe', Macmillan had told an astonished Upper House towards the end of September, 1939, 'that the board [of the BBC] has been more or less suspended and that the chairman and directors are in charge'; but Macmillan in the next breath admitted to being quite unclear as to 'exactly what the control is'. His own writ certainly did not run to 'shall I say the lighter parts of its programmes'. People who did not care for these offerings could always switch off: 'You always have the privilege of not listening, which is one of the greatest privileges I know in connection with the BBC.'

Reith wryly told himself that he must 'do better than that', and yet strive against his every instinct to respect a nominal independence which the BBC, on its own indifferent performance, hardly deserved to keep. When Sir Allan Powell, the chairman, accompanied by Ogilvie, paid a formal call on him soon after he had moved into his office, a big room in the Senate House of London University where the principal had once presided, Reith sounded them out with swiftness and tact. They seemed quite nervous about his intentions. He assured them that he would not attempt to enlarge the area of his ministerial control over the BBC 'so long as you do what you should do'. Ogilvie struck him as being 'hopelessly out of his depth and therefore all the more anxious to assert himself'. It would have been easier to deal with a stronger and much less pedantic individual than this paragon of pale, academic respectability who evidently derived an obscure satisfaction from the splitting of constitutional hairs.

'Reith came to see me yesterday' Ogilvie noted on February 23, 1940, 'the first time he had been in Broadcasting House since he left in 1938. I gave him a copy of the *BBC Handbook 1940*, inscribed with greetings and best wishes from the old firm'. Together they discussed several outstanding points: 'a daily series of talks of a "heartening kind" hitting at Haw-Haw, telling cheering stories of bravery in the fighting services or at home etc.'; the return to the Ministry of Campbell Stuart's enemy propaganda unit, which Reith mistakenly imagined to be imminent; the urgency of stepping up the broadcasting to Germany of really good programmes, including 'concerts and entertainments after the manner of Fécamp or Luxembourg'; and that familiar King Charles' head of Reith's, the statutory relationship existing between the corporation and the government.[7] As Asa Briggs has noted: 'Ogilvie, who knew little of how Reith's mind worked, was surprised by the darting references to Fécamp and Luxembourg and even more by the general turn which the discussion took when Reith turned to the constitution of the BBC. Reith stuck to the views about the wartime constitution which he had urged in 1937 and 1938 before the structural changes after his resignation. Things would have been easier if the BBC had been "taken over", by which he obviously meant—Ogilvie had no insight into this—if the right kind of Director-General had been in a position of control with a direct line to government. Ogilvie replied soberly that he was not interested in whether "things were easy or difficult for the BBC and that it was a small price to pay for independence to have the occasional nuisance of carrying a government baby" . . . Reith continued to press and to probe Oglivie. Surely the overseas services of the BBC should be thought of as "a government institution"? Ogilvie replied that a diarchy in broadcasting would be damaging and would carry with it no compensating advantages in the national interest. There the remarkable interview ended.'[8]

Reith followed it up with a telephone call some days later, seeking from the Director-General a clearer indication of his views on 'some concrete form of propaganda . . . some positive activity to which people might be urged'. Ogilvie, however, would not be drawn. He merely questioned whether morale at home was as low as Reith appeared to imply: 'There might be an absence of cheerfulness but there was plenty of determination'. Had Reith been confronting Tallents, Graves or any of his former colleagues, he might have secured the commanding foothold he wanted without contravening the letter or the spirit of his private undertaking to the Prime Minister; fortunately, perhaps, for the BBC, Ogilvie neither understood nor fully trusted him. Powell, the chairman, was naturally informed of Reith's latest démarche. He at once approached Sir Horace Wilson and extracted an oral assurance that the BBC 'would not be taken over by the Ministry of Information'. Reith persisted in clinging to his outdated illusion that there could still be a partial reversion to his original pre-war scheme of a corporation operationally interlocking with the Ministry through the Director-General and his deputy, without the useless superstructure of a board of governors which served no useful purpose in an emergency. He was backing a certain loser.

'I did not manage', he acknowledged, 'to get him [Ogilvie] to discuss the matter in a free and friendly way. He was greatly perturbed. . .' Reith was still more perturbed to discover the extent to which Sir Horace Wilson persisted in intruding into high-level policy-making. On March 27th, in the course of another desultory talk with Chamberlain at No. 10 Downing Street, Reith was invited by the Prime Minister to consider 'whether the BBC, or part of it, should be taken over,' then report back. Five days went by. Then, appropriately enough on April 1st, Wilson saw Reith and told him, in effect, that meanwhile 'he had settled the matter on his own'. Powell, the BBC chairman, had just been reassured by Wilson that there would be no move by the Ministry of Information to limit the authority or operational responsibilities of the corporation. It was a disquieting example of an over-active tail wagging the Downing Street dog; and when Reith saw the Prime Minister again on April 10th, 'he [Chamberlain] referred to the BBC as if there had never been any question of action to be settled'.[1]

Having been sworn in as a Privy Councillor and submitted to the formality of taking his seat in the Commons as the member (unopposed) for Southampton, Reith faced with equanimity the ordeal of question time which gradually became almost enjoyable. Baldwin had volunteered him some sound advice: 'Wait for freedom in replying to supplementaries until you are familiar with the idiosyncrasies of the questioner, and until you can sense the House. There is a lot of fun in answering when you have learnt the game and the House knows you know it.' He was infinitely less at ease attending meetings of junior ministers at which crumbs of measly information were doled out, while he, the minister notionally responsible, had to endure the humiliation of picking up only as many stale titbits as his masters thought fit to drop. Increasingly frustrated by the bewildering and haphazard exclusion from his trust of the propaganda activities conducted by the Foreign Office, quite apart from what he disdainfully regarded as the less than adequate home and foreign programme policies of the BBC, Reith consoled himself by tinkering with the internal structure of the rump of shadowy authority that remained, secretly bewailing his terrible impotence. His final tilt at the BBC and Ogilvie came on April 15th when far more serious issues were at stake. By then the inadequacies of his own ministry had become painfully manifest. For British forces, belatedly despatched and landed, were being hard pressed in Norway by an invading enemy determined to expel them. Every important port from Oslo to Narvik and nearly all the operational airfields as well were seized at the double. 'Hitler has missed the bus', Chamberlain had declared the week before in a broad review of the war effort, with the premonitory if misplaced glee of a woefully misinformed leader whose hold on the country, the Commons and his closest colleagues was visibly slackening.

'I suggested to Ogilvie', said Reith remounting his favourite hobby horse as though nothing else mattered, 'that he should appoint someone in whom I could have confidence to vet all news bulletins; he seemed to agree. A week later, however, after another Cabinet reference to the BBC, I arranged for Kingsley Wood to see the BBC chairman and Director-General in my office (Sir Kenneth) Lee, Monckton and (Sir Horace) Wilson being present. Kingsley Wood told them how much dissatisfaction there was: what did they propose doing about it? Ogilvie replied that they had considered the suggestions I had made and had already decided on and promulgated some changes. They thought all would be well. That was about all there was to it; but the presence of Kingsley Wood and Wilson showed them that it was a Cabinet matter, not a private persecution of mine. . . . There never was any result during the brief remainder of my tenure of office as Minister of Information.'[1]

By the droll standards of the period, Reith could hardly be described as an unmitigated failure in a post which offered him little room for manœuvre or for the uninhibited use of his undoubted powers of initiative as an organizer. To describe him as a ministerial success, however, would be just as gross a misuse of language. With a strange self-effacement which did justice only to a kind of pavlovian subservience to the demands of superior authority, however foolish or wrongheaded those demands might be, he had for the most part reverted to the passive habits of childhood and simply done as he was told. Nevertheless, the precise mode of removing him from ministerial office proved both unseemly and hurtful.

Throughout the ill-fated Norwegian expedition, Reith had to conceal his own ignorance of the confused details of the disaster as it progressively unfolded. Even Churchill agreed somewhat grudgingly with him that the Minister of Information could not fulfil the duties laid upon him except as a full member of the War Cabinet. Yet Churchill still had not forgiven Reith for supposedly 'keeping me off the air in the thirties when I wanted to broadcast about India', just as he would never forgive Montagu Norman for having supposedly over-persuaded him at the Exchequer in the mid-twenties to restore the old gold standard. Only at the critical end of Chamberlain's term as wartime premier did Reith penetrate that frigid reserve and gain his belated confidence. By then the alarms were sounding on all sides. The imminent fall from grace of each man had become inevitable, though Reith deceived himself that he might be kept on in office with increased powers. The debate which precipitated the resignation of Neville Chamberlain filled John Reith with disgust at the unprincipled fickleness of politicians as a breed:

'It was a beastly business really', he said. 'I felt throughout that Churchill was a hypocrite.' He was disgusted by the 'unseemly joy' at Chamberlain's discomfiture: men of whom he (Reith) had expected more, like Harold Macmillan, 'were yelling themselves hoarse'.[6]

Yet when, with the aid of the Labour Opposition, Winston Churchill accepted the King's commission to form a new administration, Reith's supreme belief in his own competence overcame any doubts or scruples about carrying on in the service of his political bête noire.

'I wanted a job that would bring me into direct and constant touch with Churchill', was his instinctive thought while the ex-First Lord of the Admiralty was forming his Cabinet on May 11th. Seated in Walter Monckton's room at the Ministry two days later, Reith watched the entry of a messenger with an envelope. This contained the names of further new ministerial appointments. Suddenly Monckton banged his desk indignantly and read aloud: 'Minister of Information, Duff Cooper.' Reith swallowed back his bitterness, shook hands with his erstwhile colleagues, and left the building:

'Things had run true to form to the very end', he noted sardonically. 'The Minister of Information was late with his final bit of Information'.[1]

3

'I am sure you will forgive me', Churchill wrote to Reith 'for not giving you previous intimation of the change I have thought it necessary to make. It is a matter of extreme national importance that the new administration should be installed with the least possible delay: and I have been overlaid not only with the difficult task of forming a new government, but with the course of a battle of considerable importance.'[9]

At five minutes to five on Tuesday, May 14th, the summons to see the new Prime Minister brought Reith once again to No. 10 Downing Street. He had arrived a little earlier, intent on talking first to Chamberlain whose services Churchill insisted on retaining as Lord President of the Council. In response to a direct question, Chamberlain said that Churchill would offer Reith the Transport Ministry. He had feared as much; and he admitted to the ex-Prime Minister that his inclinations were against accepting. The previous holder, Euan Wallace, had complained of not having enough to do; and that, more than any serious apprehensions about his own ability or slightly ruffled self-confidence, gave the ex-Minister of Information instant pause. Chamberlain's firm, parting advice was that he should dismiss all personal qualms and unconditionally accept. Inside the Cabinet room, Churchill greeted him with a handshake and spoke of 'the difficult and important job' he would like Reith to do:

'Transport . . .', said the Prime Minister, glancing down at a list. 'How does that appeal to you?'

As Reith hesitated, Churchill repeated the rhetorical question with gravity.

'I said I would feel differently if he had been offering me a more important job such as a service ministry. He said the war might last a long time yet. I left him, Minister of Transport and very unhappy.'[1]

What Euan Wallace had told Reith turned out to be only too true. The railways virtually ran themselves. So did the docks. In each case, there were high-powered executive committees to handle all matters of moment, however bad the emergency might become. The senior officials, suave and efficient, asserted with disarming restraint: 'All is well.' Beneath the suavity lay a deprecating hint: 'Be kind enough not to interfere.' After five months in Whitehall Reith still felt very much of an outsider, forced to temper his combative instincts and liking for direct methods to the immemorial ways of a bewilderingly impersonal but well-oiled government machine. The assumption of patronising omniscience, which the highest civil servants exuded like a suffocating fragrance, both staggered and deflated him. It was 'magnificent, if incredible'. He could do no more than settle for the undeniable truth that 'nothing was required of me except to stand by and watch this excellence at work'. As a result, Reith retreated glumly into his shell while the French armies reeled and broke under swift and brilliantly executed German armoured thrusts, and the retreating British forces moved in ragged disarray towards the Channel coast.

It was during this agonising period of uncertainty that Sir Harold Hartley, then vice-president of the London, Midland, and Scottish Railway, heard at the War Office a first-hand account of the perils confronting the British as they converged on the dunes and beaches of Dunkirk. Unable to find Reith at his office, Hartley drove out to Beaconsfield. There, in the library, the Minister of Transport, his hands clasped behind his back, was pacing up and down 'like a caged beast'. His visitor told him what he knew, then pointedly enquired why Reith was not at his headquarters. Surely, he suggested, nothing could detain him at home now that he understood the magnitude of the coming emergency?

Reith did not reply immediately. He appeared to be 'struggling for words', as if unable to plumb the depth of his own feelings. When he spoke, Hartley was completely taken aback:

'There's nothing I can do. Nothing—just nothing,' he said.

Repeating his suggestion, but in firmer terms, that Reith would be far better employed at his ministry, Hartley turned and left. The frenzied helplessness of this man, whom he knew only slightly but thought of as a human dynamo, remained clearly etched on the memory of Sir Harold for the next thirty years.[2] Neither he nor others closer to Reith in his mounting frustration could quite square the gloomy passivity of the man with that fearless aggressiveness which had once been a byword. Like a Samson in chains, Reith was reduced to powerlessness by the mystifying competence of his own civil servants.

'With the capitulation of France on June 16th, there came an increasing sense of things to be done, but I was nowhere near the planning or the doing. Great difficulty in getting any news at all. By inter-departmental committees "on official level" the civil servants knew far more than I did.'[1]

It was especially galling not to be a member of the Cabinet when he reflected that his successor, Duff Cooper, now attended meetings, having incidentally reaped all the advantages at the Ministry of Information which Reith had done his best to sow, too late. Where the first Director-General of the BBC had been obliged to treat that institution with ministerial kid gloves, Duff Cooper's right to control its activities was no longer in question. Propaganda to enemy countries also came partly under his charge. The mind of Reith had come to resemble a house over-furnished with regrets, and all too often envy dogged him like a malignant sprite. The limits of his authority continually surprised him, just as the lack of direct access to the Prime Minister distressed him. Nor did he care for the occasional personal minutes, marked 'Action This Day', which Churchill sent down the line to his subordinates when the whim took him:

'A junior should not have to be stimulated or frightened into answering quickly a note from the boss (in any business),' was Reith's unflattering comment on the practice. Churchill's broader view of his own onerous if exhilarating duties is not out of context here:

'Power, for the sake of lording it over fellow-creatures or adding to personal pomp, is rightly judged base. But power in a national crisis, when a man believes he knows what orders should be given, is a blessing. In any sphere of action there can be no comparison between the positions of number one and number two, three or four. The duties and problems of all persons other than number one are quite different and in many ways more difficult.'[10]

The restless, darting inquisitiveness of the Prime Minister did not commend itself to Reith. After all, he was in the position of number four; and he disliked being treated as a lowly servitor not necessarily worthy of trust. Queries from on high about precise plans for maintaining the flow of supplies through the ports, when enemy bombs would at length begin to fall on British cities, seemed as superfluous and impertinent to Reith as queries about preparations for laying in adequate fuel stocks to keep the nation's trains running smoothly. What irked the Minister of Transport most was the uneasy recollection that in his own halcyon days as supreme arbiter at Broadcasting House he had sometimes adopted those very methods. If only he could have had closer personal relations with Churchill, the seeds of a harmonious working partnership might have begun to take even in the rocky and barren soil of Whitehall. For Trenchard had been partly right in suggesting that these two men, so utterly dissimilar in outlook, were uncannily similar in their compulsive thirst for exemplary action. Then, before the end of September, the Prime Minister caused Reith's hopes briefly to rise.

As the nights grew longer, and the enemy failed to knock out the weakening but matchless 'few' in the skies of south-east England or to destroy the key sector airfields and radar chain of RAF Fighter Command, German air attacks on London and other large cities were intensified under cover of darkness. The Transport Ministry's plans withstood the test; but Reith wrote a careful memorandum requesting that bomb disposal squads should be placed under his direct orders in the interests of efficiency. At a special meeting of ministers, one of those normally 'perfunctory affairs' which tried his patience and caused his brain to idle along in neutral gear, Reith found the Prime Minister in a fickle mood of friendliness. He was invited to expand his arguments. He did so without trouble, noticing while he spoke that Sir John Anderson was shaking his head rhythmically in dissent and that Anthony Eden's pouting expression indicated equally firm disagreement. Before either of them could intervene, Churchill rounded on Anderson for having a closed mind:

'Reith's got an eminently reasonable case', he said.

The Minister of Transport treasured the words, yet prudently refrained from pushing home his advantage. Instead he promised to work out compromise arrangements with Anderson and Eden who appeared happy enough afterwards to meet him more than halfway. Very late that same night, before Reith retired, the telephone rang and Churchill came on the line in an exceptionally ebullient mood. How had the discussions gone, he enquired, with Eden and Anderson? Was Reith satisfied with the outcome? That idea of his for clearing up quickly after raids made good sense. In a crisis ordinary procedures must go by the board; and in this crisis of endurance the resilient spirit of the British people was, he thought, superb. As the Prime Minister went on chatting, the easy flow of his words washed over Reith in a comforting spray. Only the innate curse of a constricting shyness prevented him from telling Churchill how unhappy he still was, trying to do an undemanding job so far removed from the centre of the stage, and how happy he would be nearer to the heart of the decision-making. Yet the Prime Minister's parting sentence stuck gratefully in his mind:

'Remember, Reith. I have great confidence in you.'

For the remainder of September, the Minister of Transport worked with a rare spirit of enthusiasm. He realised, as did everyone else in Whitehall, that changes in the Government were in the offing. Neville Chamberlain's health had broken, though few outside his own family circle yet knew that he was at death's door. The nightly ordeal of the blitz continued, Reith moving off at short notice each morning to inspect damage on the spot and to supervise emergency repairs and the revision of supply schedules. In the lobbies, corridors and smoking room of the Commons, he strove to appear less aloof and ill-at-ease, buoyed up by the revived hope that shortly a call would come from No. 10 and the glum frustrations of the past nine months would be finally dissipated by a worthwhile challenge to his idle reserves of inventiveness and energy. Such was his mood of relative euphoria that during a secret debate on transport and related problems he conquered his inhibitions and delivered a respectable maiden speech that won him support and unaccustomed praise from all sides of the House.[2] For the best part of ten days, he could almost believe that the political world, that disorderly and often confounding place, lay suddenly at his feet.

The summons from Churchill came finally on October 2nd, a date that marked Reith's reversion to total disillusionment with politics and politicians. The few minutes he spent inside the Cabinet room with the Prime Minister were depressing in the extreme. Churchill came to the point at once, indicating that he wished Reith to move not only his office but his House, downwards to the new Ministry of Works and upwards through an awful optical illusion to the Lords. For a few palsied seconds, he sat in unbelieving silence, as though struck dumb. Churchill seemed surprised and slightly concerned by this lack of response.

'Must I give up my seat and cease being an MP?' Reith asked.

'Yes', said the Prime Minister, evidently mystified at the dour reception of what he evidently conceived of as the only natural means of elevating a non-political member of his team to his appropriate sphere. 'Surely you don't mind the Lords? You don't intend to remain in active politics when the war is over?'

Reith contradicted him. His intention had been to stay on in the Commons, but it was too late now for futile recriminations on this score. Yet he could not allow the Prime Minister to underrate how grievously disappointed he, Reith, was to have been passed over once more for a service ministry. Expressing regret at having been kept so far out of touch with Churchill's thinking, he went on recklessly: 'Of course, I fully appreciate that you don't like me.'

It was a fair if ill-chosen observation. The Prime Minister bridled. What reason had Reith for daring to say such a thing? He, Churchill, respected and admired his qualities, but no opening of the kind Reith wanted was at present available. In any case the war still had a long time to run. Plainly put out by the descent to personalities, the Prime Minister suggested that Reith might show some consideration for the government's difficulties and learn to temper his dissatisfaction with forbearance. He repeated his offer of the new Works Ministry, and Reith ungratefully accepted the post.

He left feeling very badly done by. Churchill, for his part, could not overlook what he regarded as a display of insufferable arrogance and presumptuousness. From that day forward Reith was earmarked as a ministerial passenger who could readily be dispensed with. 'There he stalks, that Wuthering Height', became a Churchillian catchphrase, from the moment he felicitously stumbled on it after a particularly tedious meeting with junior ministers, at which the self-righteous declamations of the first Minister of Works had apparently vexed him.[2]

If Reith could draw on ample stores of petulance, so could Churchill and with greater certainty of commanding a captive audience. It was, in a sense, a case of Greek meeting Greek. Never did either man attempt to harass or insult the other to his face. A residual respect held them far apart, so that Churchill never attempted to goad this truculent adversary into an unseemly display of temper as he often goaded less formidable men whose obsequious complaisance could be depended on:

'He usually appeared after his early afternoon sleep in the vilest of tempers', wrote Lord Brabazon, who attended many such sessions at a later stage in the war. 'He behaved as if he were a bullying schoolmaster. Everyone, in his opinion, was a half-wit; and if anyone said anything he was jumped on and snubbed. . . . I am not an admirer of Sutherland's painting of Churchill—nor do I like those of Maugham or Beaverbrook—but I do say with little fear of contradiction that his portrait exactly portrays the man as he appeared to the committee whose unfortunate duty it was to attend.'[11]

Reith cut so grotesquely forbidding a figure in committee and out that Churchill was probably wise to desist from taunting or making a butt of him. Only Sir John Anderson, the Lord President, and Sir James Grigg, whom the Prime Minister eventually promoted to the War Office, were on close enough terms with their colleague from the Ministry of Works to cajole, advise and sometimes even tease him. The sight of Reith with his lined and tormented face, 'frowning down on a huddle of seated ministers before a meeting, then turning on his heel and resuming his solitary patrol up and down a corridor, swinging the chain of his key-ring',[2] tended to frighten off those who did not know him well. Churchill had not erred in acknowledging his respect for the pristine strength and pertinacity of Reith; but the mournful rigidity of his manner as well as the prickliness of his pride were not to the Prime Minister's taste. He had no compunction in relegating this solemn man, who had twice thwarted him in the prewar days of broadcasting, to the outer perimeter of his administration. Reith thus became in Churchill's eyes a shadowy and dimly menacing intruder about as welcome as a skeleton at a feast or a Roundhead who had strayed, uninvited, into a group of roystering Cavaliers.

'I saw or heard little of the Prime Minister', Reith complained. 'My wife and I were once bid to lunch with him in a special flat the ministry had prepared for him and Mrs. Churchill in Great George Street. . . .' Again, on May 17th, 1941, two days after one night of indiscriminate terror in which much property was destroyed and over

3000 Londoners died, he crossed to the ruined House of Commons with Churchill and Beaverbrook to survey the blackened, smouldering rubble. In pensive mood the Prime Minister muttered abuse against the evil genius of Hitler for striking so useless a blow at the indestructible roots of democracy.

'I doubt whether the Germans are accurate enough to have deliberately taken aim at this place', commented Reith.[1]

He was nettled when Churchill sent him an 'Action This Day' minute less than a fortnight later, demanding a progress report on the refitting of the Lords' chamber for the use of MPs. By the end of May all was ready and the Commons soon grew acclimatized to their new surroundings. Reith's vague terms of reference, especially in the field of post-war reconstruction and planning, proved an intermittent source of wrangling and disturbance. Nobody disputed the 'great opportunity', as Attlee described it, for renovating the raddled face of Britain even before the shooting stopped. Everybody with the slightest reason to oppose the hiving-off to an upstart ministry of responsibilities that could be held back joined in resisting the claims of Reith. After his introduction to the Upper House as the first Baron Reith of Stonehaven he experienced some trouble in convincing fellow-peers that he meant, and could do, business, despite the nebulous powers he had in the planning sphere. Patching up the wrecked homes of private citizens did not enter into his field of action, though a scolding Prime Minister mistakenly assumed so until enlightened to the contrary. War buildings, including munitions plants, storage depots, camps and training centres, did: and with customary ingenuity Reith devised his own system of providing and paying for skilled workers when these were hard to find. Other government departments looked at him askance:

'Their attitude', as he put it, 'ranged from the vaguely unhelpful to the positively obstructive.' Yet he could boast with reasonable fairness that 'by July 1941 there was order and system in place of chaos'. Ernest Bevin, the forceful Minister of Labour, appreciated better than any other member of the Cabinet, except Anderson, how swiftly and neatly John Reith could tie up loose ends and nip abuses in the bud.

In mid-November 1941 there arrived another abrupt summons to No. 10 Downing Street where 'Churchill, for once, beamed on "me", and Reith caught this first glimpse of the famous "blue battle dress".' At the instigation of Beaverbrook, the Prime Minister said that he fully approved of Reith's request for confirmation of the right to decide strategic priorities in all works of construction. Churchill smiled broadly and let him see an instruction to that effect which he had just written. Only afterwards did his visitor wish that he had broken his shy silence to remind the Prime Minister that 'I wanted to be in direct touch with him'. It was, he noted immediately afterwards, 'damnable that I should feel to him as I do and that he has so deserved it'. No amount of Churchillian beaming could shift the Reithian burden of mistrust.

Harold Macmillan, then a junior minister on Beaverbrook's staff, has provided an amusing sidelight on the way in which the Minister of Aircraft Production divested his department of the vast quantities of scrap metal, including millions of aluminium saucepans sacrificed by patriotic housewives, for which no quick industrial use could be found. After some awkward questions were raised in the Commons and the press, Macmillan was charged by Beaverbrook to off-load it:

'This is a bad business', he said in his oblique fashion. 'It'll never pay. Go and sell it to someone else.'

But nobody seemed to want it, despite the carefully rehearsed, flattering overtures with which Macmillan invariably introduced the subject on his repeated errands round Whitehall ministries:

'Lord Beaverbrook wishes me to say that this immensely complicated task of presiding over the scrap collection of the country is beyond his powers,' he would begin. 'Incidentally, he feels certain that if anything happened to Churchill, you would be called upon to succeed him as Prime Minister. After the war, you are bound to play a leading role. You are the outstanding man and he begs you to shoulder this great national burden which has been too heavy for his shoulders.'

Unfortunately, the word always seemed to precede Macmillan through the corridors of Whitehall that Beaverbrook's difficulty was unlikely to be anyone's golden opportunity; and so with dwindling hope the junior minister persevered in his fruitless quest. Relief came at last. 'Eventually I came to Lord Reith, the Minister of Works,' he wrote. 'Of course, I knew him too well to venture upon the alluring appeal which I thought might suit some of the others. I could only ask him to accept this task as a help to our overburdened ministry. He accepted generously, and so we got rid of this tiresome job.'[12]

Further turmoil erupted when Reith drafted and circulated his ideas on the controlled development of the Britain which should eventually rise, phoenix-like, from the ashes of war. It was on this occasion that Churchill, while endorsing the general drift of the proposals, wrongly chided him for thinking of the future at the expense of the present and neglecting war-damage repairs. Yet the very exercise in formulating a national plan which would create new moral, cultural and economic standards, transcending the purely materialistic, briefly touched the springs of Reith's idealism. It was a pity that interdepartmental jealousies and misunderstandings hampered the translation of words into action and finally, if indirectly, led to the indefinite shelving of the project and the superseding of the minister himself. For Churchill and his small inner core of advisers had to live fully in the present with weightier matters than post-war reconstruction oppressing them and threatening to erode not only their popularity but their very credibility as the best architects of ultimate victory. By February 1942 the wiping out by the Japanese of Allied forces in the Far East, from the Philippines to Singapore, had reduced the political fortunes of the Prime Minister to their lowest ebb. The need to reshuffle and revivify his tired government had certainly become imperative to Churchill. And Reith, not unnaturally, was one of the handiest and most expendable of the pawns awaiting sacrifice.

A despatch rider roared up to his country home at 7.30 on the evening of February 19th. Reith opened the front door himself and was handed a letter from Churchill:

'I am very sorry to tell you', it began, 'that the reconstruction of my government which events have rendered necessary makes me wish to have your office at my disposal . . .'[9] Reith did not need to read on: that opening sentence was enough. He knew now how it felt to be struck on the back of the head with a blunt instrument as a preliminary to being slung up on the butcher's hook for an unsympathetic populace to stare at. The message of dismissal had the rank, sickly flavour of an obituary notice officiously passed on not for approval but for information only. Like a man suddenly brought face to face with death, he could already isolate, as he retraced the events of his ministerial life, more than one incident where someone less ingenuously trusting might have discerned the writing on the wall. Then the nausea of failure welled up in him as black as despair: his son Christopher was fortunately away at his public school; his wife and daughter, recognising the symptoms, kept their distance and prepared quietly for the worst. Whatever happened, the vicarious anguish they would suffer through and with him could hardly equal what they had endured when he left the BBC against his will.

John Reith thus reached the end of another misspent chapter. Despite the aching misery of rejection, he could see a certain irony in Churchill's timing: for only a matter of days earlier the Cabinet had at last decided to let Reith take over all the planning functions which the Ministry of Health had been resolutely opposing for many months past.

4

Reith's cantankerous gloom perturbed the handful of acquaintances whom he consulted after his dismissal. Anderson, for instance, who counselled him to do nothing rash, helped to tone down the answer to Churchill's curt and uninformative letter: 'Something else will be offered', he said repeatedly. 'Don't destroy your chances in advance.' When the Prime Minister wrote again it was with the proposal that 'you should act as Lord High Commissioner of the General Assembly of the Church of Scotland', an honourable office which, in the normal course of events, Reith would have fiercely prized. How like 'that bloody shit Churchill' to offer it now, he commented privately. The refusal was again couched in the carefully doctored language of Anderson:

'In wartime I really do not feel I could do justice to the office or be happy in it.'

Another month crept by. It lengthened into two, then three. Still no word or sign came from Churchill, and Reith grew weary of waiting. He looked gaunt and ill from constant brooding, bearing a curious resemblance to a bird of prey chained up and deprived of bare sustenance. The likeness had once impressed itself on a sharp-eyed stranger in the dining room of a club frequented by artists. The writer, D. B. Wyndham-Lewis, had looked up as Reith entered with two friends, and, catching a glimpse of his high, scarred profile, enquired with interest: 'Who on earth is that?' A neighbour gratified his curiosity, and Wyndham-Lewis stuttered in reply:

'So that's the g-g-great Sir J-J-John. I wonder why he makes me th-think of a r-ruptured vulture?'[2]

The fear that Reith might be tempted to vent his rage against Churchill and the government either by writing to the press or by speaking in the Lords troubled the few political acquaintances in whom he still chose to confide. They had no real cause for alarm. He would not have trusted himself to attack a war leader whose dislike he had learnt to reciprocate with compound interest. Besides, the rigorous law of Reith's nature forbade the pulling down of public idols and heroes from spotlit niches: it did not, however, deter him from sticking mental pins in their private images. His one speech to the Upper House during this arid and desolating period concerned the future standing, control and management of Britain's essential public services, a subject near to his heart but somewhat academic in the context of military crisis. No eyebrows were raised, no passions kindled, by his unwinking solemnity. Former associates at the BBC, some of whom had half-expected him to cuff if not to maul the thing he had once lovingly fashioned in the course of that disquisition, were correspondingly relieved or downcast by his self-restraint. During his twenty-two months as a member of Churchill's government, Reith had maintained a clandestine vigil on the activities of the corporation. As long ago as October 1940, when Beaverbrook had wanted to commandeer for his own purposes the ground floor, sub-basement and basement of Broadcasting House, he had been disedified by the unseemly haste with which Ogilvie, Powell and two attendant controllers descended on Beaverbrook's office to 'argue the toss', 'instead of declining to discuss it and turning the matter over to the Ministry of Information'. Quite unimpressed by their anxious bleatings, Beaverbrook had forthwith informed Reith that he intended to press for a decision in Cabinet. There it was decided to leave Broadcasting House alone and let the puckish Max wreak his tender mercies on other premises at Faraday House. Reith, as Minister of Works, had been present at that particular meeting.

'I became aware', he noted, 'of the intense discontent with the BBC. Churchill spoke with great bitterness: an enemy within the gates, continually causing trouble, doing more harm than good, something drastic must be done about it. The BBC to be thus spoken of. [Duff] Cooper accepted it all without protest. I wondered what Churchill would say if I offered to go back to the BBC. I nearly did so then and there. It would have been better for me if I had—and if the offer had been accepted.'[1]

The likelihood of his being asked, and by Churchill of all people, was so remote as to be almost laughable. Yet such was Reith's overmastering care for the child, created and reared in his own image, which had grown up only to cast him off, that self-deception of the sort still came all too easily to him. He was mortified by the appointment of a special Cabinet committee, consisting of Kingsley Wood, Herbert Morrison and Duff Cooper, to consider the position of the BBC. Why had he not been co-opted? Why, at the very least, did they not invite him to submit his expert views? He scarcely knew which party was the more culpably stupid, the government or the BBC. Sir Frank Pick, who had worked with Reith for a brief spell in the Transport Ministry and had since moved across to Information as its Director-General, had been highly uncomplimentary about overseas broadcasting; and Reith sympathised with Pick for warning the egregious Ogilvie that the Government might end by 'taking over the BBC'. With equal sharpness Ogilvie had retorted that 'neither the Ministry nor the BBC mattered in comparison with the national cause, and it was the business of both of us to see how we could help together to advance it, considering any means whatever (including, if necessary, taking over the BBC) without prejudice and without rushing about with head down like a bull'.[8]

What Ogilvie and his chairman, Powell, would have liked was the buffer of a Broadcasting Council to cushion disagreements and to assist Duff Cooper in providing 'a fully co-ordinated and positive direction of propaganda'. This expensive cure for the contagious ills affecting both the Ministry and the corporation did not attract the Cabinet subcommittee. It opted for a less cumbrous yet more invidious prescription: the selection of two 'General Advisers', one specialising in home policy and broadcasts, the other in foreign, with the right of appeal to the Minister himself in case of disputes. Neither Ogilvie nor Powell welcomed this departure which would entrust to two outsiders the unprecedented power of ranging freely and without hindrance over the broad and unkempt acres of the BBC's programmes and administration. For once, Reith found himself in accidental accord with the Director-General and chairman. These were 'extraordinary suggestions, muddled in themselves, humiliating to the BBC. . . . Into the organisation which the governors and Director-General were supposed to control, two individuals were to be thrust with terms of reference of their own, in no way responsible or subordinate. I wanted to forget that I had ever been in the BBC.'[1]

The introduction of Ivone Kirkpatrick as foreign policy adviser in February 1941, and the return to broadcasting of A. P. Ryan as home policy adviser the following month, presaged the effective undermining of the authority of Ogilvie and his senior controllers. It was, in Reith's view, a degradation which a weak executive and an unreasonably self-satisfied board had brought upon themselves. Too much floodwater had passed beneath the bridges for any reversion at this late date to the plans Reith himself had helped to draft before the war. These would have suspended the board and integrated the BBC with the Ministry of Information under strong, mutually interdependent leaders. The plan had been based on two premises: the first, that the BBC would have, not the hapless Ogilvie, but a chief executive worthy of the name; the second, that Stephen Tallents, now foredoomed to disappear under the new Kirkpatrick regime at Bush House, would have long ago adjusted himself to masterminding the day-to-day activities of the Ministry as its Director-General. Alas, such hopes had been swept away and lost without trace.

Yet still Reith watched from afar, very occasionally forcing himself to intervene when the need arose. It did not surprise him to discover that Kirkpatrick and Ryan, government nominees for the impracticable business of serving as fifth wheels to the BBC coach, were soon demanding the status of controllers, who, nevertheless, owed allegiance to two masters—the politicians and the corporation. What undoubtedly retrieved the still uncertain fate of the BBC, steadied its unsettled nerves, and speeded the recovery of its formerly sure sense of purpose was the appointment of Brendan Bracken as Minister of Information in July 1941. Where Lord Macmillan had behaved like a Canute, where Reith in turn had bent over backwards like a contortionist to keep the gratuitous vow extracted from him by Chamberlain, where Duff Cooper had mainly floundered out of his depth, Bracken waded fearlessly in and swam like a trained life-guard.

The BBC was in a state of acute internal crisis. Its financial and administrative controls could no longer adequately handle the massive load placed upon them by wartime expansion, notably in the new European and overseas services. Ogilvie's hesitant and uninspiring leadership quickly became apparent to Bracken who did not commit the tactical error, however, of getting rid of him at a stroke. The Treasury and the Public Accounts Committee were already taking an unhealthy interest in the 'complex wartime finances of the BBC'; and, to quote Asa Briggs, 'undoubtedly the financial and administrative confusions of the early autumn [of 1941], and the inability of the BBC and the Ministry to secure the objectives which they had themselves laid down earlier, contributed substantially to the pressure of events which led to the replacement of Ogilvie as Director-General in January 1942.'[8]

One of Bracken's decisive moves was to ask Robert Foot, the general manager of the Gas, Light and Coke Company, to spend three months inside the Corporation, investigating its financial and administrative machinery. Three months, in Bracken's opinion, should be ample. Then Foot, he said, could return to his 'bloody gas'. The Minister wanted a rough blueprint for reorganising a system which 'had become top-heavy and could no longer cope. The governors were worried, the Government was worried, and something had to be done about it.' Even so, Bracken stoutly defended the independence of the BBC in the Commons as well as in Cabinet, the friendship and complete trust of Churchill enabling him to pursue his own independent but subtle line. When Ernest Thurtle, no admirer of the corporation, made a statement in the House 'to the effect that the governors were not concerned with the war-effort of the BBC and were only concerned with culture and entertainment', the chairman at once protested to Bracken who said that Thurtle would not be allowed in future to answer questions about the BBC. 'We are not content with this', noted Harold Nicolson, then a member of the board, and point out that if what Thurtle said was really BBC policy, then we were not worth collectively £7000 a year of government money'.[13]

On Foot's first morning in his office, before he had any chance to find his bearings or even meet his secretary, the telephone unexpectedly rang. As the newcomer had been sitting alone for an hour, waiting for somebody from inside the BBC to approach him, he thought nothing of picking up the receiver out of sheer curiosity. He was somewhat sorry at his undue willingness to answer when the unmistakable voice of Reith rang in his ear:

'Is that you, Foot?'

The new broom could not deny it and half-wondered at Reith's extremely keen sense of timing. His astonishment was almost as great as his alarm.

'I've only two bits of advice to offer, Foot, so I won't keep you. First, if you really want to save the organisation, get rid of Ogilvie. Second, when you've done that, get rid of yourself.'

Then he rang off, and for a few minutes Foot sat quite still, musing over this extraordinary intrusion by a man whom he had encountered only once before.[2]

Quite independently of the BBC's founder, Foot did not take many weeks to reach the same merciless conclusion:

'Before our appointment', he wrote, 'there is no doubt that whatever Ogilvie's personal hopes and ideas may have been, the BBC was drifting nearer and nearer to control by the Government and if the change had not been made the drift would undoubtedly have continued simply because the BBC's own internal organisation was not sufficiently strong and efficient to enable it to manage its own affairs, whether financial or otherwise, without considerable interference.'[8]

Foot approached the point of decision step by step, talking to representative groups of BBC officials, to individual governors, and whenever necessary to key men in the existing structure like Lochhead, the financial controller, and Beadle, the head of administration. The latter has written:

'A few days after Foot had been appointed, he came to see me and asked me what I thought we ought to do about the organisation. I took a scheme of organisation out of my drawer and I told him this was what I had tried to get Ogilvie to adopt but without success. Whereupon he produced from his pocket an almost identical scheme which he had worked out for himself. In other words, there was, on this issue, an identity of view which made the writing of reports or recommendations quite unnecessary. All we had to do was work it out in detail and put it into effect.' It is beyond question that Robert Foot used the method of 'reorganisation' to the positive end decreed by Bracken, namely that of 'pressing the BBC's claim to freedom'.[14] If BBC financial estimates before 1942 had been 'very wild indeed', as the Treasury complained, after that the tighter system of control was judged 'reliable'. Grants-in-aid had temporarily superseded the pre-war routine of arguing with the Post Office for as much of the licence revenue as could be obtained, the Ministry of Information and Lords Commissioners of the Treasury determining the amount on representations made to the Minister by the corporation. For the remainder of the war, separate payments were allocated for home and overseas broadcasting expenditure, on the basis of forecasts of the money required to maintain and develop these services.

The overhaul of administration proved a harsher and undoubtedly greater necessity, though this could hardly be described as the ideal time for it. The unobtrusive forcefulness of Foot ensured that this radical reform went through smoothly. There were several survivors of Reith's 'old guard', Beadle among them, who held with good reason that the rigid and overcentralised system, devised by Reith and inaugurated nine years previously, should have been scrapped in the late thirties when its ineffectiveness had been sufficiently demonstrated. They blamed their founding father for foisting it on them. They were heartily glad to see its partial abolition. Any dominantly controlling unit, staffed by administrative functionaries who had to 'refer upwards' for decisions, and who rarely felt any loyalty or responsibility to the operational departments in which they worked, would have been bound to create incessant rancour in the best-regulated concern; and, by almost universal consent, the BBC under Ogilvie had not exactly been well ruled. Morale as well as creativity were at a low premium; and public disquiet, manifested in the successive appointments of outside specialists like Foot, with little knowledge of the BBC's traditions, seemed only to increase the internal uneasiness.

Just as Reith had set his face against needless professionalism in the training of producers or managers, opposing for as long as possible the establishment of production schools or management courses out of which tomorrow's leaders might naturally emerge, so he had favoured a rigid departmentalism—not for its own sake, but for the neat look of the thing on paper. Those who could roughly measure the damage caused since Dawnay's day were not unconscious of Reith's prime responsibility in the matter, while refusing to exonerate Ogilvie, a civilised but feeble successor, for resisting changes in management which he regarded as merely inopportune. In the end, of course, such changes were imposed on him; and his head was subsequently demanded on a charger, despite the formal and kindlier announcement by Bracken in the Commons that the second Director-General had resigned and not been sacked.

'We decided to retire Ogilvie', Harold Nicolson noted in his diary, on January 26th, 1942, 'and put Graves and Foot as joint Directors-General in his place. I am sure this is right, as Ogilvie is too noble a character for rough war-work. Yet I mind deeply in a way. This clever, high-minded man being pushed aside. I hate it. But I agree.'[13] The press had too little available newsprint, too many other calls upon its limited space, to play up the story as it certainly would have done in peacetime. There was bad news from the Far East and the Western Desert; the war at sea had taken a turn for the worse; Churchill himself stood politically at bay, offering 'no apologies, no excuses, no promises', yet seeking—and finally securing—a massive vote of confidence in his conduct of affairs. These were anxious days for the government; and though two or three popular newspapers hinted in passing at a successful Ministry of Information coup to get rid of Ogilvie, Bracken firmly placed the onus, where it truly belonged, at the door of the BBC board:

'The House cannot have it every way', he said, squashing the misleading rumours flat. 'Either they want the governors to have a certain amount of independence or they want the BBC to be an appendage of the Ministry of Information, which would be a very bad thing.'

Reith had small leisure to rejoice in the removal of his successor or to cavil at his replacement by Foot and Graves as joint Directors-General. For as the full scale of military reverses on land and sea became clear, the Prime Minister, querulous of growing criticism, reshaped his government and bade Reith good riddance. The BBC had meanwhile belatedly reasserted itself by cutting off the second successive top branch of a tree which could not be pruned too savagely of all needless associations with its staid, paternalistic past. It had taken nearly four years for the corporation, reinforced by detached and capable outsiders who knew how to distinguish the wood from the tree, to reorganise itself and assume the incomparably splendid role that now awaited it as the free world's harbinger of victory. The positive parts of the legacy handed down by its founder were thus rescued and adapted for a narrow but precise task, though the founder himself insisted, in the perverse spirit of a man who could brook no rivals, that nearly all of the legacy had been wantonly squandered.

5

There were not a few people in Broadcasting House and elsewhere who agreed with Reith's one-sided view. Many of those who had joined him at Savoy Hill still looked back nostalgically to the golden days, recalling the extraordinary personal magnetism and leadership of the great Sir John. He had assumed in the eyes of others, who knew him only by name or by repute, the attributes of an outsize legend. His passing had marked a watershed in history, so that the years of the corporation itself split naturally into those under Reith, 'U.R.', and those after Reith, 'A.R.'. The tales told about him were legion; and if the majority happened to be apocryphal, most of them appeared to contain an incongruous kernel of truth. Perhaps the most vivid and best-remembered cautionary tale concerned the announcer whom Reith, going round the premises late at night, had caught red-handed with a woman member of the pre-war staff in what may euphemistically be described as a compromising situation. He summarily dismissed them both on the spot, all his Calvinist self-righteousness rushing like blood to the head. Later, it was said, mitigating circumstances were pleaded on behalf of the guilty male. Even the admiral, Sir Charles Carpendale, was supposed to have put in a good word for the reprobate, and Reith relented to the point of promising that he would give the unsavoury matter 'my mature consideration'. Finally the unfortunate announcer was sent for. Reith rose and glared down at him for a few moments, then broke the silence with these imperishable words:

'You are reinstated—on one condition. Never more shall you read the epilogue.'

No more than a handful of his old employees realised that Reith's attitude to the opposite sex was neither as puritanical nor as straight-laced as his reputation for gravity might have led others to imagine. His domestic life, in fact, frequently left him feeling flat and dissatisfied, notably when the cares of office weighed most on his mind. His two children had been brought up in almost exclusive isolation from boys and girls of their own age; but their father's preoccupations did not prevent him from browbeating and even chastising his son Christopher, with or without provocation. Being four years younger than her brother, Marista was spared this treatment which in later life she came to regard as 'cruel and almost sadistic at times'.[2] Besides, she had inherited some of her father's sturdy independence of mind; and though she tried to please him, the conviction grew in her from an early age that she would be wasting her time trying too hard. The young Reiths grew up deeply attached to their mother whose efforts to protect them from their father's tempestuous moods usually proved ineffectual and drew his spleen on her as well.

It was not altogether a happy home. Yet John Reith, without being blind to his own faults, made none of those minor concessions to the imperfections of his wife and children, without which domestic harmony becomes virtually impossible. Lady Reith, whom he occasionally consulted on outside problems when these threatened to unhinge him, strove to mollify and humour him in good times and bad; but her gentleness and self-effacement were no match for his obstinate sense of always being in the right.

She was not a possessive or a jealous person: nevertheless, Reith's romantic attachments to other women, which she first discovered in the late twenties when he had already become a public celebrity, roused her vainly and repeatedly to protest. His avowals that such friendships were quite innocent and proper, and that she had nothing to fear for the stability of their marriage, failed to erase her indignant misgivings. It must be stated on the other side that, despite all the damning appearances of hypocrisy, Reith remained faithful to a wife whose natural dislike of social life and hollow public functions had become an increasing trial to him a decade before his departure from the BBC. He saw no contradiction or moral inconsistency between his stern Calvinist code and his consorting with girl-friends whose gay and attractive personalities momentarily relieved him of the pains of daily existence. These girl-friends provided an escape from the tedium of domestic and official routines as well as bringing refreshment to his spirit. They represented Reith's naïve longing to recapture his lost youth, yet he seems to have mastered the temptation to commit the unforgivable sin, as he saw it, of going to bed with any of them.

During his brief ministerial career and afterwards Reith's open and unabashed friendships caused wry amusement and even fleeting concern among acquaintances in Whitehall. The cynical if quite mistaken general assumption was that the old hero from Broadcasting House had waited rather a long time before starting to sow his wild oats. On one occasion, towards the end of the war, Sir James Grigg, who had been appointed Secretary of State for War when Reith lost his job, wrote a stiff note in his own hand to the personnel branch, objecting to their compliance with the whims of the late Minister of Works.

'I will not have my officers, ATS, shunted about to suit the convenience of John Reith', he minuted, 'who somewhat late in life has discovered the art of f——ing'.[2]

It had been no simple matter for Reith to settle down after his pride had been dealt that last, crushing blow by Churchill the unforgiving. Rejecting the idea put to him by a well-wisher that he should write his memoirs, he decided in the end to apply for a relatively humble job in the Royal Navy. He made one stipulation only: he wanted 'nothing where any brain work would be required'. The break with his recent past had to be complete. He felt 'elderly and foolish' on first wearing the uniform and insignia of an acting lieutenant-commander. When he put on his regulation navy blue burberry the effect was to make him look 'exactly like my own chauffeur, except for the cap badge'. His salary, he reflected, had now dropped to a mere thirtieth of what it had been at the BBC, but the work awaiting him surpassed his dearest expectations. Had it not been for his age and family ties, Reith would by hook or by crook have 'gotten myself into the privileges and excitements of real war' as the most desirable and dramatic method of escape.

His first assignment was to institute a new repair and maintenance service for high-speed coastal vessels, without trespassing on the preserves of the Admiralty dockyard department, under Rear-Admiral Piers Kekewich. For eight months he worked with the carefree exuberance of a man half his age. On Christmas Eve, 1942, there was a knock on Reith's door. A rating entered carrying a ladder and followed by a few senior officers. Then a Wren appeared, mounted the ladder on a word of command, and waited for Reith to obey another order to kiss her. He obliged—'anyhow she was quite pretty', he commented.[1]

By dint of concentration, and with the help of the First Sea Lord, Dudley Pound, and others of lesser rank, Reith next succeeded in establishing a special Admiralty department for the material equipping of coastal forces. He spent a further six months, from February until August 1943, as number two to its first chief, Captain F. H. Powys Maurice; but he grew restive at not having enough to occupy him in his headquarters at Queen Anne's Mansions: 'periods of real happiness', as he put it, were punctuated by 'many more of unhappiness verging on desperation'. The pretence of fulfilling himself as a junior officer wore a trifle thin when admirals almost invariably deferred to him and used his expertise as a celebrated organiser who happened also to be a peer of the realm. The Controller of the Navy, for instance, Admiral Sir Frederick Wake-Walker, asked him to investigate his empire and submit a detailed report with recommendations on how its many branches might be reduced and rendered more efficient. Reith complied, but the report was not acted on. Nothing daunted, the admiral invited him next as his extra naval assistant to suggest ways and means of streamlining the set-up of the Royal Corps of Naval Constructors. Reith's detailed proposals were 'too revolutionary', however, for Wake-Walker to submit to the Board of Admiralty.

He was salvaged from this uniformed thraldom by the urgent, exhilarating exercise of creating a new department for handling the many material requirements of combined operations in preparation for the allied invasion of France. Again Reith drafted the terms of reference. This time they were accepted. His superiors were somewhat put out when he volunteered to run it himself. And while their Lordships considered this unexpected request, Reith entertained, with fingers crossed, the extravagant fancy of seeing himself—'a two-and-a-half-striper RNVR pitchforked into a job intended for an active service rear-admiral'. He heard later that his proposed appointment had been referred to no less a person than Churchill before being ratified; which Reith took to mean, when ratification came through, that he had been removed from the Prime Minister's non-active list of possible candidates for 'proper work'.

As Director of Combined Operations Material, his own brainchild, he drew on all his reserves of versatility, thrust, concentration and bluff to instil it with his own pulsating efficiency:

'Childish or childlike', he admitted, 'but it was pleasing to be able to hold one's own in a field of which a few months earlier one had been entirely ignorant.' He had never worked so hard since his early days at Savoy Hill. His family saw little of him from one week's end to another. Almost always he would be at his desk until the small hours; often he would stay through the night, then walk across to the Athenaeum for a bath and breakfast before returning exultantly to his beloved treadmill.

A. V. Alexander, the First Lord, had originally minuted that 'if Lord Reith gives satisfaction he can be promoted commodore, RNVR, second class.' At least one senior officer objected, so Reith was deprived of the coveted rank that went with the post: by no means the heaviest burden he had to bear, since he now carried the honorary rank of captain. It was in April 1943, about the time of his promotion, that a backbench MP, learning of Reith's relegation to what he obviously regarded as a lowlier sphere of action, asked the Prime Minister how the ex-Minister of Works was employing his time. As a peer of the realm, replied Churchill evasively, the entire field of parliamentary duties and activities lay open to Lord Reith. Horror-stricken in case the Prime Minister might suspect a planted question, Reith wrote off in a panic to Churchill's secretary, disclaiming all knowledge and responsibility. On April 20th the Prime Minister followed up a 'Thank you' telegram with a brief letter:

'You may be sure that I will try my best to find suitable employment for your well-known energy and capacity', he wrote. 'I can of course make no definite promise but it would certainly be a great pleasure to me that you were pulling your full weight in the war.'[9]

Reith had heard too many promises of the kind to feel touched or grateful. Besides, he believed that he was already pulling his full weight in an anonymous but exacting role. Above all he had rediscovered his secret substitute for happiness by blotting out nearly everything and everyone outside his limited but arduous duties at the Admiralty.

6

After D-Day, the inevitable anti-climax gradually set in. The thrill of crossing twice to Normandy not long after the successful landings, of longing to go beyond the beach-head at Arromanches 'where things were really happening, where was war', did not last. He found it hard in the late summer to keep his mind on the job, now that its *raison d'être* had passed. He experienced a pang of personal sadness when Admiral Tower, his vice-controller, retired. Tower's encomium on the achievements of his subordinate, who did not long delay his own departure from the Admiralty, deserves to be quoted:

'I do assure you that you have amazed me,' he wrote to Reith, 'by the way you have grasped that vicious nettle I was responsible for thrusting into your hands over a year ago . . . The result has been astonishing . . . I am convinced that one and all recognised you as a real leader and put all they had into their work for that reason alone . . . If you had not been director the whole Overlord operation would, at the very best, have been far less efficiently done than it was, and might not have been done at all. I mean that quite definitely and I know I am right.'[9]

It was the kind of considered praise which Reith most treasured. Wake-Walker did more than endorse it. On January 1st, 1945, as Reith sat uncomfortably in a crowded Tube train reading *The Times*, he had the quiet satisfaction of hunting out his own name in the Honours List. He had just been made a Commander of the Bath (military division), an award which he learnt had never before been offered to a civilian. The war had not yet ended; but, for him, the savour had wholly gone out of it. It was time to look about him, pick up the pieces of his life, and start thinking of earning an ordinary livelihood again. The sense of public and private failure still overpowered him when he reflected on the recent past, and the future held out no glittering prospects. Yet Reith was guilty of self-indulgence in reproaching others for misfortunes which, as his conscience told him in moments of utter truth, he had, as usual, largely brought upon himself.

Epilogue

1

'I WAS tremendously serious and over-serious, I think. I was also in too much of a hurry to succeed, and I doubt if I've ever been young. I don't think I took the potential enjoyments of life as most people of my age would and did. Life itself was a head-long race for me—because of an inordinate ambition to serve others in my time.'[1]

The speaker, John Reith, might have been groping for words to fit his own epitaph. Again and again, during the final stretch of his eighty one years, he would hark back to his boyhood as if seeking definitive clues to the flawed riddle of existence. In common with a few other men and women who had gained the privilege of his confidence, I would sometimes accompany him on these mournful yet absorbing journeyings down the long corridors of memory. He took a dry pleasure in unburdening himself, a harmless form of self-indulgence. Since the world had either rejected or forgotten him, there could be no going forward, only backwards. Like Wolsey towards his end, Reith had no option but to put away ambition. Unlike Wolsey, he had too much time for brooding; and this process of erosion seemed to leave him at the last with too little faith in God or man.

Being a prodigious letter-writer and an indefatigable diarist, who could scarcely contain himself when it came to dotting the i's and crossing the t's of the most ordinary, mundane happenings, Reith gave the misleading impression at times of a man living entirely for the moment. He never shook off the habit of keeping eyes and ears alertly cocked for another improbable challenge commensurate with his deep craving to go on serving the British public. The chances of that, he knew, were negligible. Yet until his astonishingly robust health began to decline, he did not give up hoping. Among the five or six million words that poured out of him in diary entries, notes, reports and correspondence, a veritable Amazon of verbiage, there is one small rivulet of inestimable value to the biographer. Reith's written exchanges with Beaverbrook, which had begun in the early twenties when the Canadian Press magnate first met, liked and decided to help the inexperienced, unknown general manager of the British Broadcasting Company, span these declining years as well. So differently constituted in character and outlook, the two men had one common factor which drew them close together: they were sons of the manse. This endowed them with a fellow-feeling which ran deep and seemed to exclude false sentimentality. Just as Dr. George Reith had, in the considered view of his youngest son, greatly influenced public service broadcasting and its fixed standards from beyond the grave, so the puckishly hard-headed Beaverbrook had once taken a hand in bolstering up John Reith's courage and tactical shrewdness to make that achievement practicable. Now, with his pen, the bewilderingly unpredictable Max Aitken cast himself in the improbable role of Reith's father-confessor.

They had been wartime ministers, of course, under Churchill. One had been an intimate associate of the Prime Minister and a redoubtable success in 1940 as Minister of Aircraft Production. The other, as we have seen, failed to win Churchill's friendship or confidence, was sometimes scandalised by Beaverbrook's buccaneering methods, yet correctly regarded himself in moments of unsparing candour as a ministerial failure. From the historical point of view there is much to be said for the verdict of A. J. P. Taylor:

'Lloyd George's war cabinet had been a true committee of public safety, running all great affairs in common. Churchill's war cabinet rarely initiated, and overruled him even more rarely. Indeed, it is difficult to discover from the record what the war cabinet did during the war except, like the Abbé Siéyès, keep alive.'[2]

Civil servants who became ministers left no conspicuous imprint on events. Even piratical businessmen-turned-ministers, of whom Beaverbrook was the sole outstanding example, became comparative failures in due course. The political life expectancy of all but the lucky and the sycophantic was short. So Reith had not been nearly so badly done by as he contended, a fact stressed by his Canadian friend with pointed solicitude on more than one occasion. Their correspondence is notable for its brevity and open informality. It was resumed in 1948 when Reith was 'occupying miserably unoccupied time in writing memoirs'. The first draft by then had been partly completed:

'From about four million words I have gotten down to four hundred thousand. That must be reduced to about a quarter. I left the BBC years to the last, skipping 1922 to 1938. That's why I have just read your letter . . . the very kindly letter you wrote me from Deauville just ten years ago after I had a motor smash.'

Reith could not say that he was enjoying himself. The task of autobiography proved 'a melancholy process', yet what else had he to do?

'This is a great waste of material,' Beaverbrook replied by return of post, the reference being to Reith himself rather than to a manuscript which did not greatly interest the press lord. 'I think you would make an excellent head of one of the universities.'[3]

2

Not since the summer and autumn of 1944 had any piece of important public business been tossed at him like a hunk of raw meat to a caged animal. The government, through Sir John Anderson, had easily persuaded him at that time, as a newly elected member of the board of Cable and Wireless, to undertake an arduous mission of enquiry round the world. Dominion members of the Commonwealth communications council did not care for the dominant position of the commercially owned, London based, cable and wireless set-up. Despite his own business connection with the firm, Reith, with typical candour, accepted the view of Dominion critics that 'drastic constitutional changes' were probably overdue. He agreed to fly out, regardless of reservations expressed about himself and his mission both by members of Churchill's government and by a few Dominion ministers as well, 'in the hope of securing new arrangements satisfactory to all governments—something that would work'. Beaverbrook, as usual, had been purposefully hovering 'in the background of the negotiations for some time. He had finished with civil aviation; it had been rumoured that his next intervention was to be in either oil or communications.'[4] The choice of Reith as an emissary commended itself to Beaverbrook, none the less; and finally on January 22nd, 1945, Reith set off in a converted Liberator bomber of RAF Transport Command. This bore him and a small party of experts to Australia, New Zealand, India, Kenya, Southern Rhodesia, South Africa, and via Ascension Island and Jamaica to Canada. There was only one woman in the group—Reith's secretary.

Malcolm MacDonald was then Britain's High Commissioner in Ottawa. His nervousness about the Canadian Government's uncertain attitude to a proposed single telecommunications corporation, with maximum local autonomy, proved misplaced. MacDonald, in fact, admitted later that his nervousness on that score was less acute than his embarrassment on another. He knew and liked Reith well, and had been looking forward to discussing old times. The unexpected appearance of a young woman, whom Reith gladly allowed to monopolize all his available time, attention and affectionate interest, put paid to MacDonald's simpler aspirations. It also gave him several anxious moments regarding official protocol, quite apart from the disturbance to normal domestic arrangements for receiving the head of an important visiting mission and helping him to feel at home.

'It was a trying interlude,' said MacDonald. 'I had, of course, heard past whispers of his friendships with women while I was still in Whitehall. This particular manifestation admittedly took me by surprise. It complicated things in the circumstances and gave rise to some awkwardness.'[5]

The backgammon board taken on the flight by the secretary had offered Reith passing relief from the 'weary hours' in the air. As the citation scribbled on it said, in fifty-two days this 'very unusual' backgammon board had been carried 44,700 miles, crossing 'in turn the Atlantic ocean from east to west, the Pacific ocean from east to west, the Tasman sea from west to east and from east to west, the Indian ocean from south to north, the Arabian sea from north to south, the Atlantic ocean again from south to north and from west to east. It traversed the four continents of America, Australasia, India and Africa. Four times it passed over the equator. It lodged in Viceroy's House in Delhi; circled low over the Taj Mahal and the Zambesi Falls. It surveyed great rivers and mountain ranges, the cities and plains of a hundred lands. It flew by day and night through fierce tropical storms, thunder and lightning, wind and rain. It set off in blinding snow, was scorched and iced in turn. The flashing lights of aurora borealis sped it home.'

The suppressed poet in him remained as active as the unabashed romantic. He remembered that marvellous flight, and the detailed care he had lavished on its tight scheduling, long after the worries and political wrangling it caused on his return to London had ceased to bother him. It was, he boasted, 'such a journey as had not been undertaken before'. Beaverbrook, who opposed the agreed recommendations Reith brought home, wondered whether the journey had been really necessary:

'I should have thought,' said Reith, 'that he of all people would have welcomed the central, imperial co-operation of the scheme; even if he loathed corporations generally, he might have accepted this one.'[4]

At a conference of Commonwealth officials in July, 1945, the plan was unanimously endorsed. Before the delegates broke up, the general election results were announced. Churchill had been defeated, Attlee voted in as Prime Minister of the first socialist administration with a landslide majority. In due course, the new government upheld the conference recommendations, and a Bill was drafted accordingly. 'Yesterday it was coal,' said Hugh Dalton gleefully. 'Today it is cables. The socialist advance therefore continues.' But as Reith remarked with hurt self-righteousness:

'In fact the Bill neither derived from nor was inspired by socialism.'[6]

The Bill was debated in the Lords in July 1946. The Conservative peers supported it, regardless of attempts by Woolton and others to amend it. A back-handed compliment was paid to its putative father by the veteran socialist elder statesman, Addison:

'To be frank,' he said, 'I was surprised that Lord Reith turned out to be such a consummate negotiator. I had been under the impression before that he was a hard man, but he seems to have produced a measure of agreement from one end of the world to another with remarkable rapidity. All I have to say is that in that achievement he is greatly to be envied. Others of us would be glad to pursue our aims with like success.'

3

Reith's highest and vainest ambition, to become Viceroy of India, crumbled into dust when the subcontinent was partitioned under Mountbatten's lordly sway, and the rival nations of India and Pakistan were born in 1947. If the name of Churchill led all the rest in the mythical 'black book' of the people Reith loved to hate, the name of Mountbatten ran it a close second: the so-called great of his world, who had stood in their own light as well as his, deserved no less, he felt.

He had written to Churchill in January 1946, retracing the bitter and faltering steps of his short-lived career in the wartime administration. A chance remark of Anderson's, to the effect that 'Winston now admits that he treated you badly and then did nothing for you', prompted Reith to sit down and express himself plainly for once. He understood, he wrote, why Churchill had asked him to resign, but 'I doubt if a day passed that I did not hope for the word from you that never came. . . . I have like you a war mentality and other qualities which should have commended themselves to you. Even in office I was nothing like fully stretched and I was completely out of touch with you. You could have used me in a way and to an extent you never realized. Instead of that there has been the sterility, humiliation and distress of all these years—"eyeless in Gaza"—without even the consolation Samson had in knowing it was his own fault.'

Churchill's reply was couched, as Reith acknowledged, in 'kindly and understanding' terms: 'I am grieved to receive your letter of January 1st although I am glad you wrote it. I know what a sacrifice you made when you gave up your position with Airways to join Mr. Chamberlain's government and I thought you would have been fully justified in stipulating that a certain financial provision should be made for you, as has been done in other not dissimilar cases.

'So far as my administration is concerned, I have always admired your abilities and energy, and it was with regret that I was not able to include you in the considerable reconstruction of the government in 1942. This was a time of great stress, when I was unable to provide for several able ministers. Several times since then I have considered you for various posts which became vacant, but I always encountered considerable opposition from one quarter or another on the ground that you were difficult to work with. This was particularly so when, if my memory serves me right, I raised the question of your becoming again the head of Airways. My task in making political appointments in a coalition government, where a certain balance had to be preserved, was hard, and I have no doubt that under the extreme pressure of war events I often made mistakes. I am unfeignedly sorry for the pain which you felt which I understand very fully, as I was myself, for eleven years, out of office before the war, during the last six of which I earnestly desired to take part in the work of preparation.

'I admired the courage and efficiency with which you made yourself a place and a reputation in the Admiralty, and you were still often in my mind as a candidate for high employment up till the time when I was myself suddenly and unexpectedly dismissed from office by the workings of our political system. If you think I can be of service to you at any time, pray let me know; for I am very sorry that the fortunes of war should have proved so adverse to you, and I feel the State is in your debt.'[7]

However, it was not easy for any leader to provide suitable employment for a man who refused on principle to join a political party. Whether Clement Attlee would have found a sufficiently attractive task for John Reith if the latter had so far forgotten himself as to join the Labour movement may well be doubted. Reith quite wrongly assumed that Attlee disapproved of him. The facts suggest the very opposite.

'I'm certain there's at least one big task left in John Reith,' Attlee remarked to several of his colleagues during the early days of his administration. And, pursuing his own quiet method of harnessing the energies of a political outsider to one of many enlarged areas of governmental control, the Prime Minister asked his young President of the Board of Trade, Harold Wilson, to bear Reith in mind as a candidate for the vacant chairmanship of the newly created National Film Finance Corporation. Wilson complied, found Reith willing, and learnt to cherish his association with 'an outstanding character whom I respected and greatly admired'.[5] But film financing was a part-time job only. It did not extend Reith's powers, though the time and thought he devoted to it proved anything but casual. James Lawrie, his managing director, recalled that Reith 'would dearly have liked to reconstruct and reform the film industry from top to bottom'. As this lay beyond the official mandate of 'lending money for the production of British films', Reith resigned himself to taking swift, thorough and usually shrewd decisions which led to the production of a few great motion pictures by brilliant directors like Korda, Balcon and Lean in Britain's brief post-war cinema boom.

By 1950 Attlee was proposing, once more through the agency of Harold Wilson, that the stern, demanding yet dissatisfied Scot should be invited to turn his hand to something altogether more daunting.

Reith would have far preferred the Colonial Office to the functional 'hot seat' of the ill-starred Colonial (now Commonwealth) Development Corporation. For this recently created body, in the improvident fashion of pre-war Imperial Airways, had fallen on scandalously hard times. Its operations, like its constitution, 'bore all the marks of the amateur', as the future Conservative Colonial Secretary, Oliver Lyttelton, acknowledged at a later date:

'It should have been made clear from the outset that the rôle of the corporation was not to manage a whole jumble of projects, but to do exploratory work,' wrote Lyttelton whom Reith privately despised. 'No board of directors sitting in London can manage at once a rubber plantation in Borneo, a coal mine in Tanganyika, a poultry farm in Gambia, a ranch in Swaziland, an hotel in Belsize, a cement factory in Kenya, a shark fishery off the coast of West Africa and an abbatoir in the Falkland Islands. . . . I had to wrestle, with the help of Lord Reith, with what he described as this *damnosa hereditas*.'[8]

Saddled with a debt of nearly £9 million, the legacy of its early years of ill-advised and extravagant experiment earlier in Attlee's administration, the CDC slowly picked up, once Reith assumed total responsibility in the chairman's office at the Hill Street headquarters in Mayfair. How curiously experience tended to repeat itself, he mused. Was it his fate now, or was it merely his reputation as a harsh individualist capable of plucking success out of other men's failures, to be singled out for rough, ungrateful jobs like this? At odd intervals he wondered. Yet no amount of musing or suspicion of ministerial motives could prevent him from throwing himself heart and soul into the messy and sometimes inhuman business of drastic reform. The headquarters staff were inclined to admire him less than they feared him. For slovenly work, however high-ranking the official concerned, earned Reith's retribution, just as speed and thoroughness earned his warm approval.

On occasion he would fly overseas to inspect a difficult or dubious problem, whether a person or a project, on site. It was during one of these journeys, to the Caribbean area, that he decided to take a brief break from strict routine and look up Beaverbrook in Nassau:

'Almost weekly since January 30th,' he wrote to Beaverbrook in May 1955, 'I've thought to send a note to say how very glad I was to see you again and how much I enjoyed our talk. I wished it had been longer, and that I had said less and you more. You were kind to me in the old days; I hope we can meet again soon, I surely do.'

Back in London for the summer, Beaverbrook replied that very day, May 10th, asking him to lunch. 'Bring her ladyship, too,' he urged; and Reith, for once, persuaded Muriel to join him at table in the sunny dining-room of the big flat in Arlington House. Both of them enjoyed it immensely:

'Muriel, who despite a shy exterior, knows what's what, says the lunch itself was far superior to anywhere she's been; myself, though entirely appreciating both hock and food, enjoyed still more the sort of conversation I hardly ever have. . . . There's nothing more to be said than "I enjoyed it so much I'm almost sorry it happened", '[3]

It was Montagu Norman who had induced Reith to give up his teetotal ways on their Caribbean voage in 1938, not long before the enforced withdrawal from the BBC. Now, though abstemiously, he appreciated good wine and fine whisky as much as he abhorred cigarette-smoking, a habit to which he had been once addicted but which he abandoned because he suddenly found it 'filthy, obnoxious and expensive'. Like many Scots, he counted his money carefully, without suffering unduly from chronic financial neurosis. That was one reason why he still felt aggrieved at his own 'folly and weakness' in not stipulating for 'certain financial provisions', as Churchill had put it, when Chamberlain asked him early in 1940 to join his government. He could be extremely hospitable and generous; and in spite of an inveterate tendency to look on the dark side of all calculations, he was never really hard-up. As chairman of the Commonwealth Telecommunications Board until 1950, and simultaneously of the Hemel Hempstead Development Corporation as well as of the National Film Finance Corporation, he could only complain (as, of course, he did) that he barely survived spiritually in his 'well remunerated idleness'. But the task of 'an undertaker' at the Colonial Development Corporation kept him reasonably fully stretched so long as its business was in the red.

'I should like you to be the first to know,' he told Beaverbrook on December 30th, 1955, 'that the corporation (CDC) will be out of the red for the financial year ending tomorrow. . . . It has been a sickening time, the undertaker part (your word a year ago), involving a write-off of about £8 million for past errors. I've just been re-appointed for three years from March 31st, 1956. I didn't want it much, but my colleagues seemed to. I should be doing other things; and by golly I haven't changed my mind from what I said—that I've been an utter idiot and worse.'

Beaverbrook could not let that pass without a word of gentle rebuke:

'Do not believe you have made a mistake in your life in pursuit of public objects, instead of going out for private gain. It is much better to have served the people in the way you have done in these years.'

But Reith could never let well alone. The thought nagged him like a hollow tooth that he was somehow cheating himself of higher opportunities by staying on, expecially since the dirtiest work at this well-appointed funeral parlour now lay behind him:

'My second term as chairman finishes next month,' he reminded Beaverbrook in February 1959. 'So I finish then. You said it was an undertaker's job when I went to it, and so indeed it was. But now there is a first-class organisation throughout the world; and there have been profits for the past three years.' There had been increasing obstructiveness too from officials and ministers, some of whom no doubt uneasily recalled how difficult Reith could be at the head of a successful organisation. As he had written to Beaverbrook on that very subject previously:

'Some civil servants and some politicians may resent a public corporation being efficient. . . . They put a clause into the Ghana independence bill without consultation with or even information to us, and we were told not to take on any new work there or in Malaya.'

None of these minor triumphs or tribulations affected Beaverbrook. What did touch him was Reith's harrowing admission:

'When people ask me how I am, I say—well physically but ill mentally.'

Always supremely adept at stubbing out the smouldering embers of conscience, Beaverbook remonstrated with Reith for saying that he was thinking of retirement from the fray, on the pretext that 'I shall be seventy in July and forty-five of the last fifty years have been occupied in serving the State.'

22

'You must not think of retiring after the age of seventy,' Beaverbrook advised. 'That is the way to senile decay. Besides your great ability should not be lost to the country. It was wrong of you to undertake the colonial development job. But that is in the past. And you are to be congratulated on making such a wonderful success of it. But you were destined for greater things. You have been altogether too self-sacrificing throughout your life.'

Deeply distressed by Beaverbrook's unsparing worldly wisdom, Reith pondered over what his friend had told him. Then, on April 16th, 1959, he replied:

'If I'd known that you would think it wrong of me to take on the CDC in 1950 I wouldn't have done so. But I had relatively little to do, and it had the attraction of being in an awful mess. "Destined for greater things", you say; "altogether too self-sacrificing". Yes, I've been idiotic throughout. I would hate to retire, and I can't anyhow. I want to be fully stretched as if forty-five or fifty. But most people don't like me, for reasons I can well understand.'[3]

4

There were lucrative directorships enough to ensure a steadily healthy bank balance, yet seats on boards of leading insurance and industrial concerns could not thaw the wintry discontent of John Reith. His closing decade, from 1961 to 1971, was by far the bitterest.

'I have more health and energy than I can do with,' he had complained to Beaverbrook in September 1960. And when, almost three years later, he underwent a minor operation, Reith reminded his ever-solicitous Canadian friend that 'this is my first visit to hospital since the battle of Loos'.

'Your heritage of good health and your splendid character,' retorted Beaverbrook, 'are a credit to the "faith of our fathers".'[3]

Reith did not agree. If old age was in itself a hideous disease, good health and mental vigour in old age, with no practical hope of expending these on one of the innumerable, worthwhile public tasks still crying out for the imaginative touch of the born leader, could be accounted a living death.

There were many interested enquiries when the following advertisement appeared in *The Times* on May 15th, 1961:

'Lord Reith seeks advice. He has kept a diary, not a day missed, for over fifty years; it is in two parts: 12 vols manuscript, ten with letters, photographs, newspaper cuttings and such like. He is more and more minded to destroy it because: (1) he does not wish to put a burden on either of his children by leaving it to them; (2) he does not like to think of it lying in some library for a hundred years and then being scrapped (he would prefer to scrap it himself); (3) he does not want such records of himself. Has anyone any kindly advice? Write Box J.261. The Times, E.C.4.'

From the pile of more than three hundred replies by eager publishers, editors, and would-be biographers, Reith paused longest over a note from the editor of the *Evening Standard*, London. This suggested that, in the background, the insatiably inquisitive Beaverbrook had risen to the bait and was cautiously nibbling. Weeks passed, then the literary editor of the *Evening Standard*, Harold Harris, spent several days browsing through the voluminous diaries of John Reith who clearly hoped for a quick and profitable sale:

'Outright sale seems to shock or distress people,' he noted, 'though it does not shock nor distress me—provided I could feel in a certain way to the purchaser, and provided the price were not just good but very good. . . .'

And provided, of course, that the papers lived up to expectations, there was an even chance of serialisation. The alternative seemed far less attractive to Reith, who found no joy in the idea of his diary lying in a permanent home alongside the effusions of Lloyd George and Bonar Law in the Beaverbrook Foundation Library. Yet it was a relief that a realistic offer might come from that source rather than any other 'because I felt quite sure that Lord Beaverbrook, having helped me as much as he did in BBC years (and I wish he had continued it), and knowing as much about me as he does, would want me to have no regrets at losing this intimate and precious record.'[7]

Unfortunately, the scrutinising of several key sections of the personal record disappointed the careful reader from the *Evening Standard*. Mr. Harris's final report, with a number of typical extracts attached to exemplify the tenor of the whole, was fair but damning:

'The diaries are intensely personal,' he wrote, 'and indeed many parts must be incomprehensible to anyone but the writer. They show evidence of obsessive fads. . . . There are no themes, no crises in which he is involved, which can be followed through from beginning to end by the reader. There are only allusions to them, with somewhat intemperate abuse of the many people he disliked, and odd bits of gossip. Reith obviously used the diary largely for letting off steam. Each day's entry includes pretty well everybody he met and lunched with and talked to, but seldom gives more than the subject of discussion, if as much. He never seems to report an entire conversation. And it is all mixed up with family concerns. . . .

'I find him personally an interesting and, in some respects, a baffling figure. He regards himself (and he assured me this is absolutely genuine) as a failure. . . . As well as feeling a failure as a public man, the personal entries I quote show that he also regards himself as a private failure. . . . It may not be too fanciful to suggest that his diary is an attempt to establish himself—in his own eyes, not for posterity—as an individual. A psychiatrist might be interested in the mementoes which are dotted about his flat—a pair of spurs on a door handle, his wartime identity disc hanging from the lavatory cistern. It will be clear from these notes that Lord Reith's diaries cannot be regarded as a primary source of historical material, but only as a very supplementary source. . . .'

Reith's allusions to several of his former ministerial colleagues, not excluding Beaverbrook, were scurrilous and sometimes unprintable. Like a petulant, thwarted child, he furnished no reasons for his coarse indictments. I could well imagine the frisson of rage with which Beaverbrook read of himself as 'the beast', and how rage may have yielded to cynical wonder on learning that Reith had once switched off a wartime broadcast to prevent a single word from 'the beast' polluting his house. It was all very well to be assured that Reith now spoke 'in terms of the highest regard for Lord Beaverbrook, for whom he entertains the warmest feelings of respect and admiration'. The diaries spoke rather differently. And, ironically, Beaverbrook was now being asked to buy them. On balance, he decided against it:

'It seems to me that Mr. Harris should write advising him on the whole to destroy the diaries. The material will not bring credit to him and Mr. Harris can tell him that nicely.'[3]

Well before this curious interlude, I had advised Reith in the opposite sense. At our first encounter he had raised the issue, and I came to recognise its approach from afar, like an obsessive King Charles's head, at almost every subsequent meeting:

'In my view, it would be an act of vandalism to destroy them,' was my repeated advice.

As I was busily engaged at the time on a lengthy biography of Hugh Trenchard, the father of the RAF, there was little more that I could do. When I next accepted, after much deliberation, the commission to write a life of the mysterious Montagu Norman, who had been Governor of the Bank of England between the wars, Reith became less pressing in his references to the diaries. I was thankful, though once he rounded on me with mock ferocity in the course of an explanatory monologue about his past, and asked rhetorically:

'Am I your next subject?'

He knew that I intended to write his life-story one day. He would,

I think, have liked me to embark on it during his last years if only to ease the burden of his monotonous existence. I was determined to wait. For nothing would have blurred the edges of detachment more than trying to make a start with the subject peering critically over my shoulder.

Reith was fond of telling any friends who would listen: 'I've never really learnt how to live, and I've discovered too late that life is for the living.' In the company of one particular lady, whose career he helped to advance with a word in the right place, he sought frequent distraction from the fears and doubts that oppressed his soul. His indifference to what worldly and cynical observers might think or say about this and other less obtrusive friendships remained unshakable probably because, as he remarked to one of his oldest BBC colleagues, who had reluctantly accompanied Reith and his favourite confidante to a noisy party of young people:

'I assure you that my relationship with her is quite proper.'[5]

It was on the tip of the other man's tongue to suggest that if only Reith 'went the whole hog' he might work the silliness out of his system, but habitual prudence restrained him. Besides, a relationship that trespassed beyond the platonic to the carnal would have cured nothing. On the contrary, had Reith succumbed to passion through normal human frailty, his reason might have been destroyed by the terrible compounding of an already manic sense of guilt. The lure of love-making did not attract or seriously tempt him now. What drew him was something at once weird and logical: through and with these otherwise incongruous girl-friends, he could seek and find the gay companionship which had never been his in youth. He asked for nothing but the privilege of sharing their interests and cares; in their presence his own personality would briefly shed its mantle of misery, becoming sometimes as exuberant, gay and expansive as a boy's. His confidantes provided him with a magic casement from which the world transformed itself into a sunnier and more tolerable place. One evening, while dining at the home of a friend, Reith seemed to pass into a brown study. Ignoring the buzz of conversation about him, he kept staring at the wall in front of him. Then he spoke:

'My dear,' he said to the lady he was escorting, 'that wall-paper, I was admiring it. Surely it's exactly the same pattern as the wall-paper in your bedroom.'[5]

His relations with the BBC at this time, in the early sixties, were going through a relatively tranquil phase, as usually happened when recently appointed chairmen or Directors-General extended him the courtesy of a visit, a goodwill note or an invitation to lunch. Invariably the amiability would be marred by Reith's capricious inclination to take deep, personal offence at some innocent remark, some marginal programme innovation, or at some alleged lowering of standards, which inevitably led to friction and to the rupture of all contact with the corporation and its unaccountably traitorous leaders.

'What's your opinion of *Juke Box Jury*?' he asked me unexpectedly on one occasion. 'Do you regard it, as I do, as an evil and pernicious programme that corrupts the young?'

'It's not a programme I see often,' I replied. 'But surely that's pushing it a bit far. Evil? Pernicious? Corrupting the young? I know children who watch it and like it, goodness knows why; but if it's had any ill effects on them, their parents would surely have been the first to complain.'

He disagreed violently. It was, he said fiercely, the BBC's duty not to run the risk of seducing young minds. What the parents did, or did not do, hardly entered into the matter.[6] Sir Hugh Greene and Oliver Whitley soon afterwards incurred Reith's lasting animus by refusing to be cowed or influenced by his unflattering observations on the iniquities of poor David Jacobs and the panel of *Juke Box Jury*. Diplomatic relations with the BBC were abruptly severed until Greene retired, and his successor, Charles Curran, manfully, if vainly, tried to restore them.

Reith's ambivalent attitude to the BBC was wholly consistent with the feelings of a father who could never forget how his own child, originally brought up to love, honour and obey its parents, had somehow turned on him and cut him off virtually without a penny in 1938. It was an attitude in which mistrust and dislike alternated with an underlying, almost defiantly tender concern for its welfare. When Sir William Haley had joined the BBC as the fourth nominee of Brendan Bracken's during the war, after Robert Foot, Ivone Kirkpatrick and A. P. Ryan, Reith at once felt a paternal sympathy for the newcomer. Haley was suddenly elevated into the hot-seat, once 'Mr. Foot, like Ogilvie, got his yards crossed with those of the board . . . the unknown editor-in-chief of a few months was now Director-General'. Reith liked what he heard of Haley's severely practical and high-minded approach. Finally, in 1946, he wrote to him, then they met. He would have secretly relished the opportunity to work with Haley, as chairman of the board; that possibility had been vaguely mooted in 1946. Like so much else, it came to nothing. Yet Haley, in Reith's harshly intemperate view, eventually went the way of all flesh by refusing to read the signs of the times and forcibly resist the Tory campaign to promote commercial television interests in the early fifties.

'Haley,' he assured me, 'has a lot to answer for. He declined to raise a hand in the BBC's vital interests, and those of the country, when the so-called independent TV lobby was active. Yet I don't think the BBC, by things done or not done, was recognisably responsible for the introduction of commercial television. It was a political decision primarily made by a man with his ear to the ground. Any complaint against the BBC was trifling compared to the shriekings of the Tory backbenchers of the time, whose demands Woolton wanted to meet; if he kept in with the Conservative Party, he could reckon on being made chairman and being given an earldom. I offered to help Haley by taking a room in Broadcasting House and the job, unpaid, of fending off the commercial lobby, Woolton, Profumo, dogmatists like Heath, Powell and Macleod, and the indifferent Churchill, too.'*

Perhaps Haley was wiser in his generation than Reith realised. There would have been no peace from any quarter if Reith had installed himself solidly once more inside the citadel itself. Yet to this day Haley remains puzzled by Reith's additional remark: 'I hope there will be an explanation from him, some day.' For the commercial TV lobby, like the commercial radio lobby nearly twenty years later, would undoubtedly have succeeded in smashing the BBC's monopoly, no matter how cleverly Haley or anyone else had anticipated and exposed their every move. Reith took a typically contrary view. 'Haley's attitude astonished me. In his place I'd have resigned, but the need wouldn't have arisen. I think he had an abhorrence, maybe a congenital abhorrence, of public relations especially when as in this case, it was a matter of taking arms against the government. The aversion,' he concluded with an obscure dig at the *Guardian* and its Liberal traditions, 'may have derived from C. P. Scott.'

Recalling Churchill's offer to help 'if I can be of service to you at any time', Reith had belatedly approached the Prime Minister. It was the second week of June 1952. Both Lords and Commons had debated the measure for introducing commercial television; so to Winston Churchill he turned in anguish as though to a sympathetic, supreme judge of appeal. Lord Moran, Churchill's personal physician, was himself in hospital when the Upper House discussed the Bill. Yet, reading Hansard next day, he was conscious of 'the long shadow of that gaunt old covenanter, Lord Reith, across its pages. I could see him as he rose in his place like another John Knox to scourge the infidel. "I am slow at speech," he began, "reluctant to waste your Lordships' time and my own." He claimed no credit at all for what

* Discussing with me why he dissented from the findings of the Beveridge Committee's 1951 report on broadcasting, Mr. Selwyn Lloyd said: 'What mainly put me off was the appalling evidence of Reith—and the rolling eyes of William Haley.'

had been done when he was Director-General of the BBC during the first sixteen years of its existence. He had tried to do as he had been taught in the manse of the College Church in Glasgow. He believed that he was peculiarly helped in plan and execution. Of the worth and consequence of British broadcasting, its flower and essence, he spoke with pride: today it commanded the respect and admiration of the whole world. "What grounds are there," he cried, "for jeopardising that heritage and tradition? . . . Need we be ashamed of moral values or of intellectual and ethical objectives? It is these that are here and now at stake." '

It was the heart-cry of a prophet wasting his words in a wind-swept wilderness. Moran himself was moved to write an eloquent letter to *The Times*, protesting, as one debarred by illness from participating in the debate, against the light assumption of the Lord Chancellor (Simonds) that the people and their tastes should be trusted and pandered to: 'Was he arguing that we should now be better off if the Reith dynasty had been cut off and broadcasting had been sponsored from the outset? We have not heard the last of this issue. . . .'

Chancing to meet Moran a few days after that letter appeared in *The Times*, Reith said to him:

'I wrote to Winston the day after the debate, but he has not answered. I always thought he was a courteous man. I said I had not seen him for ten years, and would like to talk to him about it. I was shocked at the Lord Chancellor's speech.'

Moran was moved and somewhat upset by Reith's appearance:

'His gaunt, scarred face expressed his grief and alarm. England was going to the devil, and his soul yearned to do something for the shattered state of the country.

'The next morning I found Clemmie in Winston's room, when the following conversation took place.

'Clemmie: "Have you read Charles's letter in *The Times*?"

'Winston: "It is not a subject I feel very strongly about. I do not worry about it as I do over the solvency of the country."

'Moran: "But is not the issue fundamental?"

'Winston (peevishly): "I don't see why it is fundamental. It is not at all fundamental."

'It was plain that he did not want to discuss the question; he was not interested in abstract issues. And then, on the spur of the moment, he said:

' "But I am against the monopoly enjoyed by the BBC. For eleven years they kept me off the air. They prevented me from expressing views which have proved to be right. Their behaviour has been tyrannical. They are honeycombed with socialists—probably with communists."

'He spoke hotly; his detachment had quite gone.

' "I first quarrelled with Reith," he went on, "in 1926, during the General Strike. He behaved quite impartially between the strikers and the nation. I said he had no right to be impartial between the fire and the fire-brigade. The nation was being held up. It did not matter so much to me, as the Columbia Broadcasting Corporation [*sic*] was ready to let me speak at any time, and would pay me £500 for doing so. But it might have happened to others." '[9]

In the teeth not of Churchill's indifference but, as he thought, of his unabated animosity, Reith still absurdly contended that, had he stood in Haley's place, he would not have run away but rallied the 'thinking part of the nation' to his standard. The fact that, lined up against him, there were doctrinaire supporters of free enterprise, apart from avaricious men anxious for a slice of the equity and vainer men no less keen than Churchill had ever been to obtain an alternative outlet for their opinions, probably occurred to him but by no means deterred him. Anyway, it was by then too late for resistance. The pass had been sold.

5

Twice during these years John Reith submitted himself to trial by interview on the television screen, despite his incessant querulousness about BBC policy, standards and objectives. Before John Freeman cross-examined him during the *Face to Face* series in 1960, he was shown round the studios by Gerald Beadle. As they walked across a wide, workshop area where the carpenters had been sawing and planing all day on elaborate designs for programmes, Reith noticed the pictures of scantily clad pin-up girls that festooned every locker-door except one. Halting in his tracks before a postcard representation of a Henry Moore sculpture on this unique locker-door, he exclaimed:

'A third-programme carpenter, I presume.'[5]

The lengthier, three-part interview he agreed to record with Malcolm Muggeridge in 1967 was a memorable contribution to broadcasting history, though much of the original film and sound-track ended up, sadly, on the cutting-room floor. By now Reith had become acclimatised as Lord Rector of Glasgow University, while Muggeridge had recently won election to the same honorary office at Edinburgh. In one of G. K. Chesterton's lesser-known essays there is a reference to the obituary notice of an obscure sea-dog, a fleeting glance at which caused one reader to blurt out: 'Good gracious, I see Admiral so-and-so is dead,' and his neighbour to comment: 'Admiral so-and-so dead? I didn't realise he'd been born.' For many viewers the appearance of John Reith on the small screen must have been like the conjuring up from some neglected tomb of an extraordinarily vivid and not unappealing ghost, reincarnated by a trick of light in the camera's eye. He reminded Muggeridge forcibly of Charles de Gaulle, that other despotic giant who had answered the call of destiny also, but with none of the flattering ingenuousness Reith had repeatedly displayed in his dealings with devious politicians.

'In a word, what do you think is the best form of government?' asked the interviewer at one point.

'Despotism tempered by assassination,' was Reith's unexpected reply.

'I know perfectly well that I'm not a complete failure,' he said at another juncture. 'I consider that my life has been about one half as successful as I think it might have been. . . . I would have been very happy to have seen the BBC through the war period, and immensely happy getting things settled down after the war. Might I possibly have the conceit to imagine that the *mores* would have been somewhat different to what they are if I had stayed there?'

Radio he seldom listened to, or so he claimed. I knew that one August night in 1945, with subdued rejoicing going on in London after the unexpectedly swift surrender of Japan, a reveller had rung up the BBC from Wales. The stranger said he was John Reith. He denounced the corporation for its appalling programmes. The duty officer, who had never heard the authentic voice of the master, was quite taken in by the impersonation. The complaint and the name of the complainant were duly logged. A thunderous plea of 'not guilty' came from Reith when an old colleague gently upbraided him for an indiscretion of which he was wholly innocent.

'You always got a clear, definitive answer from him,' declared another of his earliest collaborators, Sir Harold Bishop. 'When he was once asked the traditional question: "What single book would you take with you if you were cast away on a desert island?" he answered simply: *Thomas' Guide to Practical Shipbuilding*.'[5]

Yet it was with wry horror that Reith spurned an invitation to appear on *Desert Island Discs*; and to a solemn young producer who employed flattery in an effort to induce his unlikely participation in a religious series entitled *What I Believe*, Reith replied shortly: 'I would not broadcast under any circumstances.' He took some delight later in poking fun at me for my association with *The World at One*, an innovation in radio-journalism which he wholeheartedly deplored.

'It's inconceivable,' he would say, 'you of all people being mixed up in that.' Then, employing a familiar mannerism of failing to remember a proper name he preferred to forget, that of William Hardcastle, he would continue: 'Let me see, isn't there someone called William Ancaster—no, not Ancaster, William McMaster—that's it, McMaster, who introduces himself, then hands back to another reader who hands back to him for a lot of rubbishy, trivial snippets that are supposed to be news? I wouldn't have allowed it in my day. I like mine straight.'

It was a point of minor disagreement between us. I recognized from the vehement way he pulled my leg that he was puzzled as well as distressed at my low taste in journalism if not in literature. 'I don't think I'd have survived in your time at the BBC,' I once said to him. 'I wouldn't be so sure,' he replied. 'I never much liked yes-men.'

Only the heavy fall which crippled him about the time of his eightieth birthday prevented him from keeping a date with me to record what might have proved a blistering if partly unbroadcastable interview on *Landmarks in My Life*. By then I had long mastered the elusive art of drawing him out without becoming in the process a personal target for his spleen.

Television as such he continued to regard as 'a social menace of the first magnitude'. He would, as he frequently said to me, have restricted its use by restricting the hours, so maintaining by rarity value the loftiest possible standards. As regards his own *mores*, the overweening arrogance, the lack of humility, the impatience and intolerance, the occasional lapses into the romantic follies of irrecoverable youth, such blemishes were for the Almighty alone to judge. Very few of his shrinking band of friends realised even then, as the shadows of death approached, that John Reith in his own embittered eyes stood already condemned by the Almighty. A partial failure in this world, he was foredoomed by himself to an eternity of loss in the next.

His wife could seldom reach his self-tortured spirit. His children, who had grown up largely relieved to be free of his moralising, saw him at intervals only. When his only daughter announced that she intended to marry a Presbyterian clergyman, Dr. Murray Leishman, Reith reverted to type and sternly put his foot down. He did not want Marista to do it; he schemed hard, bullied and raged harder, in a futile attempt to forbid the banns. Only after Lord MacLeod of Funeray, the leader of the Iona community, recalled him to his sense of duty as a father did Reith reluctantly appear at the wedding. He stayed for as short a time as seemed obligatory, then made his excuses and glumly left. The whole episode disturbed him so profoundly that he entered a psychiatric clinic for treatment soon afterwards, walking out of the place in disgust at the inability of the specialists to alleviate his *accidie*.

If Reith, in his socially pretentious way, posed as a disappointed father who felt that his daughter might have 'made a more acceptable match', that was not the main reason for his outrageous behaviour. I caught a strong whiff of the truth one evening at his club, when he spent over an hour lambasting in turn the various relatives who had been 'sponging on me like leeches' for many years past. Quite unfairly, he feared that the good Dr. Leishman would instantly join the queue of family spongers, and might even rob him of his last halfpenny.

'It will be a hundred years at least before Britain gets over the malign influence of that unscrupulous man', Reith said to me one January day in 1964, while the body of Winston Churchill still lay in state on its catafalque in Westminster Hall, not many yards away. He was sitting hunched over a drink in the bar of the Upper House. Despite the inappropriateness of time and place, his sentiments were brutally sincere; he doubted indeed whether the country 'will ever recover from Churchill's influence, especially after the war when he gave no moral lead whatever'. His words carried to the far side of the room where an Anglican Bishop turned a startled head for a moment, then turned it quickly back. Reith glared across, almost daring the prelate to indicate dissent.

Six months later, Reith decided that he would celebrate his seventy-fifth birthday by climbing for the last time to the top of Cairngorm, accompanied by a Scotswoman with whom he had been on close terms for many years, though she had seen him only on rare occasions since her marriage in the mid-thirties. When she received his letter with this wild-sounding proposal, she wondered what he meant by the remark that he was 'in training'. Reith rang her up impatiently two nights later. Why had she not replied? Would she please go up the mountain with him? Yes, he would be quite fit for the ascent in a few days' time: 'There are forty or so steep stairs to our flat at the top of Lollards Tower. I've calculated how many times those stairs go into the height of Cairngorm, and I'm getting into proper training.' Once, in his endless, purposeful ascending and descending, the housekeeper gave him a 'queer look' and enquired if he was feeling all right. 'Oh yes', he said, 'I haven't gone off my head yet, if that's what you mean.'

He told his friend on reaching Aberdeen, that he had one great hope and longing in pursuing this apparently foolhardy enterprise: 'It's only a dream, but I've a feeling I may meet my father again at the summit. I'd like to die up there and go away with him.'

The lady burst out laughing. Then she tried to tease him out of his eagerly sombre mood:

'What good would I be with you up there if you decided to die? Do you expect me to carry your body down? No, I don't want to come, thank you.'

So Reith climbed Cairngorm uneventfully with his son Christopher.[5]

Death, that equal foot at all men's doors, was a visitor whom he would have bidden and welcomed prematurely when, as happened with increasing frequency in Reith's old age, there seemed nothing challenging or enjoyable to live for. Honours he still coveted, less for their own sake than for the supposed recognition attendant on them.

'I know my father would have hated to hear me ask for this', he told an amiably surprised Lord Longford one afternoon by way of preamble to a blunt piece of special pleading, 'but could you do something to get me a higher grading in the peerage which previous governments have denied me?'

Longford, then leader of the Labour lords, promised to forward this oddly phrased but honest plea to the proper quarter. He was not shocked by Reith's inordinate longing to be created a Viscount, but was faintly puzzled for two reasons: first, he could see only the pointlessness of such a longing; second, he thought it was already common knowledge, though John Reith evidently did not appear to share it, that Harold Wilson had long set his face against all but life peerages. The Labour Prime Minister retained his affectionate, respectful regard for this 'extremely able and active old man who, almost until the last, seemed to expect a call to high office in the event of some unexpectedly grave crisis in the nation's affairs'.[5]

The other, darker side of Reith's spirit remained veiled from the majority of people. The death-wish would come to him almost naturally when he permitted himself the self-indulgence of excessive brooding on the past and its recurring disappointments:

'Do you realise', he said one day to an old friend from the academic world, 'that by taking thought I could *will* myself to die?'

His friend pretended not to hear him, so Reith flung down this black gauntlet again, forcing the other to comment coldly:

'Coming from someone whom I've always held in high regard for sensibility and intelligence, that's one of the silliest things I've ever heard you say.'[5]

Like a sharp slap across both cheeks, the comment appeared to bring Reith back to the land of the living. He loved returning to Scotland. He gloried in the pomp and ancient ceremonial inseparable from the office of Lord High Commissioner, the coveted post offered to him by Churchill and rejected during the war, offered again by Harold Wilson and this time gratefully accepted. With resplendent maids of honour, courtiers, officials, equerries and a dignified retinue of servants to wait on him and his guests in the banqueting hall and state apartments of Holyrood, Reith was restored to his natural element. Somewhat hesitantly he took sound advice and appointed Dr. Leishman, the once suspect son-in-law, as his chaplain. Lady Reith, who really preferred homely, simple food and clothes to the richer fare and more formal attire expected of a hostess in those stiff surroundings, suffered her husband's recurring rebukes in self-effacing silence. The RAF equerry, an experienced flight lieutenant, was standing to attention in the courtyard one morning as the Reiths came down to enter their waiting car. A slightly flustered Lady Reith stepped forward and lowered her head to climb in first, but her husband reached out a long arm and tugged her back:

'D'ye not yet realise, woman', he snapped, 'that I'm the Queen's representative in this land.'[5]

The heavy fall, which badly incapacitated him during the final three years of his life, also taxed his limited reserves of patience. While the torn ligaments of both legs were mending in hospital, he became the prey to so deep and corrosive a depression that he consented to an eminent consultant's suggestion that he should submit to electro-convulsive treatment. He did not fear death; he appeared stoically nonchalant about his fate in the hereafter. What afflicted him chiefly was a melancholic uncertainty about the future in this world of the most loyally attentive of his confidantes. His heart, meanwhile, had begun to trouble him. A pace-maker was inserted and, mustering what small stamina he could, Reith learnt to hobble about the two bachelor apartments that had been knocked into one large flat at the top of Lollards Tower; this had been his grace-and-favour home since leaving Harrias House at Beaconsfield in the early sixties. He moved north in the late summer of 1970 to a bigger, more fashionable, but chillier abode: The Queen's House in Moray Place, Edinburgh. None of his remaining friends doubted that he had deliberately decided to uproot himself, no matter how much he disliked the upheaval, to end his days on Scottish soil.

His last illness struck him down in June 1971. It was mercifully brief. He had never been a good patient, and the nurses relieved his pain of body and spirit with heavy sedation. Who can tell whether that valiant, proud, despairing being, so obsessed by the repeated foiling of his worldly ambitions, found true peace on the brink of eternity? He had always shrunk in an access of false humility from trying to calculate the incalculable good he might have done as a public servant. His personal faults were many, perhaps the worst being the subtlest of all—that terrible sense of being foredoomed to damnation which had haunted him since boyhood. John Reith was a remarkable man cast in no common mould. Greatness had not been thrust upon him by destiny entirely; through the impetus of that messianic force, he had achieved it by his own single-minded efforts before the age of forty. The flaws in his character, in the superstitious marrow of his very bones, gradually led to his undoing after that. Like Jonah, he was too easily swallowed by the whale of the establishment; and as a captive in the darkness of the whale's belly, he voyaged helplessly, no longer the master of his destiny, for the next forty years. During his long inglorious confinement as a prisoner of the 'mini-men' he despised, John Reith did not learn how to live in peace with himself or with the stern God of his fathers. Nor did he shed the tenacious illusion that fame and glory and success in the eyes of the worldly-wise were prizes infinitely worth coveting, in spite of setbacks and rebuffs.

He left a living monument in the BBC, yet believed in his obstinately childish fashion that his heirs had wantonly defaced it. He left everything too late, his own departures from public responsibilities included, even his reluctant departure from life itself. If any great man can ever be said to have atoned for his misdeeds on the elaborate rack he made of his own conscience, that man was surely John Reith. We in our generation shall certainly not look on his eccentric like again.

Malcolm Muggeridge was at his bedside shortly before he died. Reith lay in a drugged sleep. His face, usually so severe, had an unfamiliar look of serenity. Then, as he watched, there flashed into Muggeridge's mind a death-bed scene strangely similar in its poignancy. The words used by Kent to hush his companions while Lear drew his final breath might have been fashioned by Shakespeare for the dying Reith:

> 'Vex not his ghost: O! let him pass; he hates him
> Who would upon the rack of this tough world
> Stretch him out longer.'

References

Chapter 1: The Boy (pages 29–38)

1. J. C. W. Reith, *Into the Wind*, Hodder & Stoughton, London, 1949, p. 5
2. Reith conversations
3. Information to author from René Cutforth, whose televised profile of Reith, including interviews with contemporaries, was indefinitely shelved

Chapter 2: The Misfit (pages 39–54)

1. *Into the Wind*, pp. 10–16
2. Reith conversations
3. Edmund Gosse, *Father and Son*, Heinemann, London, 1907, p. 206
4. Private information to author

Chapter 3: The Warrior (pages 55–84)

1. Reith conversations
2. John Reith, *Wearing Spurs*, Hutchinson, London, 1966, pp. 13 et seq.
3. Reith correspondence
4. *Into the Wind*, p. 20

Chapter 4: The Seeker: (pages 85 to 102)

1. Reith conversations
2. *Wearing Spurs*, p. 221
3. Reith correspondence

4. Private information to author
5. *Into the Wind*, pp. 64 et seq.

Chapter 5: The Opportunist (pages 103 to 137)

1. Reith conversations
2. Reith correspondence
3. Confirmatory evidence from Beardmore's successors
4. *Wearing Spurs*, pp. 149–50
5. Private information to author
6. Lord Beaverbrook, *The Decline & Fall of Lloyd George*, Collins, London, 1963, pp. 173 et seq.
7. *Into the Wind*, pp. 81 et seq.
8. Frances Stevenson, *Lloyd George, A Diary*, Hutchinson, London, 1971, p. 262
9. Asa Briggs, *The History of Broadcasting in the United Kingdom*, Oxford University Press, London, 1965, Volume One, pp. 136–8 et seq.
10. A. R. Burrows, *The Story of Broadcasting*, Cassell, London, 1924, p. 68
11. BBC Archives

Chapter 6: The Visionary (pages 138 to 178)

1. BBC Archives
2. A. J. P. Taylor, *English History 1914–1945*. Oxford University Press, London, 1965, p. 204 et seq.
3. BBC Archives (Reith correspondence)
4. Asa Briggs, Vol. 1, pp. 174 et seq.
5. *Into the Wind*, pp. 90–1 et seq.
6. C. A. Lewis, *Broadcasting from Within*, Newnes, London, 1924
7. Private information to author
8. Peter Eckersley *The Power Behind the Mike*, Cape, London, 1941, p. 80
9. G. K. A. Bell, *Randall Davidson*, Volume II, p. 1211, also Briggs, Volume 1, p. 241, op. cit.
10. Frederick Sykes, *From Many Angles*, Harrap, London, 1942, p. 321.
11. J. C. W. Reith, *Broadcast over Britain*, Hodder & Stoughton, London, 1924, pp. 78 et seq.
12. Harold Nicolson, *King George V, His Life and Reign*, Constable, London, 1952, p. 384

13. Andrew Boyle, *Montagu Norman*, Cassell, London, 1969, pp. 166 et seq.
14. Gainford Papers (Reith correspondence), Nuffield College, 51A.
15. Gainford Papers (Bull correspondence), Nuffield College, 125–1
16. A. G. Gardiner, *Certain People of Importance*, Cape, London, 1926, p. 127
17. Stanley Baldwin, *On England*, Philip Allen, London, 1926, pp. 196 et seq.
18. Reith conversations

Chapter 7: The Hostage (pages 179 to 214)

1. Asa Briggs, Volume I, pp. 403 et seq.
2. Reith conversations
3. BBC Archives
4. Crawford Committee Evidence and BBC Archives
5. Reith Papers as quoted by Briggs, op. cit. Volume I, pp. 326 et seq.
6. Andrew Boyle, *Montagu Norman*, pp. 195 et seq.
7. A. J. P. Taylor, p. 242
8. John Evelyn Wrench, *Geoffrey Dawson and Our Times*, Hutchinson, London, 1955, p. 249
9. *Beatrice Webb's Diaries*, 1924–1932, Longman, London, 1956, pp. 91 et seq.
10. Richard Hoggart, *The Uses of Literacy*, Pelican, London, 1958, pp. 228–9
11. *Into the Wind*, pp. 108 et seq.
12. Private information to author
13. BBC Archives (Davidson correspondence)
14. BBC Archives (MacDonald correspondence)
15. *Radio Times*, May 28, 1926, Gilbert Murray
16. Robert Blake, *The Private Papers of Douglas Haig, 1914–19*, Eyre & Spottiswoode, 1952, p. 279

Chapter 8: The Autocrat (pages 215 to 246)

1. Information to author from Lord Shinwell
2. Reith conversations
3. *Into the Wind*, pp. 118 et seq.
4. Asa Briggs, Volume 11, pp. 426 et seq.
5. Gainford papers (Snowden correspondence)
6. Private information to author
7. Aberdeen papers (Reith correspondence)

8. Gainford papers (Reith correspondence)
9. Gainford papers (Clarendon–Rendall correspondence)
10. BBC Archives
11. Mary Agnes Hamilton, *Remembering My Old Friends*, Jonathan Cape, London, 1944. p. 28
12. Information to author from Lord Boothby
13. Val Gielgud, *Years in a Mirror*, Bodley Head, London, 1965, pp. 50 et seq.
14. A. J. P. Taylor, p. 233, et seq., op. cit.
15. Francis Meynell, *My Lives*, Bodley Head, London, 1971, p. 255
16. Lord Vansittart, *The Mist Procession*, Hutchinson, London, 1958, pp. 367 et seq.
17. Nicolson, (George V), p. 458, op. cit.
18. Christopher Hassall, *Edward Marsh*, Longman Green, London, 1959, p. 570
19. Andrew Boyle, *Montagu Norman*, p. 279. op. cit.

Chapter 9: The Paternalist (pages 247 to 295)

1. *Into the Wind*, pp. 158 et seq.
2. BBC Archives
3. Asa Briggs, Volume II, pp. 358 et seq.
4. R. S. Lambert, *Ariel and All His Quality*, Gollancz, London, 1940, p. 150
5. D. G. Bridson, *Prospero and Ariel*, Gollancz, London, 1971, p. 41
6. Ralph Wade, *Early Life in the BBC*, typed *mss.*
7. Val Gielgud, p. 65, op. cit.
8. Reith correspondence
9. Reith diary extracts quoted by Briggs, Vol. 11, p. 444, op. cit.
10. Private information to author
11. Reith conversations
12. Harman Grisewood, *One Thing at a Time*, Hutchinson, London, 1968, pp. 90–1
13. Ullswater Committee proceedings
14. Andrew Boyle, *Trenchard, Man of Vision*, Collins, London, 1962, p. 691
15. A. J. P. Taylor, p. 383, op. cit.
16. Maurice Gorham, *Sound and Fury*, Percival Marshall, London, 1948, pp. 62 et seq.
17. Keith Feiling, *Life of Neville Chamberlain*, Macmillan, London, 1946, pp. 434 et seq.
18. M. A. Hamilton, p. 287, op. cit.
19. Stuart Hibberd, in *Prospero*, Christmas 1971

Chapter 10: The Outsider (pages 296 to 328)

1. *Into the Wind*, pp. 337 et seq.
2. Private information to author
3. Beaverbrook correspondence
4. Andrew Boyle, *Trenchard*, op. cit.
5. Information to the author from Lord Runciman
6. Reith conversations
7. BBC Archives
8. Briggs, Vol. III, p. 331, op. cit.
9. Reith correspondence
10. Sir Winston S. Churchill, *The Second World War*, R.S. Volume II, p. 28
11. Lord Brabazon, *The Brabazon Story*, Heinemann, London, 1956, pp. 206–7
12. Harold Macmillan, *The Blast of War*, Macmillan, London, 1967, p. 95
13. Nicolson, *Diaries and Letters*, Volume 1, p. 187 et seq.
14. Sir Gerald Beadle. *Television: A Critical Review*, Allen & Unwin, London

Epilogue (pages 329 to 351)

1. Reith TV interview with Malcolm Muggeridge
2. A. J. P. Taylor, p. 483, op. cit.
3. Beaverbrook correspondence
4. *Into the Wind*, pp. 500 et seq.
5. Private information to author
6. Reith conversations
7. Reith correspondence
8. *Memoirs of Lord Chandos*, Bodley Head, London, 1962, pp. 201–202
9. Lord Moran, *Winston Churchill: The Struggle for Survival 1940–1965*, Constable, London, 1966, pp. 387–90

Index

Index compiled by Ann Field

Aberdeen, Lord, 220
Adam Smith, Janet, 263–4
adolescence, 36–54
Aircraft Production, Ministry of, 338
Aitken, Max: see Beaverbrook, Lord
Alexander, A. V., 326
Allen, Hugh, 150
Amalgamated Press, 188
Anderson, Major, 123
Anderson, Sir John, 156, 192, 310, 312, 316, 333
Anderson, P. F., 138
apprenticeship, engineering, 412, 48–51, 53–4; completion of 54
Archibald, R. R., 52
Army career, 55–84; Reith's adjutants, 70–7, 79–80; administration, 63–4, 67, 70–1; attitude, 57, 86–7; cadet corps, 38, 57; civilian life, 102; destiny, 56; Fifth Scottish Rifles, 53, 59–60, 82; First Lanarkshire Rifle Volunteers, 51; France, 64–84; Glasgow University O.T.C., 39, 51–3; horsemanship, 61–2, 73–5; militia certificate of proficiency, 54; mobilisation, 59–60; parents' attitude, 64–5; relations with men and superiors, 67, 74–5; Royal Engineers, 101; application for transfer to, 76–7, 80–1; transport section, 61–3, 66–76; trenches, repair of, 82–83; wounded, 83–7; parents' anxiety, 86–8
Ashbridge, Noel, 256, 259
Asquith, H. H. 158–60, 162–3
Astbury, Mr. Justice, 199, 205
Astor, Hon. J. J., 136, 266, 273
Attlee, Clement, 270, 302, 313, 332, 334,
autobiography, 26, 35, 331
Aviemore, 44

Backgammon, 332
Baldwin, Oliver, 262
Baldwin, Stanley, 139, 145, 158, 162, 165–169, 176–8, 183–4, 194, 196, 201–2, 206, 214, 222, 236, 269, 275, 281, 285; Abdication crisis, 281–4; BBC and broadcasting, attitude and influence, 153–4, 163, 165–7, 179, 203–205; industrial crisis, 1926, 190–3; Reith, meeting, 164
Bank of England, 167, 193, 209, 243–4
Banks, Sir Donald, 265–6
Barker, Ernest, 266–7
Barrington, Jonah, 262
Bartlett, Vernon, 260
Barton Street residence, 137, 274
Beaconsfield home, 274, 350
Beadle, Gerald, 292–3, 321, 345
Beardmore, Sir William, 107, 109
Beardmore's, 107–9, 122, 148–9
Beaverbrook, Lord, 115, 133, 145, 150, 173, 185–6, 236, 300, 313–4, 317, 331–332, 337–40; BBC and broadcasting, attitude to, 133–4; Reith, meets, 133; correspondence with, 330, 336
Beecham, Sir Thomas, 273
Beerbohm, Max, Reith cartoon, 234
Beharrell, Sir George, 298
Bell, Dean G.K.A., 150, 214
Benn, Wedgwood, 237
Berry, group, 188
Bevin, Ernest, 313
Binyon, Major Basil, 128, 173, 180, 213
biography, 340–1
Birkenhead, Lord, 114, 116–7, 166–7, 194
Birkenshaw, Douglas, 277

Bishop, Sir Harold, 346
Blanesburgh, Lord, 177
Bonar Law, Andrew, 115–8, 138–9, 145, 158
Boosey, William, 189
Booth, George, 90
Boothby, Lord, 230, 288
Boult, Adrian, 258, 261, 273
Brabazon, Lord, 222, 312
Bracken, Brendan, 319–22
Bridges, Robert, 150
Bridgeman, Lord, 269
Bridie, James, 52
Bridson, D. G., *Prometheus the engineer*, 253–4
Briggs, Professor Asa, *History of Broadcasting in the United Kingdom*, 26, 120, 127, 141–2, 149, 151, 153, 155, 157, 171, 175, 180, 183, 189, 195, 197, 204, 212, 217–8, 255, 257, 271, 280, 288, 290–1, 303
British Airways, 298–9
British Broadcasting Company (later Corporation), 24, 97, 122, 125–6, 133, 213, 316–7, 322–3, 330, 341–2
  administration, 256–7; reorganisation, 321
  advertisements for executives, 118–9
  advertising and sponsored programmes, 124–5, 145, 186–7, 211–2, 271–3, 288
  advisory committees, 173, 223, 318
  Arabic service, 287
  board, 127–8, 143, 153–4, 169–71, 180–181, 219, 221–2
  Broadcasting House, 247, 249–50
  bureaucracy, 255–9, 277
  Cabinet committee, 317–8
  Cardiff station, 130
  censorship, 253–4
  centralisation, 147–8, 264
  chairman, 226–7
  Charter, 212–3, 224–5, 265–6, 273; draft, 210–11
  children's programmes, 273
  Christian values, 152, 174–5, 230–1
  Christmas Day royal broadcast, 254
  class ignorance, 204
  commercial interest, 185
  committees, reliance on, 252–3
  concerts, 145
  constitution and status, 169–71, 180–1, 268; change, 171, 183, 189–90
  control, 251–2, 277
  controversial subjects, 172–4, 187, 208, 211, 260, 290
  Crawford Committee, 170, 174, 177, 181–90, 196, 266; acceptance, 209–210; Post Office evidence, 183; Postmaster General, 183; publication, 189–90; recommendations, 184–5, 207–8; Reith's evidence, 182–3
  creative section, 256–7
  Daventry long-range transmitter, 176
  Director-General (Reith), 22, 212, 259, 276; authority, delegation of, 252; campaign to oust, 291–95; control of programme content, 238–9; decline, 277–8, 286; departure, 293–5; image, 240: inhibiting presence, 290; relations with board, 215–26, 245; relations with P.M.G., 266–7; resignations, threatened, 220, 289; role, 215, 234–5, 246, 250–1, 265; salary, 223; staff attitude, 252–9, 262–3, 296
  dissolution of company status, 212–3
  drama, 188, 231–2
  education, 150
  Empire broadcasting service, 251, 256, 273–4, 287
  engineering, 149, 259
  English, standard of, 150, 198
  finance, 128, 143–5, 161, 170, 182, 187, 207–11, 228–9, 243, 266–8, 273, 286–287, 319, 321
  function, 185
  General Manager (Reith), 119–22, 126–127, 146–78; acknowledgement of efforts, 146; board's support, 149; dominance, 155; reorganisation, 128–130; Savoy Hill office, 149–50
  General Strike, 193–203, 205–6, 345; effect of, 178, 191–2, 203–5
  government service, 193–4
  governors, 210–12, 273; meetings, 219, 223; relations with Director-General, 215–227, 235–6; status and powers, 224–5, 245 6
  growth, 179, 251
  impartiality, 193–4, 197, 199, 205–6, 271, 292, 345
  independence, 196–7, 240
  international reputation, 240–242
  licences, 123–8, 131–2, 134–5, 142, 146, 161, 169, 187, 210, 287
  light entertainment, 272
  Magnet House, 123, 128
  Managing Director (Reith), 146, 180–1; status, 182
  Marconi House, 129–30
  mass tastes, 151, 157
  monopoly, 124, 217–8, 133–5, 139, 143, 153, 175, 179, 182–3, 185–6, 189–90, 207, 235, 271, 344–5

BBC, *cont.*
moral responsibility, 150, 214, 239–40, 259, 344
music, 146, 150, 188–9, 258, 261, 273
news service and staff, 125, 140–1, 172–173, 194–7, 204, 254–5, 273–4, 290; development of, 191–99, 207–8
organisation, 250–1
overseas service, 286–8, 303
policy control board, 155
political, electoral and ministerial broadcasts, 158, 162–3, 174, 191–2, 203–5, 222, 236–7, 244, 282
Portuguese service, 287
producers, 252–3
programmes: abdication crisis, 281–4; advertising of, 130–1; artistic and creative policy, 189; board, 155–6; criticism, 157; expenditure, 228–9; scope, 140–1, 173, 213–4, 238; specialist tastes, 186; unimaginative, 252
public opinion, 179–80; influence on, 240–1, 289
public relations, 228–9, 259
public service, 141, 181–2, 198, 214, 229, 251
regional stations, 125, 147–8, 155; controllers, 219, 264–5
Reith, programmes, 346
relayed programmes, 271–2
religious broadcasting, 150, 175
respectability, 161, 171–2
royalty, attitude to, 233, 281
Savoy Hill, 147, 249
simultaneous transmission, 155, 174
Spanish service, 287
sporting programmes, 172
staff, 147–9, 216, 223–6, 231, 247, 251, 259; association, 261, 270–1, 274, 280–1; conditions, 292, grievances, 261–2; moral code, 230; qualities, 227; recruitment, 227, 267, 273; relations, 261–3
standards, 143, 147, 151, 155, 157, 171–172, 186, 252–3, 289, 342–3, 346–7
structure, 146–7, 250–2, 256–7, 277–8, 321
Sunday broadcasting, 272
Sykes Committee, 136–44, 170, 179; press evidence, 140–1, 145–6; publication, 144–5
'talking mongoose' episode, 279–80
talks programmes, 258, 290
television, 272, 277, 343–4; experimental, 251, 259
Ullswater Committee, 266–71, 272–5; BBC evidence, 268; Parliamentary debate, 276–7; recommendations, 273–4
wartime role, 302–6, 308–9, 317–22
British Gazelle, 192, 195–6, 199, 202
British Overseas Airways Corporation, 299–300
British Worker, 199
Broadcast over Britain, 152, 154
broadcasting:
advertising and commercial, 124–5, 143, 186–7, 211–2, 271–3, 288; United States, 124
development, 121–4, 134–5, 154
Crawford Committee: see under BBC above
interests, 127, 142
international visits by Reith, 241–2
mystery of, 119–20
public control, 141
public opinion, 179–80
public services, 181
Sykes Committee: see under BBC above
Ullswater Committee: see under BBC above
Brown, Mr. F. J., 124, 136–7, 147
Buchan, John, 260
Bull, Stephen, 112–3
Bull, Sir William, 114–7, 118–21, 128, 136, 149, 162, 171, 185, 213; meets Reith, 112–3
Bunbury, Sir Henry, 141
Burnham, Lord, 136, 213, 226
Burnham, W. W., 128
Burrows, A. R., 122–3, 129, 146, 155–6
Butler, Richard Austen, 16

Cable and Wireless, Reith's tour, 331–2
Cadman report, 291
Cairngorms, love for, 20, 44, 348
Cameronians, 66–7
Campbell case, 162–3
Canada, touring holiday, 300
Caradon, Lord, 19
Caribbean, visit to, 336
Carlton Club, 115
Carpendale, Sir Charles, 147–8, 155–6, 179, 212, 214, 218–9, 223–6, 231, 254–7, 323
Cavendish Club, 112
Chamberlain, Austen, 115–8, 116–7, 244
Chamberlain, Neville, 135, 244, 276–7, 285–6, 290, 293, 297, 301–2, 304, 306, 310; as P.M.G., 132
Chanak, crisis, 114–5
childhood, 24, 29–38, 329; birth, 29; bullying, 37; code of conduct, 30–1;

childhood, *cont.*
Glasgow, 17; infant memories, 31–2; petulance, 33, 72–3; reserve, 24; restriction, 33; self-indulgence, 32; sullen behaviour, 33; unhappiness, 32
Churchill, Winston, 26, 114, 116–7, 166–8, 190, 192, 194, 196, 200, 209, 243–4, 275, 300, 306, 309–17, 322, 326, 330, 343–5, 348; BBC, attitude to, 193–197, 200, 236–7; correspondence with Reith, 333–4; defeat, 332; general strike, 192–3; Prime Minister, 306; relations with Reith, 200–1, 203, 306–327
Clarendon, Lord, 210–11, 215–9, 220–7, 232–4
Clyde Navigation Trust, 20
Clynes, J. R., 111
coal industry, 168–9, 190; crisis, 177–8; Royal Commission, 177–8, 190–1
Coatman, John, 254
Cock, Gerald, 277
College Church Manse, 33–4
Colonial Development Corporation, 335–8
Columbia Broadcasting Corporation, 345
Commander of the Bath, 327
Commonwealth Telecommunications Board, 336
communists, 162, 193
Conservative Party, 115–8, 222; BBC, attitude to, 263–4; commercial television, 342–4
Cooper, Duff, 236, 306, 308, 317–9
Crawford, Earl of, 177
Crawford Committee of enquiry: see under BBC above
Cripps, Sir Stafford, 280
Crocombe, Leonard, 157
Curran, Charles, 352
Curzon, Lord, 138–9

Daily Express, 132–5, 145, 173, 185
Daily Herald, 145
Daily Mail, 191
Daily Telegraph, 180
Dalton, Hugh, 333
daughter: see Reith, Marista
Davidson, J. C. C., 191, 193, 196, 199–200, 206–8
Davidson, Dr. Randall, 150, 152, 201–2
Davies, Clement, 266
Davies, Walford, 150
Dawnay, Colonel Alan, 253, 255–9, 277
Dawson, Geoffrey, 195–6, 282
Dawson of Penn, Lord, 278
de Gaulle, Charles, 25, 346
death, 349, 351
Defence: Forces objections to broadcasting, 125; rearmament, 275–6, 286, 290
Desert Island Discs, 346
Dewar, Mungo, 148
diary, 26, 56–8, 60, 69, 119, 142, 232, 321, 338–40
Dill, Major-General Jack, 270
Dunardoch, 112

Eccles, Mr. J. R., 113
Eckersley, Peter, 146, 149, 151, 155, 166, 189, 227, 230, 256, 272
Eckersley, Roger, 227–9, 257, 259
economic situation, 167–8, 190, 208–9, 240, 242–4
Economist, The, 207
Eden, Anthony, 287, 310
Edinburgh, 20, 350
education, 32–3, 35–8; desire for, 110–1; difficult pupil, 33; family attitude, 37–43; Glasgow Academy, 33, 36–7, 51; Gresham's School, 37, 39–41, 45; revisited, 112; improvement, 39–40; lack of, 15, 40–1; Park Preparatory School, 33, 52; performance, 36–7; reputation, 46–7; subjects of interest, 39, 41, 46; technical college, 46, 48–51; university, desire for, 40–2
Edward VIII, 281–4
Elgar, 260–1
Eliot, T. S., 253–4, 264
Elliot, Walter, 51–2, 57, 118
Elton, Lord, 266, 273
Emerson, 47
Empire Free Trade, 236
Empire Press Union, 273
employment, search for, 103–4
engineering industry, 89
entertainment business, 188–9
Establishment, relationship with, 203, 233, 237–8, 248, 296–7, 307, 351
Evening Standard, 145, 339

Face to Face, 345
family: age difference, 32; attitudes, 42; brothers and sisters, 31–3, 35, 42; father: see Reith, Dr. George; Glasgow, 20; grandfather, 20, 35, 49; holidays, 43–4; life, 30–1; mother; see Reith, Mary; parents, 24, 33, 36, 76, 90–1, 103; Presbyterianism, 35; religious atmosphere, 34; Southwick, 104; Stonehaven, 31
finance, 108, 112, 121, 336, 338
Fisher, H. A. L., 289
Fisher, Sir Warren, 265–6, 269, 283, 293
Fleet Street: see Press

Foot, Robert, 319–21, 322, 342
Fraser, Captain Ian, 177, 185, 189
Freeman, John, 345

Gainford, Lord, 146, 155, 161, 168, 171, 207, 210, 212, 220–1, 225–6, 228–9, 268
Gas, Light and Coke Company, 104
Geddes, Sir Eric, 298
General Strike, 178, 191–205; BBC coverage, 173, 191–205
George V, 159; broadcast, 161, 254; death, 275; meets Reith, 69–70
George VI, 285
Germany, visit to, 241
Gielgud, Val, 231–2, 254
Gill, Eric, 249–50
Gilmour, Sir John, 250
gold standard, 167–8, 190, 209, 243–4
Glasgow, 35, 145–7; affinity for, 20–1; College Church, 30; Hydepark, 42, 48–51; University, 15; Lord Rector, 15–27, 345; West End, 30
Gorham, Maurice, 279
Gosse, Edmund, *Father and Son*, 43
government administrations: Attlee, 332–333; Baldwin, 144–5, 162–3, 166–9, 222; Bonar Law, 116–7, 138–9; Chamberlain, Neville, 285–6, 306; Churchill, 306; influence and of BBC, 139, 153–4, 158, 160–1, 183, 191–203, 254–5; Labour, 242; Lloyd George, 114–6; MacDonald, 159–63, 222, 238–9
Graham, William, 177, 199, 205
gramophone records, 189
Graves, Cecil, 227, 257, 259, 298–9, 322
Gray, John, 128
Greene, Sir Hugh, 342
Greenwood, Sir Hamar, 117
Grey of Falloden, Earl, 199–200, 227, 299
Grigg, Sir James, 312, 324
Grisewood, Harman, 267, 281–3
Guardian, 343
Guest, Frederick, 117
Gwynne, H. A., 262

Hadow, Sir Henry, 177
Haley, Sir William, 342–3
Halifax, Lord, 289
Hamilton, Mrs. Mary Agnes, 290
Hankey, 269, 276
Hardcastle, William, 347
Harding, Archie, 253–4, 264–5
Harrington, General 'Tim', 114
Harris, Harold, 339–40
Hartley, Sir Harold, 308
Hartshorn, Vernon, 160
Haunting of Cashen's Gap, 279
health, 47, 71, 80, 329, 337–8, 350
Hemel Hempstead Development Corporation, 336
Hibberd, Stuart, 204, 294
Hitler, Adolf, 260, 269, 275, 290
Hoggart, Richard, 198
Hoover, President Herbert, 124, 241
Hore-Belisha, Leslie, 285, 292
Horne, Robert, 116
Howson, G. W. S., 37–8, 40

Ibsen, Henrik, *Ghosts*, 254
Iliffe, Lord, 187–8
Imperial Airways, 291–3, 297, 334; chairmanship, 298–300
Imperial Defence, Committee of, 125
India, 333; broadcasting, 269–70; Viceroy, ambition for, 270, 333
industrial situation, 108–9, 177–8, 190
Information, Ministry of, 300–6; relations with BBC, 302–6
Inskip, Sir Thomas, 276
International Broadcasting Company, 271
Into the Wind, 26
Invergordon naval mutiny, 243
Isaacs, Sir Godfrey, 121, 127
Italy: Abyssinian invasion, 275–6

James, A. Lloyd, 150
'Jix': see Joynson-Hicks, Sir William
Johnston, Tom, 169
Joynson-Hicks, Sir William, 134–7, 139, 193–4, 197, 206
Juke box Jury, 342

Kekewich, Rear-Admiral Piers, 325
Kellaway, Frederick, 117, 120, 124, 171, 180, 213
Keynes, Lord 190
Kipling, Rudyard, 150, 177
Kirkpatrick, Ivone, 318, 342
knighthood, 214

Labour Party, 111–2, 117–8, 205–6; administration ,159, 222–3, 238–9, 242; BBC, attitude to, 199–200, 263, 270–1
Lambert, R. S., 279–80
Landmarks in my life, 347
Lang, Dr. Cosmo, 253
Laski, Harold, 232
Laurie, James, 335
League of Nations, 275, 290
Lee, Sir Kenneth, 305
Lees-Smith, F., 226, 234
Leishman, Dr. Murray, 347–8, 350

letters, 329
Lever, Sir Hardman, 298
Levita, Sir Cecil, 279–80
Lewis, C. A., 122–3, 146–7, 156
Listener, The, 263–4, 279–80
Lloyd, Lord, 270
Lloyd, Mr. Selwyn, 343 fn.
Lloyd George, David, 114–7, 162, 165–7, 202
Locarno Pact, 167, 222
Lochhead, Mr. T., 228
Lollards Tower, 348, 350
London: job-hunting, 110; move to, 55; property, 107; return to, 109; settlement in, 59
London Evening News, 133
London Scottish Rugby Club, 78
Longcroft, Charles, 61
Longford, Lord, 349
Lord High Commissioner of the General Assembly of the Church of Scotland, 20, 316, 350
Lord President of the Council, 268
Lords, House of, 311; speeches, 316, 343–344
Lough, Thomas, 159
Lyttelton, Oliver, 335

McClintock, Sir William ,266
MacDonald, Malcolm, 331–2
MacDonald, Ramsay, 158, 160–2, 199–200, 205, 214, 222–3, 226, 234, 238–239, 242, 245–6, 260, 266, 269, 276
McKenna, Lord, 190, 266
McKinstry, Archibald, 127, 171
Macleod, Iain, 19
Macleod, of Funeray, Lord, 347
Macmillan, Lord, 190, 301–2, 315, 319
Macmillan, Harold, 314
Macpherson, Ian, 177
Mair, D. B., 267
Manchester Guardian, 195
Marconi Company, 120, 125, 127
marriage and family, 232–3, 274, 300–1, 323–4, 326, 347–8
Martin, Kingsley, 230
mass-production methods, 95, 286
Masterman, Sir John, 255
Matheson, Hilda, 238, 262
Mavor, O. H., 52
Member of the Queen's Bodyguard, 20
Meynell, Francis, 235
Millbank Hospital, 85, 88
Milligan, Spike, 19
miners, 168–9, 177–8, 190–1, 207–8
ministerial posts, rumours and offers, 276–295
Mitchell-Thompson, Sir William, 169–74, 176, 180–1, 193, 196, 208–12, 266, 270, 272
Mitcheson, Mr. G. G., 250
Moir, E. W., 41, 89–92
Moir, Mrs. E. W., 89
Monckton, Walter, 284, 305–6
Moran, Lord, 343
Morning Post, 192
Morrison, Herbert, 141, 317
Mosley, Sir Oswald, 238–9
motor accident, 296
Mountbatten, Lord, 333
Muggeridge, Malcolm, 22, 345–6, 351
Munitions, Ministry of, 90, 92, 96, 104, 106
Murray, Sir Evelyn, 183, 211
Murray, Gilbert, 206
Murray, W. S. Gladstone, 173, 194, 208, 257, 259, 279
musicians and music publishers, attitude to BBC, 188–9

Nairne, Sir Gordon, 210, 221, 223–5, 233
National Film Finance Corporation, 335–6
New Statesman, The, 239
Newman, John Henry Cardinal, 23–4
Newnes Ltd., 157–8
news agencies, 125, 140, 194
News of the World, 145
Newspaper Proprietors' Association, 130–131, 140
Newspaper, Society, 139
Nicholls, Basil, 259
Nicolson, Harold, 319, 322
Nobel's, 56
Noble, Sir William, 119–21, 127–9, 132, 140, 149, 185, 272
Norman, Sir Henry, 136
Norman Montagu, 159–60, 164, 168, 190, 209, 233–4, 242–3, 268–9, 291, 306, 336
Norman, Ronald, 234, 268–9, 277–81, 289, 291, 293
Norway, British forces in, 305–6

Odhams, Muriel, meets Reith, 104–5
Odhams, 188
Ogilvie, F. J., 299, 302–5, 317–20, 322
old age, 23, 330, 349
Owen, Sir James, 139–41, 187

Pall Mall Gazette, 131
Parkinson, C. Northcote, 258
Parliament: maiden speech, 310–11; Southampton seat, 304
Payne, Walter, 188

Pearson's, 55–6, 89–90, 92
Pease, Henry Mark, 128, 171
peerage, 311
Performing Rights Society, 189
Philco, 271
Pick, Sir Frank, 317
Plugge, Captain L. F., 271–2
Polish visit, 240, 242
politics and politicians, attitude to, 24, 52–53, 100, 158, 222, 237–8, 278; career, 110–1, 114–21; disenchantment, 118, 311; education, 128, 113–8
Post Office, responsibility for broadcasting and BBC, 123–8, 131–2, 134–7, 141, 143–6, 153, 170–4, 180, 207–12; relay services, 272
Postmaster General, responsibility for broadcasting and BBC, 123–8, 134–7, 143–6, 169–75, 196, 206–12, 266–9, 273
Pound, Dudley, 325
Powell, Sir Allan, 302, 304, 318
Powys Maurice, Captain F. H., 325
Presbyterianism, 20–1, 24
Press, 127, 240–1; BBC and broadcasting, attitude to, 125, 128, 130–3, 139–41, 145, 157, 170, 180, 187, 172–3; General Strike, effect of, 191, 194; Ullswater Committee evidence, 273; wireless periodicals, 187–8
press-cuttings, 232
Price, Harry, 279
Privy Councillor, 304
psychiatric treatment, 23, 348
public service ideal, 18, 24, 141–2, 151, 153, 214, 241, 329
public speaking, 98–100, 112, 261
publishers, evidence to Ullswater Committee, 273

Radio Luxembourg, 271–2
Radio Normandie, 271–2
Radio Society of Great Britain, 132
Radio Times, 131, 157–8, 187–8, 231
railways, Caledonian line, 48–9
Rayleigh, Lord, 177
Rediffusion Ltd., 272
Reith, Beth, 32
Reith, Christopher, 232, 274, 315, 323, 349
Reith, Dr. George, 20, 22–3, 29–30, 32, 41–2, 44, 46–7, 53, 55, 64–5, 76, 91, 99, 106, 110–1, 117, 137; death, 105–6; Glasgow reputation, 30, 47–8; influence on John Reith, 21, 23, 35, 48–9, 99, 106, 123, 153, 176, 330: Moderator of the General Assembly of the United Free Church of Scotland, 55, 105; rift with John Reith, 41, 45–47, 65, 72–3, 106
Reith, Marista, 274, 323; marriage, 347–348
Reith, Mary, 29, 31–2, 108, 176, 214, 220, 233; death, 274–5; religious faith, 29, 36
Reith, Lady Muriel, 214, 233, 294, 296, 323–4, 336, 347, 350
Reith, John Charles Walsham:
ability, 27, 338; accidie, 24–5, 222, 278, 348; actor, 16, 18, 68, 152; administrative and organising ability, 24, 62–64, 77, 101–2, 121–2, 143, 147–8, 155–6, 182, 305; aggression, 232; aloofness, 57, 234; ambition, 27, 56, 78, 97, 235, 247, 270, 329, 351; aplomb, 170, 285; arrogance, 27, 212, 311, 347; astuteness, 16; authority, 63–4, 101, 129, 154–5; awkwardness, 72–3
bias, 239; bitterness, 294; book-keeping ability, 117; books, 34; bureaucracy, attitude to, 24, 183; business propriety, 158
Calvinism, 17, 34, 47, 187, 232; candour, 248; cantankerousness, 47; caricature and jokes, 234; change, resistance to, 251; charm, 25; Christian attitudes and values, 17–8, 24, 123; church, 35–6; combat, love of, 126; commonsense, 183; competence, 121; complacency, lack of, 156, 179; conceit, 77; confiding in self, 43; conformist, 97, 122, 151; conscience, 17, 23, 48, 327; conscientiousness, 55–6; conservative tastes, 152; consideration, 148, 234; contacts, useful, 89; conventional values of others, 53; conversationalist, 25; countryside, love of, 20, 44–5, 51; courage, 27, 95, 334; credibility, 240; criticism, 157, 182, 232, 251, 277; crochetiness, 248; cultural deficiencies, 150–1
delegation of work and authority, 152, 218, 220, 252; delicacy, lack of, 251; democracy, 18, 229; depression, 23, 76, 95, 112, 222, 350; despair, 22, 27, 110; destiny: see Providence below; detail, 79, 155; determination, 146, 170, 232, 297; dignity, 19; difficulty, thriving on, 126; disenchantment, 288; disinterestedness, 293; divine justice, 34; dominance, 53; doubt, 112; doubts, spiritual, 43; dreamer, 19, 21, 33, 36, 47, 73; drilled precision, 39;

Reith, John Charles Walsham, *cont.*
drive, 183; duties and responsibilities, sense of, 52, 105, 297
earnestness, 151; efficiency, 71, 97, 121, 334; egoism, 218; energy, 143, 269, 310, 338; envy, 308; excellence, desire for, 150
failure, sense of, 17, 21–2, 25, 197, 233, 346–7; fairness, 206; faith, 122; farsightedness, 298; fatalism, 23; fervour, 277; firmness, 298; flattery, 260; foreboding, sense of, 25, 351; free will, 34; freedom, 47; frustration, 17, 42
God, concept of, 23, 34, 36, 45, 65, 73, 121; greatness, 88; guilt, 21
handling of men, 63, 74–5, 87–8, 107, 109, 122, 152; happiness, 325; hard-bargaining, 107, 210; health, spiritual, 47; helplessness in eyes of God, 36; hierarchy, sense of, 152; honesty, 293; honours, desire for, 161–2; 275, 349; humility, 25, 27, 214, 347; humour, 25, 152, 294; hypersensitivity, 24, 233; hypocrisy, 23, 324
idealism, 153, 164–6, 180, 193, 218, 239, 314; identity, 58; image, 61–2; imagination, 33–4; immaturity, 122; 151; impatience, 248, 288, 347; impulsiveness, 73, 108; inadequacy, 233; independence, 77–8, 196; indifference, 15; inefficiency, attitude to, 77; infallibility, 277; inflexibility, 251; ingenuity, 313; initiative, 62, 305; innocence, 203; inscrutability, 22; interest, 19; intolerance, 216, 219, 347; inventiveness, 310
judgement, 17; justice, 78
leadership, 53, 156; loyalty, 24, 293
mastery, 151, 232; melancholy, 70, 222; memory, 46, 152; mercy, 78; messianic approach, 121–2, 143, 183, 203, 247, 351; 'mini-men', attitude to, 25; mission, sense of, 156; moods, 79; moral values, 100, 142–3, 165, 229–230, 344
negotiator, 333; newspapers, 122; nightmares, 85–6; nostalgia, 16
obstinacy, 258, 297; occasion, sense of, 16; omniscient manner, 24; opportunity, 143; orderliness, 297–8
panache, 260; passionate nature, 197; patience, 146, 251; patriotic ardour, 39; perception, 21; personal crisis, 235; persuasiveness, 107, 298; petulance, 176, 221, 312; plain-speaking, 16; power, 154–5, 214; practicality, 122; predestined role, 26, 73, 121, 153; prejudices, 53; presumptuousness, 311; 'prevailing', 126; pride, 21, 40, 101, 184, 197, 233, 283, 297, 299, 312, 324; principles, 234; privacy, 47; prophetic quality, 17; Providence and destiny, 20, 23, 42, 45, 53, 57, 73, 77, 85, 95, 121–2, 130, 170, 176, 215, 241, 351; public and private life, 17, 22–3
reasoning, 107; reassurance, 233; religious faith and inspiration, 32, 42–3, 118–9, 137, 176; remorse, 233; resilience, 24, 130; responsibility, 217; restlessness, 276; ritual, 18, 205, 247; romanticism, 34, 44–5, 78, 347; royalty, attitude to, 281–4
self-abasement, 21; self-belief, 88; self-condemnation, 25, 278; self-confidence, 16, 51, 61–2, 81, 109, 151, 180, 183; self-conscious foolishness, 72; self-deception, 21; self-doubt, 19, 24, 270; self-dramatisation, 78; self-effacement, 305; self-esteem, 297; self-indulgence, 327, 329; self-justification, 19, 58, 251, 262, 276; self-knowledge, 17, 232; self-pity, 95, 278; self-recrimination, 293; self-righteousness, 77, 229, 323, 333; self-sufficiency, 38, 48, 112; sentimentality, 97; seriousness, 121; shrewdness, 27; shyness, 57, 62, 148, 216, 248; singlemindedness, 60, 108, 151, 170, 206, 242, 351; snobbery, 233; solemnity, 22, 212, 248, 312; spiritual struggle, 297; standards, 24, 35; strength, 130, 312; 'striving', 126; stubbornness, 97; success, 17–18; superiors, attitude to, 60–1, 63, 69, 70–1, 74–5, 104, 151, 293, 305; suspicion, 50–1; symbolism, 20, 78
tact, 117, 302; temper, 122, 176, 212; theatrical, sense of, 25–6, 283; thoroughness, 297–8; toughness, 24; triumphs and successes, 25; truth, 18
uncompromising manner, 22; unfairness, 240; unhappiness, 25, 325
vanity, 104; vigour, 27, 248; vindictiveness, 36; vision, 181; vulnerability, 22
will, strength of, 21–2, 32; wisdom, 25; worldly fame, 21, 27
Remington-Delaware plant, 92–3
Rendall, Dr. Montagu, 210, 221, 249
retirement, 337–8
Rice, 156
Riddell, Lord, 140–1, 170, 172, 187, 194
Robertson, Dr. Ivor, 118–9
Robertson, Field Marshal Sir William, 137
Rothermere, Lord, 236

Royal Air Force, 286, 309
Royal Navy: acting lieutenant commander, 324–7; Director of Combined Operations material, 326
rugby, 36, 39, 46
Runciman, Lord (Leslie), 298–9
Ryan, A. P., 318, 342

St. Andrew's Society, Philadelphia, 98
St. John Pym, W., 292
Salisbury Plain, military housing scheme, 102
Salter, Lord, 244
Samuel, Sir Herbert, 178, 190
Sarnoff, David, 124
Schuster, Leonard, 277
Scott, Sir Walter, 34
Selfridge, Gordon, 11
Selsdon, Lord: see Mitchell-Thompson, Sir William
Sèvres, Treaty of, 114
sex, attitudes to, 234, 323
Shaw, George Bernard, 150, 175, 260–1, 302
Shields, Miss F. I., 146
Shinwell, Lord, 215–6, 218
Siemens, 116
Siepmann, Charles, 238, 257, 260
Simon, Sir John, 260, 286
Simpson, Mrs. Ernest, 281–4
Smith, Gypsy, 31–2
Smith, W. C., 146
Smyth-Piggott, Major, 91–3
Snowden, Mrs. Ethel, 215–30, 232–3, 235–236, 261
Snowden, Philip, 160, 199, 210, 238, 244
socialism, 111, 141, 183, 289
Somerville, J. A. C., 150
son: see Reith, Christopher
South Africa: broadcasting work, 275; visit to, 269–70
Stamp, Sir Josiah, 190
Stanton-Jeffries, L., 146
Stevenson, Frances, 116, 146
Street, Sir Arthur, 299
Stuart, Sir Campbell, 301–2
Swarthmore: see United States, Philadelphia
Sykes, Major-General Sir Frederick, 136, 138–9, 141, 153
Sykes Committee of enquiry: see BBC

Talbot, Dame Meriel, 177
'talking mongoose', 279–80
Tallents, Sir Stephen, 259, 279, 318
Taylor, A. J. P., *English history, 1914–1945*, 163, 175, 234–5, 282, 330
Telegraph Act, 1869, 123
television, 272, 347; commercial, 342–4; experimental, 251, 259; Reith interviews, 345–6
theatres, 188–9
Thomas, Sir Godfrey, 283
Thomas, J. H., 199
Thurtle, Ernest, 319
Times, The, 192, 194–6, 199; Reith advertisement, 338–9
Titbits, 145, 157
Tovey, Professor, 150
Tower, Admiral, 327
trade unions, 168
Trades Union Congress, 177–8, 191, 198; BBC attitude during General Strike, 197–9
Transport, Ministry of, 307–11; bomb disposal, 309–10
Trenchard, Lord (Hugh), 61, 270, 275, 300, 309, 340
Trevelyan, Sir Charles, 136, 141, 199
Turkey, relations with Great Britain, 114
Twain, Mark, 34, 97

Ullswater, Lord, 266
Ullswater Committee of enquiry: see BBC
unemployment, 145, 158, 160–1, 168, 231, 222, 238–9
United States: broadcasting and radio, 124, 241; career and experience in, 90–101, 107, 122; emigration, thoughts of, 110; National Guard, 100; Philadelphia, 92–8

Vansittart, Lord, 269, 286, 288
Vauclain, Sam, 96

Wade, Ralph, 148–9, 252, 294
Wake-Walker, Admiral Sir Frederick, 325, 327
Wallace, Euan, 68, 307
Wallace, Robert, 64
war, attitude to, 56–7, 59–61, 64–5, 83
War, First World, 53, 56–84; armistice, 103; employment, 89–90; industry, effect on, 107; small-arms, U.S. production, 89–98, 104; United States, 98–100
War, Second World, 299; D-Day, 327; Far East, 315, 322; France, 308–9, 326; German bombing, 309–10; industries, reorganisation of, 300–27
War Office, 106, 292
Wearing spurs, 26
Webb, Beatrice, 198–9, 204
Wellington, Lindsay, 264–5
Wembley Exhibition, 1924, 161

West Indies, visit to, 291
Weston, W. E., 181
Wheatley, John, 160
White, Graham, 266, 273
Whitelaw, 63, 68, 80
Whitley, John, 226–7, 234–7, 240, 245–6, 269
Whitley, Oliver, 342
wife: see Reith, Lady Muriel
Wigram, Sir Clive, 242
Wilkinson, Ellen, 205–6
Wilson, Harold, 335, 349
Wilson, Sir Horace, 261, 280–1, 283, 292–293, 297, 300, 304–5
wireless and radio trade, 116, 126–7, 134–137, 140–1, 143–5, 179–80; Conservative attitude, 184; crisis in trade, 138; demand for sets, 184; development of industry, 120, 122–5, 131–2 184–5; interests in broadcasting development, 142, 170–1, 184
Wireless Association, 186
wireless exchanges, 271–2, 274, 288
Wireless League, 185–6
Wireless Telegraph Board, 125
Wolmer, Lord, 183
women, attitude to, 65, 68, 99–100, 217, 323–5, 332, 341, 348–9; ideal, 108; in old age, 22–3; timidity, 105
Wood, Kinglsey, 245, 259, 265–6, 276–7, 287–8, 291–3, 297, 305, 317
Woods Humphrey, 291–2, 298
Woodward, 214
Woolton, Lord, 333, 343
Wordsworth, William, 45
Works, Ministry of, 235, 311–5; post-war reconstruction, 314–5
World at One, 347
Worthington-Evans, Sir Laming, 139, 144–5, 158
Wyndham-Lewis, D. B., 316

Young, Filson, 189
Young, G. M., 192

Zinoviev, 162